# ADVANCE PRAISE FOR *In Defense of Public Debt*

"Discussions of sovereign debt are always the same, yet always different. Why debt finance? How much can we borrow? Should creditors worry? The authors take us on a fascinating 2,500-year tour of sovereign debt through the ages, the discussions, the successes, and the failures. The bottom line: Well-used, debt finance has been and is precious. The latest example: The use of debt during the Covid crisis. A must read for anybody interested in current debt debates."

—**Olivier Blanchard**, Professor of Economics Emeritus, MIT, and Senior Fellow, Peterson Institute for International Economics

"An exceptionally comprehensive and readable history of public debt from ancient Greece to modern Greece and from Argentina to Australia to Asia to America. This book is rich with detail, studded with lessons learned, forgotten, and learned again, and packed with analytical perspective that reflects decades of scholarship. It is a timely reminder to governments, lenders, investors, and ordinary citizens that, if you don't know where you've been, you probably don't know where you are going."

—**David Wessel**, Director, Hutchins Center on Fiscal and Monetary Policy, Brookings Institution

"Repeatedly since the 1980s, Americans have been told to worry about the size of the federal debt. And yet the debt has continued to grow absolutely and as a share of gross domestic product, with few of the predicted adverse consequences. Building expertly on large and complex literatures in history, economics, and political science, *In Defense of Public Debt* offers a balanced account of the positive and negative aspects of public debt, showing the vitally important role government borrowing can play in a time of crisis, but also the very real problems that can arise when debts grow too large. At a time when too many policymakers subscribe to naive ideas about public finance, this is a book that cries out for a readership beyond the academy."

—**Niall Ferguson**, Milbank Family Senior Fellow, Hoover Institution

"For a typical citizen, protection in war-time or in a pandemic reveals their government to be a problem-solver rather than 'the problem.' Yet the legacy of such episodes in the accumulated national debt is widely misunderstood, opening the way to too rapid a turn to austerity. *In Defense of Public Debt* provides enlightenment and reassurance by inviting the reader to follow how public debt—warts and all—has helped create the modern world."

—**Wendy Carlin**, Professor of Economics, University College London

"*In Defense of Public Debt* could not be timelier. It is an engaging and informative account of the use and misuse of government borrowing, from early times to the Covid pandemic. The unquestionable expertise of the authors, and their non-partisan reading of the evidence from our past, will serve to guide the intelligent reader as they wrestle with one of the most important issues of our time: Are we borrowing too much?"

—**Raghuram Rajan**, Professor of Finance, University of Chicago

"How much debt should a country accumulate during a crisis? And afterwards? To know what works and what doesn't requires verdicts on past performances. The authors deliver the verdicts, applying sound principles in a definitive global history of public debt."

—**Peter H. Lindert**, Distinguished Professor of Economics (Emeritus), University of California – Davis

"With so much nonsense about the public debt in the air, it is refreshing to discover a work of such intelligence, balance, and erudition. Read *In Defense of Public Debt* for fun and profit. Then send an excerpt or two to your favorite politicians."

—**Alan S. Blinder**, Gordon S. Rentschler Memorial Professor of Economics and Public Affairs, Princeton University

"In this fascinating and comprehensive history, the authors provide a much-needed antidote to the simplistic accounts that so often dominate debates about government debt. From its earliest origins to today, public borrowing has sometimes led to spectacular failures, but it has also allowed societies to achieve objectives that would have been impossible in its absence. As we ask where we stand with public debt today, there is no better book to remind us of the lessons of history."

—**David Stasavage**, Julius Silver Professor of Politics, New York University

# In Defense of Public Debt

# In Defense of Public Debt

BARRY EICHENGREEN, ASMAA EL-GANAINY,
RUI ESTEVES, AND KRIS JAMES MITCHENER

OXFORD
UNIVERSITY PRESS

# OXFORD
UNIVERSITY PRESS

Oxford University Press is a department of the University of Oxford. It furthers
the University's objective of excellence in research, scholarship, and education
by publishing worldwide. Oxford is a registered trade mark of Oxford University
Press in the UK and certain other countries.

Published in the United States of America by Oxford University Press
198 Madison Avenue, New York, NY 10016, United States of America.

CIP data is on file at the Library of Congress
ISBN 978–0–19–757789–9

DOI: 10.1093/oso/9780197577899.001.0001

1 3 5 7 9 8 6 4 2

Printed by LSC Communications, United States of America

# CONTENTS

1.  Introduction  1

2.  Debt in Service of the State  10

3.  States and the Limits of Borrowing  25

4.  Democratization and Globalization  45

5.  Caveat Emptor  63

6.  Managing Problem Debts  77

7.  Successful Consolidation  93

8.  Warfare to Welfare  106

9.  Cycles of Debt  128

10. Oil and Water  149

11. Missed Opportunities  165

12. Debt to the Rescue  181

13. COVID-19  199

14. Conclusion  211

*Acknowledgments*  225
*Notes*  227
*References*  267
*Index*  291

# 1

# Introduction

On December 21, 2020, as the number of Americans who had died from COVID-19 approached 319,000, Senator Rand Paul, Republican from Kentucky, took to the floor of the Congress, not to address the public health emergency but to express concern about the government's spiraling debt. "How bad is our fiscal situation?" he asked. "Well, the federal government brought in $3.3 trillion in revenue last year and spent $6.6 trillion, for a record-setting $3.3 trillion deficit. If you're looking for more COVID bailout money, we don't have any. The coffers are bare. We have no rainy-day fund. We have no savings account. Congress has spent all of the money."

From fiery rhetoric, the senator pivoted to economic analysis. "Today's money is gone," he explained, "so Congress is spending tomorrow's money. . . . When we talk about spending tomorrow's money, this is not just money we will need next month; this is money we will need in a decade—money we will need in one, two, and three generations from now. For national defense. For infrastructure. This is money that your children and grandchildren will pay back with interest, and it is going up by more than a trillion dollars every year. Instead of enjoying the same wealth and opportunity that we have enjoyed in this country, our children will be stuck paying our bills—with interest."[1]

Senator Paul's appeal built on an important insight, namely that government is the steward of the nation's finances. If it mismanages them by borrowing excessively, worrisome economic and financial consequences will follow. But the implication he drew—that the government should balance its budget, just as a household should balance its budget in order to avoid mortgaging the future—was fundamentally flawed. Indeed, a government that did not borrow in order to provide essential services during a deadly pandemic—or to ensure the national defense during a security emergency, or to invest adequately in the productive infrastructure of which Senator Paul spoke—would be accused of dereliction, and rightly so. Such a government, to continue the analogy with a household, would be like parents who refused to borrow to obtain life-saving surgery for a child.

A government that badly mismanages its finances and ends up saddling the state and future generations with an unsustainable debt will not long retain its legitimacy. But neither will a government that stubbornly refuses to borrow to meet an emergency, or to invest in the future when productive investment opportunities present themselves.

Public debt, then, has its uses. It enables a government to continue providing basic social services when revenues fall. It helps in undertaking productive investments, and in supporting aggregate demand when aggregate demand needs support. It allows the state to ramp up defense spending when faced with a military threat, to intervene to stabilize the banking system when a financial crisis erupts, and to provide humanitarian assistance when a hurricane, earthquake, pandemic, or other natural or manmade disaster strikes.

But public debt, like any potent instrument, can cause damage if misused. The ability to issue debt creates a temptation to put off hard decisions. It allows legislators to finance deficits, instead of facing hard choices about what spending programs to cut or taxes to raise. It allows incumbents to manipulate the budget for political gain, ramping up spending before an election in the hope of attracting swing voters, or boosting programs favored by their constituents prior to leaving office. Borrowing can be relied on excessively, since future generations that lack political voice bear the burden of the government's obligations. The heavy debts incurred by those who succumb to these temptations cause problems. The higher interest rates that are needed to place additional debt can crowd out productive investments. Doubts about the government's willingness and ability to pay can dent confidence and jeopardize financial stability. This is especially true when a government's debt is held by foreigners, who enjoy the least legal protection and are therefore inclined to liquidate their investments at the first sign of trouble, in turn causing debt prices to crash.[2] It is especially the case when the debt is held by banks, in which case a sovereign debt crisis can quickly become a banking crisis.

These issues have a long history. Borrowing by monarchs and states traces back at least a thousand years, to the period following the fall of the Carolingian Empire, of Franks and Lombards who ruled much of Europe in the first millennium CE. From that point, Europe was divided, for geographical and political reasons, into literally hundreds of city-states and princely kingdoms. Proliferating border conflicts resulted in burgeoning offensive and defensive wars. Rulers borrowed not only to expand their territories, but to defend the realm and survive. Specialized lenders, initially Italian family-run banks, mobilized resources on an unprecedented scale and developed elaborate contracts to meet the state's financial needs. Debt served the sovereign. It enabled him to retain power. It legitimized his reign by helping him protect his subjects. Equally, debt served the lenders, who were rewarded, amply if not uniformly, for their services.

Not uniformly, that is, because, then as now, things could go wrong. Sovereigns sometimes borrowed for reckless and poorly conceived military adventures or simply to line their pockets. This failure to repay inflicted losses on their lenders, extending to bankruptcy in the case of some of those selfsame Italian banking houses.

One might think that this less-than-happy experience would have spelled the end of sovereign borrowing and lending. To infer this, however, would be to underestimate the value of debt to the state and belittle the ingenuity of the lenders. As military technology became more elaborate and costly, sovereigns again turned to their lenders, borrowing even larger sums to defend themselves and their subjects. As long-distance trade gained importance, they borrowed to protect their ships and trading routes. They devised new taxes and means of collecting them as ways of mobilizing the resources to service additional debts.

Lenders, for their part, developed mechanisms for protecting their interests. They gained a firmer hold on the taxes earmarked for debt service by monitoring collection and even raising those taxes directly. Banks formed syndicates, enabling them not only to lend more, but also to diversify their holdings and spread the risk. They securitized their loans and organized secondary markets on which government bonds could be traded. This permitted the sovereign's obligations to be held by a still-larger population of investors and the risk to be spread even more widely. Again, things didn't always go smoothly. Defaults happened. Investors took losses. But it is revealing that this market survived, and indeed thrived, for the better part of five hundred years.

The seventeenth and eighteenth centuries were the period of transition to the modern age of public finance. First in England and the Netherlands and then elsewhere, investors secured protections against arbitrary action by the sovereign. They established legislatures and parliaments, in which creditors were represented, to advise and consent to the state's fiscal policies. With checks and balances in place, interest rates came down, and borrowing became easier. Acquisition of these additional fiscal and administrative resources allowed the formation of larger territories, leading to the emergence of the modern state system. Public debt played a substantial role in the advent of the nation-state and then, in the nineteenth century, following the Treaty of Vienna, in a declining incidence of interstate conflict. It is no coincidence that England and the Netherlands, two countries that were early to develop markets in public debt, were in the vanguard of this process.

Advances in public debt management meanwhile fostered the development of private financial markets. It helped that government bonds were liquid. They were easily traded and could be readily converted into cash and other financial assets. Because they were liquid and safe, they were widely accepted as collateral when lenders extended credit to other borrowers. And wider availability of collateral, packaged in this standardized form, made for more lending. Government bonds were also the benchmark for pricing riskier assets and setting interest rates on riskier loans. In these ways, public debt was integral to the development of financial markets that served as a cornerstone for the Commercial and Industrial Revolutions of the eighteenth and nineteenth centuries. It is no coincidence, from this standpoint, that modern economic growth emerged first in Northwest Europe, the cradle of modern sovereign borrowing and lending.

Contemporaries were aware of these positive implications of public debt, although they tended, like twenty-first-century observers such as Senator Paul, to emphasize the negative aspects. In chapter 3 of *The Wealth of Nations*, Adam Smith warned that it was all too easy for governments to borrow against future taxes and to accumulate debt that placed an onerous burden on future generations.[3] Of the various justifications for sovereign borrowing, Smith emphasized, appropriately for his time, the exigencies of war. As modern military technology gave rise to an increasingly expensive arms race, state survival hinged on the sovereign's ability to borrow. But this blessing, Smith cautioned, was mixed. Cognizant of their ability to borrow, sovereigns and states failed to accumulate adequate reserves in advance, rendering them dangerously dependent on debt finance. "The government . . . is very apt to repose itself on this ability and willingness of its subjects to lend it their money on extraordinary occasions," as Smith put it. "It foresees the facility of borrowing, and therefore dispenses itself from the duty of saving."

Efforts to raise taxes once the conflict passed, Smith went on, would be resisted by influential stakeholders, and attempts to surmount their resistance risked provoking a backlash. But assuming that this stakeholder rebellion was contained, the additional state borrowing and taxes required to service heavy debts could still crowd out productive investments and, in so doing, damage the economy. Either way, Smith glumly concluded, these "enormous debts presently oppress, and will in the long run probably ruin, all the great nations of Europe. . . ."[4]

Among public finance specialists, Smith is best known for these dire predictions, much as twenty-first-century debt scolds in the mold of Pete Peterson are known for their apocalyptic warnings of unsustainable public-sector obligations.[5] In fact, however, Smith was aware of the positive aspects of public debt. Governments also borrowed, he acknowledged, to build roads, canals, and bridges. In the best of all worlds, their investments might so increase the extent of the market as to generate revenues sufficient for the state to repay its creditors with interest, and have a surplus left over.[6]

In addition, Smith understood that the government's debt securities could be resold on the secondary market to other investors, ensuring that they remained in willing hands. "The security which [the government] grants to the original creditor is made transferable to any other creditor," as he put it, "and, from the universal confidence in the justice of the state, generally sells in the market for more than was originally paid for it." The transferability of public debt securities, of which Smith spoke, in turn conferred other advantages. Merchants and manufacturers could still pursue productive investments when these presented themselves, despite having lent previously to the state. Savers, seeking a secure repository for their funds, could acquire one in the form of government debt securities; saving itself would be encouraged. Not just additional saving and investment but also further deepening and development of financial markets would ultimately result.

This positive view is underappreciated, perhaps because it is less sensational than the apocalyptic warnings of a Peterson or a Smith. Our goal here is to rehabilitate it by providing a balanced account of the positive and negative aspects of public debt. Balance in this case means placing more weight on the positive aspects than is typical of the literature. Hence our title, which conveys our theme that public debt is not all bad—that, contrary to the impression left by much popular discourse and political rhetoric, public debt is not always and everywhere dangerous and destructive.

In what follows, we focus on the debts of national or central governments as distinct from state and local governments. Sovereign debt, as this is also known, is special in that responsibility for repaying it can't be assumed by a higher power.[7] It is also special because it is not subject to the jurisdiction of a court.[8] Prior to the rise of the modern city-state, the sovereign, or king, was the embodiment of the state and by definition the highest earthly power. Subsequently, the governments of sovereign states enjoyed immunity from legal judgment under prevailing judicial doctrine.[9] This makes lending to sovereigns uniquely risky and, from a conceptual standpoint, uniquely interesting.[10]

We use history to illuminate both the positive and the negative aspects of public debt. A historical perspective on the negative aspects illuminates much, if only because defaults on sovereign debt, although not exactly rare, are not as commonplace as defaults on other financial obligations. Studies limited to recent years are hamstrung, therefore, by their focus on a limited number of events. History helps by increasing sample size, subject of course to the caveat that consequences will differ when historical circumstances differ. In what follows, we go to some length to take such differences into account.

In addition, placing sovereign borrowing in different historical settings helps in understanding some of the more perplexing questions surrounding debt. Why, for example, do governments pay when, unlike other debtors, they can't be compelled to do so by the courts? Why do we observe differences in the design of debt contracts, in their enforceability, and in the prevalence and costs of default?

But a long-term perspective is equally relevant for illuminating the positive aspects of public debt. History shows how states have employed debt to secure their borders, invest in infrastructure, and supply social goods, and how this has helped to build durable polities and foster economic growth. It illustrates how sovereign debt evolved into a safe asset, as governments and investors took steps to enhance its attractions. It indicates how this contributed to development of financial markets and the economy more generally. And it demonstrates how governments used their borrowing capacity to dampen business cycles and limit the incidence of economic depressions, and in the course of doing so how they enhanced their own ability to repay.

If history brings out these commonalities, it also documents changes over time in the uses to which debt is put and the reasons it is incurred. To be sure, wars have accounted for spikes in indebtedness throughout history, not least in the twentieth century, when two world wars occasioned dramatic increases. Over time, however, governments also expanded their borrowing for other purposes. With the development of financial markets, they borrowed to create banks and raise the resources needed to resolve financial crises. In effect, they moved from borrowing to provide the public good of national defense to borrowing to provide the public good of financial stability. In addition, they borrowed to finance railways, urban infrastructure, and social overhead capital associated with modern economic growth.

European governments, building on their earlier success at developing debt markets, pioneered these efforts. Subsequently, governments in other parts of the world, such as those of the newly independent Latin American republics in the early nineteenth century, emulated their example, some more successfully than others. Those that had not yet put in place the prerequisites for an active debt market sought to capitalize on the success of their predecessors, issuing debt in the principal international financial centers. Their foreign borrowing created perils as well as opportunities. For example, debt denominated in foreign currency was especially risky. Paying it back required a country and its government to generate not just revenue, but specifically foreign exchange. This exposed the borrower to the uncertainties of global commodity and financial markets. A decline in commodity prices that reduced export receipts, or a decline in the exchange rate that made foreign-currency debt more burdensome, could abruptly render a previously sustainable debt unsustainable.

Moreover, foreign investors might be imperfectly informed about local conditions and the intentions of a government. Where they lacked information, they attempted to infer it from the behavior of other investors, creating the danger that they would all exit, en masse, in a panic. With industrialization and economic growth, developments themselves not unrelated to the prior evolution of public debt markets, a more dramatic imbalance in economic, technological, and military capabilities then opened up between the West and the rest. This allowed foreign investors and their governments to intervene by force to extract payment from the debtor, at the cost of the latter's fiscal and sometimes even political sovereignty.

Gunboat diplomacy was a last resort. More often, investors relied on financial pressure for enforcing contracts and regulating the market. To underwrite bond flotations, they looked to investment banks with long experience in organizing debt issues and possessing contacts with foreign governments, and took the involvement of those banks as a signal to invest. They organized stock exchanges on which the securities of foreign sovereigns could be listed and traded subject to rules designed to protect investors—including rules that barred new listings by governments in default. They formed bondholder committees to represent their interests in negotiations with governments that were behind on their payments.

These mechanisms did not work perfectly. But they worked tolerably well, as shown by the fact that the global market in public debt continued to expand in the second half of the nineteenth century. Although defaults were not uncommon, sovereign debts were repaid with sufficient regularity, and yields on foreign bonds were sufficiently high, that overseas lending paid. For European investors, lending to foreign sovereigns paid better than lending to their own governments. As for the debtors, foreign borrowing was positively associated with investment and growth, not always but more often than not. Countries that borrowed more invested more and grew faster on average, suggesting that issuing sovereign debt paid.[11]

Subsequently, and starting again in Europe, governments moved from borrowing for infrastructure investment and for providing social overhead capital to borrowing to provide social services. Although they continued to invest in railways, canals, and ports, they now also built schoolhouses, libraries, and hospitals. They provided state-sponsored disability insurance, unemployment insurance, and old-age pensions. The five decades from 1880 to 1930 saw early inklings of what became the twentieth-century welfare state. Its social insurance and transfer functions reconciled the insecurity of urban, industrial life with the economic dynamism afforded by the operation of markets. The welfare state protected workers against risks from which they couldn't protect themselves. In this way it reconciled workers and society at large to the operation of the market economy.[12] It lent legitimacy to the state, which was now seen as not only the guarantor of markets, but also a mediator of distributional outcomes.

It is less clear why the public sector's expansion and advent of the welfare state should have been associated with increased indebtedness. In principle, social insurance and transfer payments can be fully financed out of current revenues. If there was additional demand for these public services, then taxes could have been raised. Part of the explanation for the association with debt is that the pressure to expand these programs was most intense in hard economic times— when unemployment was high, dislocations were extensive, and the government lacked revenues adequate to meet immediate demands. Calls for increases in provision of social insurance and transfer payments were intense following World War I, when economic conditions were turbulent and the political establishment sought to head off proto-revolutionary movements. Pressure for their provision was acute in the 1930s, when the Great Depression and the Soviet experiment raised questions about the future of the market system. It intensified again in the economically difficult aftermath of World War II, when an iron curtain descended over Europe and Western governments were anxious to maintain the allegiance of the populace and its faith in the market system. It was strong in the 1970s, when growth slowed and unemployment rose across the advanced-economy world. In all these instances, revenues lagged, causing governments to borrow to finance their programs.

Of course, this explanation only begs a further question: If governments borrowed in bad times, why didn't they repay when times were good? The answer is: sometimes they did. High public debts were successfully reduced, either absolutely or relative to gross domestic product (GDP), in the nineteenth century, in the 1920s, after World War II, and even, in a few national cases, in the final decades of the twentieth century. In some instances, such as France before World War I, debt consolidation was a matter of natural security. Reducing the debt and restoring the capacity to borrow ensured that the state would be able to mobilize resources the next time it faced an existential crisis.

In other instances, debt consolidation was facilitated by limits on the extent of the franchise. With the right to vote limited to the propertied, creditors were disproportionately represented in decision making and could make their preferences felt. And when an absolutist leader, Romanian Premier Nicolae Ceaușescu, determined in the 1980s that foreign indebtedness was a threat to his personal rule, and made debt repayment an absolute priority, there was nothing to stop him. Nothing, that is, except the revolt of the Romanian people, who, rebelling against the resulting privations, overthrew the regime and executed Ceaușescu and his wife just eight months after he triumphantly announced having extinguished the foreign debt.

Democratization may thus be part of why debt levels are higher today and why over-indebtedness is more of a problem. In democratic societies, creditors are only one of many interest groups with the vote. The larger the number of groups with representation, the greater the "common-pool" problem, where each group insists on additional public spending on its favored programs but none fully internalizes the implications for indebtedness. In addition, greater national security may have reduced the perceived urgency of bringing down high debt. This is not to deny the existence of security threats in Europe and Japan, two parts of the world where public debts are heaviest. That said, both Europe and Japan have enjoyed seventy-five years of peace, or at least seventy-five years free of all-out wars like those they endured in the first half of the twentieth century. European and Japanese officials advance various arguments for why bringing down high debt levels would be prudent, but an imminent national security threat is not one.

In the twenty-first century, national emergencies take on a different cast. They come in the form of systemic economic and financial crises, as in 2008–09, and global pandemics, like that in 2020–21. The Global Financial Crisis and the COVID-19 crisis were nothing if not emergencies; they were enormously costly in economic, financial, and humanitarian terms. Governments ramped up public spending to stabilize the financial system, steady the economy, and stem the spread of a deadly disease. In 2008–09, it was enormously costly to recapitalize and otherwise repair broken banking and financial systems. Since those costs could not be met out of current revenues, they resulted in large increases in public debt. In 2020–21, keeping firms alive, furloughed workers on payroll, and children fed entailed vast increases in public spending and debt. Critics complained about the design of these disaster-relief programs. They warned of the troubling implications of exploding public debts. But a state that did not prevent the collapse of its banking and financial system, or that did not do whatever it took to contain the spread of a deadly virus while limiting damage to its economy and citizenry, would not have retained legitimacy in the eyes of the public. To refuse to borrow and incur debt under such circumstances would have been for the state to default on its essential functions.

History shows that the heavy debts bequeathed by wars are challenging to manage, more so to the extent that they must be reduced to restore the state's capacity to borrow to meet similar threats in the future. The same is true of the heavy debts bequeathed by recessions, financial crises and pandemics. No question, managing this financial legacy will be a serious challenge going forward. But this is different from saying that, when confronted with a financial crisis and then a pandemic, not borrowing would have been better.

# Debt in Service of the State

We begin with the role of debt in state building: in enabling the state to carry out its essential functions, to repel internal and external threats, and to survive. Discussing this topic requires understanding the purposes to which sovereign debt is put. It also requires a description of how sovereigns gained access to credit by pledging collateral and delegating prerogatives to their lenders, how debt once closely held by bankers came to be traded more widely, and how the emergence of markets on which such trading took place fostered commercial and economic development.

## An Origin Story

Exactly when sovereigns first borrowed is hard to pinpoint. Two criteria can help to identify when sovereign entities began making concerted use of marketable debt instruments. The first one is the presence of the legal and political infrastructure needed for issuing public debt: durable cities, states, and nations; laws recognizing political entities as capable of borrowing; and ledgers for recording payment and repayment (what we today call accounting systems). Second is the presence of the necessary economic conditions: on the supply side, a polity whose spending needs sometimes exceed its revenues; and on the demand side, individuals with resources sufficient to lend.

The written record points to public borrowing as long as two thousand years ago.[1] Greek city-states such as Syracuse regularly borrowed from their citizens. A treatise attributed to Aristotle contains a set of fiscal vignettes for the period up to the fourth century BCE. One passage records an early episode of debt, debasement, and default:

> [Dionysus of Syracuse (432–367 BCE)] borrowed money from the citizens under promise of repayment, [and] when they demanded it back,

he ordered them to bring him whatever money any of them possessed, threatening them with death as the penalty if they failed to do so. When the money had been brought, he issued it again after stamping it afresh so that each drachma had the value of two drachmae, and paid back the original debt and the money which they brought him on this occasion.[2]

Syracuse was not an isolated case; other city-states engaged in similar practices. They borrowed not only from their citizens, but also from religious foundations known as temples, which bore more than a passing resemblance to banks. To generate income, temples managed estates, which required their managers to develop accounting skills. Putting that financial acumen to use, they offered depository services to the treasuries of city-states. In exchange for these services, temples were permitted to lend out their accumulated capital, receiving interest in return.

As the passage from Aristotle describes, not all borrowing went smoothly. One of the earliest recorded international debt crises involved the Temple of the Delians on the Island of Delos. The temple, famous for its impressive statuary of crouching lions, attracted thousands of pilgrims to annual religious festivals. (We can think of Delos as a precocious example of a Greek island that moved from relying on agriculture to specializing in tourism.) From there, Delos (unlike most Greek islands) developed into a commercial hub and ultimately a financial center.

In the fourth century BCE, thirteen city-states contracted loans from the Temple of the Delians.[3] An inscription on a marble slab at the Fitzwilliam Museum in Cambridge, England, details the increasingly perilous state of these loans.[4] By 377–373 BCE, ten were in partial interest arrears, the other three in full arrears (Table 2.1). Nearly three-quarters of interest due to the temple was late. Although the ultimate fate of these loans is unclear, some scholars conclude that interest and principal were never repaid.[5] It is apparent in any case that this early experience with international lending did not meet the creditors' expectations.

The Roman Republic had a more sophisticated financial system. In its early years, lending was peer to peer. A Roman merchant or gentleman needing cash or credit would turn first to family and friends and, after that, to business acquaintances. Written records were kept, generally in duplicate.[6]

In addition, financial services were provided by *societates*, partnerships in which two or more individuals pooled their resources and shared the profits. Some *societates* persisted beyond the initial venture that occasioned their formation, at which point they began functioning as bankers. However, all but the largest such entities, *societates publicanorum* that provided services such as tax

*Table 2.1* **Greek Cities' Loans from the Temple of Delos, 377–373 BCE (values in Drachmae)**

| City-states | Principal | Interest | |
|---|---|---|---|
| | | Paid | In Arrears |
| Mykonos | 4,200 | 1,260 | 420 |
| Syros | 18,000 | 2,300 | 4,900 |
| Tenos | 21,000 | 6,000 | 2,400 |
| Keos | 24,000 | 5,473 | 4,127 |
| Seriphos | 4,000 | 1,600 | |
| Siphnos | 13,200 | 3,191 | 2,089 |
| Ios | 2,000 | 800 | |
| Paros | 72,000 | 2,970 | 25,830 |
| Oenoe of Icaria | 25,200 | 4,000 | 6,080 |
| Thermae of Icaria | 2,000 | 400 | 400 |
| Naxos | 24,000 | | 9,600 |
| Andros | 30,000 | | 12,000 |
| Karystos | 21,000 | | 8,400 |
| **Total** | **260,600** | **27,994** | **76,246** |

*Source:* Bogaert (1968).

*Note:* 260,600 dr = 1,120.6 kg of silver.

collection to the government, lacked legal personalities and did not enjoy limited liability. In other words, each partner was responsible for the entirety of the partnership's obligations, which limited their expansion.[7]

Beginning in the second century BCE, specialized Roman bankers (*argentarii*) emerged, taking deposits and making payments on behalf of clients.[8] Some of these bankers operated multiple branches and provided services to governments. There is even evidence of an interregional, interbank market, in which transactions among banks created a degree of financial integration that complemented the Roman Empire's high degree of product-market integration.[9]

Finally, credit was provided by public endowments, again primarily temples that managed resources for civic and religious purposes. These lent out idle funds to generate income to help support their religious and charitable activities. Interest rates on loans were officially capped at 12 percent, making this the payout on the endowment of the representative temple, which was thereby able to keep its capital intact.[10]

This financial system may have been elaborate, but the Roman state made only limited use of its services. There was some borrowing by state authorities and individual generals in military emergencies and during the civil war that marked the end of the Republic. In 242–241 BCE, the Roman Republic borrowed from citizen-bankers to finance war with Carthage. It borrowed at home and abroad (mainly from Syracuse) to finance the Second Punic War in 218–202 BCE. In 70 CE, Vespasian asked the Senate to approve a loan of 60 million sesterces to finance his civil war with Vitellius.[11]

Other than this, however, the Roman state does not appear to have borrowed. Religious doctrine discouraged ambitious leaders who might have been tempted to borrow for additional campaigns to augment their power. Stoic teaching emphasized the moral perils—for the individual as well as the Republic—of falling into debt. This doctrine was a sort of pre-modern equivalent of twenty-first-century Germany's *schwarze Null* (black zero)—the belief that the budget should be balanced under all but the most exceptional circumstances, justified on not only economic but also moral grounds.[12] This case is a reminder that development of a sovereign debt market is subject not only to supply-side constraints, meaning the presence or absence of capable lenders, but also to constraints on the demand side. It depends as well on the willingness of the state to borrow.

One reason the Roman Republic was able to avoid falling into debt was that it enjoyed a monopoly of coinage. This was an important difference from the Greek city-states, where coins of different polities circulated alongside one another, and even the largest city-states were unable to suppress their competition. Rome, in contrast, used its administrative and military prowess to ensure exclusive circulation of its coins. If expenses exceeded current revenues plus cash reserves in the state treasury, then the emperor could debase the currency. Because the public possessed no other circulating medium, the emperor could reduce the specie content of his coins, lighten their weight, or announce an increase in their nominal value with impunity.

But even this impunity had limits. As their troubles mounted, emperors increasingly resorted to debasement. The result was higher inflation, as is invariably the case when governments turn to the inflation tax. Diocletian tried to halt inflation in 301 CE by fixing prices and salaries in his *Edict on Maximum Prices*. But this early experiment with price controls worked no better than at other times and in other places. It resulted only in shortages and evasion.[13]

## Europe, the World's Debtor

There is no record of public borrowing in Europe between the later stages of the Roman Empire and the High Middle Ages. Starting in the second millennium

CE, however, sovereign borrowing resumed. Scholarship points to 1000–1400 CE as the key period when borrowing agreements with sovereigns and states were concluded with regularity and debt contracts were standardized.

The terms of these late medieval loans were stringent, reflecting their risks. Loans such as those provided by Italian bankers to the English monarch Edward III during the Hundred Years War (1337–1453) ran no more than one or two years and bore double-digit interest rates.[14] Both high rates and short duration were justified by the risks. (Edward defaulted as early as 1345, with devastating consequences for the lenders.) But rates were elevated, in addition, by limited competition on the lending side, the Tuscan bankers as yet having few rivals.

Outside Europe, borrowing was less common. Chinese rulers did not borrow, funding their expenses instead by taxation and, occasionally, debasement.[15] Japanese feudal lords (daimyo) similarly engaged in only limited borrowing. The Ottomans first borrowed internally, mostly from Jewish, Armenian and Greek financiers, in the sixteenth century, and externally, in Western Europe, in the nineteenth.[16]

Europe was the second millennium's public-debt pioneer because of the prevalence of war. After the collapse of the Carolingian Empire in 888, the continent was divided into literally hundreds of princely states, many no more than cities with modest hinterlands.[17] Europe's geography as a landmass riven by mountain ranges and river valleys posed a natural obstacle to formation of more extensive territorial states.[18] This division into a multitude of jurisdictions tempted rulers to seize territory and resources when they could. As the sociologist and historian Charles Tilly put it, war was the normal condition in Europe from the dawn of the second millennium CE.[19]

War being a matter of state survival dictated mobilizing all available resources. So states borrowed. They borrowed more with the decline of feudal obligations for military service, requiring them to employ paid militias. The intensity of their competition spurred them to invest in expensive military hardware.[20] They purchased swords, lances, and armor, while commissioning firearms, artillery, and ships carrying guns. They built fortifications to defend against these implements of war. Offensive and defensive battles became more expensive, and emergency borrowing rose accordingly.

All this was specifically the case for Europeans, whose geography provided singular incentives for developing and investing in these elaborate military technologies. It was less so on other continents, where geography and political history were different.[21] And with the exceptional expense of warfare in Europe came an exceptional need to borrow.

# A Higher Calling

An initial spurt of lending came from the papal finances, the Roman Church being no less engaged geopolitically than other more terrestrial bodies. The Church, though nominally rich, was hampered by geographic dispersion of its property and income, chiefly the tithe, but also "donations" such as Peter's pence.[22] It faced the challenge of collecting funds in a variety of monies and physically conveying them to Rome.

These issues were of long standing, but they became pressing once the Church found itself in a lengthy conflict with the Holy Roman Emperor, spanning the period 1254–1302. The Church needed to pay the troops of its Italian allies.[23] Military considerations thus provided impetus for the development of debt finance no less in the papal case than in others.[24]

For a solution, the pope turned to his Tuscan bankers. Having started out as merchants, the Tuscans had experience underwriting long-distance trade and reaped large profits from doing so.[25] This commercial success was a source of income and wealth that could be put to wider use. From underwriting trade it was a short step to making loans unrelated to their commercial interests and attracting additional capital and deposits to fund those operations. Having bought and sold goods internationally, the Tuscans were familiar with different monies. They had developed the bill of exchange as a mechanism for transferring funds between locations, including on behalf of the Church.[26] (A bill of exchange is a payment order through which the issuer instructs an individual in another location to settle a debt on his behalf.) Possessing financial resources, the Tuscans could anticipate income from religious dues and advance money to the papacy.

From the early thirteenth century, the merchant-bankers of Siena, Lucca, Florence, and Pistoia competed in providing financial services to the Roman Curia.[27] Boniface VIII, pope from 1294 to 1303, favored the Florentines, who consequently acquired a quasi-monopoly.[28] Their favored position meant profits and, hence, resources for additional endeavors. As the Florentines spread their wings, they became bankers to the papacy in Avignon, France (which housed the pope for nearly seventy years in the fourteenth century), and to Edward III in England. International lending is sometimes portrayed as a uniquely modern phenomenon. In fact, Tuscan bankers engaged in sovereign lending across borders already in the fourteenth century.

The Church encouraged the banks to incorporate as joint stock companies as a way of furthering their provision of credit. Thus, in contrast to the bankers of the earlier Roman Republic, these banking firms had legal personalities independent of their investors. They had transferable shares. They had partners overseeing different regional branches and a single master account at the head office in Tuscany. Organizationally, they emulated their earliest client, the Holy See. In the same way that the pope issued instructions in letters to his far-flung bishops, the head offices of the Tuscan banks sent written instructions to their foreign branch offices.

This new corporate form enabled what started out as family firms to increase their capital base by selling shares to additional investors. It allowed them to attract deposits from wealthy individuals as a way of expanding their lending capacity without further diluting their control.[29] Over time, these Tuscan banks developed into some of the largest economic organizations in medieval and Renaissance Europe. Knowing where their bread was buttered, they continued granting advances to the Church.

## Mountains of Debt

In time, other city-states of the Italian peninsula elaborated the Tuscan model. These cities were heavily involved in trade, so they had to defend their ships and secure their trading routes. They had voyages to finance, and they were in the business of extending credit to their suppliers and customers. All this required financial resources and acumen. Not incidentally, this same trade was a source of income and wealth that they could turn around and lend.

Accordingly, Genoa and Venice became home to banking houses not unlike those of the hilltop towns of Tuscany. Their banks pioneered innovative financial contracts and accounting systems. Double-entry bookkeeping, under which each and every financial transaction has equal and opposite effects in two accounts, may not have been invented in Venice, but it was most certainly popularized there. The bankers for their part found ready customers in the governments of these same commercial city-states.

Importantly, Italian city-states appear to have been able to borrow at longer maturities than other thirteenth- and fourteenth-century debtors. City walls offered protection from hostile forces; they supported regime survival, which was a prerequisite for repayment. Cities, to which merchants migrated for protection from marauding gangs and invading powers, overtook the smaller towns that hosted regional fairs, now becoming the leading commercial centers. Their mercantile expansion in turn provided a pool of resources for lending.

Moreover, unlike sovereigns, whose powers were absolute and therefore arbitrary, republican city-states could credibly promise to repay. They were dominated by merchants.[30] Were the state to default on its debts, those merchants would be defaulting on themselves. The debt was an obligation of the commune, which might outlive any one individual, including a monarch with infinite powers but finite life.[31] Hence city-states were able to issue long-term debt earlier and more successfully than other polities.

In particular, republican city-states such as Venice, Genoa, and Florence possessed representative assemblies in which the creditors had voice. Geographical compactness allowed them to meet despite high travel and communications costs.[32] The cities' limited geographical scope meant that landowners did not outnumber merchants in the ranks of the elite. Those merchants, as a source of credit to the state, had an obvious interest in prioritizing repayment.

Genoa's case is illustrative. The Commune (later the Republic) faced the repeated need to finance military campaigns, first in conjunction with the Crusades and then to secure trading routes and colonies. As early as 1149, it ceded control of direct taxes to a consortium of bankers, known as a *compera*, as a way of expanding its ability to borrow. Subsequent expeditions then required additional taxes be assigned to ship construction and related costs. Some debt issued in this context was retired, but some was rolled over (new loans were extended as soon as the old ones matured), thereby forming the basis for a permanent stock of debt.[33]

Other Italian city-states emulated Genoa's example, raising loans by assigning specific revenues to the creditors. In Venice, the Doge, advised by senior magistrates elected by the Senate, raised loans to fight the Republic's many wars. In 1164, the Doge borrowed from twelve leading families in exchange for controlling, for eleven years, rents paid to the city by the merchants of the Rialto market.

This practice of delegating revenues had limits, however; if taken to the extreme, it might leave the Republic with no funds with which to meet emergencies. The Venetian government consequently changed tack. Starting in 1172, it demanded contributions from wealthy citizens in the form of forced loans.[34] Venice was divided into six districts, in each of which officials collected declarations of wealth.[35] Although citizens were required to subscribe to the loan on the basis of those declarations, they received an interest rate of 4 percent. Taxes on vendors' stalls at the Rialto Market were again set aside for interest payments, as were revenues from the weigh house, where other merchandise was weighed and assessed. Although the revenues were still controlled by the government, records were maintained by the Procurators of San Marco, prominent citizens appointed by the Doge and subsequently by the Grand Council (the communal assembly in which the creditors were represented).[36] These institutional arrangements can be seen as an early forerunner of the International Monetary Fund's Fiscal Transparency Code, which is designed to provide "legislatures, markets, and citizens with the information they need to hold governments accountable for their fiscal performance and use of public resources."[37] These arrangements were intended to enhance the credibility of the commitment to repay, as they did.

The initial expectation was that the debts of the Venetian Republic would be repaid at the first opportunity. As in Genoa, however, the ability to borrow proved alluring, and the state's obligations were rolled over. As more obligations then accumulated, questions arose as to their being retired. This reality was acknowledged in 1262 when the Republic's debts were consolidated into long-term loans known as *monti* (Italian for "mountains" [of debt]). Owners of *monti* could trade them on an informal secondary market, where prices reacted to the military successes and setbacks of the state (a pattern that will be important for our story).

*Monti* bore a 5 percent return, lower than on the earlier, unconsolidated loans. To be sure, 5 percent was better than nothing—considerably better, since merchants and other wealthy citizens, operating through the Grand Council, were imposing this restructuring on themselves. After all, if the Republic's earlier debt was unsustainable, and if the state collapsed under its weight, then those creditors would receive nothing. But if everyone agreed to a reduced income, then the state might still be able to commission voyages and mount military campaigns. The creditors all had to agree, however, which led to the forced nature of the conversion. This, in effect, was an early example of the collective-action problem that regularly bedevils a state's creditors and that, over history, has been addressed in many ways.[38]

To manage the *monti*, the Grand Council created a special board of worthies with ties to the commercial elite. Members were required to swear an oath that they would use the revenues accruing to the city to pay interest, after deducting just 36,000 lire for essential civic services.[39] It is sometimes argued that delegating authority to individuals with a stake in debt repayment was a mechanism through which territorial states acquired the ability to borrow in the seventeenth and eighteenth centuries.[40] Venetian history indicates that city-states already had resorted to this practice fully five centuries earlier.

When Venice then became embroiled in a life-and-death struggle with its rival Genoa in the war of Chioggia (1378–81), the prices of Venetian bonds fell to deep discounts on the secondary market (as shown in Figure 2.1). This reflected not only the vagaries of the war, which Venice ultimately won, but also the mixed nature of the loans. Desperate times requiring desperate measures, the Venetian state required its citizens to subscribe up to 40 percent of their wealth in new forced loans. The resulting bonds changed hands for less than their face value, again reflecting the uncertain outcome of the war. Citizens compelled by circumstances to sell their bonds might get only 8 soldi on the lira (40 cents on the dollar). Conversely, in buying those bonds, speculators (the equivalent of the vulture funds that dog twenty-first-century sovereign debt markets) stood to make large gains if Venice emerged victorious and continued to pay the 5 percent coupon.

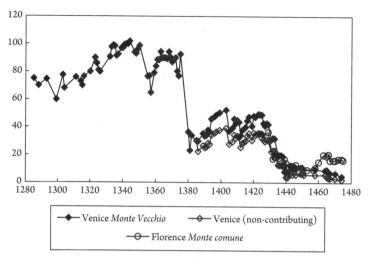

*Figure 2.1.* Prices of Venetian and Florentine Bonds, 1285–1475 (percent of par)
Sources: Luzzatto (1963) and Conti (1984).
Note: Venice's *Monte Vecchio* and Florence's *Monte Comune* were long-term bonds that consolidated past debt (in 1262 and 1343, respectively) and new forced loans. These bonds were freely tradable and bore an initial coupon of 5 percent. From 1382, Venice paid a lower rate of interest to bondholders who bought the *monti* in the secondary market from citizens who had been forced to subscribe them. The market prices of these "noncontributing" bonds were correspondingly lower.

High returns accruing to speculators, well into the double digits, led the Venetian authorities to reduce the interest rate unilaterally, in another early example of an involuntary restructuring.[41] The coupon rate was cut from 5 to 4 percent in 1382. In 1386 the state then reduced the coupon paid to investors who had bought its bonds in the secondary market from 4 to 3 percent and then in 1444 to 2 percent. The price of the bonds held by noncontributing investors was correspondingly less than that of bonds still in the hands of the Venetian citizens who had originally subscribed to the war loans.

By the early sixteenth century, having raised a series of forced loans to fight increasingly costly wars, the Venetian authorities were unable to force more *monti* onto their citizens.[42] They therefore sought to cultivate voluntary demand. New subscribers, many from the less-wealthy classes, were offered annuities, payments administered by the state mint (the *Zecca*). These annuities bore a market rate of return and were actively traded.[43] Each issue was secured by state revenues earmarked for the purpose. The initiative proved successful. In this way, a broader market for Venetian state debt was born.

After the loss of Cyprus in 1573, Venice enjoyed a long period of peace, during which the authorities sought to consolidate the debt. By extending new taxes imposed during wartime, the government was able to repay most of its debts to the *Zecca* between 1577 and 1584, saving itself half a million ducats annually in interest. As we will see, debt consolidations are not always this fast; nor are they pursued with such resolve.

## Florence Follows

The public finances of the Florentine Republic evolved along parallel lines. From 1201, the state administration followed a strict pay-as-you-go policy, relying on a direct tax, the *estimo*. For much of the thirteenth century, the *estimo* covered the state's spending needs, given that Florence, unlike Genoa and Venice, was not a maritime power defending seaborne trade routes or possessing overseas ambitions.[44]

With commercial expansion, however, came conflicts with neighbors. By the late thirteenth century, military expenses were rising faster than revenues. The Florentine state, like Venice, relied initially on forced loans. These were allocated following official assessments of household wealth, as in Venice, and the city was divided into districts for purposes of fiscal administration. But in contrast to Venice, where wealth was self-assessed, five committees were established in each district to produce independent estimates of wealth for each household. The high and low estimates were discarded, and the average of the middle three formed the basis for the assessment. This procedure was designed, as one historian has put it, to "diminish the corruption and favoritisms to which any assessment of fiscal burdens of neighbors by neighbors was vulnerable. . . ."[45]

These widely held loans transformed Florence into a republic of citizen creditors who pushed for arrangements to protect their interests.[46] The administrative responsibilities of the state were delegated to consuls, who served for a fixed period and lived in monklike isolation in order to limit patronage and other earthly temptations, including financial. Debt service and amortization were overseen by committees on which the major creditors served. Committee members were accountable to communal assemblies and, later, to representative councils in which creditors were again among the most active participants.

In 1315 the *estimo*, paid mainly by the wealthy, was abolished in "a political decision, made by, and in the interests of, the class of wealthy merchants and property owners."[47] Those merchants and property owners hoped that higher taxes on consumption goods, such as wine, olive oil, and hogs, and which fell primarily on the poorer segments of society, would provide adequate revenues, and free them of the burden of taxation. Instead, receipts declined as the tax rate rose.[48] Meanwhile, Florence faced mounting military expenses owing to its conflict with the Ghibelline forces of Lucca, supporters of the Holy Roman Emperor. Something had to give. So, as in Venice, the state considered forced loans. But forcing more loans on the citizenry threatened to provoke a rebellion. The Republic thus turned to its large banking houses, the Bardi and Peruzzi. Aware that lending to a penurious sovereign was risky, the bankers demanded an interest rate of 15 percent.

Such a high rate obviously made it hard for the state to stay current on its obligations.[49] Accordingly, Florentine officials in 1343 resorted to a restructuring.[50] They converted the public debt into a collective *Monte Comune*, writing down the principal and attaching a reduced 5 percent interest rate to the balance.[51]

Given this checkered history of repayment, securing voluntary subscriptions to subsequent debt emissions wasn't easy. The Florentine authorities responded in 1424 with a new financial instrument tailored to the needs of the investing public. This was the *Monte delle doti*, a dowry fund that promised to repay the money subscribed by families in 7.5 to 15 years. Funds invested in this new instrument, unlike the *Monte Comune*, did not pay interest periodically, but instead provided a balloon payment on maturity. This security was designed to meet the needs of parents planning ahead to pay for festive weddings for their daughters, as well as for the associated dowries. Unlike earlier loans, which were only as credible as the current financial circumstances of the state, the dowry fund was integral to social life. It was unlikely to be defaulted on because the commune's leading citizens, and more importantly their wives, wouldn't stand for it.

Subscribers to the *doti* could purchase shares with the bonds of the old *Monte Comune*, alleviating the burden of earlier loans. Moreover, because the dowry fund paid interest and repaid principal only at the end of the contract, the Florentine state's debt-service obligations were backloaded. Together, these provisions reduced the immediate interest burden and in so doing stabilized the prices of the state's debt securities.[52]

This conjoining of political and financial elites, cemented by joint governance arrangements, allowed Italian city-states to borrow long and cheap before anyone else. The power and representation of the creditors prevented the state from overborrowing and discouraged it, when things went wrong, from mandating excessively costly cuts in interest and principal (what modern finance specialists call haircuts). The corresponding limitation was that foreigners were reluctant to purchase Italian securities, since they were not represented in these city-states' governing assemblies. Hence Italian city-states were able to attract and use only modest amounts of foreign capital prior to the seventeenth century.[53] In an era of limited government, the capacity to tap the local market was enough. In the long run, however, this reluctance to access regional, national, and international markets turned out not to be a winning model.

## The Development of Secondary Markets

Territorial monarchs with god-given powers were not subject to oversight by representative assemblies. By implication, they were not easily deterred from repudiating their debts. For bankers to lend, those monarchs consequently had to hypothecate valuable assets, pledging them as security. Pledging the crown jewels was the ultimate form of hypothecation, since their loss would fatally compromise a monarch's reputation.[54]

A more cautious monarch might grant his bankers the proceeds of salt monopolies or customs duties and tolls, and authorize the bankers to collect those taxes directly, in the manner of the republican city-states of Venice and Genoa. Thus, as a condition for lending to the king of England, Italian bankers were given the authority to collect payment directly from sheriffs, bailiffs, and other local officials. They oversaw operation of fishing ports and the mint.[55] This was a way not only of securing the loan, but also of helping to solve the information problem surrounding the adequacy of the sovereign's income. It prevented the king from claiming less income than actually received. It thereby resolved uncertainty about whether a sovereign's debt problems reflected inability to pay—or unwillingness. And with resolution of that ambiguity, debt renegotiation became easier, something that was important for sustaining debtor-creditor relations.

But what the sovereign could give, the sovereign could take away, also by royal decree. Some of the largest Italian merchant-banking houses were destroyed by a royal customer repudiating a debt. We have already described how Edward III's default reduced the Peruzzi and Bardi to bankruptcy in 1345.

For sovereign lending to continue, therefore, it was necessary to find a better way. One better way was diversification, through which individual lending houses limited their exposure to any one borrower. Some diversification could be achieved by syndication, through which the bankers assigned portions of the loan to other bankers. But more extensive diversification presupposed development of secondary markets on which shares of debt contracts could be sold to retail investors.

These share contracts were called *rentes* or *renten*. They specified that the holder would receive a stream of interest payments over his lifetime (in the case of "life rents") or in perpetuity. *Rentes* were pioneered by municipalities in northern France; from there they spread to towns and cities in Flanders, the Holy Roman Empire, and Spain.[56] The first documented case was Troyes, one of the towns hosting Champagne fairs and thus possessing a regular source of income, which sold life *rentes* in 1228. The purchasers were mostly financiers from nearby towns such as Arras, St. Quentin, and Rheims, who then resold their securities to retail investors in those neighboring municipalities. Thus, we see here the embryo of a secondary market infrastructure, in which primary dealers (the financiers) vetted the issuer (the government) before marketing shares to the final investor (the residents of other municipalities). And what worked at the municipal level was quickly emulated at higher levels of government.

In these developments we also see local financial markets beginning to evolve into what ultimately became national and even international markets. This was in contrast to the loans of the Italian city-states, which could be forced only on citizens and consequently were exclusively traded locally.

Perpetuities had yet further advantages. The payment stream was assigned to the loan contract rather than the initial purchaser, in contrast to the case of life annuities. Hence perpetuities were more easily traded, which in turn rendered them more attractive to investors.[57] This was evident in perpetuities bearing lower yields.[58] Since perpetuities didn't expire and could be redeemed only if the borrower raised revenue sufficient to repay the principal, an unlikely event, they formed the basis for a permanent stock of debt.

Yet another advantage of perpetuities was that they allowed lenders to circumvent religious doctrine on usury. Since perpetuities were not automatically retired, theologians regarded them as legitimate contracts in which one party purchased a stream of future income from the other, rather than as usurious debts to be repaid.[59] This allowed perpetuities to trade at market-clearing interest rates, which again made for more transactions.[60]

The repercussions of these developments extended beyond the state's own finances. Since these instruments were liquid and negotiable, investors were prepared to accept them as collateral when lending to other borrowers.[61] The existence of this state-backed collateral thereby secured and facilitated borrowing and lending by nonstate actors.[62] It increased the number and range of customers to which bankers were prepared to lend. In this way the sovereign's debt securities were transformed into a financial public good.

Through its acceptability as collateral, this stock of government bonds thus increased the availability of credit and the liquidity of secondary markets. It stimulated the development of short-term money markets on which credit was obtained by merchants, markets that consequently emerged first, and operated most vigorously, in Europe. Expansion of local and long-distance trade—what economic historians refer to as the Commercial Revolution—was a key factor in setting the stage for industrialization and modern economic growth. It was a factor in whose development sovereign debt played no small part.

The acceptability of government debt as collateral also reduced the interest rate required of sovereigns by increasing the utility of their negotiable securities. Investing in the debt securities of a territorial monarch was still risky, to be sure, given the borrower's ability to repudiate his debts, so a risk premium was demanded of the borrower. But diversification enabled investors to avoid putting all their eggs in one royal basket. The existence of liquid secondary markets allowed risk-averse investors to reduce their exposure when these dangers arose and, in this way, greased the wheels of sovereign finance. In turn, the development of short-term money markets, aided by availability of sovereign debt as collateral, encouraged investment.[63] And the healthier economy made possible by financial development worked to strengthen the royal regime and enhance the sustainability of its debts.[64]

## A Market Comes into Focus

By the sixteenth century, then, many of the prerequisites were in place for the operation of sovereign debt markets. Credit being critical for military success and state survival, there was no lack of demand for finance. Investors had developed mechanisms for securing their claims, including the hypothecation of revenues and pledging of collateral, and were increasingly willing to lend. The outline of the modern sovereign debt market came into focus, with liquid secondary markets and dedicated bankers and financiers acting as broker-dealers. And the same institutions and instruments that greased the wheels of sovereign finance increasingly invigorated private capital markets, with wider consequences for commercial and economic development.

These mechanisms did not prevent periodic defaults and restructurings, which mark sovereign debt markets through the ages. But neither did such problems prevent those markets from expanding to the point where they were ready to accommodate a new class of borrowers, come the emergence of the modern nation-state system.

# States and the Limits of Borrowing

The next stage in the development of public finance came with the rise of nation-states. The size and stability of the European states created after the Peace of Westphalia, which ended the Thirty Years War in 1648, permitted new and more efficient forms of taxation and, as a consequence, more extensive public borrowing. Meanwhile, the growth of public debt provoked a reaction from creditors, who won seats at the fiscal table. In some instances, those creditors forced sovereigns into commitments requiring them to balance their territorial ambitions with fiscal probity. In the best case, those same commitments also conferred benefits to the sovereign, in the form of lower borrowing costs.

Europe's political geography then coalesced into a system of nation-states, as governments used modern military technology to consolidate their rule and secure their borders. Commerce expanded with the elimination of internal tariffs and mercantilist restrictions. Financial markets developed along with production and trade, undergirded by negotiable public debt securities eligible as collateral. More production made for more powerful and extensive states, and more powerful and extensive states made for additional tax revenue, enabling governments to service more debt. One can here begin to discern the positive feedbacks that facilitated modern public finance and, ultimately, modern economic growth.

With political centralization came stronger internal checks and balances. Representative assemblies could be organized at the national level, transportation costs having declined from Venetian days. Landowners and merchants thus were better able to push back against arbitrary action by the sovereign. Although tax centralization allowed rulers greater access to funds, political elites required that a portion of that finance be devoted to debt service and that another portion support the provision of public goods, rather than being dissipated in military adventures.

To be sure, this transition to limited government was uneven. It was completed earlier in England and Holland than in France and Spain. But the direction of travel was clear.

## Dutch Treat

The Netherlands was the transitional case, where the polity created institutions requiring the sovereign to share the power of the purse. Movement began in the sixteenth century, following the declaration of independence from Spain by the seven provinces that formed the Republic of the Netherlands. From this point, fiscal prerogatives were delegated to the States-General, an assembly of provincial delegates who oversaw the finances of the central government. Most provincial representatives were merchants and investors, who followed the instructions of those responsible for governance of their home provinces, where merchants and creditors were again influential. This made the States-General a voice for fiscal probity.[1]

The central government had a source of direct income in the tariff, used for funding the navy, which was organized into five regional admiralties.[2] This use of tariff revenues was appropriate, since the admiralties kept shipping lanes open and did battle with pirates, two key state-building functions for a maritime power.[3] Other central-government functions were funded by taxes administered by the provinces, portions of which were transferred according a formula inherited from the Spanish period.[4] In practice, some 80 percent of the resources of the central government derived from this revenue sharing.[5]

To ensure that import duties were collected and revenues were allocated according to formula, the States-General appointed a treasurer-general to keep the books. The States-General worked with a Council of States, made up of members drawn from the various provinces.[6] The Council was concerned with administration of the military, for which purpose it presented a report of common expenses to the treasurer-general annually. This transparency was designed to enhance accountability for those responsible for raising and spending revenues. The system did not work perfectly, as we are about to see. But it imposed a degree of uniformity on the still partly decentralized Dutch system.

Each province individually attempted to implement similar checks and balances. In Holland, for example, debt holders doubled as political decision makers.[7] They sat in the Estates of Holland, to which eighteen towns and cities sent delegates. The chief executive of this body was the councilor pensionary. The councilor served a fixed five-year term and had his own budget and staff. However, because decisions in the Estates of Holland required a qualified majority, he had to build a coalition with other representatives.[8] This meant reaching understandings specifically with other merchants and creditors. The leading seventeenth-century councilor pensionary, Johan de Witt, was himself an investor in government securities and able mathematician. His most famous work, *The Worth of Life Annuities Compared to Redemption Bonds*, developed formulae for comparing returns on annuities and redeemable debt.[9] Life annuities, as we saw in Chapter 2, were relatively illiquid and therefore bore high interest rates. Using his findings, de Witt converted most of the province's life annuities into long-term redeemable securities, reducing Holland's debt service payments and enhancing its ability to borrow.

By the second half of the seventeenth century, these arrangements allowed Holland and other Dutch provinces to acquire what only the stablest city-states had achieved before, namely the ability to issue long-term debt at interest rates of 3–4 percent. These rates fell from 5 percent in the first half of the seventeenth century and the 6–8 percent paid previously—higher rates that were still attached to borrowing by other authorities.[10] Figure 3.1 displays Holland's fiscal achievement: it shows the real interest rates that the province paid for its long-term borrowing.[11]

Clever marketing accompanied this clever financial engineering. Government revenue offices were established in each city to distribute the debts among retail investors. "Receivers" responsible for those offices were empowered to tailor their offerings to local tastes.[12] These arrangements, together with a large middle

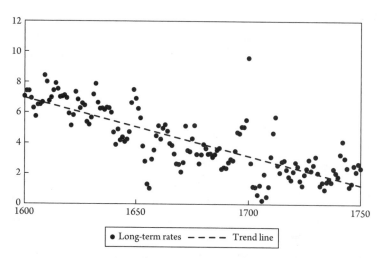

*Figure 3.1.* Long-term Borrowing Costs for Holland, Real Interest Rates, 1600–1750 (percent)

Source: Schmelzing (2020).

Note: Inflation expectations are one-step-ahead forecasts from an ARMA(1,1) GARCH(4,1) model of Dutch price inflation.

class and the state's reputation for financial probity, enabled the Netherlands to become the first state to successfully mass-market its debt. Such marketing prowess in turn created a constituency supportive of fiscal prudence. This synergy helps to explain how the provinces of the Dutch Republic were able to issue large amounts of new debt in the final decades of the Eighty Years War, from 1618 to 1648, at declining interest rates—just the opposite of what one would expect when the debt burden was rising.

## Failure from Success

The Dutch model was transitional in that it involved only a partial move toward fiscal centralization. The individual admiralties collected the common tariff at their respective ports.[13] Those admiralties varied in their tolerance of smugglers and hence in the tenacity with which they collected duties. Moreover, because vigorous application of duties might divert business to other less-taxing ports, there was a tendency to undercollect.[14] The smaller provinces also tended to shirk on their obligation to transfer a portion of their receipts to the center, claiming fewer revenues than they actually raised. The largest province, Holland, which had the least ability to free-ride, sometimes made up the shortfall, but only partly.

Thus, while the Dutch system limited overspending, it also limited receipts. This was a happy balance in normal times, but it could be problematic in exceptional circumstances. The War of the Spanish Succession, from 1701 to 1714, was just such a circumstance. With military expenses rising sharply, Holland tested the limits of its borrowing. As interest rates on its bonds rose from the customary 3–4 percent to 6 percent and higher, the province reintroduced the costly life annuities that de Witt had eliminated some years earlier.

But if higher interest rates enabled the state to maintain its market access, they also augured problems. By 1713, Holland's debt service had come to exceed its ordinary tax revenues, understandable given wartime circumstances, but not sustainable. The state could meet its interest obligations only by issuing additional debt, an ability it now predictably lost. The Estates had no choice but to announce a reduction in the interest rate—in effect, to declare a default.

Evidently, the Dutch system of partial fiscal centralization, with its associated free-rider problems, had its limits. There followed, in the course of the eighteenth century, a series of reform proposals intended to address these limitations, none of which gained political traction. The provinces and admiralties remained jealous of their prerogatives. Full centralization was achieved only after more than a century.

In the meantime, the central and provincial governments were forced to compress their spending, leading to what economic historians Jan de Vries and Ad van der Woude label the Dutch Republic's "undisguisable military impotence."[15] Lacking resources, the Netherlands adopted a foreign policy of studied neutrality. Having taken the lead for four decades in an international coalition to contain the French, the Dutch now steered carefully between France on one side and Britain and Austria on the other, placating neither. Dutch armies and navies acquitted themselves poorly in war with the British (provoked by Dutch support for the North American revolutionaries) and war with the French (provoked by the French Revolution).

Reasons for the decline of the Netherlands as a military and maritime power are complex. The East India Company, the most important Dutch business enterprise, faced growing competition from foreign trading companies. The Dutch were less successful than the British in establishing colonies. Lack of coal became a handicap with the transition to steam power and the Industrial Revolution. But the lag in moving to fiscal centralization and consequent limits on borrowing and debt-servicing capacity are important parts of the story.

Thus, the Netherlands' early success at modernizing the public finances of a territorial state gave way, ultimately, to failure. The experience is a reminder that the history of public debt, like other history, is not linear.

## Glorious Fiscal Revolution

In England, what came to be known as the Glorious Revolution limited the prerogatives of the monarch and enhanced the parliamentary influence of the creditors. In a famous paper, Nobel Laureate Douglas North and his coauthor Barry Weingast argued that the events of 1688 were revolutionary not just politically but also financially.[16] In their telling, by creating a constitutional monarchy the Glorious Revolution credibly committed the sovereign to repay what he borrowed. This led in turn to a sharp reduction in the sovereign's borrowing costs.

Subsequent revisionism suggests that imposition of constitutional checks and the decline in borrowing costs were more evolutionary than revolutionary. Already in the thirteenth century, the king's ability to levy taxes was subject to the advice and consent of his Great Council of church elders and wealthy landowners.[17] In 1362, Parliament then adopted a statute asserting its right to approve all taxes, where a major purpose of taxation was to service and repay debt. In 1407, King Henry IV conceded that this right to approve taxes resided with the House of Commons, the chamber where merchants and creditors had the loudest voice. When Charles I attempted to force loans on the wealthy,

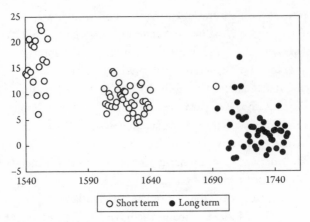

*Figure 3.2.* Borrowing Costs of the English/British Crown, Real Interest Rates, 1540–
1750 (percent)

Sources: Epstein (2000) for short-term rates and the Bank of England database "A Millennium of
Macroeconomic Data for the UK" (Bank of England, 2017) for yields on long-term debt (consols) and
prices.

Note: Inflation expectations are one-step ahead forecasts from ARMA(2,4) model of English price
inflation.

Parliament asserted their illegality, setting the stage for the English Civil War,
fundamentally a conflict over who controlled the power to tax and borrow.
That same assertion ultimately led to the Glorious Revolution that North and
Weingast celebrate as a turning point.

The sovereign's borrowing costs in fact came down gradually over a long
period, reflecting the evolutionary nature of these developments. Figure 3.2
shows their long retreat from double-digit levels in the sixteenth century to just
3 percent in the eighteenth century. Already by the 1650s, prior to the Glorious
Revolution, two-thirds of this reduction had been achieved.

Still, there was a sense in which the Glorious Revolution constituted an important break. For the first time, all sovereign promises and obligations were
brought under exclusive parliamentary control; loopholes through which the
king's ministers had previously eluded parliamentary control were closed,
rendering ministers now directly answerable or, technically, responsible to
Parliament.[18] The sovereign was now able to reliably issue long-term debt,
averting his earlier need to resort to short-term loans, on which interest rates
were more volatile. English kings began to regularly issue the perpetuities
that came to be known as consols. (The term was derived from "consolidated
annuities" and came into common use after the consolidation of nine separate
government bonds into a single 3 percent bond in 1751.) This newfound stability, rather than a sudden reduction in interest rates, was the financial legacy
of the Glorious Revolution.

# Absolute Monarchs and Their Debts

Absolute monarchs with unchecked powers found borrowing more difficult. Some, such as Philip II, king of Spain from 1556 to 1597, had little choice but to fund their military campaigns by borrowing short term from European bankers, the "payday lenders" of the era.[19] Although problems with these loans were chronic—Philip, for example, defaulted four times—the king's Genoese bankers succeeded in encouraging him to restructure, rather than repudiate his debt outright. They used the modern mechanism of loan syndication to form a cohesive cartel that prevented lenders from competing with one another. That cartel was held together by "linkages of blood and marriage" and a tapestry of interwoven business ties.[20] These connections enabled the bankers to threaten Philip that failing to meet them halfway would result in his indefinite loss of market access, a result with catastrophic consequences when borrowing was a matter of state survival. We will see in subsequent chapters how, with further development of financial markets inhabited by more numerous lenders not bound together by ties of blood and marriage, it became more difficult to form a coalition and effectively threaten a defaulting debtor with loss of market access. Evidently, financial development, though not without benefits, also creates problems.

Despite Philip's serial suspensions of debt-service payments, Genoese bankers charged a sufficiently high interest rate on their loans to earn a healthy return.[21] This explains why they continued to lend despite Philip's repeated debt-service interruptions. Put another way, Philip's unchecked powers and inability to commit—and the bankers' absence of recourse other than to deny him market access—meant that the king paid a pretty penny in order to borrow.[22]

Like Spain, France failed to pursue political reforms along Dutch or English lines, which again limited the sovereign's ability to borrow. Nominally, the French constitution provided for a representative assembly, the Estates General, that met to approve the king's requests for new taxes and funds. Unlike other assemblies that sat regularly, however, the Estates was called by the king. In practice, the frequency of meetings was among the lowest of all representative assemblies in Europe.[23] Moreover, the Estates were dominated by landowners, not by the government's creditors. Members hailed from the provinces and lacked sympathy for the Parisian elite, who disproportionately held the government's debt. All this limited the political representation and influence of the creditors, which in turn limited the king's ability to borrow.

The resulting political vacuum was filled by a network of *parlements*, led by that of Paris. Notwithstanding their name, these were courts, not assemblies. Although the king possessed extensive executive and legal powers, his edicts and laws had to be registered by these bodies to acquire the force of law.[24] Mostly filled by ennobled legal officers, these courts could refuse to register his edicts, including those creating new taxes.[25] Louis XIV famously asserted "l'état c'est moi" when he came into conflict with the *parlement* of Paris in 1655. In 1673 he went so far as to abolish the courts' right of registration, which gave him unprecedented power to rule by edict.[26] After his death, the regent ruling in the name of the new king, Louis's five-year-old great-grandson, returned this power to the *parlements* in an effort to solidify their support for the regency. Still, the lesson was that what the king granted he could also take away.

A further problem was the decentralization of fiscal arrangements. Regions absorbed into the French state relatively late retained their own archaic tax systems. The Church, the nobility, and other special interests received exemptions in return for their political support.[27] This was a more chaotic version of the fiscal decentralization characteristic of the Netherlands and had similarly destabilizing consequences.

The inefficiency of French taxation, a consequence of these limitations, made it difficult to raise revenues adequate for servicing and repaying debt. Collection of indirect taxes on consumption goods was delegated to tax farmers, for the most part accountants and notaries organized into large groups or syndicates.[28] The king received a fixed sum, and the tax farm kept the rest. In practice, the tax farmers had a better sense of that revenue potential, given the size and diversity of the French economy and the fact that they had boots on the ground. Moreover, there was little competition for contracts, since it was challenging to organize an army of private-sector tax collectors.[29] The king might have increased his income by negotiating a revenue-sharing arrangement, but this would have exposed him to income fluctuations. And income fluctuations were potentially damaging given the Crown's difficulty in borrowing and smoothing its spending.[30]

Only the main direct tax, the *taille*, levied on land, was administered directly by the Crown. Unfortunately, this too was riddled with exemptions based on regional privileges and social status. Chief among these was exemption of property owned by the Church and the nobility, where the latter controlled more than 40 percent of all land.[31] In an attempt to shore up the system, successive kings and finance ministers sought to create new taxes, but these ended up foundering on the opposition of vested interests.[32]

Although the real value of tax receipts increased sixfold between the sixteenth and eighteenth centuries, this was not enough to keep pace with the country's rivals. England, a nation with a third to a half of French population and a smaller national income, was able to mobilize more revenue, enabling it to service more debt and, in times of need, to borrow more extensively.[33] It evidently helped to have universal taxation, a Parliament that sat regularly, and rule of law.

A third factor limiting French fiscal capacity was the sovereign's late embrace of modern borrowing methods. Compared with the long-term annuities and consols marketed by the Dutch and English to a large public of middling investors, French long-term debt instruments were complex and illiquid. Like Spanish kings, French monarchs borrowed from financiers at high interest, for short terms. But unlike the Spanish, who relied on Genoese bankers, French kings borrowed at home. Their main lenders were the tax farmers and officials who collected and transferred the funds they were responsible for raising. Both controlled large capital sums that the king sought to tap.

But as in Spain, the capacity of French kings to grow the tax base fell short of their military ambitions. This being the case, lenders relied on short-maturity debt as a disciplining device. The monarchy issued short-term treasury notes that were endorsable, negotiable, and readily traded but that had to be reissued as they matured. In turn, this required the king to take visible steps to shore up investor confidence.[34]

These frequent debt rollovers did not entirely protect the creditors: in the seventeenth and eighteenth centuries, defaults followed wars on no fewer than ten occasions. As a result, French kings, like Spanish kings, were forced to borrow more expensively than their rivals.

## The *Rente* Comes Due

In an effort to circumvent this problem, the French sovereign piggybacked on the creditworthiness of other institutions. Rather than borrowing from individual investors, the sovereign borrowed from the Church and the Municipality of Paris, which had their own incomes and would have been formidable enemies had the king reneged.[35] The government of Paris was controlled by merchants rather than the landed elites who dominated the Estates General. Those merchants, often also bondholders, were concerned that their obligations were promptly and fully serviced, and to that end sought to ensure that they were safely collateralized. This in turn lent credibility to the king's promise to repay.

Starting in 1522, the Municipality sold perpetual annuities (*rentes*) to local investors, passing the proceeds to the king. In turn, the king signed a contract assigning specific future revenues, initially from consumption taxes levied in and around Paris, for use in servicing these obligations. The municipal authorities were well informed about commercial conditions in Paris, enabling them to verify the Crown's claims concerning revenues. The *bureau de ville* (the Paris city council) collected the taxes, so it could allocate them to debt service directly. The *bureau* had to approve issuance of additional *rentes* and didn't knuckle under easily. In effect, it acted as gatekeeper, preventing the king from overborrowing.[36]

This system worked smoothly so long as the Crown limited these arrangements to Paris. Eventually, however, the pressure of war led the monarch to ask the Municipality to also market *rentes* in other cities. To service these debts, the Crown pledged revenues from all over France. But monitoring tax collection in multiple towns was more complicated than just monitoring it in Paris. Ultimately, consumption tax revenues fell behind interest payments, leading to a suspension of payments in the 1570s.[37]

A final source of indirect borrowing was the sale of public offices. This practice, dating to the fourteenth century, involved everyone from the accountants who managed the state's finances to municipal dignitaries, attorneys, notaries, judges, and, eventually, wigmakers. The king assigned income from the office in return for a loan, known as a *finance*. Like the British consol, the *finance* was perpetual; it could be passed down to future generations, along with the office itself. Although the Crown might pay interest, the holder's income derived mainly from the functions of the office. Since offices were transferable (they could be bought and sold), they were popular investments.[38] They went through periods of substantial price inflation, reflecting rising income accruing to officeholders, until the French Revolution terminated their sale.[39] Interest rates on *finances* were low, given expectations of increases in valuation.

Even Jacques Necker, the astute Genevan banker hired to rescue the French sovereign from bankruptcy, recommended the sale of offices as a revenue-raising device. A report commissioned by Necker in 1778 calculated that the effective interest paid on offices was as little as three-quarters of a percentage point. Its authors concluded, accordingly, that "there is no other form of borrowing ... that is less onerous to the state."[40] What the authors didn't realize, or at least didn't emphasize, was that selling offices mortgaged the sovereign's future. The state received a low interest rate loan now but relinquished sources of income that would expand along with the economy.[41] This shortsightedness would come back to bite the French sovereign in 1789.

Increasingly desperate for a market, the French monarchy experimented with various financial innovations in the final years of the Ancien Régime. It tailored its debt securities to the tastes of investors, à la the Dutch, seeking a wider market. It mass-marketed life annuities (those familiar instruments that paid a fixed interest rate over the course of the purchaser's life), but also tontines— collectively purchased annuities that paid installments only to survivors, in the manner of a lottery. Tontines were also marketed elsewhere, but they were relied on most heavily in France. Survivors received attractive returns, compensating them for the risk of holding claims on a government with an unreliable revenue stream.[42]

As a result, the next time the monarchy faced a fiscal crunch, owing to the costs of the American War of Independence (1775–83), there had been a material change in the relation between the king and his creditors. Those creditors were no longer just a financial elite of tax officials and farmers. A default was now more dangerous politically, since it would touch more of the king's subjects. Returning to save the day, Necker recommended that the king recall the Estates General, which he did in August 1788. Things didn't turn out as intended. Less than a year later, the Ancien Régime was swept away by what became the French Revolution.

## Neither Holy nor Roman

The Holy Roman Empire, encompassing much of modern-day Germany, was yet another laggard in the transition to modern public finance. It was composed of 170 secular and 136 ecclesiastical fiefs and 83 imperial cites that guarded their autonomy jealously. Emperors were chosen by princes who exacted fiscal concessions. Those same princes, who along with the magistrates of imperial cities were responsible for collecting imperial taxes, met with the emperor to negotiate their amount. They withheld funds when the emperor sought to strengthen the prerogatives of the center. They husbanded information about their wealth and fiscal capacity to avoid attracting attention from the imperial court.[43]

As a result, the empire lacked many of the normal *accoutrements* of a state, including a standing army, a unitary tax system, and a capital city.[44] In the first half of the seventeenth century, this unstable equilibrium degenerated into the Thirty Years War, during which the Catholic Habsburgs and Protestant princes engaged in internecine conflict rather than defending their collective borders, much less building commercial capacity.

The larger cities of the empire had developed relatively sophisticated fiscal administrations, tax structures, accounting practices, and banking systems by the medieval and early modern periods. As in the case of the Italian city-states, these achievements grew out of their experience as commercial and trading centers and relatively cohesive governance. The towns in question were able to issue perpetuities and life annuities. As early as the fourteenth century, their bonds were treated as negotiable. By comparison, princely fiefdoms and terri-torial administrations lagged behind. The cities therefore lent them funds. In addition, city residents acted as consultants to territories seeking to modernize their fiscal systems. An example was the Leipzig merchant Jacob Blasebalg, who reorganized the financial affairs of the Duchy of Saxony in 1487–90.

Where the cities led, princely territories followed, eventually anyway. They consolidated and reorganized their fiscal affairs to support standing armies, something for which the Thirty Years War provided impetus. Not so the em-peror, who remained cash strapped. The imperial domain was mortgaged in the fourteenth and fifteenth centuries, when successive emperors pledged property, jewels, and revenues for short-term loans.[45] "The central feature of German fiscal history," as one historian puts it, "was that once the king lost both his domain and, increasingly, his feudal rights during the latter Middle Ages, he found no way of compensating adequately for this loss through the development of new forms of revenue from the Empire."[46]

## Positively Modern

Notwithstanding these problems, by the mid-seventeenth century European states had accumulated debts that look positively modern, as high as 60 percent of GDP.[47] Their obligations, no longer in the hands of a small number of well-connected bankers, were widely held. The credibility of the commitment to repay was, as always, less than complete. Still, that such large debts were held by a growing population of investors suggests the ability to commit was significantly greater than before.

The Dutch provinces, as we have seen, were first to scale up this model. The seven provinces and most of the principal cities took advantage of the demand for fixed-income securities from charities, schools, and a growing middle class by issuing short-term promissory notes (*obligationen*), long-term bonds (*losrenten*), and life annuities (*lijfrenten*). In an important innovation, the Dutch then added an international twist by marketing their securities beyond their borders.[48]

Holland's sworn enemy, England (the two countries clashed over fishing rights and Asian trade), was able to mobilize even more finance by developing the indirect tax known as the excise, levied on everything from beer, spirits, and wine to leather, soap, and candles. Indirect taxes were more elastic than the land tax, the government's earlier source of finance, since revenues rose with commercial activity.[49] As at other times and places, these fiscal developments were a response to military imperatives. England itself had been late to raise a standing army, given the natural protection afforded by the Channel. It relied instead on the muster, which required able-bodied men to assemble when called, in the manner of an army reserve (more precisely, a militia reserve).[50] With the expansion of militaries on the continent, however, this cost-saving practice no longer sufficed. Then there was the Civil War, one legacy of which was the presence of a permanent standing army on English soil.[51] That army's existence created the need to mobilize additional revenues and lent legitimacy to the excise.

This fiscal system was supported by centralization, which England achieved earlier than other European states (see Table 3.1).[52] The excise was collected by a state commission, whose members had the pleasurable task of sampling ("tasting" in official parlance) beer, wine, and spirits in order to determine their taxability. Less palatable was the requirement that they advance a portion of

*Table 3.1* **State Revenues Per Capita and Fiscal Constitutions, 1650–1815 (revenues in grams of gold per capita)**

| Country | Fragmented | | Centralized | | Date of Centralization | Date of Limitation |
| --- | --- | --- | --- | --- | --- | --- |
| | Absolutist | Limited | Absolutist | Limited | | |
| England | | | 2.61 | 9.89 | 1066– | 1688– |
| France | 3.32 | | 6.45 | | 1790– | 1870– |
| Netherlands | | 12.15 | 11.52 | | 1806– | 1572–1795 |
| Portugal | 0.69 | | | | 1832– | 1851– |
| Prussia | 3.66 | | 2.78 | | 1806– | 1848– |
| Spain | 0.93 | | | | 1844– | 1876– |
| Sweden | 2.78 | | | | 1840– | 1866– |

*Source:* Dincecco (2011).

*Note:* Fragmented states are those in which revenues are raised by local authorities; centralized states are those where revenues are raised by the central government. Absolutist governments are not checked by a countervailing political institution such as a parliament, whereas limited governments are.

the taxes they were expected to collect, effectively allowing the state to borrow short term. This gave rise to mixed motives: the more efficient officials were at collecting taxes, the more they were expected to lend. The dilemma was not unlike that of a factory manager in the Soviet system, for whom increasing the efficiency of production only gave rise to an increased production quota.

Still, through the operation of this tax commission, the domain over which taxes were raised was extended beyond London and the Home Counties, which traditionally contributed the bulk of resources. In a sense, the tax commission constituted the embryo of Britain's independent, meritocratic civil service. It is sometimes said that the state is a network of agencies.[53] If so, then creation of this fiscal agency was central to the development of the modern English state.

Such reforms made for more revenues and debt-servicing capacity than in the fiscally fragmented Netherlands, altering the balance of power. It transformed what had been a royal debt, dependent on the personal credit of the sovereign, into a national debt supported by Parliament's right to levy and oversee collection of taxes. The excise, assignment of specific excises to servicing specific debts, and creation of a standing excise commission thereby enlarged the government's capacity to borrow. Officials seized the opportunity with both hands. As English historian John Brewer puts it, "borrowing reached such heights that if eighteenth-century Britain had gone to the modern International Monetary Fund for a loan it would certainly have been shown the door."[54]

The innovations that made this public borrowing possible also fostered the development of private financial markets. With the advent of the excise came excise-backed securities, also known as public-faith bills, which allowed the state to anticipate revenues. The government issued these in advance of tax receipts, reducing its dependence on advances from the tax commissioners. These bills were sold to retail investors with help from goldsmith-bankers, the forerunners of modern investment banks. Importantly, issuance of public-faith bills was subject to Parliamentary authorization. Presentation and discussion of accounts, reports, and papers in the House of Commons provided information enabling investors, most immediately members of Parliament but also others, to price these financial instruments. Trading of these securities on secondary markets, notably on the London Stock Exchange, began almost immediately. Public-faith bills were used as collateral for other financial transactions, extending further the collateral practices of the Florentine banking houses described in Chapter 2.[55] It is hard to imagine a clearer example of public debt in service of financial development.

## Backstopping the Market

Still, this fiscal system was not always able to meet the demands placed on it, especially when these stemmed from catastrophic military engagements, such as William III's defeat at the hands of Louis XIV in the Nine Years War (1688–97). By 1694, William had exhausted his credit. In response, he launched perhaps his most consequential financial innovation: the Bank of England. William allowed the founders to incorporate as a limited-liability joint-stock company with a banking license and the right to issue notes in London. In return, they extended him a £1.2 million loan at 8 percent. Simply put, William obtained an immediate cash infusion in return for mortgaging his right to issue notes.[56]

Compared to the French practice of selling offices, William's trading a bank charter for cash had more favorable implications for economic and financial development. These became evident when the Bank of England began buying and selling government securities on the London Stock Exchange. Its operations steadied the prices of those securities.[57] This stability reassured investors that government bonds could be reliably converted into cash at or near their face value. The bonds in question were then accepted as collateral even more widely than before. In these ways, the pledgeability of the government's debt securities, now backed by a bank prepared to ensure orderly market conditions, lent yet additional impetus to the development of credit markets.

The Bank of England next issued its own notes against the collateral of government bonds in its vaults. Doing so enabled it to provide liquidity to other banks and lend to the nonfinancial sector.[58] Such services were especially valuable in a period when Britain was engaged in expensive wars, when the government was borrowing heavily, and when public debt issuance threatened to crowd out private investment. Whatever crowding out occurred was limited by the bank's successful efforts to keep the credit market afloat.[59] In addition, Bank of England notes were accepted as money from the outset. They were used to settle a variety of transactions in addition to those in whose connection they were issued, and they were relied on as a store of value.

Thus, an act of desperation—creation of the Bank of England in response to William III's exhausted credit—gave Britain not just an active credit market but also a reliable money supply. Again, this was public debt in the service of commercial and financial development.

## Above the Law

Other financial innovations were rather less admirable. The 1710s saw episodes of financial speculation and manipulation in both France and Britain. In 1716, John Law, the son of a prominent Scottish goldsmith, banker, and gambler, created the Banque Générale on behalf of the French regent, the Duke of Orleans, who held the throne, as we have seen, on behalf of the child-king, Louis XV. Law simultaneously took control of the Company of the Mississippi, a state-chartered trading company that he renamed the Company of the West. It received a twenty-five-year monopoly on trading privileges in a vast region encompassing the Mississippi River Valley, nearly half the present-day continental United States. In return, Law's bank purchased sovereign bonds at prices favorable to the government, financing those purchases by issuing shares.

Effectively, the regent had committed the state's income from the Mississippi territory to servicing the debt by assigning that income to its principal creditor. In exchange for their bonds, investors received a claim on the prospective profits of Law's bank, in a kind of debt-for-equity swap.[60] As we will see elsewhere in this volume, sovereigns convert their debt into equity, arbitrarily modifying their creditors' claims, only when they are no longer able to service that debt in full. It follows that debt-for-equity swaps typically entail a "haircut," or partial write-down, of the value of creditors' claims, while indexing the earnings accruing to holders of that equity to future economic conditions. Law, however, failed to apply a haircut, which should have raised questions about the sustainability of his scheme.

The government needed revenue on the spot, but income from the Mississippi trade stood to materialize only over time. For Law, this was no impediment. Having inherited his father's gambling gene, he began issuing additional shares to complete the swap. Doing so put downward pressure on share prices, of course, which did nothing to attract additional investors. In January 1720, Law therefore began using the good offices of the Banque Générale to issue additional banknotes to himself, which he used to buy back shares when their prices dipped. The predictable result was the depreciation of banknotes, which were putatively convertible into fixed amounts of precious metal but in practice lost two-thirds of their value in a matter of months. Law then sought to prop up share prices in still more creative ways, by making banknotes the exclusive form of legal tender, by nationalizing the stock of gold, and by getting the authorities to prohibit capital outflows. Such measures only sent negative signals. None had the desired effect.

The Mississippi Company and Banque Générale were clearly careening toward bankruptcy. Seeing the writing on the wall, Law fled France in a very personalized act of default, leaving behind the Place Vendôme in Paris and twenty-one chateaux for his creditors to attach. He knew the way; this was actually the second time Law had fled across the Channel, having done so in 1694, in the opposite direction, to escape death by hanging for having killed a rival in a duel.

In England, meanwhile, the promoters of the South Sea Company, transfixed by Law's early successes, hatched a similar scheme. This involved swapping the government's debt for shares in the new company, which was backed by a monopoly on trade with the Spanish American colonies.[61] This proposition turned out to be even more dubious than Law's. Trade with the Spanish American colonies consisted mainly of importing African slaves into the region. Moreover, the company's access to Latin America depended on good relations with the Spanish Crown—relations that did not exist. For a time, the promoters succeeded in driving up share prices with publicity, announcing that King George I had made a £100,000 investment of his own funds, and by extending credit to purchasers of shares, requiring them to put down only 20 percent to secure title.[62] Soon enough, however, the realization dawned that the South American trade was unlikely to expand at a rate sufficient to finance dividends on highly priced shares. In September 1720, the bubble burst, jeopardizing banks that had lent against the security of shares. The government then pressured the Bank of England to assist in containing the fallout from the failure, which it did by advancing funds to the directors of the South Sea Company, helping to stabilize the market.

Though this episode was disruptive, it did not prevent the English state from continuing to borrow. This was in contrast to the failure of the Banque Générale, which interrupted the market access of the French government for the better part of a century. In England, as we have seen, the government persuaded the Bank of England to support the price of South Sea shares in order to prevent avoidable bankruptcies. The bank's intervention as market maker and liquidity provider of last resort lent a modicum of stability to the markets, thereby helping preserve the English government's ability to borrow. Since the French government possessed no analogous banker, the consequences lingered. A half century would pass before a banking charter was again issued to a joint-stock company, the Caisse d'Escompte, in 1776. This bank too would become unhappily entangled in the French government's finances; its heavy exposure to the state and the turmoil of the Revolution forced its closure in 1793.[63]

Already by the eighteenth century, then, a central bank capable of backstopping the market was a precondition for stability of the public finances and maintenance of market access. Eventually, institutions such as these would be recognized as important for preserving the public credit and be established in a growing range of countries.

## A Republic Founded in Debt

The United States is a final case where public debt had a role in political consolidation and state building. The nation emerged from its war of independence with a debt burden unevenly split between the states. Massachusetts had more debt than Connecticut, New York, and New Jersey combined, despite the states having waged a common war. Massachusetts farmers consequently complained of burdensome taxes levied to finance interest and amortization. They petitioned their state legislature to write down the debt unilaterally. In 1786, a rabble of armed farmers led by Daniel Shays threatened Northampton courts acting against delinquent taxpayers; this was only the most visible manifestation of broader discontent.[64] The fiscal imbalance thus threatened to poison the internal relations of the new Republic. If left unaddressed, it threatened the Republic itself.

This was not the stable nation-state to which American federalists aspired. Providentially, however, the new nation possessed a statesman, Alexander Hamilton, with the political vision to address the problem. Hamilton proposed that the federal government should assume the obligations of the states and consolidate them into a new federal debt. A precondition was federal revenue sufficient to pay the interest and repay the principal. The early Articles of Confederation had delegated to the states the decision of what taxes to levy, whether for themselves or for funding the common treasury. The free-rider problem that resulted will be familiar from our earlier discussion of Dutch provinces.

The first step in rectifying it came on March 4, 1788, with ratification of the new US Constitution.[65] This document, influenced by Hamilton's contributions to the *Federalist Papers*, included a clause vesting in the Congress the power to levy and collect taxes, duties, and excises. This was not simply a feat of financial engineering; it was a feat of political engineering, in which the union was preserved by endowing the federal government with powers to be used to relieve the states of debts that threatened national solidarity. Overcoming the opposition of Republican followers of Thomas Jefferson in Southern states, which had relatively light debts and opposed a strong federal government, wasn't easy. It required agreeing to move the federal capital from Philadelphia to the banks of the Potomac River bordering Virginia and Maryland. It required convincing the opposition that all states, even the less heavily indebted, would benefit from this transfer of powers, since the federal government, now possessing additional resources, would have greater ability to borrow abroad, specifically in times of war, when the new nation's survival was at stake.

On July 4, 1789 (notice the date), President Washington signed an act authorizing the federal government to apply duties to imported goods. Four weeks later, Congress established the US Customs Service to collect those duties. Since imports would almost certainly rise over time, this ensured that the government would have revenues commensurate with the needs of a growing economy. It would not have to beg the states for funds in order to carry out essential functions.

To reassure investors and the public of the efficacy of the associated debt-market operations, Congress created a Treasury Department responsible for their administration and appointed Hamilton as its head. Hamilton proposed, and Congress agreed to establish, a federally administered sinking fund that would apply surplus revenues, generated mainly by the federal postal service, to secondary market purchases and retirement of government bonds. In effect, the government was committing to pay interest on its debt but also to support the prices of its securities and redeem them in timely fashion.[66] To assure investors that the sinking fund would operate responsibly, its commissioners included some of the highest officers of the land: the vice president, the secretary of state, the secretary of the Treasury, and the chief justice of the Supreme Court.

These steps had their intended effect of enhancing the creditworthiness of the new federal debt. Barely a year after adoption of Hamilton's recommendations, market makers in New York, Philadelphia, and Boston, doing business out of coffeehouses, were trading federal government securities. In New York, trading started in December 1791 with establishment of the "Six Per Cent Club" by William Duer, a speculator who also just happened to serve as assistant secretary of the Treasury under Hamilton. This, of course, was a conflict of interest, and it did not burnish Duer's already dubious reputation.[67] But even this did not prevent the market from getting up and running. The founding of what became the New York Stock Exchange, initially in a small office at 22 Wall Street, followed on March 8, 1792.

Everything did not go smoothly in this brand-new market; brand-new markets are rarely smooth. Duer quickly moved to corner the market in 6 percent US government bonds. When his funding proved inadequate and bond prices plummeted, he was carted off to debtors' prison. Fearing a panic, Hamilton mobilized the resources of the sinking fund to intervene in the markets and stabilize bond prices. Again, we see here the utility, indeed the indispensability, of a lender and liquidity provider of last resort.

But the sinking fund's resources were limited; Hamilton therefore proposed establishing a Bank of the United States, modeled on the Bank of England, to provide more extensive liquidity services. Unlike the Bank of England, this bank was owned in part by the government itself. Hamilton made allowance for additional investors in the bank, authorizing them to purchase shares using the new US government's bonds. This indirectly supported the prices of those securities and aligned the government's fiscal interests with those of the bank's promoters. Once chartered, the Bank of the United States extended loans to the government, again following the English model.

In a final reform, Hamilton oversaw replacement of the myriad colonial and state currencies that circulated before and during the War of Independence by a single, uniform US dollar. Achieving this took several years. But by 1793 the United States had a national mint, headquartered in Philadelphia, with branches in other cities, to produce gold and silver coins in the new dollar unit of account. It had a uniform currency to foster the development of integrated national markets, including, not least, a market in public debt. The entire scheme was so successful that one can almost imagine a Broadway musical about it.

## Looking Forward

Sovereign debt has existed as long as sovereigns, since states and their rulers frequently need to borrow. But sovereign debt as a well-defined asset class, issued and exchanged subject to standard conditions, developed only with the emergence of stable supplies and demands. A stable supply presupposed the existence of durable cities, states, and nations. It required an evolution from kingdom to nation-state, making the debt an obligation of an entity that outlived any one individual. It rested on the existence of polities capable of defending their borders, which meant borrowing for military needs whose cost could exceed current revenues. A stable demand for debt obligations meanwhile presupposed a commercial environment in which merchants possessed expertise derived from extending credit to fellow merchants, then to other customers, and finally to the state.

These observations take us some way toward understanding when and where markets in sovereign debt developed. They developed in Europe because of the continent's geography and history, which made war especially prevalent. By implication, borrowing to finance urgent military needs was especially prevalent as well. As for when, this market emerged after 1000 CE, when Europe's disintegration into warring states heightened these financial imperatives.

In addition, these practices developed in Europe because the Champagne fairs and Levant trade of the Italian city-states bequeathed a community of merchant bankers with the requisite financial acumen and profits to invest. Europe was not the only continent possessing merchants, but it was the only place where commercial activity combined with history, geography, and military imperatives in quite this way.

The emergence of this asset class also presupposed the development of financial instruments, accounting practices, and contracting conventions. Widespread trading in debt securities required a secondary market, allowing investors to diversify and dispose of their claims. A high volume of transactions required the standardization of contracts and development of legal doctrine according to which claims on the sovereign could be asserted not just by the individual who originated the loan but by whoever currently held the contract.

Finally, development of this asset class presupposed institutional arrangements that gave creditors reason to think that sovereigns would pay. This belief could be encouraged by assigning specific revenues to debt service or granting creditors the privileges and territories generating those revenues, and doing so in ways that were difficult to revoke. The process was cemented by political reforms that gave creditors leverage and that limited sovereign prerogatives. The capstone was when a royal debt, which depended on the personal credit of the sovereign, was transformed into a national debt, and when the power to levy taxes and oversee their collection was vested in a representative assembly.

Borrowing capacity and the financialization of public debt had come a long way. By the end of the eighteenth century European states had accumulated debts as large, relative to national income, as those of many governments today. The stage was thus set for the globalization and democratization of the market, the dual processes that came next.

# Democratization and Globalization

Fiscal capacity developed with the efforts of states and rulers to secure their borders, expand their territories, and survive. Larger, more centralized states increasingly possessed the fiscal machinery to pursue these objectives. After 1650, the European continent consequently crystallized into a system of territorial states with stable borders and national identities, reducing the incidence of interstate conflict.[1] The capacity to issue debt and the stability of the state system thus went hand in hand, each reinforcing the other.

Spending then shifted from financing wars to supplying public goods and services. This evolution was consistent with a model in which states, as they acquire the capacity to tax, regulate, and withstand challenges from nonstate actors, spend more on public goods.[2] As city populations expanded, demands arose for clean water, sewers, and electricity. In response, governments issued bonds to finance investments in transport infrastructure, power, and sanitation. The practice made sense from an economic standpoint, since construction costs were incurred up front but returns accrued only over time. From a political standpoint, this transition again illustrates the role of public debt as an instrument of state building—as a mechanism that lends legitimacy to the state by enabling it to meet the needs of its constituents.

Where savings were low and financial markets were underdeveloped, governments were unable to finance such projects at home. This was true, for example, of the new governments of Greece and Spain following their 1820 revolutions. It was true of Latin American republics following their wars of independence.[3] Financing armies and public works therefore required tapping global capital markets. Some governments, in Latin America for example, relied almost entirely on foreign investors. For their part, investors searching for yield found it in debt backed by infrastructure projects.

Issuing debt abroad could be risky, as we saw in earlier chapters. Individual countries are small relative to global financial markets; they are like dinghies on choppy seas. Capital flows and the availability of foreign funding can be disrupted for reasons beyond their control—by a crisis in a foreign financial center, for example. When an obligation is denominated in foreign currency, a change in commodity prices or the exchange rate can eliminate the government's ability to service its debt. And when things go wrong, the central bank and the government, lacking the ability to print foreign exchange, can do little about it.[4]

Unseasoned borrowers paid a premium when tapping international capital markets.[5] They lacked a track record. Information about their economies and politics was sparse. They therefore relied on intermediaries able to substitute their own reputations and on promoters claiming knowledge of the country and its leaders.[6] This gave such intermediaries power. Baring Brothers and N. M. Rothschild were "the true lords of Europe," as Byron put it in Don Juan.[7] A loan organized by one of these prestigious houses was viewed as sound not only because the organizers had privileged access to government officials, but also because the bank's reputation rested on a positive outcome.

But along with these reputable houses were also "more aggressive bankers less inhibited by traditions of sound finance, and . . . swarms of promotors, go-betweens, and people who knew 'the right people.'"[8] The most sensational, surely, was Gregor McGregor, the Scottish adventurer who, in the tradition of his fellow countryman John Law, floated £200,000 of bonds on the London Stock Exchange on behalf of the mythical Central American Kingdom of Poyais.[9] McGregor's 1822 loan was organized by Sir John Perring, Shaw, Barber & Co., a banking house with stately offices in the City of London but otherwise of a somewhat dubious reputation. More generally, there was no shortage of opportunistic bankers prepared to organize loans earning them generous commissions but offering hapless investors little prospect of repayment. Meanwhile, the British government, anxious to open Latin America to the products of industry, was happy to see evidence of commercial development and, when confronted with questionable undertakings, to look the other way.

McGregor's fundraising success was indicative of broader enthusiasm among investors for what today are called emerging markets (late-developing economies located outside Western Europe). What had once been a niche market dominated by a handful of sovereigns now featured more than a score. This marked the creation of a new asset class. It was a further step in democratizing the market, as an expanding population of retail investors, impressed by publicity campaigns, plunged into this new class of securities. It is hard to improve on the summary of Frank Whitson Fetter, Haverford College professor (and son of Austrian School economist Frank Albert Fetter): "Only a combination of a political interest of Great Britain in the new countries of Latin America, a speculation-mad investing public in Great Britain, a group of loan contractors whose profits were an important motivation in the transactions, and finally Latin-American ministers of finance who seemed willing to agree to any terms, no matter how outrageous, as long as they brought in current funds to a hard pressed exchequer, can explain the transactions of the 1820's."[10] Economic theorists of the Austrian school emphasize credit boom-and-bust cycles. The views of the younger Fetter, evidently, were influenced by his father's.

Moreover, at the very time this process was getting underway, the Bank of England and HM Treasury were pushing down interest rates on domestic securities, thereby encouraging investors to search for yield abroad. Treasury sold short-term bills to the bank and used the proceeds to retire long-term debt, depressing long-term rates.[11] Retail investors seeking higher yields therefore scooped up emerging-market debt, not just the bonds of newly minted Latin American republics, but also the debt securities of Spain, Portugal, Greece, and other peripheral European credits.

Finally alarmed by this speculation, the Bank of England began curtailing its provision of credit in 1825. As credit became dear, the bubble burst. In the words of Leland Jenks, one of the early historians of this market, "Investors came to a sudden realization that the only interest they had received had come out of the principal of successive loans. . . ." The South American republics, for their part, "suddenly discovered that they had borrowed beyond their means. . . ."[12] By the end of the decade, all but a handful of loans to the new nations of Latin America had lapsed into default, along with loans to Portugal, Spain, and Greece.

This was an early example of a regular pattern: tightening by a money-center central bank, a sudden stop in capital flows, and financial distress in emerging markets.[13] In this instance, as in others, decades would pass before the detritus was cleared away.

## The Heyday of International Lending

In the third quarter of the nineteenth century, Latin America returned to the market. Once the successor states of Gran Colombia—Colombia, Ecuador, and Venezuela—agreed on apportioning their predecessor's debt and renegotiated their defaulted obligations, their governments sought to borrow again. They succeeded beyond their wildest dreams.

Carlos Marichal, the leading financial historian of the region, characterizes the period from 1850 to 1873 as marking "the rediscovery of Latin America."[14] The first loans, in the 1850s, were refinancing issues, money lent by bankers and their clients so that governments could resume repaying a portion of what they owed those selfsame bankers and clients. Defaulted debts having been regularized, new offerings were then organized. With the acceleration of global growth and international trade, Latin America's prospects brightened. Britain's imports from the region tripled between 1850 and 1873. Latin America's own imports, financed in part by foreign money, more than doubled. Central and South American governments sought to modernize their economies by building railways, roads, and ports, all of which required cash.

Table 4.1 shows how the spending priorities of Latin governments shifted from defense to public works. Despite the now-heavier burden of debts extended to settle past defaults, the share of loan revenues devoted to public works rose to 60 percent of foreign borrowing in the 1870s. More infrastructure meant more trade, which allowed governments to collect additional import duties and thereby access additional external funds.[15]

The four decades leading up to World War I were the heyday of overseas lending to sovereigns, railway companies, and other borrowers. Foreign assets rose from 7 percent of world GDP in 1870 to 18 percent in 1913.[16] Great Britain, the leading capital exporter, allocated more than 4 percent of its GDP to investment overseas on average every year for fully forty years.[17] By 1913, 32 percent of the country's net national wealth was held abroad. On the eve of the Great War, government debt held by foreigners represented more than 5 percent of world GDP, or almost a third of the total stock of foreign assets.

Colonial governments with limited local resources similarly tapped European capital markets. In the four decades leading up to World War I, colonies (both self-governing and dependent) absorbed more than 40 percent of British investment abroad.[18] French and German investors were attracted less strongly to colonial issues, partly because of their countries' less extensive empires (and fewer settler colonies in particular), allocating 6 and 14 percent of their overseas portfolio to them, respectively.[19] Colonies paid lower rates of interest than sovereign nations, because they lacked sovereign immunity and because (in the case of settler colonies) nonpayment meant defaulting on one's fellow countrymen. There was a clear pecking order of colonial borrowers: colonies with large European settlements had superior market access and issued more debt as a share of GDP than territories with indigenous majorities.[20] Together, foreign and colonial government bonds accounted for more than a quarter of the value of all securities,

*Table 4.1* **Foreign Loans Issued by Latin American Governments, 1850–75**

| Period | Number of Loans | Nominal Value (£ Millions) | Use (percent of total) | | |
|--------|-----------------|----------------------------|------------------------|-------------|------------|
| | | | Military | Public Works | Refinancing |
| 1850–59 | 9 | 10.9 | — | 32 | 68 |
| 1860–69 | 20 | 56.7 | 41 | 12 | 47 |
| 1870–75 | 22 | 73.3 | — | 60 | 40 |

Source: Marichal (1989), Table 3.

stocks and bonds alike, quoted on the London Stock Exchange in 1883.[21] They accounted for 21 percent in 1913, outstripping the share of domestic public debt.[22]

Colonial or dominion status was no guarantee against problems and in some cases actually compounded them, as illustrated by Australia. Prior to federation, borrowing was necessarily done by the individual colonies (later states). Funds borrowed in London were invested mainly in railways and in housing and urban infrastructure, above all in Melbourne. In the late 1880s, net capital inflows were running at 8 percent of GDP per annum, extraordinary sums for what we would now call an emerging market.[23]

At this point, the Argentina-Baring Crisis erupted, and Australia's access to new issues dried up.[24] (It didn't help that the Australian subcontinent was at the same time being overrun by a plague of rabbits; these had been recently imported to provide game for wealthy settlers and possessed no natural predators.) Capital inflows abruptly declined from 8 to 1 percent of GDP.

In response to this reduction in financial resources, the housing boom collapsed. Banks in Victoria, the state in which Melbourne was located, were forced to close their doors. Real GDP fell by fully 17 percent in just one year, 1892–93, if historical statistics are to be believed.[25] Surviving banks were then restructured with government help. But colonial governments were unwilling to default on their kith and kin in Britain.[26] As a result, Australia endured painful deleveraging for more than a decade, as households, firms, and governments reduced their spending in order to pay down debt and repair their balance sheets.

This was the only period other than during World War I when GDP per capita fell in Australia. Other settler economies exporting many of the same commodities, Canada, New Zealand, and even Argentina, had bounced back from the slump induced by the Argentina-Baring Crisis by the mid-1890s. In contrast, the Australian economy did not start growing again until 1904.[27]

As this Australian experience indicates, one should not overlook subsovereign borrowing, even if the focus in this book is on sovereign debt. Subsovereign states and municipalities didn't borrow to conquer territory or secure borders, but rather to invest in infrastructure and compete in financial development. Subsovereign borrowing might be seen as safer for this reason, and also because it was not subject to sovereign immunity.

This, however, was a misunderstanding.[28] Although creditors might have recourse to the courts, there was still the problem of collecting on a judgment. Local officials made this as difficult as possible. In the 1870s, one Kansas county embroiled in a bond lawsuit elected its officials on the understanding that they would stay in hiding for their term in office and conduct all official business under cover of darkness, thereby avoiding the creditors. The commissioners of one Arkansas county regularly resigned on completing pressing business in order to avoid being served, with the understanding that they would be reappointed when new business arose.[29]

Moreover, it was hard for creditors to impose trade and military sanctions on subsovereign borrowers, insofar as the defaulting state or municipality was part of a larger economy. Cutting off trade credit from abroad was ineffective because much of a state or municipality's trade and credit came from other parts of the home country. And the government of the creditor country lacked justification for military action or financial sanctions against the larger jurisdiction of which the subsovereign was part.

US state debts in the early nineteenth century were especially notorious. Between 1820 and 1839, nineteen states, along with the Florida and Wisconsin Territories, issued bonds to establish banks and finance canals, turnpikes, and railways.[30] Northern states concentrated on transport improvements, Southern states on land banks to provide planters with working capital (see Figure 4.1).[31] A substantial fraction of this debt was held by foreign investors, either by their American agents or abroad. By the end of the period, state-issued and guaranteed debt was approximately $200 million, compared to a nominal US GDP of roughly $1.6 billion.[32]

In 1839, concerned that shipments of specie to the United States in payment for purchases of American securities might jeopardize its sterling peg to gold, the Bank of England tightened credit.[33] On cue, the borrowing binge collapsed.[34] With railway and canal networks still incomplete, and with newly established banks in the South unable to withstand the downturn, a majority of state governments lapsed into default.[35] Some states repudiated their bonds outright, and foreign creditors pressed the federal government to assume responsibility for the debts.

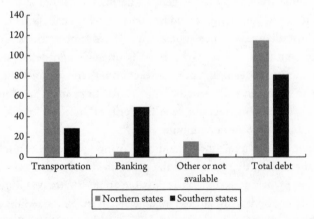

*Figure 4.1.* State Debt in the United States, September 1841 (millions of dollars, by purpose of issue)
Source: English (1996), Table 1.

This time, in contrast to 1790, the US Congress refused. In 1790, as Alexander Hamilton had recognized, the issue was holding the new nation together. Now it was bailing out the bondholders—foreign bondholders, no less—which was rather less appealing.[36] Although the federal government's ability to borrow might be affected negatively by state defaults, the federal authorities had limited responsibilities and faced no military emergency. The states themselves would be unable to borrow, but they were already stuffed to the gills with debt. As one Florida newspaper responded to the observation that foreign investors would hesitate to lend, "Well, who cares if they don't?"[37]

The US case was distinctive in that the country's founding fathers (Alexander Hamilton notwithstanding) envisaged a limited role for the federal government.[38] But similar patterns were evident elsewhere. For example, the only public loan obtained by newly independent Argentina was contracted not by the Republic itself but by the Province of Buenos Aires. This Buenos Aires loan was among those swept up in the wave of defaults that followed the Bank of England's tightening in 1825.

In the Argentine case, three decades would pass before the province settled with its creditors. The Republic itself then went to the market in 1866.[39] It continued borrowing for two-plus decades ("Public borrowing abroad took wing for Argentina from 1870" is how one historian puts it), relying on its customary underwriter, Baring Brothers.[40] Much of this foreign capital went into "opening" the Pampas (clearing and fencing land and building rail links to the coast). But, as is often the case, interest obligations materialized faster than exports. Meanwhile, an expansive credit policy, of the sort favored by heavily mortgaged landowners everywhere, fueled inflation and currency depreciation, making maintenance of debt service on sterling-denominated bonds even harder for an Argentine government whose tax revenues were denominated in pesos.

By 1890, interest payments were absorbing 40 percent of government revenues. In November the government sent a delegation to London to seek Baring Brothers' help in rescheduling its payments and securing a new loan. The timing was not propitious; the Bank of England had only just intervened to rescue Baring Brothers, the bank's finances having been battered by its failure to find takers for an earlier Argentine issue.[41] With its usual financial agent sidelined and finding itself shut out of the market, the Argentine Republic suspended payment on its bonds.

The Republic and its creditors settled in 1893, but defaults by Argentinean provinces and municipalities took longer to resolve. The provinces, like the federal government, had borrowed in foreign currency but had even less capacity to generate foreign exchange. Several had borrowed in order to set up the equivalent of provincial development banks under the Guaranteed Banks Law of 1887. There having been little actual development, default followed the crunch in 1890.[42]

The situation was not unlike that of the Southern US states that had borrowed in the 1830s, also for the purpose of capitalizing development banks. But unlike in the United States, Argentina's federal government assumed responsibility for these defaulted provincial and municipal loans. The US government was not running significant deficits and had no need to borrow in the 1840s, but the Argentine government had large deficits and was desperate for new money to pay its creditors and also to finance its ongoing expenditures.[43] The committee of Argentine bondholders, now chaired by Rothschilds rather than the disgraced Barings, made federal government assumption of these subsovereign obligations a condition for arranging new money.[44] The provincial elites were well represented in the Argentine Congress, especially the Senate, so opposition from other quarters was overcome. Under the provisions of a law adopted in August 1896, the federal government replaced the outstanding provincial and municipal bonds with a new external loan in an operation that added 20 percent to the national debt.[45]

These events illustrate at least one way in which the creditors of subsovereigns could get their money back, namely by having a higher level of government assume responsibility for it.

## Lenders of Different Stripes

The United Kingdom, though the leading lender, was not alone. Whereas average annual capital export was 5.2 percent of British GDP between 1880 and 1913, it was 2.7 percent of GDP for France and 1.4 percent of GDP for Germany.[46] Not just London but also Paris, Hamburg, Berlin, Brussels, Amsterdam, and Zurich were consequential international financial centers. This is a comprehensive enumeration: Britain, France, Germany, Belgium, the Netherlands, and Switzerland together accounted for nearly 90 percent of all overseas investment in the decades preceding World War I.

Careful readers will have noticed the absence of the United States. As the *Journal of Commerce* observed in 1905, "Probably less than a dozen foreign securities are listed on the New York Stock Exchange, and even these, outside of the Mexican and Canadian Railways, are rarely dealt in."[47] Benito Juárez attempted to borrow in San Francisco and New York in the 1860s to fund establishment of the Second Mexican Republic, but was unsuccessful. The Province of Quebec and cities of Winnipeg and Montreal had better luck, successfully marketing debentures in New York and St. Paul. Although US investors at the turn of the century subscribed to loans of the British government (then prosecuting the Boer War) and of the government of Japan (engaged in war with Russia), these instances were exceptional.[48]

Longstanding suspicion of concentrated financial power slowed development of the infrastructure needed for New York to become an international financial center. National banks were prohibited from opening branches abroad, while state banks lacked resources and contacts.[49] The correspondent system, in which country banks deposited their liquid balances in regional reserve centers, facilitated dispersion of financial resources across multiple cities instead of concentrating them in a single center. National banks were required to hold US government bonds as backing for their liabilities, to the exclusion of foreign public debt. Private banks such as J. P. Morgan & Co. and Kuhn, Loeb & Co. had foreign contacts, but the resources they could mobilize were limited to the capital of their partners.[50]

Then there was the awkward fact (at least from the viewpoint of building an international financial center) that the federal government issued little debt. It actually retired much of its Civil War debt in this period, as we will see in Chapter 7. Its functions were limited, reflecting the lasting influence of Jeffersonian democracy and the country's decentralized political system. Lack of indebtedness may have been a happy fiscal condition, but it meant there was limited trading in government bonds and hence less expertise than in London, Paris, and Berlin.

Finally, the United States lacked a central bank to ensure market liquidity. The result was financial volatility and recurrent crises, which rendered the country a less-than-reliable source of international finance. Only in 1913, with congressional passage of the Federal Reserve Act, was a central bank established and were national banks authorized to branch abroad. Following the outbreak of World War I, governments then turned to the United States for finance. Until then, however, international lending was almost entirely a European affair.

## A Globalized Market

Table 4.2 summarizes the geographic distribution of European investments in sovereign debt prior to World War I. The first three columns show new issues of external debt by all levels of government in twenty-eight independent countries.[51] The data come from securities listed in London, Paris, and Berlin.

The table shows that intra-European debt flows still accounted for the largest share of new issues, European economies having been first to turn to sovereign borrowing and lending. The rediscovery of Latin America is also apparent in the first three columns: the region was responsible for almost half of all new issues in the 1880s. After that, Japan and China appear as significant borrowers. The United States and Canada also placed securities abroad, although rapid population and economic growth and strong fiscal positions meant that they relied less on foreign debt.

*Table 4.2* **Geographic Distribution of Sovereign Debt, 1880–1914**

| | New Debt Flows | | | Cumulative Debt Stocks | | |
|---|---|---|---|---|---|---|
| | Foreign | Foreign | Foreign | Foreign | Foreign | Total |
| | 1880–89 | 1890–99 | 1900–1913 | 1913–14 | 1913–14 | 1913–14 |
| Europe | 36.8 | 48.5 | 37.4 | 47.3 | 48.9 | 73 |
| North America | 7.9 | 10.6 | 9.3 | 2.4 | 2.3 | 4.3 |
| Latin America | 47.8 | 12.3 | 21.3 | 9.2 | 9.8 | 5.1 |
| Africa | | | 0.4 | 7.8 | 7.4 | 2.6 |
| Asia | 7.5 | 28.6 | 25.9 | 26.1 | 24.9 | 9.6 |
| Oceania | | | 5.7 | 7.1 | 6.7 | 5.3 |
| Memorandum: Total (USD m) | 957.6 | 1,284.5 | 4,398.6 | 12,729.1 | 13,453.1 | 40,171.8 |
| # of sovereigns | 26 | 26 | 29 | 29 | 45 | 45 |

*Sources:* Bent and Esteves (2016) and United Nations (1946).

*Note:* Values in percent unless otherwise noted. Each column is made up of percentages that sum to 100. Only independent sovereign nations are considered. Total debt (in the last column) is the sum of domestic and foreign.

The last three columns of Table 4.2 are from a United Nations report tallying sovereign debt stocks on the eve of World War I. This tabulation encompasses both foreign and domestic debt and includes data for a larger number of economies. It shows that the total stock of debt in 1914 topped $40 billion (16 percent of global GDP), $13.5 billion of which was foreign. The distribution among regions does not change much with this broader geographic coverage. This presentation highlights the importance of domestic debt, while underscoring that it was mainly European countries that were able to borrow at home.[52]

A contemporary financial handbook (*Fenn's Compendium of English and Foreign Funds*) singled out five European nations as issuing the largest stocks of domestic and foreign debt, in declining order France, Britain, Italy, Austria-Hungary, and Spain, which together owed £2.9 billion (or $14 billion). This represented, according to the same source, 54 percent of the total debt of sovereign nations and their colonies.[53]

The spending priorities of these European debtors evolved over time, not unlike those of their Latin American counterparts. Table 4.3 splits European public expenditure into traditional state functions (defense and administration), new economic and social functions (provision of infrastructure, education, healthcare,

*Table 4.3* **Structure of Government Expenditure in Europe (percent of total government expenditure)**

|      | Traditional Functions | New Functions | Debt Charges |
|------|------|------|------|
| 1850 | 63.1 | 19.5 | 20.7 |
| 1870 | 53.8 | 17.1 | 29.2 |
| 1890 | 48.4 | 28.9 | 22.8 |
| 1910 | 45.9 | 34.2 | 21.9 |

*Sources:* Flora et al. (1983), Mata (1993), and Carreras and Tafunell (2005).

*Note:* Traditional includes defense, police, and judicial expenditure and general administration. New includes economic services, transport/communications, health, education, and social security.

and social security), and debt service.[54] Although traditional functions remained the largest, the share accounted for by social and public goods increased markedly in the decades leading up to World War I.[55]

Foreign borrowing was strikingly important for investment. A third to a half of all investment in Canada, Argentina, Brazil, and of course Australia was financed by foreign capital.[56] Few economies in the twentieth and twenty-first centuries have been able to finance such large shares of investment by borrowing abroad. Since 1960, it has been hard to find a correlation between foreign borrowing and investment or between foreign borrowing and growth. Those correlations were clearer in the decades prior to 1913.[57] The difference in this earlier period reflected both the extent to which foreign finance was directed toward investment and the fact that much of that investment was productive.[58]

To be sure, this dependence on foreign finance meant that a sudden stop in capital flows could destabilize investment and the economy. This happened in 1873, when crises engulfed Berlin and Vienna, infecting other European financial centers and causing flows to emerging markets to dry up and multiple defaults to ensue.[59] It happened with the Argentina-Baring crisis in 1890–91, when other Latin American countries and Australia felt the repercussions.

## Market Macrostructure

When is a debt sustainable? The answer lies in part in the relationship between the interest rate $(r)$ and the rate of economic growth $(g)$. If $r$ is less than $g$, the government's interest obligations will rise more slowly than its capacity to service and repay its debts. If the economy grows faster, then government revenues will grow faster. And if revenues rise faster than interest payments, the debt will become easier to service.

Hence, an important factor supporting the growing volume of sovereign and private indebtedness in the nineteenth century was the diffusion of new industrial technologies. Recent scholarship emphasizes that new machinery and techniques were adopted in a limited number of sectors initially, and that these sectors had to reorganize before growth could accelerate.[60] By the third quarter of the nineteenth century, however, new technologies had infiltrated a growing range of sectors and industries, and the necessary reorganization was well underway. The pace of global growth had accelerated from perhaps 0.3 percent per annum from the sixteenth through eighteenth centuries to 1 percent per annum in 1820–70. It then doubled again to 2 percent per annum between 1870 and 1913, at the same time that the market in sovereign debt was globalizing.[61]

Moreover, at the same time that global growth was rising, interest rates were falling (Figure 4.2). Financial markets and institutions were mobilizing savings through development of new financial instruments, as detailed in Chapter 3. Governments signaled their creditworthiness, whether through political reforms or by delegating sovereign prerogatives to bankers and foreign powers. To be sure, neither process was smooth. Political reforms could be rolled back by coup or counterrevolution, as happened in Italy in 1821 and Spain in 1823. Delegating oversight of revenues to foreigners might incite a political reaction, as in China

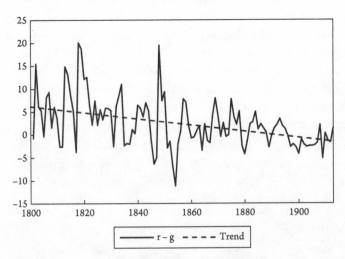

*Figure 4.2.* Global Interest Rate-Growth Rate Differential, 1800–1913 (percent)
Source: Schmelzing (2020).
Note: The global series is an average (weighted by GDP) of the *r – g* differentials of eight economies: France, Germany, Italy, Japan, Netherlands, Spain, the United Kingdom, and the United States. Schmelzing reports the real (inflation-adjusted) interest rate and rate of real economic growth (although because he adjusts both nominal series using the same price index a graph of the difference between the two nominal rates would look the same).

in 1900.[62] The evolution of interest rates and growth rates varied across countries. From a macroeconomic standpoint, however, the favorable evolution of the growth-rate–interest-rate differential was critical in supporting the borrowing process.

When debt was sold to foreigners, it was important for exports to expand along with the economy. Exports generated the hard-currency receipts needed to service debt denominated in those same hard currencies. The government couldn't just print money and depreciate the value of foreign-currency-denominated debt. It had to earn foreign exchange by exporting goods and services.

Another factor supporting sovereign borrowing, therefore, was expanding international trade. Between 1870 and 1913, global exports rose half again as fast as global GDP. The trade boom touched all continents, as shown in Figure 4.3, although it was strongest in regions recently opened to European commerce and settlement. This trade expansion was yet another corollary of the Industrial Revolution. With development of the railway and the steamship, augmented by the steel hull, dual screw propeller, and refrigeration, trade costs fell by a third from 1870 to the eve of World War I (Figure 4.4).[63]

Trade was boosted further by tariff reductions. Britain eliminated its agricultural tariffs in the 1840s, signaling the declining political power of agrarian interests and the growing sway of industry. London and Paris negotiated the first modern trade agreement, the Cobden-Chevalier Treaty, in 1860. Other

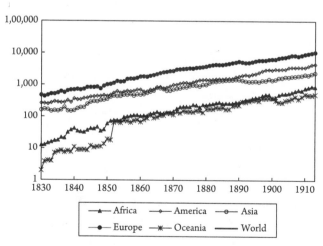

*Figure 4.3.* World Exports, 1830–1913 (millions of 1913 US dollars)
Source: Federico and Tena (2017).
Note: Values are in logarithmic scale.

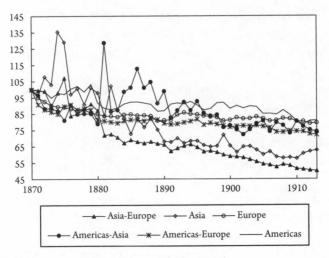

*Figure 4.4.* Trade Cost Indices, 1870–1913 (1870 = 100)

Source: Jacks, Meissner, and Novy (2011).

Note: The trade cost measure is derived from a gravity model of international trade such that the implied trade costs are consistent with the observed bilateral trade flows in the period.

countries inserted most-favored-nation clauses into their trade agreements, enabling them to share in the benefits of agreements negotiated by their partners.

Trade was also fostered by the spread of the gold standard. The arrangement was not universal: China never adopted it, nor did Spain, which inherited a heavy debt from its 1868 revolution. Japan and various Latin American countries went onto gold only at the very end of the nineteenth century. But where just ten countries were on the gold standard in 1875 (ten if we include British dominions such as Australia under this heading), more than two dozen had adopted gold-coin and gold-exchange standards by 1895. The stability and predictability of their exchange rates encouraged firms and merchants to export.[64] In turn, this positioned governments to borrow.

Maintaining gold convertibility at a fixed domestic-currency price required fiscal and financial discipline, since governments living beyond their means would suffer gold losses. If their reserves fell, they might be forced to suspend the convertibility of domestic currency into gold, as happened in Greece and Argentina after 1885 and Brazil after 1889. Membership in the gold club did not eliminate risk premiums, since in the same way that gold convertibility could be adopted, it could also be abandoned.[65] Still, adherence provided at least some reassurance to domestic and foreign investors.

# Market Microstructure

Channeling European savings into sovereign bonds involved specialized institutions such as investment banks and organized secondary markets. In London, the leading market for the bonds of foreign nations, an independently governed Foreign Stock Market opened in 1823, literally next door to the London Stock Exchange.[66] Many of the regulatory trappings of modern securities markets, such as listing requirements, depository trusteeships, and procedures for dealing with defaults, developed in London in this period as well.[67]

In the 1820s, when lending to the newly independent Latin American republics took off, foreign offerings were informal and ad hoc.[68] An agent acting on behalf of a government, either an official or an individual operating on commission, would contact a bank active in arranging loans.[69] The contractor would agree with that representative on the amount of the loan. The contractor would then encourage his "narrow circle of friends and family" to purchase bonds.[70] If these personal and familial connections contributed less than expected, the contractor took up the difference. The commission, generally upwards of 6 percent of the value of the loan, reflected not just the contractor's ability to mobilize friends and family, but also this obligation to absorb the residual balance.[71]

As sovereign loans grew in size, this risk became greater. By the 1860s, issuers were forming loan syndicates, where the contractor entered into a written agreement with other financial institutions. Syndicate members agreed to share the task of placing the bonds, along with the commission. In this way, less formal practices, where the London Rothschilds wrote the Paris Rothschilds to request their assistance, gave way to signed contracts between financial institutions with no familial connection.[72]

In the 1880s, the task of contracting the loan was separated from responsibility for guaranteeing the funding. One set of institutions marketed the issue while another committed to buying up unsold shares. Typically, the bank negotiating the contract relied on stockbrokers with whom it worked to organize the investors responsible for buying up the residual share. This second set of investors might include not only banks but also insurance companies, merchants, interested individuals, and stockbrokers themselves. In this way, the risk of bringing a large loan to the market was spread more widely.[73]

This distinction between banks that negotiated contracts and institutions that guaranteed the funding is subject to some confusion, since both are referred to as underwriters. But the lead or contracting bank was the crucial agent. It retained a portion of the guarantee and was expected to buy and hold part of any issue so organized, ensuring that it had skin in the game. As originator of the issue, its good name was on the line. The ability to syndicate a portion of the guarantee hinged on that reputation, which derived from the performance of earlier issues. Since the lead bank's reputation, along with its portfolio, depended on the performance of the bonds, it was expected to intervene in the market, supporting their price in periods of weakness, and to supply the market with liquidity.[74]

Hence, when a reputable banking house organized a security issue, its involvement was a positive sign. Bond prices and interest rates responded accordingly.[75]

Over time, additional sources of information developed—from financial handbooks specialized in providing analyses of sovereign bonds to publications of the London-based Corporation of Foreign Bondholders, the representative organ of investors. The financial press provided more timely coverage of the market, aided by the telegraph, the telephone, and advances in printing.[76] The *London Times* and *Morning Chronicle* published "money columns" and "City articles" on foreign bonds. These broadsheets were supplemented by specialized newspapers such as *The Economist*, founded in 1843, and *The Banker's Magazine*, founded in 1844. They were complemented by handbooks offering up-to-date data on foreign sovereigns, chief among which were *Fenn's Compendium*, already encountered, which went through fourteen editions between 1837 and 1889, and *The Statesman's Yearbook*, started in 1864 and still publishing today.[77]

As these innovations enriched the information environment, the lead bank's signaling function became less important.[78] Where formerly the bank underwriting the loan had put its good name and reputation on the line, now the underwriter denied responsibility for anything other than advertising and marketing the security. As one contemporary described the contrast, "While the old financial firms called themselves contractors for the loan, the firms acting on commission styled themselves agents," asserting that "they had had no original connection with the loan, knew nothing of the country for which it was raised, had no influence there, and left to others to exert themselves for the fulfilment of the conditions."[79] The trend continued. A century later, in the 1990s, when emerging market bonds were again issued and traded, sources of information about securities had grown even more numerous and diverse. At this point, the identity of the lead bank mattered hardly at all.[80]

Although London moved first, it faced growing competition from the Continent. In 1872, more foreign sovereign bonds were listed in London than in Paris and Berlin combined.[81] By 1900, in contrast, Paris had overtaken London in the number of listings.[82] Until the 1870s, the value of a London quote, meaning that a bond was continuously priced and traded there, was universally recognized and desired. It made for ready acceptance among British investors and also those of other countries. In the forty years following, as other European markets came to compete with London on all relevant dimensions, the premium associated with a London quote diminished accordingly.

Complementing these supply-side changes were changes in the investor base. In 1800, most sovereign bonds were still held by relatively wealthy individuals. Over the course of the century, these individuals were joined by a growing population of middling investors. In addition, institutional investors, such as banks and insurance companies, increased their holdings, enabling small savers holding claims on these institutions, in the form of bank shares or insurance policies, to gain indirect exposure to foreign debt markets.

A related development was the rise of the managed investment fund. The Dutch had pioneered this model in the eighteenth century, when they established funds to invest in the securities of the new United States of America.[83] Investing through a mutual fund was a way for Dutch investors to obtain the stabilizing benefits of diversification. British funds, starting with the Foreign and Colonial Investment Trust established in 1868, invested in a globally diversified portfolio of "well-selected Government Stocks" (stocks being a nineteenth-century term for bonds) and, eventually, in the securities of colonial governments and US railroads.[84] As described in its prospectus, the trust was designed to "to give the investor of moderate means" an opportunity to invest in dividend-paying foreign stocks. With yields on British government bonds falling in the mid-1860s, retail investors were attracted to alternatives. There was also greater appreciation, following the panic of 1866, that investors with an internationally diversified portfolio were best placed to cope with volatility.[85]

By 1875, more than a score of London-based investment trusts were in operation.[86] By 1890, on the eve of the Baring Crisis, there were more than fifty.[87] One set of scholars found a total return of 3.4 percent per annum for investment funds active in London from 1872 to 1907, a figure that bests the return on British government bonds (which averaged 2.7 percent).[88] Although the investment trust industry did not beat the stock market return of 4 percent, it delivered gains to investors of moderate means, who would have otherwise been unable to replicate the stock market index and obtain that fully diversified 4 percent. And since investment funds held securities not listed in London, they offered British investors an even greater degree of diversification.

Today, emerging market mutual funds are ubiquitous. They allow nonspecialists to dabble in the bonds of sovereigns and reap the benefits of international diversification. A look back at the nineteenth century shows that we have been here before.

## Making a Modern Market

Sovereign debt has long had an international dimension, tracing back to the lending activities of the Bardi, Peruzzi, and Scali of Florence, Genoa, and Venice.

Over time, these names were superseded by others, like N. M. Rothschild and Baring Brothers, in locations such as Amsterdam and London. The practices of these banks resembled those of their early modern predecessors. After a government and bank agreed on a contract, the bankers reached out to family members and associates to take up shares, in much the same manner as the Italians. Family and personal connections were still paramount in the operation of sovereign debt markets.

The centuries saw some broadening of this market, with sale of life rents and perpetuities by French towns and then retailing of life annuities by the French state. But most retail investors stuck close to home. They invested in the bonds of their own or neighboring municipalities, in which they had confidence bred by familiarity, or similarly in the bonds of their sovereign. The nineteenth century was the first time when the market was simultaneously globalized and democratized. It was the first time when an expanding base of retail investors adventured their savings in bonds issued by sovereigns in all parts of the world.

As is not infrequently the case of innovations, particularly financial innovations, this new departure unleashed a wave of enthusiasm, and attracted ambitious operators seeking to exploit it. In the lending boom of the 1820s, there arose a grab bag of new entities flouting financial credentials and seeking to interest investors in the latest government bonds. These investments performed poorly, and the market in foreign sovereign debt took decades to recover.

When it did recover, in the 1850s and 1860s, it assumed a more mature cast. The steamship and telegraph gave more timely access to information about foreign conditions and economic policies. Specialized services helped to digest and disseminate that information. The investing public, in Britain and elsewhere, diversified its holdings. Investors bought policies from insurance companies, purchased shares in banks, and subscribed to managed investment funds that selected portfolios of government bonds on their behalf.

By the late nineteenth century, then, the global market in sovereign debt had acquired its modern appearance. But lending to sovereigns, then as now, posed risks. When a government defaulted on a loan contracted abroad, it was inflicting losses on foreign investors. Those foreign investors were not a domestic political constituency, which limited their ability to extract political concessions. Investors had long sought to develop mechanisms for deterring opportunistic behavior by sovereign borrowers. Now, with democratization and globalization of the market, they faced the challenge of developing them further.

# ‖ 5 ‖

# Caveat Emptor

Investors' appetite for foreign government bonds reflected the belief, or at least the hope, that projects funded by borrowing would yield the hard-currency receipts needed to pay the money back. Because much foreign finance was devoted to infrastructure investment in the context of an expanding world economy, often they were right. But it didn't always turn out this way. There also were instances where things went spectacularly awry—where investment projects were ill conceived, bondholders and borrowers were poorly served by banks and promoters acting as gatekeepers, money was squandered, and worse.

## From Sea to Shining Sea

Honduras, Gregor McGregor's old stomping ground, was a case in point. The country re-entered the market in the 1860s before lapsing into default in 1873. "The audaciousness of the frauds perpetrated, both upon the investors and upon the government of Honduras, by the unscrupulous promotors who engineered these loans in London and Paris" was, in the words of an early observer, "almost unparalleled."[1] Such is the language of market participants when money is lost.

Honduras had inherited a heavy debt from the 1820s. In the 1860s it then sought to construct a railway across the isthmus and develop the adjoining territory, which in practice meant harvesting its mahogany forests. To borrow for these purposes, the government first had to issue new bonds to regularize its outstanding debt, including four decades of interest arrears. To this end, it enlisted the London house of Bischoffsheim & Goldschmidt, not one of the city's most reputable investment banks.[2] Secured by the prospective income of the railway and forestry enterprise, bonds were issued at an interest rate of 10 percent and an issue price of just 60, pushing the yield well into double digits.[3] A tenth of the money raised was retained by Messrs. Bischoffsheim & Goldschmidt for "commissions and expenses."

Even at this lucrative yield, subscriptions were not forthcoming. As Don Carlos Gutierrez, Honduras's consul in Britain, put it, "the first Honduran loan . . . was received [in London] with perfect indifference . . . there were hardly any other subscriptions than one of about 10,000 *l*. made by the firm of Bischoffsheim itself."[4] The balance of the loan was placed privately with the help of one Charles Joachim Lefevre, a shadowy operator who, it was later recalled, had once been charged with financial crimes and served two years in prison.

Building a railway through the Honduran highlands was not easy, and oversight of construction was lax. When funds proved inadequate, further loans were issued in 1869 and 1870. The 1870 issue was actually marketed not by Bischoffsheim & Goldschmidt but by Lefevre himself, who enlisted the stockbroker Barclays to buy and sell the bonds at inflated prices and create the appearance of a strong market. Bischoffsheim & Goldschmidt lent its good name in return for a side payment, despite making no investment of its own.[5] Apparently the bankers, if no one else, had learned something from their 1867 experience.

In 1872, still desperate for funds, the Honduran government and Lefevre sought to launch an even larger loan for an imagined "Transoceanic Ship Railway" that would transport fully loaded cargo ships across the isthmus. When they failed to find takers, Lefevre fled to France, like McGregor before him. The Honduran government lapsed back into default and took another thirty years to reorganize its finances and regain market access.

In the end, fewer than 53 miles of railroad was completed. A century and a half later, in 2019, construction of a 246-mile-long "dry canal" linking Honduras's Atlantic and Pacific coasts was still underway. Some investments, evidently, have long gestation periods.

## Passing the Baton

Other flotations were less preposterous but no more satisfactory. The roll of unfamiliar European borrowers included such recently autonomous nations as Romania in 1864, Serbia in 1867, and Bulgaria in 1888. In addition, German unification and the Italian Risorgimento created new borrowers through political amalgamation.[6]

As we saw in Chapter 2, Ottoman sultans shunned external finance, fearing foreign entanglements. The empire relied instead on domestic lenders, notably non-Muslim private bankers in the Galata Quarter of Istanbul.[7] Starting out as traditional moneylenders, the Galata bankers used their connections to source short-term funds in Europe, which they then lent to the state.[8] For much of the period, the Galata bankers had the field to themselves. Until the second half of the nineteenth century, the sultan regulated the operations of foreign merchant houses, as a result of which "there was little of a platform within the Ottoman Empire for the transmutation of resident foreign mercantile houses into foreign banking houses."[9]

The situation was transformed, as often is the case, by military imperatives. The Crimean War, fought from 1853 through 1856, finally overcame "the resistance of the Sultan and the more conservative ministers to raising long-term loans in the money markets of western Europe. . . ."[10] It helped that the 1854–55 external loans were guaranteed by the British and French governments, which were allied with the Ottoman Empire against Russia.[11] The Ottomans provided collateral in the form of the annual tribute received from their semiautonomous Egyptian province.[12] The British tranche of the loan was managed by the Bank of England, which forwarded the funds to the Porte without deducting a commission.[13] The French tranche was underwritten by none other than the Paris-based Bischoffsheim, Goldschmidt et Cie, which took its customary 10 percent.[14]

Once the Ottomans acquired a taste for foreign finance, their debt grew quickly, supported by high cotton prices owing to the "cotton famine" caused by the US Civil War. The 1860s, recall, was another boom period for foreign lending, when Latin American republics reentered the market and European investors turned their attention to opportunities overseas. But it was unclear whether the Ottomans could sustain a heavy debt, absent further guarantees from France and Britain. The economy was dominated by subsistence agriculture. The empire exported little other than cotton, for which high prices were not guaranteed. The Porte relied on tax farming, with its associated inefficiencies. Much of Constantinople, the capital city and center of the economy, enjoyed traditional exemptions from taxation. Foreign businessmen and their domestic associates similarly enjoyed tax concessions as a result of the capitulations, or agreements between the empire and foreign governments designed to attract foreign business.[15]

Still, none of this constituted an insurmountable obstacle to borrowing. The only prerequisite, it seemed, was putting in place the relevant financial infrastructure. A private bank, the Ottoman Bank, was established in 1856, ostensibly as a joint venture of British interests, the French Banque de Paris et des Pays-Bas and the Ottoman government, although foreigners owned 98 percent of the shares. Leveraging its British connection, the bank organized another external loan in 1858. Then, in 1863, having been renamed the Imperial Ottoman Bank, it was given responsibility for managing the note issue. With help from the Crédit Mobilier and Glyn, Mills & Co., it raised funds in Paris and London. The Imperial Bank withdrew currency notes injected into circulation during the Crimean War, stabilizing the exchange rate and enabling the regime to float additional foreign loans. This marked the economy's definitive transition from domestic to international finance. As Cottrell puts it, creation of the Ottoman Bank and its reestablishment as the Imperial Ottoman Bank represented "the passage of the 'baton' of Ottoman banking from local individuals . . . to London bankers and the Parisian haute banque."[16]

Over time, the Imperial Ottoman Bank acquired additional central banking functions. Besides regulating the note issue, it provided the state administration with short-term loans and transferred payments to its creditors. It seemed as if the government now had a market maker and liquidity provider of last resort to backstop credit and bond markets. (Notwithstanding the supposed "passing of the baton" to foreign bankers, half the state's debt was still to the Galata bankers and to local holders of treasury bonds.[17]) However, the operations of the Imperial Ottoman Bank were overseen by its dual boards in London and Paris.[18] Whether the bank's mandate was to provide a bridge to foreign finance and turn a profit or to backstop domestic markets thus depended on whom you asked. In practice, the bank did more to facilitate the government's access to external funding than to stabilize and develop domestic finance.

Some of the foreign finance so sourced was committed to railway construction in the empire's European provinces, but much was dissipated in current spending. Then, in 1873, the expedient of resorting to new borrowing to pay old debt service was foreclosed by the financial crisis in Vienna and Berlin.[19] In an effort to get a handle on the problem, responsibility for collecting taxes and controlling government expenditure was turned over to the technocrats of the Imperial Ottoman Bank.[20] Almost immediately, however, this attempt to consolidate the empire's finances was swamped by insurrections in Bulgaria and Bosnia-Herzegovina. Putting down these revolts, at whatever cost, was imperative for an empire whose internal unity was in doubt.

In September 1875, the extent of the resulting budget deficit was revealed, causing bond prices to collapse. Six months later, with access to finance foreclosed, the state defaulted on more than £190 million ($900 million) of foreign debt obligations, in what, at that time, constituted the single largest default in recorded history.[21]

The weakness of the economy in the wake of this bankruptcy doomed efforts to hold together the far-flung empire. Christopher Clay, writing of the geopolitical consequences of Turkey's foreign financial entanglements, argues that this default was "one of the key events of late Ottoman history, and arguably of modern history in general. . . ."[22] The default and its repercussions, he concludes, shaped the Balkan context leading to World War I and, through this channel, determined the political configuration of the modern Middle East.

But geopolitics could wait; the immediate task was normalizing the government's financial affairs. Arrears to domestic creditors were settled in 1879, when the government assigned revenues from stamp, spirit, fishing, and silk taxes and salt and tobacco monopolies to repay the debt. Following its default, the government had turned again to the Galata bankers, but these loans also quickly fell into arrears. Not resuming payments to the Galata bankers would have threatened their solvency and disrupted the provision of credit, critical for keeping the economy afloat.[23] Beyond this, domestic creditors were an important political constituency. From this it followed that domestic renegotiation and settlement came first.

Renegotiating the foreign debt took longer but was culminated successfully in 1881. The government was anxious to regain access to international markets, while foreign bankers saw opportunities in new lending for infrastructure and tobacco cultivation. This sufficed for a meeting of the minds. The principal amount was cut by half, and interest on the residual balance was reduced.[24] In return, the sultan agreed to create an Ottoman Public Debt Administration, an autonomous organ that controlled more than a quarter of the state's revenues, paying them directly to European investors and exercising a veto over new borrowing.[25]

This, clearly, was a heavy price. The reluctance of earlier sultans to borrow abroad for fear of foreign entanglements had been more than fully warranted, so it now appeared.

For those unconcerned with matters of sovereignty, there were advantages. The Public Debt Administration developed into a bureaucratic organization with upwards of five thousand employees in twenty cities. It was efficient by local standards, so starting in 1888 the Porte tasked it with collecting additional taxes not also earmarked for debt service. The Debt Administration promoted silk weaving and exports. It provided instruction on planting and cultivating mulberry trees, and sent agents to India to promote sales of salt mined from the Red Sea.[26] The Porte, having enhanced its credit, was able to return to the market to fund infrastructure projects, including the Constantinople-to-Baghdad railway. This was another case of public debt stimulating economic, financial, and administrative development, if through distinctive and, ultimately, untenable channels.

## Union and Confederate Borrowing

It was not only Turkey and Latin American countries that entered the market in the 1860s. In addition, the Union and Confederate governments of the not-so-United States borrowed to finance their civil war. A total of $400 million of Union government bonds were placed with foreign investors.[27] Many of these were domestic bonds purchased by J. W. Seligman and Co., a US investment bank whose principals saw an opportunity to resell them to European investors.[28] Although the securities in question were denominated in dollars, the Legal Tender Act of 1862 specified that interest on Union government bonds would be paid in gold or dollars of constant gold content, making them attractive to foreign investors. The $400 million placed abroad amounted to roughly 7 percent of the Union's wartime expenditure. The remaining bonds were sold to ordinary citizens or held as reserves by federally chartered banks, as required by the National Banking Act of 1863.[29] The National Banking System served the country for half a century. It was born out of the Union government's emergency wartime recourse to public debt.

The Confederacy initially placed its bonds with local investors. New Orleans was a banking center and home to cotton merchants with income and savings to invest. But war disrupted the cotton trade. Not only was the New England textile industry cut off, but the Confederate government ordered 2.5 million bales of cotton to be burned in an attempt to coerce Britain, which depended on the South for this input into its textile industry, into the Confederate camp. Evidently, Confederate leaders failed to anticipate that this would make bond flotations more difficult.

The Confederacy's ability to raise external funding turned out to be limited, given that the new government lacked the Union's track record. In 1862, the Paris-based firm of Emile Erlanger & Co. agreed to guarantee the sale of $15 million of bonds in five European financial centers, taking a 5 percent commission. It was the South's good luck that Erlanger, a German-born Parisian aristocrat, was attracted to, and some months later married, the daughter of a Louisiana merchant and politician, John Slidell, who just happened to be the Confederacy's emissary to France.

When loan negotiations opened, the South's battlefield position was good. Still, the interest rate of 7 percent and sales price of 77 made for a yield of more than 12 percent, indicative of the uncertainty surrounding the Confederacy.[30] Union government bonds, by comparison, bore a coupon of 6 percent and traded at more than 90 percent of par, sometimes even more than 100 percent.[31]

Erlanger & Co.'s initial placement was successful—the offering was five times oversubscribed, reflecting the high yield on offer. Within a week, however, the bonds fell below the issue price of 77 (see Figure 5.1). The Confederate government, to preserve its market access, felt compelled to use the loan proceeds to support bond prices. As a result, it netted only $3 million from the $15 million flotation. The shortfall did not make repayment seem likely. Then, in the days leading up to the deadline for retail investors to transfer their payments to Erlanger & Co., the Union's financial agent in London, Robert Walker, circulated a pamphlet insinuating that Confederate officials, including Jefferson Davis, were discussing the possibility of defaulting on their obligations. Walker blanketed the City with his pamphlets, dropping them from hot-air balloons.

Investors also questioned the collateral. Lacking gold, the Confederacy collateralized its bonds with cotton, which, according to the loan contract, could be converted into sterling at a price of 6 pence per pound. This might have been attractive to investors in normal circumstances, but not in wartime. The price

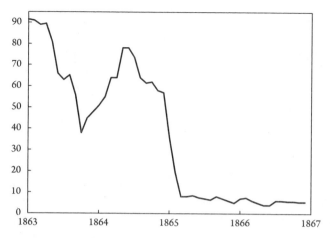

*Figure 5.1.* Confederate 7% Cotton Bond Price in London (US dollars), monthly, January 1863–December 1866
Source: Bloomberg.

of cotton had been rising since the outbreak of hostilities. Already in 1862 the price of American cotton in Liverpool exceeded 17 pence.[32] Moreover, the fine print specified that the bonds could be redeemed for cotton only within the Confederacy, not in Liverpool, and only within ten miles of a railroad or a stream navigable to the ocean so long as the region remained at war.[33] Investors were not reassured when the Confederate army's battlefield position deteriorated and retreating troops burned the government's store of cotton to prevent it from falling into enemy hands.

Unsurprisingly, the Erlanger loan was not just the Confederacy's first foreign loan but also its last. Total Confederate government spending on the war exceeded $2 billion, but foreign debt financed less than 1 percent.[34] Like its other debts, these obligations were "swept away when the Confederacy fell."[35]

## Enter the Dragon

Europe and the Americas were the principal sovereign debt issuers, but they were not alone. Qing China was able to borrow in London despite a litany of problems. In 1853 it lost the city of Nanjing to the God Worshipping Society, a cultlike group led by the self-proclaimed prophet Hong Xiuquan.[36] When Britain and France occupied Canton in 1856 in the latest of a series of disputes over the opium trade, Russia saw an opportunity to take Northern Manchuria, forcing China to sign the Treaty of Aigun and concede an indemnity. Defeat in the Second Opium War in 1860 then required China to make additional concessions. These included extending an earlier agreement limiting the customs duty on imports to 5 percent, hamstringing the government's main revenue source.

Clearly, China was not the kind of sound and stable regime with defensible borders that ordinarily appealed to foreign investors. Nonetheless, the Qing Dynasty was able to borrow abroad in the mid-1860s, when it obtained a £1.4 million loan from an English bank to finance war compensation payments to Russia. China floated an 8 percent sterling-denominated bond in 1875, a 6 percent bond in 1885, and a 5 percent loan in 1896. It launched a 4.5 percent issue in 1898 to finance the Japanese indemnity following defeat in the Sino-Japanese War.[37]

Nor was this all. In 1900 the Boxers, a militant group of martial arts practitioners, launched an armed insurrection against foreign presence in the country. When their nationals became casualties, Japan, Russia, Britain, France, Germany, Austria-Hungary, Italy, and the United States all landed troops. The occupiers demanded a $330 million indemnity for damage from the uprising, which China financed by borrowing. Organized as a thirty-nine-year, 4 percent loan, this doubled the foreign debt at a stroke.[38]

Notwithstanding this burden, the Chinese government was able to contract additional loans between 1900 and 1911 to finance railway construction and establish and improve telegraph and telephone services. It did so despite the weakness of the Qing government and the fact that the country was not on the gold standard.[39]

China's market access thus takes some explaining. Explanation starts with a set of arrangements tailored to reassure foreign investors. Specifically, investors were reassured by an autonomous tax administration, in the form of the Chinese Maritime Customs Service established in Shanghai in 1854 by foreign consuls concerned that the trade taxes financing the operation of the port were being diverted to other uses. When the arrangement demonstrated its utility in Shanghai, it was extended to other cities.

The Customs Service was run by foreigners, predominantly Britons. But while foreigners oversaw its operation, actual collection of duties was delegated to Chinese inspectors. Still, because foreign superintendents were on the spot, they were able to accurately assess the revenues, preventing spurious claims that these were inadequate to service debts.

Initially, customs revenues were the exclusive security pledged to service debt. Over time, however, the government's interest obligations came to outstrip revenue from import duties; other sources of government income, such as taxes on salt and opium, were placed under Customs Service oversight, echoing the Ottomans' experience with their Public Debt Administration.[40] Covenants attached to China's foreign bonds stipulated that these provisions would remain in place for as long as the securities in question were outstanding.

Complementing the Customs Service were the market-making activities of the Hongkong and Shanghai Bank. HSBC, to use the modern name, was established in 1864 by a group of prominent taipans (foreign-born businessmen) to finance trade with Japan and the Philippines. Since credit for this trade, as for much nineteenth-century commerce, was sourced in London, the bank forged a British connection. Within months of its foundation, it had a relationship with London and Westminster Bank. Before long, it was run by British managers and was majority-British-owned. It had a head office in Hong Kong and a branch in Shanghai but also an agency in London.[41] It developed expertise in moving funds across borders, this being the essence of trade finance. Its staff learned to manage the balance-sheet consequences of fluctuations between China's silver-based currency and the gold-backed pound sterling. This came in handy when underwriting Qing China's loans, two-thirds of which were in pounds.[42]

It was then a short step from trade finance to public finance, and from sourcing trade credit in London to placing government bonds. HSBC supported issuance of some bonds and discouraged others, playing the gatekeeping role of a Rothschild's or Barings. It invoked the security of the Customs Service by having customs commissioners endorse its bonds.

Given their involvement in bond underwriting, HSBC executives appreciated that a stable market enhanced the bank's reputation. Consequently, HSBC intervened on the secondary market, buying bonds when their prices fell and selling when they recovered. It acted as a quasi-central bank, not just through these market-making activities but also as a lender of last resort, as in 1910 when it organized a group of foreign banks to lend to the government of Kiangsu province to stem a bank run.[43] China lacked a proper central bank prior to 1928, when the Nationalists finally established one.[44] In the meantime, HSBC stepped into the breach, in much the same manner as the Imperial Ottoman Bank.

HSBC's gatekeeping periodically broke down, for example in 1887, when a rival group placed a Chinese loan in Germany. It collapsed again in the 1890s when a consortium of French and Russian banks, with encouragement from their governments, banded together to lend the Chinese government 400 million francs (the equivalent of £16 million or $80 million).[45] These episodes aside, the government relied on HSBC's seal of approval. Doing otherwise might have jeopardized the market-making and lender-of-last-resort services received in return. For its part, HSBC was not shy about reminding the authorities of their dependence on its services. In 1912–13, for instance, when a new republican government attempted to cut a deal with financial interlopers from Japan, HSBC threatened to halt its stabilizing market interventions. China's novice republican leaders then quickly abandoned their negotiations with the Japanese bankers.[46]

Some authors suggest that these institutional arrangements—a gatekeeping bank and an independent revenue administration—were entirely responsible for China's market access.[47] A problem with this argument is that actual collection of revenues by the Customs Service was still in the hands of Chinese inspectors, not foreign supervisors. Consequently, it was still necessary to ensure that the funds earmarked for debt service were not diverted to other uses. The problem was not only one of information, which the Customs Service was in a position to address, but also of commitment, which the Customs Service alone could not solve.

The additional factor supporting China's market access is easy enough to detect. It was floating offshore, with guns pointed at the mainland. When the Boxers rebelled against outside cultural and financial influence in 1900, foreign governments landed troops, as noted earlier, to protect their citizens and financial interests. Everyone understood that debt default might provoke the same response.

The 1911 revolution illustrates the point. Uncertainty about the intentions of the new republican government prompted the British to finally seize control of customs duties. Rather than entrusting collection to Chinese inspectors, British staff took immediate control of the receipts and deposited them with HSBC.[48] This was done, in the words of Francis Aglen, acting inspector general of the Customs Service, so that "they will not be used by the Revolutionary Party to finance their military forces but are preserved to pay back foreign debt."[49] That Britain and other foreign powers had gunboats moored in the Yangtze and Xiang Rivers eliminated resistance to this step.

Surprisingly, in light of the Chinese Revolution of October 1911, but unsurprisingly given this floating commitment device, there was little movement in Chinese bond prices in London despite the disorderly change in regime. Indeed, the new government and its successors were able to place additional loans in London in 1917, 1918, and 1922. As late as 1941, foreign gunboats continued to patrol the Yangtze, with the stated purpose of protecting foreign business, but also creating pressure for maintenance of interest payments. For its part, the Chinese government, despite all manner of turbulence, continued servicing its debt.[50]

# Rising Sun

Where China had a mixed record of state building, Japan was a classic case of public debt in service of the state. The new Meiji government issued its first domestic bond in 1873 to resolve outstanding debts of the *daimyo*, powerful feudal lords who had ruled much of Japan. The new government assuming their debts effectively sealed the centralization of power by assigning to the national government both fiscal responsibilities and duties; this was not unlike what Alexander Hamilton achieved in 1790 in the United States. The next issues were devoted to paying off the hereditary stipends of the samurai class. Instead of receiving periodic payments, these military nobles and officers, who might have otherwise challenged the state, received a one-time payment in the form of a bond.

The samurai had other ventures in mind. Requiring more cash than they received in the form of periodic interest payments, they sold their bonds to raise liquidity. Some samurai sought to establish banks; they purchased those same bonds to capitalize their new depository institutions. Both transactions required a secondary market to facilitate trading. It followed that 1878, the same year the bonds were delivered to the samurai, saw the creation of stock exchanges in Tokyo and Osaka.[51] Government bonds accounted for the majority of turnover on both exchanges. "Although the stocks of the exchanges [themselves] and of banks were later listed," one account explains, "public debt accounted for most of the trading for some time."[52] In 1882, the government then established a central bank with the capacity to backstop the bond market. Using the liquidity so provided, Japan developed a commercial banking system modeled after the National Banking System in the United States.

This effort to develop financial markets facilitated placement and secondary-market trading of debt. In turn, the existence of a benchmark asset, government bonds that could be priced and traded subject to standard conditions and therefore could be used as collateral, further stimulated those markets. Public debt and private finance developed hand in hand.[53]

Over the next quarter century, the Meiji government regularly issued domestic debt for railway construction and other purposes. It also floated loans in London in 1870 and 1873.[54] This can be understood as the response of a brand new regime to the absence of the infrastructure needed for successful issuance and secondary market trading at home—a deficiency, as we have seen, that was remedied quickly. Once that domestic market was up and running, there was then no further need to access foreign capital markets, so there was no more foreign borrowing.[55]

Interest rates on the 1870 and 1873 foreign loans were even higher than those paid by other risky borrowers, such as Egypt and Romania, reflecting doubts about the Meiji government's hold on power and the time needed to build a functioning tax system.[56] Those high yields were indicative of the novelty of the issue, this being Japan's first appearance on foreign financial markets and the country being "totally unknown . . . to many Western investors."[57] Japan, in effect, was an emerging market that could access public credit only by borrowing abroad, in foreign currency at high interest rates, because it lacked both a track record and the financial infrastructure to borrow at home. The difference between Japan and other emerging markets was that Japan was able to achieve redemption from this "original sin" in less than a decade.[58]

With the outbreak in 1894 of the Sino-Japanese War, fiscal pressures intensified. The government continued to rely on domestic debt issuance, but military requirements eventually surpassed the funding capacity of residents. In 1897, the authorities sought to resell domestic bonds in London. This was the War Loan Bond of 1895–96, repackaged as the Imperial Japanese 5 percent bond of 1897. That it succeeded is, at first sight, a surprise. The government finally determined to go on the gold standard only in early 1897, and the new currency act took effect late in the year. But this made little difference for market access, since the Bank of Japan guaranteed the principal and interest in units of constant gold content; £4.4 million of sales were completed at an interest rate of 5 percent. Another £10 million were then issued in London in 1899, with additional amounts placed in Hamburg and New York, ostensibly for investing in railways and telephone systems, but in reality in preparation for the Russo-Japanese War. These bonds bore a 4 percent interest rate. The issue price was 90, but since the bond ran an impressive fifty-five years to maturity, the yield was only modestly above 4 (see Table 5.1).[59]

When Japan first accessed foreign capital markets, in 1870 and 1873, it was required to pay yields of 10.8 and 8.7 percent. The contrast between then and now was impressive for a country about to embark on a war with a much larger adversary. It reflected economic progress in the interim, notably export growth

Table 5.1 **Japanese Bond Issues in London**

| Year | Value (£ million) | Interest Rate (percent) | Maturity (years) | Use of Proceeds |
|------|------|------|------|------|
| 1870 | 1.0 | 9 | 13 | Railways |
| 1873 | 2.4 | 7 | 25 | Miscellaneous |
| 1897 | 4.4 | 5 | 53 | Military |
| 1899 | 10.0 | 4 | 55 | Railways, telephone |
| 1902 | 5.1 | 5 | 55 | Military, telephone |
| 1904 | 22.0[a] | 6 | 7 | Military |
| 1905 | 60.0[a] | 4.5 | 25 | Military |
| 1905 | 25.0 | 4 | 25 | Miscellaneous |
| 1907 | 23.0 | 5 | 40 | Miscellaneous |
| 1910 | 11.0 | 4 | 60 | Miscellaneous |

Source: Sussman and Yafeh (2000).

Note: [a] Denotes total proceeds raised in two separate issues of bonds of similar terms.

(particularly silk). It testified to success at financial institution building: creation of stock and bond markets, a commercial banking system, and a central bank.[60] And it benefited from credibility derived from political institution building—adoption of the Meiji Constitution in 1889 and a functioning Diet—and no less from Japan's victory in the first Sino-Japanese War.

When war with Russia broke out in 1904, foreign lenders added a default-risk premium to the Japanese government's bonds. The war loan, secured by a lien on Japan's customs revenues, bore an interest rate of 6 percent. It ran seven years to maturity, which translated into a yield of 7.2 percent. This was higher than five years earlier, but only modestly. Given that the country was engaged in an uncertain war with an enemy several times its size, the surprise was that rates weren't higher.

The explanation lies in a bit of good luck. Half of the 1904 issuance was floated in New York by the US investment bank Kuhn, Loeb. This was an exception to American investors' general lack of interest in foreign government bonds. Korekiyo Takahashi, the loan negotiator, had been fortuitously seated next to Jacob Schiff, senior partner in Kuhn, Loeb, at a dinner party in London.[61] Schiff was concerned with czarist oppression of the Jews and hoped that Russia's defeat at the hands of Japan might lead to establishment of a more tolerant constitutional government. So motivated, Schiff allied Kuhn, Loeb with National City Bank and the National Bank of Commerce to underwrite the Japanese government's bonds and market them to American investors.[62] Schiff eventually got his revolution, just not the constitutional government for which he hoped.

When its forces made battlefield gains in 1904, the Japanese government was also able to attract foreign investors to the latest domestic issue. It did so despite this being denominated in yen and secured only by the general credit of the country.[63]

Thus, by consolidating power, demonstrating its military prowess, and implementing financial reforms, the Meiji government transitioned, in just thirty years, from a novel credit, "totally unknown to Western investors," to a seasoned sovereign borrower. It gained the ability, otherwise limited to a small handful of mature economies, to borrow abroad in its own currency. Few other emerging markets of that day were able to graduate from original sin so successfully.[64]

# Conclusion

For Japan, issuing public debt paid. The government used the resources so mobilized to foster economic and financial development, succeed on the battlefield, and lend legitimacy to the state. Holding public debt paid also for investors with well-diversified portfolios of foreign and colonial government bonds. But there were also cases where funds were devoted to less rewarding uses, governments stopped paying, and investors incurred losses. We have seen examples of both kinds in this chapter. We have also encountered devices, from military incursion to fiscal administration, to which investors and governments turned when seeking to recover their funds. In the next chapter we will consider them further.

# Managing Problem Debts

The nineteenth century saw a considerable increase in governments' use of debt finance. Countries with little in the way of domestic financial markets floated bonds in foreign financial centers. From the new nations of Latin America to members of the British Empire such as Canada and Australia and politically dependent entities such as Egypt, every newly independent or quasi-independent entity turned to this market once they obtained a modicum of fiscal autonomy.

There were ample problems along the way, including when governments stopped paying. Investors developed a range of mechanisms for dealing with these defaults. They formed bondholder committees to organize negotiations. They worked with the stock exchange to prevent defaulting debtors from launching new issues. They lobbied their own government to impose economic and political sanctions and, in the limit, for foreign financial control.

Figure 6.1 shows the number of new defaults and the percentage of countries in default from 1800 to 1910.[1] Although there were defaults in all eleven decades, their number spiked in the 1820s, 1870s, and 1890s, decades marked by the principal international debt crises of the era. In the 1820s, the probability of default rose to 5 percent per annum, and by the end of the decade close to a third of all independent nations were behind on payments.[2] Not until the 1860s were these loans normalized and did the fraction of countries in default fall below a quarter. Even this normalization was short-lived, however: the ensuing lending boom collapsed already in 1873, when banking problems in Vienna and Berlin, mentioned in Chapters 4 and 5, infected other European financial centers, and the unconditional probability of default shot up to 2.5 percent.[3]

The third wave of defaults followed yet another lending boom, this one in the 1880s. This was the boom that ended in 1890, when financial problems in Argentina jolted the House of Baring and spilled over to other countries.[4] The default rate rose to 4 percent, its highest since the 1820s, with payment suspensions by Argentina, Brazil, Colombia, the Dominican Republic, Ecuador, Greece, Guatemala, Liberia, Nicaragua, Paraguay, Peru, Portugal, and Venezuela.

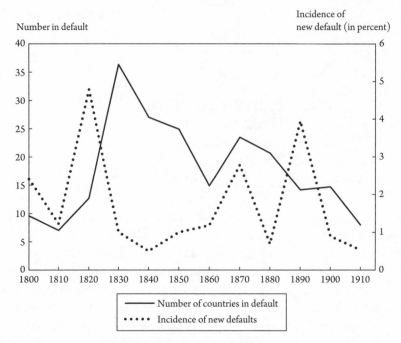

*Figure 6.1.* Sovereign Default Prevalence, 1800–1913
Sources: Reinhart and Rogoff (2009) and authors' calculations.
Note: Composition of coverage: forty-seven nations that became independent some time before 1913.
The sample includes emerging and advanced economies. Countries in default refers to the number
of independent nations in default in a given year over the total number of independent nations in the
same year. Incidence of new defaults refers to the unconditional probability of default per annum, i.e.,
the number of defaults per year in a given decade, divided by the number of independent nations in
the same decade. The data refer to external public debt.

The incidence of new defaults declined more rapidly this time, however, and settlements were reached more quickly. By 1907, all countries other than Guatemala that defaulted in the 1890s had settled with their creditors. The average duration of default fell from fourteen years before 1870 to eight years in the 1870s and 1880s and a mere two years thereafter.[5] Bondholder committees, stock exchanges, investment banks, and creditor-country governments all played a role in this more smoothly functioning adjustment process.

Defaults occurred for a variety of reasons. Some authors emphasize problems in the borrowing countries: political instability, weak fiscal systems, and civil conflict.[6] Others highlight the questionable incentives of the lenders.[7] Although some underwriters screened out dubious credits and discouraged overborrowing, others attached more importance to the commission earned up front than to the performance of the loan.[8] Investors were not always able to distinguish one from the other.

Nor did the desire for market access necessarily deter a borrower in straitened circumstances from contemplating default. This was true of countries with unstable, short-lived governments, which might dismiss loss of market access as a problem for their successors. It was even more the case when investors displayed short memories and were quick to reopen the market to defaulting debtors. The conclusion of economic historians Peter Lindert and Peter Morton that "investors seem to pay little attention to the past repayment record of the borrower" would seem a bit overdrawn.[9] Still, their observation points to the frequency with which sovereigns were able to placate their creditors by negotiating a settlement and undertaking a bond exchange. In so doing, they might regain market access relatively quickly.

But for some countries, reentering the market only meant more problems. Colombia, Mexico, Spain, and Venezuela all defaulted five times between 1800 and 1913. This chronic condition becomes apparent when we calculate, for the countries in Figure 6.1, the probability of default conditional on the number of previous defaults. For countries with no more than one prior default, the probability of default in a given year was a relatively low 1.5 percent per annum. After two defaults, the probability rose to 2.2 percent per annum; after three, it rose to 4.7 percent.

# Debt Renegotiation

Whatever the source of the problem, it was in the common interest of the borrower and lenders to negotiate a settlement. For investors, partial payment was better than none, while for the indebted government, partial payment could be an acceptable price for regaining market access. In principle, there was scope for an agreement in which interest arrears were added to the existing debt, old bonds were exchanged for new ones, and a fresh loan was provided.[10]

But neither party knew for sure what concessions might be wrung from the other. The more anxious a government was to regain market access, the more likely it would table a generous offer. But if officials suspected that investors were even more impatient, then the government had an incentive to hold out to see whether the creditors would accept less costly terms. Conversely, if investors thought it at least possible that the debtor was even more impatient to regain market access, then they had an incentive to demur and see whether the government might make a more generous offer.

Thus, the greater the uncertainty, the stronger the incentive to delay as a way of obtaining additional information. In effect, the debtor and its creditors were locked in a war of attrition that could drag on, perhaps indefinitely.[11]

One explanation for the decline in the duration of defaults in the course of the nineteenth century, it follows, was better information. Investors gained knowledge of countries and governments, and officials learned about the attitudes of investors. Specialized financial publications and institutions helped to overcome information asymmetries. Even prior defaults revealed information. Ironically then, the same countries defaulting more than once was itself a factor helping to break the latest impasse.

Although investors sought to mount a united front as a way of exerting pressure on the debtor, bondholders' circumstances varied. A debtor could sow division by offering investors in one issue more generous terms and asserting that its settlement constituted sufficient grounds for readmission to the market.[12] Even when a majority of investors were of the view that the debtor had tabled an acceptable offer, it was still necessary to pressure the holdouts. Otherwise, the will of the majority could be frustrated, and other bondholders or the government might have to buy out the holdouts at an exorbitant price.

Common law courts, including those of London, adhered to the doctrine of sovereign immunity, refusing to hear cases against governments.[13] Officials hesitated to involve themselves in private financial affairs. Investors had an incentive, therefore, to adapt their loan contracts to address the obstacles to collective action. In 1879, Francis Palmer, an English barrister, introduced the first majority-action clause, under which a majority vote by the holders of a bond could force a dissenting minority of investors to accept the agreement. These majority-action clauses, which facilitated post-default settlements by disenfranchising holdouts, were counterbalanced by other legal provisions, such as the *pari passu* clause, which required equal treatment of all bondholders and was widely used following its inclusion in a Bolivian bond in 1872.[14]

## Bondholder Committees

Given the advantages of coordination, bondholders formed committees as vehicles for reaching agreement among themselves. Early committees were ad hoc, purpose-built, and organized along national lines. An example was the Committee of Greek Bondholders, established in 1826 by investors assembled at the City of London Tavern, with Jacob Ricardo, brother of David and co-organizer of an ill-fated 1825 Greek loan, in the chair.[15]

Not all committees were chaired by experienced financiers. Some were organized by fly-by-night operators more interested in the commission earned when old bonds were exchanged for new ones than in the welfare of investors. In other cases, competing committees representing different investors undercut one another's negotiating position.[16]

Early British committees worked hand in glove with the London Stock Exchange and its governing board, the Committee for General Purposes, which counted important bondholders among its members.[17] Starting in the 1830s, the committee moved to suspend trading in the securities of governments in default on application by a bondholder committee.[18] It permitted new bonds to be listed and quoted only when the bondholder committee reported that a majority of its members was prepared to accept a government's restructuring offer. In this way, the London Stock Exchange provided a degree of institutional continuity. Bondholder committees might come and go, but the Committee for General Purposes endured. The exchange's ban on trading allowed bondholders to pressure the defaulted government. It was also a mechanism for pressuring holdouts, who might see the market for new issues start up again when an agreement was supported by a majority.

With the resumption of lending in the 1860s, efforts were made to regularize these irregular arrangements. A November 1868 meeting of British investors, again at the London Tavern and presided over this time by the merchant banker, politician, and future Chancellor of the Exchequer George J. Goschen, founded the Corporation of Foreign Bondholders, a standing committee of claimants on governments. The banking firm of which he was a partner, Frühling and Goschen, had helped to float the Egyptian loans of 1862–66.[19] By 1868, these loans had lapsed into default and were of understandable concern to the bondholders, not least to Frühling and Goschen itself.

In 1873, the corporation was restructured as a nonprofit and received a license of incorporation from the Board of Trade.[20] Its governing board, or council, was dominated by bond brokers and underwriting banks. Other members objected that this rendered the council too quick to accept settlement offers, since its bankers and brokers were interested in resuming underwriting as soon as possible. As the *Economist* wrote in 1896, "a powerful influence is exercised upon bondholders by the issuing houses, who find it practically impossible to do fresh business with the borrowers while the default lasts, and who are, therefore, naturally anxious that some sort of settlement be arrived at, more especially as settlements . . . are frequently followed by new loans."[21] Bondholders could decide whether to accept an offer by majority vote at a general assembly, but the agenda for that meeting was controlled by the council. These complaints caused the corporation to be reconstituted in 1899 by an act of Parliament, with members of the council now nominated by the London Chamber of Commerce, in which the bondholders were represented.[22]

In addition to organizing the bondholders, these committees addressed information problems. The Corporation of Foreign Bondholders organized public lectures. It maintained agents in financially consequential countries. It published reports on the debt situation. It operated a reading room and library where investors could consult reports, press clippings, and other market-relevant materials.[23]

Parallel committees were founded in the Netherlands in 1876, France and Belgium in 1898, and Switzerland in 1912, mirroring these countries' rise as foreign lenders. Like the Corporation of Foreign Bondholders, these committees originated as creatures of banks and bond brokers. Some, like the *Association Nationale des Porteurs Français de Valeurs Mobilières*, were created in response to pressure from the government, which feared that bondholders might attempt to enlist government officials as advocates if they lacked representation.[24] In Germany, where the market was controlled by a small handful of banks, investors continued to rely on ad hoc committees organized by bank underwriters.[25]

Although the Corporation of Foreign Bondholders worked closely with the London Stock Exchange, it worked less well with its foreign counterparts. Inadequate coordination with foreign stock exchanges and bondholder committees could be a problem, since a government that settled with one national committee and resumed issuing bonds on that market could take a harder line in negotiations with others. Bondholders of different nationalities disagreed over who would be paid first. Creditor coordination was a casualty of such disagreements.[26] Thus, Guatemala was able to resume borrowing in France and Germany shortly after the turn of the century, despite remaining in default on its British loans.[27] Similarly, British bondholders saw no choice but to settle with the Portuguese government in 1902 because Portugal had settled with French and German investors a year earlier.[28]

Although the bondholder committee was a work in progress, its effects were discernible. Negotiations were concluded more quickly when bondholders were represented by a permanent organization.[29] Defaults took longer to resolve when bondholder representation was split between multiple committees. Rates of return were a fifth again higher when negotiated by a standing organization rather than an ad hoc committee.[30]

Committees such as the Corporation of Foreign Bondholders pursued the bondholders' claims for many years. The corporation was still seeking to collect on defaulted Russian bonds more than sixty years after the Bolsheviks repudiated the debts of the czar.[31] The longer a default persisted, of course, the more remote were the prospects of a favorable settlement. Moreover, with a quiescent international bond market following the defaults of the 1930s, there was a dearth of new claims and of bondholders to pay membership dues. Rent being an operating cost, the Corporation of Foreign Bondholders first abandoned the Square Mile for the exurbs of London. It closed down in 1988, mere months, ironically, before issuance and trading in emerging market bonds started up again.

## Pyramids of Debt

In the extreme, debt mismanagement could result in loss of not just market access but also financial and political autonomy. Egypt illustrates the perils.

Though a province of the Ottoman Empire, as we have seen, Egypt acquired a degree of political sovereignty thanks to the efforts of Muhammed Ali, who ruled from 1805. In an 1841 political settlement, the Porte, formally in charge of all things Ottoman, granted Ali and his successors the title of governor (or khedive) and financial autonomy in return for an annual tribute.[32]

Although this settlement did not expressly authorize issuance of debt, neither did it preclude it.[33] Capitalizing on the ambiguity, the second khedive, Said (1854–63), began issuing short-term treasury bonds. When the market proved limited, in 1860 he obtained a personal advance from the Comptoir d'Escompte, a French institution set up with government sponsorship following the 1848 Revolution.[34] The funds so obtained were used to finance, among other things, construction of the Suez Canal, in which the French had an obvious interest. At least the funds financed the inauguration of construction. Before long, more finance, much more, would be required.

The era of modern Egyptian state finance, as opposed to the personal loans of the khedive, commenced in 1862 with a £2.2 million bond issue floated in London and other European centers. It was helped along by the strong cotton prices associated with the US Civil War.[35] This was the first of the ill-fated loans in which Frühling and Goschen was involved. Said received just 60 percent of the face value of the bonds, since these were purchased by investors at 80 and subject to extraordinary commissions and service charges of 20 percent (split between Frühling and Goschen and its German partner—Frühling and Goschen having originally been a German bank). Someone, presumably the firm, evidently understood that the undertaking was risky.

On assuming power in 1863, Khedive Ismail Pasha inherited this debt. Rather than consolidating, he borrowed more to finance everything from a national road system to an opera house. Since tax revenues didn't rise commensurately, new loans had to be raised to fund interest payments. The khedive resorted to increasingly creative measures, pledging the revenues of his personal estates (*Dairas*), precollecting taxes (in exchange for a 50 percent discount), and selling 45 percent of Suez Canal shares to the British government. By 1876, long-term debt had risen to £54 million, short-term debt to £26 million. The combined total was roughly 120 percent of GDP, an extraordinary sum for an emerging market still at the early stages of economic development.[36]

Cotton prices predictably declined with the end of the American Civil War. The Egyptian government contracted a final external loan in early 1873, after which the financial crisis in Europe and the 1875 Ottoman default foreclosed the market.[37] In a last-ditch effort to preserve market access, Ismail turned over customs duties, tobacco-monopoly revenues, and provincial taxes to his French and British creditors.[38] The plan was crafted by the same George Goschen who chaired the meeting leading to establishment of the Corporation of Foreign Bondholders and whose firm had underwritten Egypt's bonds.[39]

This was one of the first applications of foreign control to the finances of an impecunious debtor and a model for subsequent interventions, such as that in the Ottoman Empire in 1882.[40] The Caisse de la Dette Publique, the creditors' special-purpose vehicle, received the assigned revenues directly and exercised a veto over new borrowing and changes in taxation.[41] In return, it consolidated the external debt into a single 7 percent loan.[42]

External control understandably went down poorly in Egypt. In 1882 it incited demonstrations and riots in which Europeans lost their lives. The British government's "proportionate" response was to bombard Alexandria, occupy Egypt, and take control of its finances.[43] The British government's stated policy was not to intervene in foreign countries on behalf of commercial interests. Exceptions were made on strategic grounds, however. And the Suez Canal was nothing if not strategic.[44]

Egypt's finances were stabilized with help from an 1885 loan guaranteed by Britain and five other European governments concerned to maintain the navigability of the canal, not to mention repayment of earlier loans. Under this arrangement, half of any budget surplus went to retiring outstanding debt, while the other half went to reviving the economy, principally by investing in irrigation projects. This was an improvement over the preceding arrangement, under which the controllers had mandated that 100 percent of any increase in revenues go toward debt retirement. Attaching 100 percent of the increase eliminated all incentive for the Egyptian authorities to do anything to increase revenues. (This is what economists refer to as a debt overhang.) But now, with investments in irrigation, the economy began to revive, and the state's finances improved. The creditors, by taking less, received more. Revenues devoted to debt service rose by 50 percent between 1882 and 1904.[45]

After the turn of the century, once the Caisse de la Dette Publique had accumulated sufficient reserves, the creditors loosened their grip. The Egyptian government used its flexibility to return to the market and convert old debt into new loans, paying half the previous rate (Table 6.1). Through these operations, the outstanding debt was reduced from ten times government revenues in 1882 to half that in 1913. Gaining fiscal space, the government began borrowing again, for railway improvements and other purposes.

This was successful debt consolidation, albeit under circumstances that did not recommend themselves to other countries. Moreover, the Caisse, enjoying adequate revenues, did little to encourage more fundamental fiscal reforms.[46] On the eve of World War I, as a result, Egypt had one of the weakest fiscal capacities among its peers. This left it even less prospect of regaining full political and financial autonomy than other economies also under international financial

*Table 6.1*  **Foreign Borrowing by Egypt before and after Financial Control**

| Period | Foreign Loans (nominal value in £m) | Effective Interest Rate (in percent) | Debt Per Capita (in £) |
|--------|------------------------------------|--------------------------------------|------------------------|
| 1862–76 | 69.0 | 8.5 | 7.2 |
| 1876–1913 | 55.0 | 4.5 | 7.5 |

*Source:* Tunçer (2015).

tutelage. Those other economies reacquired at least a modicum of independence following World War I. Egypt, in contrast, regained its fiscal sovereignty only after World War II. This was not treatment that Egyptians who lived through the interwar period found easy to forget.

## Sanctions and Sovereignty

Egypt was not alone, of course, in enduring this insult to its sovereignty. One study identifies eighteen pre-1914 instances when military pressure was applied or foreign control was imposed in response to debt problems.[47] Defaults followed by such sanctions were settled more quickly than other defaults.[48] Subsequent default became less likely, and problem borrowers were better able to issue new debt on international markets. The political consequences were more problematic. With hindsight, it is not surprising that after suffering through a long period of foreign financial and political control, Egypt turned to a highly nationalistic leader, Gamal Abdel Nasser, on finally gaining independence.

Nor could investors necessarily rely on sanctions. British foreign secretaries from Canning to Palmerston insisted that British bondholders should not expect help from their government.[49] As Canning summarized the position, it was not "any part of the duty of the Government to interfere in any way to procure the payment of loans made by British subjects to foreign powers, States, or Individuals."[50] Not that the creditors were shy about asking. They persisted, Palmerston complained, "beyond endurance in their roguery and impudence."[51]

There were other counterweights as well. British merchants and manufacturers worried that a naval blockade would interfere with trade. Consequently, military intervention was more likely when British commercial interests were at risk and the positions of commerce, industry, and finance were aligned. This was the case, for example, when it appeared that foreign governments might use debt problems as a pretext for seizing the Suez Canal.

When Britain intervened, it often did so in conjunction with other powers. Such cooperation tended to make a blockade more effective. This was the case in Venezuela, for example, which experienced a revolution starting in 1898 and ceased payment on its debts. Germany had substantial interests there and took the lead in this intervention. The British foreign office was swayed; it appreciated that it would bear only a fraction of the cost and feared that a unilateral German blockade might secure superior terms for German investors.

So in 1902, Britain and Germany blockaded the ports of La Guaira and Puerto Cabello and seized their customs houses, while Germany bombarded the fort at San Carlos in a show of force and in an attempt to enter Lake Maracaibo. US President Theodore Roosevelt declined to deter them on the grounds that the Monroe Doctrine, which warned European governments against interventions in the Western Hemisphere, applied to seizures of territory but not to efforts to enforce debt contracts. Eventually, Roosevelt grew impatient and dispatched a US fleet under Admiral George Dewey to force Germany to the bargaining table. Under terms reached in Washington, DC, Venezuela agreed to devote 30 percent of its customs income at La Guaira and Puerto Cabello to interest owed to the United States and nine European countries. It was in little position to resist: the blockade was maintained throughout negotiations. For its part, Venezuela was represented in its discussions with the Germans by the US ambassador to Caracas, Herbert Wolcott Bowen.[52]

This incident set the tone for US intervention in the region. In 1904, when Santo Domingo (modern-day Dominican Republic) ceased payments on its debt, Germany and Italy blocked its ports. This time, however, the US president issued the proclamation that became known as the Roosevelt Corollary of the Monroe Doctrine. This was a warning to European governments and indebted countries alike. "If a nation shows to act with decency with regard to industrial and political matters," it read, "and if it keeps order and pays its obligations, then it need fear no interference from the United States." However, "[b]rutal wrong-doing, or an impotence which results in a general loosening of the ties of civilized society, may finally require intervention by some civilized nation, and in the Western hemisphere the United States cannot ignore the duty."[53]

The United States then dispatched a battleship and took control of the customs house in Santo Domingo, preempting the Germans and Italians. Investors took this action as a signal that there was renewed hope of settling the outstanding defaults of Latin American debtors; bonds rallied on the news. As the New York Times commented on May 5, "London stockbrokers are driving a roaring trade in South Americans, which have become a subject of lively, speculative interest on the theory that President Roosevelt has practically guaranteed all South American obligations."[54]

The United States threatened Costa Rica in 1911, Nicaragua in 1912, and Guatemala in 1913 with gunboats and seizure of the customs house. In doing so, it was only following the example of the European powers in Greece, Egypt, Turkey, and elsewhere.

# Impact of Default

How did default affect countries economically? The simplest approach to answering this question is to compare economic growth before and after the event. The experience of nineteen sovereigns that defaulted between 1880 and 1914 for which historical national income estimates are available indicates that the loss in GDP, relative to the five years preceding the event, was as high as 10 percent, after which the effect tapers off.

Of course, defaulting and nondefaulting countries also differed in other respects. Sovereigns are prone to default precisely because they overborrow and artificially stimulate the economy in the preceding period, leading to an even larger collapse when market access and credit stimulus are withdrawn. One way of circumventing this problem is the "narrative approach."[55] This uses contemporary sources to distinguish defaults resulting from this kind of overborrowing (so-called endogenous defaults) from defaults that occurred for reasons not of the country's own making ("exogenous defaults," resulting instead from, say, global commodity price shocks or problems in other borrowing countries or financial centers). Figure 6.2 shows the result, distinguishing the response of GDP in the full sample and in endogenous default cases.[56] As expected, the GDP loss was smaller in cases of exogenous default, although the decline is still there.

Figure 6.3 shows sovereign spreads, the additional premium that investors demanded in order to hold a sovereign's bonds over and above the yield on safe assets (e.g., British consols). It indicates that spreads rose significantly and remained elevated after a default. Four years after default, spreads were still 50 percent higher than before the crisis. The increase was similar across the

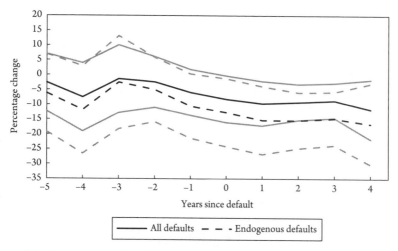

*Figure 6.2.* Output Costs of Sovereign Defaults, 1800–1913
Source: Authors' calculations.
Note: GDP figures are from Bolt et al. (2018). Gray lines depict 95-percent confidence intervals.

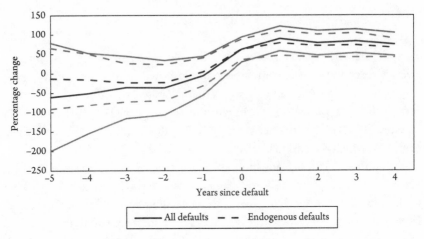

*Figure 6.3.* Impact of Defaults on Sovereign Spreads, 1800–1913
Source: Authors' calculations.
Note: GDP figures are from Bolt et al. (2018). Gray lines depict 95-percent confidence intervals.

two samples, suggesting that exogenous and endogenous defaults were not always clearly distinguished by investors. This finding supports the view, still held today, that markets are not as discriminating as one might think when it comes to country risk.

## Realized Returns

How did investors fare? We have a considerable body of evidence on foreign debt issued in the principal European financial centers, but less on domestic debt. In the research cited earlier, Lindert and Morton compute returns to investors on foreign government bonds outstanding in 1850 and issued between 1850 and 1913. They consider four Latin American issuers (Argentina, Brazil, Chile, and Mexico) and six other prominent borrowers (Australia, Canada, Egypt, Japan, Russia, and Turkey).[57] Their calculations, in Table 6.2, show realized returns ranging from –0.7 percent for Mexico to 4.8 percent for Canada and 6.4 percent for Egypt. Other government bonds offered returns in the 2–3 percent range, not dissimilar from British consols.

This dispersion is a reminder of the very different circumstances in which debt was incurred and repaid. The disastrous returns on Mexican loans reflect the 1910 revolution, which caused payments to be suspended. Negotiations with an International Committee of Bankers on Mexico, chaired by Thomas Lamont of J. P. Morgan & Co., commenced already in 1919, but only sporadic payments were made until 1941. At that point, the debt was restructured on

*Table 6.2* **Realized Real Returns on Lending to Ten Foreign Governments, 1850–1914**

| Borrowing Nation | Number of Bonds | Amount Lent ($ millions) | Real Rate of Return (percent) |
|---|---|---|---|
| Argentina | 113 | 928.1 | 3.5 |
| Brazil | 79 | 841.8 | 2.3 |
| Chile | 32 | 249.7 | 2.8 |
| Mexico[a] | 37 | 475.7 | −0.7 |
| Sum | 261 | 2,495.0 | 2.2 |
| | | | |
| Australia | 232 | 1,525.2 | 3.0 |
| Canada | 62 | 65.7 | 4.8 |
| Egypt | 18 | 367.9 | 6.4 |
| Japan | 32 | 914.9 | 1.9 |
| Russia[b] | 48 | 3,340.9 | 1.3 |
| Turkey | 42 | 695.4 | 1.6 |
| Sum | 434 | 6,910.0 | 2.1 |
| **Grand total** | 695 | 9,405.0 | 2.1 |

*Source:* Lindert and Morton (1989).

*Note:* 'Sum' is total number of bonds, total amount issued, and average return for the countries listed immediately above. Grand total is for bonds of these ten countries. Rates of return are constructed by subtracting from the nominal return the ex post rate of consumer-price inflation in the lending country. Flows are deflated by the lending-country consumer price index. Amount lent is in current US dollars before commission and expenses are deducted.

[a] Two unsuccessful Mexican conversion loans from the 1915–45 period are included.

[b] Two loans in dollars issued to czarist Russia in 1916 are included.

terms favorable to Mexico, with pressure from the US State Department, which wished to mend fences with America's neighbor to the south given the outbreak of World War II.[58]

The very different performance of Egyptian bonds reflects the foreign financial control described earlier. The returns on Canadian issues indicate that this faithful Commonwealth member serviced its sterling-denominated debt in full.[59]

Overall, returns on the bonds of the four Latin governments averaged 2.2 percent, slightly higher than returns to investors purchasing consols (1.7 percent). On balance, then, the premium demanded by investors to compensate for default risk by these four Latin sovereigns more than offset the impact of debt service interruptions. In contrast, returns on the bonds of the six other debtors, which averaged almost exactly the same in absolute terms (2.1 percent), slightly underperformed consols.[60] All told, returns on foreign bonds and consols, at 2.12 and 2.26 percent, were all but indistinguishable for buy-and-hold investors.

These returns are calculated for the life of the loan, imagining patient investors. Not everyone who bought in fact held, of course. The existence of a secondary market allowed investors to rebalance their portfolios and liquidate unwanted positions before the maturity date. This makes it useful to have an alternative gauge of returns. The obvious alternative is total annual returns.[61] The economists Benjamin Chabot and Christopher Kurz make the necessary calculations and find that the return on the bonds of foreign governments listed in London averaged 8.4 percent between 1866 and 1907, while British government securities delivered an average return of 2.1 percent.[62] The premium paid by foreign governments was driven by risk and volatility. Even when one adjusts returns for the volatility of bond prices, however, these numbers suggest that it paid to invest in the bonds of foreign sovereigns.[63]

These calculations provide a sense of why investors were attracted to sovereign bonds despite the risks of international lending. The risk premium more than compensated investors for losses from defaults. This should not come as a surprise: as we saw in Chapter 3, this was the same reason foreign bankers in an earlier century continued to lend to Philip II of Spain despite his serial defaults. Supranormal returns also compensated investors for the volatility of bond prices. And those investors enjoyed the benefits of portfolio diversification— stabler returns overall—since payments on domestic and foreign bonds were only loosely correlated with one another.[64]

## Domestic Debt

Sovereigns issuing debt in domestic currency had to compensate investors not just for default risk, but also for currency risk—for the risk that the bonds would lose value if the currency depreciated. This was especially a concern for the bonds of countries that exported a single commodity. Many countries at the periphery of the gold standard relied on exports of one or a small handful of primary commodities: meat and wheat in Argentina, coffee and rubber in Brazil, copper in Chile, tobacco in Colombia, guano in Peru, cacao in Venezuela. If commodity prices fell, the balance of payments and government budget would move into deficit. Reserves would flow out, and the authorities might be forced to depreciate the currency.[65] The value of the interest payments would be correspondingly less.[66]

Investors understood. On average, governments were required to pay an additional 220 basis points as compensation for currency risk when issuing domestic debt.[67] They continued to pay this premium even after adopting the gold standard, since what was adopted could also be abandoned.

We have two snapshots of domestic debt, one for 1883 and another for 1914. The economic historians Marc Flandreau and Nathan Sussman consider all bonds outstanding in London and Paris in 1883, classifying them by currency of denomination.[68] They show that only a handful of European countries—Britain, Germany, and the Netherlands—issued debt exclusively in their own currencies. France can be added if one ignores the 1871 indemnity loan following the Franco-Prussian War.[69] Belgium and Switzerland can be added if one ignores the denomination of their bonds in French francs, effectively the common currency of the members of the Latin Monetary Union.

Even by this liberal interpretation, the resulting list is limited to a handful of relatively advanced European countries. In most cases, their currencies were used internationally, allowing their bonds to be bought and sold on liquid markets. They produced manufactures as well as primary commodities, stabilizing their terms of trade. Creditors had voice in their political systems. Latin American countries lacked these prerequisites and therefore mainly issued bonds in foreign currencies or included exchange clauses tying payment to those currencies. The English-speaking dominions and other British colonies did likewise.[70]

A few countries outside Europe were able to place domestic-currency bonds with local investors. Japan, discussed in the previous chapter, was one. The United States was another. In other cases, however, the sovereign was able to issue only token amounts of domestic debt. For some, the constraint was a dearth of wealthy investors, underdeveloped financial markets, or weak political institutions. For others, it was the volatility of exports and instability of the currency.

Our second snapshot of domestic debt is for 1913 (Table 6.3). There is a clear contrast there between Europe and North America on the one hand, where

*Table 6.3*  **Government Debt Composition in 1913**

|  | Government Debt ($ millions) | |
|---|---|---|
|  | *External* | *Domestic* |
| Europe | 6,576 | 22,752 |
| North America | 311 | 1,419 |
| Latin America | 1,314 | 743 |
| Africa | 991 | 69 |
| Asia | 3,355 | 520 |
| Oceania | 906 | 1,216 |
| Total | 13,453 | 26,719 |

*Source:* United Nations (1948).

domestic debt was close to 80 percent of government borrowing, and other continents. These figures also disguise considerable variation within continents. Having built a working tax system and liquid secondary markets, Japan was now able to interest foreign investors in its domestic, yen-denominated bonds, as we saw in the previous chapter. By 1914, several Latin American countries, typically larger ones, had gained the capacity to issue additional domestic debt, along with the British Dominions and Scandinavian countries.[71] But little had changed for Greece, Egypt, Turkey, Mexico, Peru, and others, which continued to rely on foreign currency bonds issued overseas.

## Modern Markets, Modern Problems

Despite defaults and delays in resuming payments, investors purchasing foreign government securities did at least as well as when holding domestic government securities. They were compensated for volatility. They enjoyed the benefits of portfolio diversification. That realized returns were favorable explains why investors lent despite the risks.

The practice had risks not just for investors but also for borrowers. The behavior of secondary market prices of sovereign bonds quoted on the London Stock Exchange following the Argentina-Baring Crisis in 1890 illustrates the point.[72] The risk premium (i.e., the current yield minus the risk-free rate) charged to Latin American governments rose explosively, by 840 basis points between 1890 and 1891 and by fully 1,600 basis points by 1895. These are very large numbers; not surprisingly, they had marked recessionary consequences. And not just in one region: we described earlier how these events originating in Latin America resulted in a lost decade in Australia. In addition, governments might be forced into painful fiscal, commercial, and political concessions by investors claiming title to their tax receipts. At worst, sovereignty itself could be a casualty.

But borrowing also had positive effects, which is why governments persisted in the practice. Countries used borrowed resources to strengthen their defense and secure their borders. As a result, irregular border changes were fewer between 1815 and the onset of World War I than in earlier centuries. In addition to national defense, governments invested in ports, railways, and other forms of infrastructure capable of supporting additional exports, helping them smooth their borrowing and manage their debts. And even when default ensued, borrowing left behind a legacy of railways, ports, sewers, and incandescent streetlamps, not unlike how the dot-com bubble of the late 1990s, after it burst, left behind a legacy of fiber-optic cables.

# || 7 ||

# Successful Consolidation

Debt problems get all the attention, but not all borrowing ends in tears. There also have been instances, including before World War I, when high debts were successfully reduced. In this chapter we describe three such episodes: Britain after the French and Napoleonic Wars, the United States after its Civil War, and France after the Franco-Prussian War. We focus on these cases because they involved three of the largest economies of the nineteenth century, and because their public debts were among the heaviest.[1]

In all three instances, high public debts were reduced as shares of GDP. But the way in which they were reduced differed from the twentieth-century episodes we consider later. There was no involuntary restructuring or renegotiation of debts, as occurred in emerging markets and developing countries. No measures were taken to artificially depress interest rates. Nor were debts inflated away. Rather, debt-to-GDP ratios were reduced "the old-fashioned way," by running budget surpluses and growing the economy. The question is how these countries did it, and whether something similar is feasible today. Do these tales of debt consolidation have implications, positive or negative, for heavily indebted economies emerging from the COVID-19 pandemic?[2]

## Pity of War

The French and Napoleonic Wars, the Franco-Prussian War, and the US Civil War were three of the most expensive conflicts of the nineteenth-century. The French and Napoleonic Wars spanned more than two decades, from 1792 through 1815. The US Civil War, as the first major conflict of the industrial era, saw unprecedented investments in war materiel; it entailed the use of industrial-era technology in the form of railroads and steamships to deploy armaments and troops.[3] And where the US Civil War involved one industrial power (the Confederacy being primarily agricultural), the Franco-Prussian War opposed two.

In all three instances, governments and banks were forced to suspend the convertibility of currencies into gold and silver, and to resort to money creation. In fact, however, additional money creation (what economists refer to as "seigniorage") did not account for a large fraction of war finance in any of these cases, something that stands in contrast, as we will see, to the experience of the principal combatants during World War I.

Instead, war expenditure was financed mainly by levying taxes and issuing debt. Thus, Britain financed the Napoleonic Wars primarily by borrowing and, as the war ground on, by raising taxes. This behavior is consistent with economic logic (with what economists refer to as "the theory of optimal tax smoothing"). This theory suggests that the costs of a short war can be spread over time—e.g., by borrowing—but that a government in a semipermanent state of war will have to raise taxes.[4]

Once gold convertibility was suspended in 1797, the Exchequer also relied on the Bank of England to purchase government securities, primarily short-term bills. But the increase in the bank's holdings of government debt was limited, from £21 million in 1797 to £34 million in 1815. A 50-percent increase is not peanuts, but it required two decades to achieve. Compare the Federal Reserve's response to the COVID-19 pandemic, when it increased its holdings of US government securities by 71 percent in just the first four months of the outbreak.

The Bank of England's most important wartime role lay not in directly financing the Exchequer, but rather in ensuring that the payment system and therefore the economy continued to function. The bank achieved this by providing short-term financing to merchants and manufacturers. It advanced credit against their receivables, what were known as private bills. Between 1797 and 1816 the bank's holdings of these nearly quintupled, from £5 million to £24 million.[5]

By implication, the majority of the debt securities issued by the British government were placed with individual investors. The authorities cultivated investor support by signaling their commitment to maintaining the value of their obligations and by continuing to pay into the sinking fund, set up in 1786 by William Pitt, the Younger.[6] The sinking fund was a special account whose receipts were earmarked for debt retirement.[7] Investors were understandably reassured by its existence and by the continued transfer of funds. The authorities further reiterated their intention of restoring gold convertibility at the prewar parity once the emergency passed, whenever that might be.[8] England already had a relatively efficient tax administration, in the form of the excise described in Chapter 3. When it became apparent that the war would be lengthy, Pitt added the country's first income tax.[9]

Pitt proved to be an astute debt manager. During the war, he faced the decision of whether to issue bonds paying 3, 4, or 5 percent. He understood that a 5-percent coupon would have required the government to make heavier debt-service payments during the war, so he opted for 3 percent. However, this implied a heavier postwar debt burden, since 3 percent debt had to be sold at a higher discount but was redeemed, eventually, at par. Still, this was a worthwhile trade-off at a time when every penny counted.[10]

Price-level trends also had implications for the debt. Having risen by 90 percent between 1791 and 1813, the price level was pushed back down to within 10 percent of 1791 levels by 1821, permitting gold convertibility to be restored at the prewar parity, as promised.[11] The authorities had long since signaled this intention, as noted, assuming that the war was won. This can be thought of as another bit of clever financial engineering, effectively transforming government bonds into state-contingent securities. If the country emerged victorious from its war with the French, then the authorities would be able to make good on their promise to restore the prewar parity, and the bondholders would enjoy capital gains. If Britain was defeated, on the other hand, it was likely that the prewar parity would be abandoned. In this case, bondholders would suffer losses—appropriately insofar as the wealthy should not escape the pain of defeat, financially or otherwise.[12]

Public finance during the US Civil War was broadly similar in its outlines. The majority of wartime spending by the Union government was financed by issuing bonds and raising taxes, as described in Chapter 5. Bonds held by banks and low-denomination notes held by the public rose from $65 million to more than $2 billion between 1861 and 1865; this, clearly, was a revolution in American finance. Although taxes accounted for only a small fraction of the Union government's resources in 1861–62, their share rose as the war dragged on, with increases in tariffs and excises and introduction of the first US income tax in 1861, again consistent with tax smoothing logic.[13] However, putting in place an income tax administration took time, and in the interim the Union was desperate for funds. Treasury Secretary Salmon P. Chase bridged the gap by selling additional Treasury bonds to banks in New York, Boston, and Philadelphia in anticipation of revenues.

The most controversial element was issuing greenbacks (currency notes not backed by gold), which accounted for 15 percent of wartime government spending. Their emission was associated with a cumulative 75 percent rise in the price level, slightly less than in Britain during the period of the French and Napoleonic Wars. Not until 1878 did prices return to prewar levels, and gold convertibility was restored only in 1879, making for a more gradual readjustment than in Britain.[14]

The Franco-Prussian War was less expensive than the Napoleonic and US Civil Wars, although there was also a postwar indemnity with which to contend. The contemporary statistician and financial journalist Robert Giffen estimated that France's war-related outlays totaled 3 billion francs, or about 15 percent of GDP.[15] By comparison, British military spending in the Napoleonic Wars represented five times national income, while the combined war outlays of the Union and Confederate governments totaled 75 percent of US GDP.[16]

The French government financed roughly half its wartime expenses with taxes and half with debt.[17] The Bank of France suspended specie payments in 1870. It then provided direct advances, collateralized by Treasury notes, to the government; these accounted for a third of wartime borrowing.[18] In 1871 the bank also provided advances to the Paris Commune, the city's short-lived revolutionary government. The Communards used the funds to pay their citizen militia and to meet other expenses. In return, they refrained from taking over the bank, a concession for which they were criticized by Marx and Engels.[19] Even while financing the Commune, the bank also continued providing credit to the conservative Thiers government in Versailles. That's called hedging one's bets.[20]

The postwar indemnity to Germany amounted to 5 billion French francs, or another 25 percent of GDP. It was also more than 200 percent of a year's taxes, which meant that it had to be financed.[21] This was accomplished by placing two large bond issues, half of which were subscribed by foreigners.[22] The 6 percent yield was relatively modest given that France was defeated and still in turmoil. The first loan was twice oversubscribed, remarkably for a country that had just suffered both a battlefield defeat and a domestic revolution. As the French financial historian André Liesse put it, "this result was obtained in June, 1871, not long after the civil war, and while the monuments of Paris were still smoking from the fires set by the insurgents of the commune."[23] This investor enthusiasm testified to confidence that the authorities would stabilize prices, restore gold convertibility, and honor their obligations, as they in fact did.

## Accounting for Consolidation

Some simple debt accounting can help us understand how these debts were successfully consolidated. We can divide changes in the debt-to-GDP ratio into three components. The first is the cumulated primary budget balance, that is, the budget surplus excluding interest payments. (This is sometimes referred to as fiscal effort—the effort a country makes to retire its debt.) The second term is the product of the inherited debt-to-GDP ratio and the difference between the nominal interest rate on debt and the nominal GDP growth rate. This term captures how debt, as a share of GDP, will rise with the interest rate, since additional debt service will have to be financed with additional debt issuance (assuming nothing else is done), and how that debt, again as a share of GDP, will fall with the economy's growth.[24]

The third term, which captures everything else, is known as the stock-flow adjustment.[25] Factors contributing to the stock-flow adjustment include capital gains and losses on foreign currency debt due to exchange-rate changes, restructurings that write down the value of previously issued debt, and other exceptional financial operations.[26]

In each case, the starting point for our calculations is the year in which the debt-to-GDP ratio peaked, and the endpoint is the eve of World War I. Table 7.1 shows the result. It confirms that the reduction in the British debt-to-GDP ratio was the largest and spanned the longest period. Debt fell from 194 percent of GDP in 1822 to 28 percent nine decades later (as shown also in Figure 7.1).[27] The French public-debt-to-GDP ratio fell from 96 percent in 1896 to 51 percent in 1913, after which consolidation ended with the outbreak of war (Figure 7.2). This case ranks second in size but first in pace; France's debt-reduction efforts spanned less than two decades.[28] Union government debt at the end of the US Civil War was not as high as in France, and the subsequent consolidation was more leisurely. But this case is notable for having essentially eliminated the debt on the eve of World War I (as shown in Figure 7.3).

In contrast to the post–World War II debt reductions described in Chapter 9, the growth-rate–interest-rate differential did not contribute materially to the decline of debt burdens in any of these episodes, as Table 7.1 shows. In fact, since nominal interest rates exceeded nominal GDP growth rates, this term slowed down debt consolidation.[29] This negative effect was least significant in France,

*Table 7.1*  **Decomposition of Large Pre-1914 Debt Consolidations**

| Country | Period | Debt-to-GDP Ratio (percent) | | | Contribution to Decrease (percent) | | |
|---|---|---|---|---|---|---|---|
| | | Starting Level | Ending Level | Decrease | Primary Balance | Growth-Interest Differential | Stock-Flow Adjustment |
| United Kingdom | 1822–1913 | 194.1 | 28.3 | 165.8 | 299.3 | −158.5 | 25.0 |
| United States | 1867–1913 | 30.1 | 3.2 | 26.9 | 40.6 | −12.5 | −1.3 |
| France | 1896–1913 | 95.6 | 51.1 | 44.5 | 44.7 | −0.8 | 0.7 |

*Sources:* Authors' calculations. For the United States: Carter et al. (2006); for France: Flandreau and Zumer (2004); for the United Kingdom: the Bank of England's database *A Millennium of Macroeconomic Data for the UK* (Bank of England 2017).

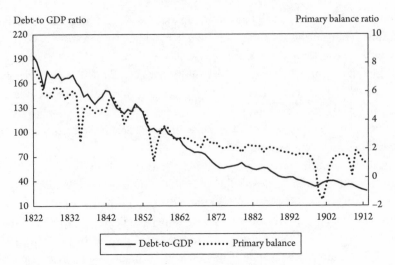

*Figure 7.1.* Public Debt and Primary Balance in the United Kingdom (percent of GDP)
Sources: Bank of England database "A Millennium of Macroeconomic Data for the UK" (Bank of England, 2017) and authors' calculations.

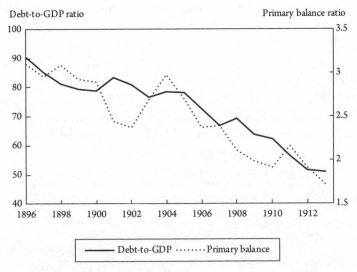

*Figure 7.2.* Public Debt and Primary Balance in France (percent of GDP)
Sources: Flandreau and Zumer (2004) and authors' calculations.

since it operated over the shortest interval and because price levels increased in the 1890s, inflating nominal GDP.

The drag of the growth-rate–interest-rate differential on debt consolidation reflected not only high coupon rates on debts placed in wartime, but also relatively modest economic growth. As noted in Chapter 4, scholars have highlighted that growth rates were slow during the Industrial Revolution, by modern standards, because productivity increases that arose from mechanization were limited to a

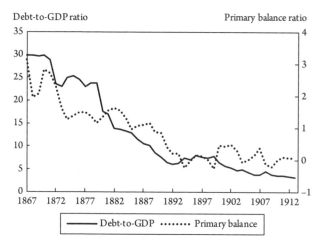

*Figure 7.3.* Public Debt and Primary Balance in the United States (percent of GDP)
Sources: Carter et al. (2006) and authors' calculations.

narrow range of sectors. As our accounting makes clear, what mattered for Britain was not simply the rate of economic growth, but the growth-rate–interest-rate differential. The behavior of this differential reveals that growth did not reduce the debt.[30]

Debt reduction in France similarly did not benefit from a favorable growth-rate–interest-rate differential. France too saw only a gradual acceleration in productivity and GDP growth. The country was burdened as well by a notoriously low rate of population increase, less than 10 percent between 1871 and 1911. Germany's, by comparison, grew by 60 percent, Britain's by 54 percent.

The US population, in contrast, more than tripled over the country's consolidation period, boosting aggregate growth. Yet there was no contribution to debt consolidation from the growth-rate–interest-rate differential even in the United States. A popular misconception is that the United States was able to shed its status as a debtor because of immigration—that the rise in population so increased the scale of the economy that the country was able to painlessly outgrow its debt. Table 7.1 shows that the story is more complicated: the economic growth rate may have been high, but interest rates on debt were higher still.[31] The US is probably best classified as an emerging market in this period. Politically, its Civil War was still a very recent memory. Financially, the country did not return to the gold standard until 1879. And until adoption of the Gold Standard Act of 1900, its prospects of remaining on gold were unclear.

Similarly, inflation did little to erode the real value of the debt. Price levels trended down from 1873 through 1893 and then upward to the eve of World War I, ending more or less where they began. On balance, there was essentially no inflation in any of these countries in their periods of consolidation. Governments, meanwhile, did little to bottle up savings at home or to use regulation and legislation to otherwise depress yields. There was little in the way of financial repression, to put the point in modern terms. British governments did not discourage outward foreign investment; to the contrary, they encouraged it as an instrument of British soft power. French foreign investment, although less extensive, was encouraged even more actively by government officials as a device for building and solidifying alliances.[32]

## We Are All Victorians Now

Because governments did not simply grow out from under their debts, fiscal effort was required to consolidate debt. That these consolidations took place tells us that large and persistent primary budget surpluses more than compensated for the negative effect of the growth-rate–interest-rate differential. Britain achieved the impressive feat of maintaining an average primary surplus of 1.6 percent of GDP for nearly a century. The only deficit in Figure 7.1 was during the Boer War, a time of exceptional financial need. One of the political legacies of Peel and Gladstone was a fiscal philosophy of sound finance that emphasized budget surpluses, low taxes, and limited government expenditure.[33] Sound finance was integral to the Victorian strategy of free trade, peace, and retrenchment, according to which trade promoted peace, which in turn limited military expenditures. It allowed the government to service debt and reduce its burden, thereby positioning the Exchequer to borrow more in a future conflict, in turn helping to deter aggression. Under the Victorians, it was sometimes said, the public credit was no less vital to the national security than the Royal British Navy.

In political terms, this outcome reflected the balance of interests and institutions. Budgetary reforms starting in the 1820s gave Parliament control over expenditure and allowed it to apply the surpluses made possible by spending restraint to stabilizing the debt. The franchise was still limited to 2.5 percent of the British population, predominantly owners of freehold property or land worth at least 40 shillings.[34] This created a considerable overlap between public creditors on the one hand and voters and members of Parliament on the other.[35] In the words of one historian, "The most obvious reason for the firmness of the British commitment to its public debt was the predominance of public creditors within the political system."[36] This was still true after the 1832 and 1837 Reform Acts, which expanded the franchise. Even then, it was hard to find a member of Parliament who was not also an investor in government bonds.

Spending on welfare relief for the disenfranchised masses was held in check by this political configuration. It was held in check even more firmly after the

Reform Acts than before, as newly enfranchised voters identified more with large landowners, who opposed more generous welfare relief, than with the working class. In return, the self-taxing class of income-tax-paying electors relieved nonelectors of the burden of direct taxation. Budget surpluses then made feasible further reductions in tariffs and taxes, which limited the cost of living for the working class.[37]

This was the recipe by which the British debt ratio was steadily reduced over nearly a century. Only with the electoral reforms of the 1880s did the urban and rural poor gain representation in Parliament. The earlier political equilibrium reached its limit with these political reforms, and with the organization of unskilled trade unions whose members could not afford self-help (could not afford to organize themselves as a mutual-aid society). The result was a growing demand for social spending at the same time military costs were ramping up. Fortunately, by the time these pressures materialized in the late nineteenth century and early twentieth, Britain's heavy debt burden had been dramatically reduced. In any case, the fact that politics are drastically different today, in the era of universal franchise, suggests this is not a debt-reduction strategy that is easily replicable.

In the postbellum United States, the political equilibrium was different, given universal (white male) suffrage. Still, creditor influence was considerable. This is evident in the decision to return to the gold standard in 1879, despite its deflationary consequences. It is also apparent in populist complaints about powerful bankers and trusts, and in the inability of the complainants to do much to rein in that power before the turn of the century.

The nature of the political constellation is evident, finally, in the federal government's reliance on the tariff, a regressive form of taxation, as its principal revenue source. The income tax put in place during the Civil War, which fell primarily on the wealthy, was removed following the conclusion of hostilities. In contrast, higher import duties stayed: tariff revenues as a share of imports, having tripled between 1861 and 1871, remained at their elevated level. From the standpoint of debt consolidation, this was not an unhappy situation; the tariff, championed by the Republican Party, provided an elastic supply of revenue in this period of expanding trade. Farmers saw the tariff as favoring manufacturing over agriculture and were not pleased, but their Populist Revolt gained only limited traction at the national level.

On the spending side, the stars were aligned for restraint. Southern states opposed expansive federal spending, given that the social priorities of the federal government were not their own. Transfers and entitlements were limited to Civil War pensions. The pressure for redistributive taxation and additional transfers was further lessened by the country's relatively equal distribution of income, as a result of which the median voter's income was close to that of the rich.[38] Thus, federal government spending remained less than 5 percent of GDP prior to US entry into World War I. With revenues expanding along with the economy, the federal government was able to maintain primary surpluses. Although these came to an end with the Panic of 1893, the ensuing recession, and then the Spanish-American War, subsequent deficits were minimal.

In France, debt reduction was again achieved by running primary surpluses. Special tax treatment of the nobility, clergy, and certain provinces and corporations had been abolished during the Revolution, widening the tax base. New taxes on income from real estate and stock-market investment were then added in the latter part of the nineteenth century.[39] The governing elites saw taxation as putting the country on a stronger financial footing in the event of another German war.[40] French leaders blamed the country's serial defeats, from the Seven Years War to the Franco-Prussian War, on the weakness of the state's finances, a problem they now sought to remedy.[41] In the two decades preceding World War I, primary budget surpluses exceeded even British levels, averaging 2.5 percent of GDP.[42] From the turn of the century, renewed tensions, particularly after the first Moroccan crisis in 1905, created pressure for additional military spending. At this point, primary surpluses gave way to deficits, and the debt stabilized at a low level.

Finally, these three episodes did not see involuntary restructurings, as indicated by the last term in our decomposition. Only in Britain did the stock-flow adjustment, which captures such operations, account for a discernible share of debt reduction. Its 15 percent share captures conversion of the stock of perpetual debt (consols) from 3 percent to 2.75 percent and then to 2.5 percent—an operation engineered by Goschen in 1888.[43] Interest rates having fallen, consols were trading above par. Goschen offered debtholders either conversion into new 2.5 percent securities or immediate redemption at par, as provided for by the bond covenants. The majority of outstanding securities were so converted, with the remainder paid off in full, using excess Treasury balances. Some tabulations classify this conversion as a default or involuntary restructuring. We see it as a run-of-the-mill debt-management operation and regard the consequent reduction in debt obligations as voluntary.

In sum, the British, US, and French governments went to great lengths to repay their debts. This was partly a consequence of the enfranchisement and political influence of the creditor class and of the fact that most debt was held by relatively affluent, politically influential citizens. It was partly a function of prevailing conceptions of limited government and the absence of intense popular pressure for public programs, entitlements, and transfers. It reflected the priority attached to maintaining creditworthiness in order to augment the capacity to mobilize resources in the event of a future conflict. Finally, it reflected good luck—a limited number of major wars, crises, and other disturbances during the consolidation period.

# The Politics of the Possible

Debt crises are dramatic and colorful, which is why they attract so much attention. But instances when heavy debts are successfully stabilized and reduced as shares of GDP deserve their limelight in the history of public finance as well. Debt consolidations were achieved in the nineteenth century in a number of economies, not just Britain, the United States, and France, but also in Canada and Italy.[44] Consolidations are less sensational than crises, but they show that heavy debts can be successfully managed. The episodes considered here demonstrate that even heavily indebted sovereigns can restore their ability to borrow when they anticipate future circumstances requiring them to tap capital markets. This was accomplished in a number of countries in the pre–World War I period. The question is whether something similar will be possible under post–COVID-19 circumstances.

These nineteenth-century debt consolidations were not achieved by inflating away debts. Nor did economies simply outgrow their obligations. Rather, debt consolidation was accomplished by running primary budget surpluses—in France for two decades, in the United States for four decades, and in Britain for the better part of a century.

Political circumstances made this possible. In Britain, the franchise was heavily skewed toward owners of property and other assets, including government bonds. The United States and France had universal male suffrage, but in both national cases, creditors enjoyed disproportionate sway. The resulting political configuration meant that inflation and debt repudiation were beyond the pale.

On the spending side, contemporary conceptions of limited government meant that demands for transfers and social spending were slow to develop. The 1800s were hardly a century of peace, but until 1914 additional conflicts involving these countries were relatively few. Thus, pressure for military spending did not overwhelm debt consolidation. Where war was a worry, governments prepared by keeping their powder dry. Britain relied on the Victorian strategy of substituting commercial ties for military intimidation ("the imperialism of free trade," as it is sometimes called). It reduced the debt-to-GDP ratio as a way of preserving the ability to borrow, and ensuring the capacity to ramp up military spending as needed. France similarly reduced its debt ratio to safeguard its ability to borrow if political and military tension with Germany again came to a head. For its part, the United States prepared for foreign entanglements, such as the Spanish-American war, by essentially extinguishing its debt. Thus, politics—both domestic and international—were integral to the consolidation process.

Of course, nothing pointed up the central role of this political constellation as dramatically as the Great War itself, which shattered the prevailing political equilibrium and, in doing so, created a very different landscape for public debt.

# Appendix: Details on Debt Decomposition

In this appendix, we provide details on the debt decomposition used in this chapter. Specifically, we decompose debt changes as follows:

$$d_T - d_0 = \sum_{t-1}^{T} p_t + \sum_{t-1}^{T} \frac{i_t - \gamma_t}{1 + \gamma_t} d_{t-1} + \sum_{t-1}^{T} sfa_t \tag{1}$$

Equation (1) says that the change in the debt-to-GDP ratio $(d_T - d_0)$ can be decomposed into three parts. The first term is the primary budget balance $(p_t)$: that is, the budget surplus excluding interest payments. This captures the impact of fiscal policy on debt dynamics. The second term is the product of the lagged debt-to-GDP ratio and the difference between the nominal interest rate on debt $(i_t)$ and the nominal growth rate of GDP $(\gamma_t)$.[45] This term captures endogenous debt dynamics. It shows how debt, as a share of GDP, will rise with the interest rate, since additional debt service will have to be financed with additional debt issuance, assuming that nothing else is done, and how that debt, as a share of GDP, will fall with the economy's growth, which increases the denominator of the ratio. This differential is multiplied by the lagged debt-to-GDP ratio because the magnitude of the effect depends on the inherited level of debt.[46]

The third term captures everything else, and is known as the stock-flow adjustment (or *SFA*). This is the adjustment needed to reconcile the flow of new debt issued to finance current government spending with the increase in the reported stock of debt. Factors contributing to the *SFA* include capital gains and losses on foreign currency debt due to exchange-rate changes, debt restructurings and exchanges that write down the value of previously issued debt, and other exceptional financial operations. The *SFA* captures valuation effects (on foreign currency debt due to changes in the exchange rate, for example), timing effects (deficits are measured in accrual terms, while debt is a cash concept), assumption by government of debts of nongovernmental entities, debt restructurings, privatizations, and bank recapitalization costs. It may be affected by other measures designed to support the financial sector that increase the debt but not the deficit, any drawdown or buildup of government deposits, transactions in financial assets, and—of course—measurement error.

According to current convention, measures aimed at supporting the financial sector affect both the deficit and the debt. Unless they are financed from cash reserves, they will increase gross debt. They may also affect the budget balance, depending on whether the operation presents a clear loss for the government. If so, they are classified as a capital transfer—for example, through acquiring financial assets at above-market prices and injecting capital to cover bank losses. However, if the government receives shares in a bank or debt securities of value equal to the capital injection, the support measure is classified as a financial operation that affects only the government gross (and not the net) debt.[47] Reclassification of entities from the financial sector to the general government sector (e.g., nationalization of banks) also increases government debt, but not the deficit.[48]

Interpretation of the *SFA* depends on its sign and on whether the decomposition exercise is undertaken for debt-accumulation or debt-reduction episodes. In a debt-accumulation episode, a positive *SFA* increases debt. In a debt-consolidation episode, a negative *SFA* means that the debt fell by less than the growth-rate–interest-rate differential and the primary surplus together would lead one to expect. Put differently, if the *SFA* is positive in a consolidation episode (implying that it contributed to a reduction in debt), then the decline in debt would have been larger than what was observed, assuming that the contributions of the primary balance and the growth-rate–interest-rate differential are the same.

Although large *SFAs* tend to be common during debt surges, they can also occur in consolidation episodes.[49] They reflect a host of country-specific factors, including institutions (such as those affecting budgeting transparency) and politics (elections sometimes affecting the timing of when expenditures are booked). The scale of such discrepancies again depends on the extent of transparency in the budgeting process, among other factors.

# Warfare to Welfare

Rationales for issuing public debt broadened in the course of the nineteenth century, as we described in earlier chapters. Previously, governments had borrowed mainly to mobilize the resources needed to secure borders and launch military campaigns. Debt issuance was concentrated in times of war. Now, in addition, they borrowed to finance infrastructure investments designed to foster economic cohesion and growth. Debt issuance became regular and ongoing.

In the twentieth century, the focus shifted again, this time toward debt issued to finance social services and transfer payments. That there were calls for governments to provide such services was a corollary of democratization. Meeting this demand was a means of legitimation for states and leaders; it was what modern states and leaders were supposed to do. Inevitably, calls for the state to provide social services and income support were loudest when times were tough. These were the very times, of course, when revenues declined. So governments borrowed to bridge the gap.

To be sure, war finance remained important: World Wars I and II were major engines of debt accumulation. And social spending was still limited compared to what came later. In time, however, the advent of the welfare state, to give the phenomenon its modern name, would have far-reaching implications for public debt.

## Welfare State Dynamics

The hallmarks of the welfare state are its redistributive, insurance, and income-maintenance functions. The simplest interpretation of its rise associates spending on social services and income guarantees with higher income per capita. As incomes rose in the late nineteenth and early twentieth centuries, so too did demands for social and income security of a sort that only the state could provide.

Democratization also worked to mobilize support for social programs with a redistributive component. Eliminating property requirements for the franchise and extending voting rights to the working class strengthened the political influence of groups whose members saw themselves as prospective transfer recipients.[1] The formation of socialist and social-democratic parties, which rely on working-class support and for which social solidarity and redistribution are points of emphasis, amplified their voice.

Table 8.1 shows how public spending on pensions, housing, health, income maintenance, and unemployment compensation rose to as much as 5 percent of GDP by 1930. Five percent is not impressive by twenty-first-century standards;

*Table 8.1* **Social Transfers, Including Welfare and Unemployment Relief, Pensions, Health, and Housing, 1910–30 (percent of national product at current prices)**

|                | *1910* | *1920* | *1930* |
|----------------|--------|--------|--------|
| Australia      | 1.12   | 1.66   | 2.11   |
| Austria        | 0.0    | 0.0    | 1.20   |
| Belgium        | 0.43   | 0.52   | 0.56   |
| Canada         | 0.0    | 0.06   | 0.31   |
| Denmark        | 1.75   | 2.71   | 3.40   |
| Finland        | 0.90   | 0.85   | 2.97   |
| France         | 0.81   | 0.64   | 1.08   |
| Germany        | +      | +      | 4.96   |
| Ireland        | ns     | ns     | 3.87   |
| Italy          | 0.0    | 0.0    | 0.10   |
| Japan          | 0.18   | 0.18   | 0.22   |
| Netherlands    | 0.39   | 1.10   | 1.15   |
| New Zealand    | 1.35   | 1.84   | 2.43   |
| Norway         | 1.18   | 1.09   | 2.39   |
| Sweden         | 1.03   | 1.14   | 2.60   |
| Switzerland    | +      | +      | 1.2    |
| United Kingdom | 1.39   | 1.42   | 2.61   |
| United States  | 0.56   | 0.70   | 0.56   |

*Source:* Lindert (1994).

*Note:* + denotes that public spending is established but not its amount; 0 denotes no public spending for a country/year; ns denotes not a sovereign state at the beginning of that year.

social spending in many advanced countries today exceeds 20 percent of GDP. But neither is it negligible.

Much of the action, especially in Europe, occurred between 1920 and 1930. This timing is consistent with the income-growth and democratization hypotheses, given the spread of industrialization and rising living standards to much of the European continent and its regions of overseas settlement, and extensions of the electoral franchise before and after World War I. Nor is it incidental that the highest level of social spending was in Germany, which pioneered health insurance, accident insurance, and old-age insurance in the nineteenth century; Otto von Bismarck championed these programs as ways of deradicalizing the working class. Given the revolutionary upheavals of 1918–19, deradicalization now became more pressing still.

Table 8.1 also highlights the extent to which social spending varied internationally. It was greatest in countries with high old-age dependency ratios, the elderly valuing pensions and health services.[2] It was highest where women had the vote, though it is unclear whether this reflected women's support for welfare-state programs per se, or the fact that the same social, political, and economic factors conducive to women's suffrage were also associated with support for such programs.[3]

Finally, social spending ratios were highest where there existed an urban, industrial labor force. In bad times, the chronic condition in the countryside was underemployment rather than unemployment, as workers turned to the farm for subsistence. This meant less need for unemployment insurance and pensions for the aged.[4] But an urban, industrial proletariat couldn't live off the land and tended to protest, sometimes violently, against inadequate state support. As workers organized through unions and political parties to lobby for public spending on unemployment insurance, poor relief, and support for the aged, governments accommodated the pressure.

If the half century from 1880 to 1930 saw the birth of the welfare state, then the subsequent half century saw its maturation. In advanced economies, public spending on social transfers rose to 10 percent of GDP in 1960, 12 percent of GDP in 1970, and 17 percent in 1980.[5] Living standards were rising, and social insurance was a normal or superior good (meaning that spending rose with income).[6] Trade unions, social-democratic parties, and Christian-democratic parties all pressed the state to supplement the charitable efforts of religious and civic groups. The political upheavals and economic hardships of the 1930s reinforced arguments for publicly financed transfers on social-solidarity and anti-revolutionary grounds, while unemployment highlighted the difficulty individuals have in adequately insuring themselves.

The question, of course, is why the welfare state, with its redistributive, insurance, and income-maintenance components, should have been less than fully financed by current revenues. Aging populations are part of the answer; with fewer remaining years of life, the elderly worry less about future debt-service burdens when deciding on current social spending and transfer payments. Part of the answer may also be political fractionalization: each political group, although regarding certain social programs as indispensable, has just enough power to block taxes on itself but not enough to impose taxes on others. Yet another part of the answer may be electoral uncertainty, which leads politicians to advocate more spending on their favored programs when in office, since they may be in a weaker position to push such spending later, and since additional debt incurred today will be someone else's problem tomorrow.[7]

These theories suggest that excessive indebtedness may especially be a problem in democracies and in periods of political instability and rapid executive turnover. The aftermath of World War I was just such a period.

Figure 8.1 shows the wartime jump in the debt-to-GDP ratio in the advanced economies from 20 percent in 1914 to more than 80 percent in 1920. The European belligerents came away with especially heavy debts: the 1920 debt-to-GDP ratio was 170 percent in France, 160 percent in Italy, and 140 percent in Britain. In Germany, Reich (or federal) debt was somewhat lower, in the

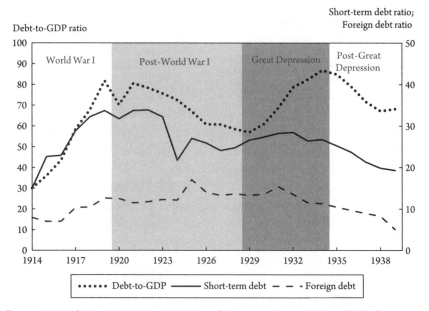

*Figure 8.1.* Debt-to-GDP Ratio, Maturity and Currency Composition of Debt for Advanced Economies

Source: Abbas et al. (2014b).

Note: Debt-to-GDP ratio in percent. Short-term debt ratio and foreign debt ratio are measured as a percent of total debt. The sample includes Australia, Belgium, Canada, France, Germany, Ireland, Italy, Japan, Netherlands, Spain, Sweden, the United Kingdom, and the United States. Data for Ireland start from 1924. Purchasing-power-parity (PPP)-GDP weighted averages.

neighborhood of 100 percent of GDP.[8] The German government had put aside a war chest of gold, obtained from the French in the wake of the Franco-Prussian War, to prefund military expenses. Whereas other countries took steps to halt inflation in 1919–20, inflation in Germany continued to rip, ballooning the denominator of the debt-to-GDP ratio. By these European standards, the US debt-to-GDP ratio was relatively light at 28 percent, the country having entered the war late, at a time when the federal government was virtually debt-free.

Inherited debt burdens were reduced in the 1920s through a combination of economic growth, primary surpluses, and inflation. But these consolidations did not last. Debt rose again in the 1930s with the collapse of incomes in the Great Depression. The growth that brought down debt burdens in the 1920s was unsustainable—it was achieved by engineering a credit boom that substituted private debt for public debt. Where high inflation had been used to liquidate the debt, the experience left society polarized, unable to respond when the Depression struck. Either way, debt ratios that had come down in the 1920s went back up in the 1930s.

## Financial Consequences of the War

The financial legacy of World War I was not just more debt in general, but more short-term debt in particular. By the war's end, 42 percent of the debt of the Reich and German states was floating (meaning short-term). France, Italy, and Russia were in similar positions: their short-term debt shares were 44, 43, and 48 percent.[9] Governments issued short-term debt to meet immediate wartime needs and then replaced it with long-term loans as conditions allowed. But conditions varied, and arranging long-term loans took time. Military needs were ongoing, so short-term debt was issued all the while. Short-term debt can be especially risky, since it enables investors to scramble out at any time.[10] European governments would soon learn this hard lesson.

Alone among the combatants, the United States was able to finance virtually its entire wartime borrowing with long-term loans. It helped that it entered the war, as we have seen, with minimal debt.[11] In addition, the banking system could be force-fed government bonds through a combination of regulation and moral suasion.[12] America was also the birthplace of the large, multidivisional firm, with companies like the U.S. Steel Corporation having their own treasury departments and investing massively in government bonds. Much was made of how the US Treasury issued small-denomination "war savings certificates" targeted at the working class. In fact, only 20 percent of Liberty Loan bonds were in small denominations suitable for retail investors.

Britain too was able to access this US market. London banks had long marketed British bonds in the United States in limited amounts, with assistance from New York correspondents such as J. P. Morgan and National City Bank.

That Britain maintained the façade of the gold standard now reassured American investors.[13] The Franco-British loan issued in the United States in December 1915, in which the French government piggybacked on Britain's credit, found a ready market, including among American firms in the business of selling commodities and merchandise to the Allies and therefore interested in their buying power.[14] Other countries lacking access to the US market were limited to issuing bonds at home and, when this was difficult, relying on floating debt.[15]

Once America entered the war, the US Treasury extended loans directly to America's allies, acting on authority granted it under the Liberty Loan Acts. Between its entry into the war in 1917 and the armistice two and a half years later, intergovernmental lending by the United States totaled $8 billion, or roughly

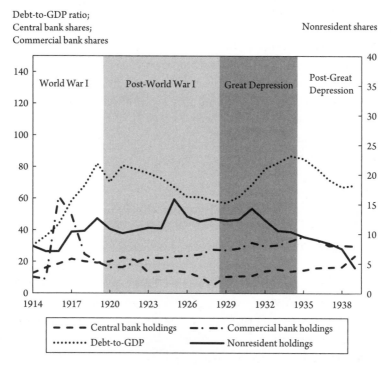

*Figure 8.2.* Debt Composition in Advanced Economies

Sources: Abbas et al. (2014b) and Ferguson, Schaab, and Schularick (2014), with updated data from the authors.

Note: Debt-to-GDP ratio in percent. Central bank, commercial bank, and nonresident holdings all as percent of total debt. For central bank holdings, the sample includes Australia, Belgium, Canada, France, Germany, Ireland, Italy, Japan, Netherlands, Spain, Sweden, the United Kingdom, and the United States. For commercial bank holdings, the sample includes Italy, Netherlands, the United Kingdom, and the United States. Data for France start in 1936, for the United Kingdom in 1920, and for the United States in 1916. For nonresident holdings, the sample includes Australia, Belgium, Canada, France, Italy, Japan, Netherlands, Spain, Sweden, the United Kingdom, and the United States. Data for Ireland start from 1924, and for the United Kingdom from 1920. Purchasing-power-parity (PPP)-GDP weighted averages.

10 percent of America's 1918 GDP. The United States then advanced another $2 billion the following year, including to countries that were not its wartime allies.

A final change, evident in Figure 8.2, was the higher share of public debt held by the banking system.[16] US commercial bank holdings of government debt rose by 233 percent between June 1917 and June 1919. The rise in central bank holdings was less dramatic but still notable: Federal Reserve holdings of US government securities increased by $122 million to fully $300 million over the war years. The Bank of England nearly quadrupled its holdings of government securities over the war. Note circulation and the broad money supply (including not just currency but also bank deposits) both rose by nearly 150 percent. Germany, which was unable to borrow abroad, except to a limited extent in Amsterdam, relied even more heavily on central bank financing and saw its money supply quadruple between 1913 and 1918.[17] In France, advances from the central bank again provided a significant fraction of government wartime funding; the Bank of France's note issue rose fivefold between 1914 and 1919.[18] All this meant that when wartime controls were lifted, inflationary pressure would be released.

Thus, advanced-country governments emerged from World War I with heavier debts. More of it was foreign, creating political complications. It was shorter in term, heightening the danger of debt runs. It was held to a greater extent by banks, meaning if there was a problem with the debt, there would be problems for the financial system.

## Pious Ejaculations

Financially, the 1920s are not typically portrayed in positive terms. One constructive aspect, however, was debt consolidation as measured by declines in debt-to-GDP ratios.[19] The problem, as noted, was that those consolidations did not last.

Table 8.2 shows that debt reduction was achieved, in roughly equal measure, by running primary budget surpluses and maintaining favorable growth-rate–interest-rate differentials. The role of primary surpluses was similar to that in the United Kingdom, the United States, and France in the nineteenth-century episodes discussed in Chapter 7. But the positive contribution of the growth-rate–interest-rate differential contrasts with the nineteenth century, when its contribution ranged from negative to inconsequential.

The growth-rate–interest-rate differential did not contribute positively everywhere, however. In the United Kingdom, for example, interest rates remained elevated because inherited debts were heavy and high yields were required to attract investors when maturing obligations needed refinancing. The Bank of England kept interest rates high in order to attract capital from abroad and rebuild its gold reserves, with the goal of returning to the gold standard at the prewar gold parity, an objective achieved in 1925. Keynes warned that sterling would be overvalued if the

*Table 8.2* **Decomposition of Large Debt Consolidations in Advanced Economies, 1920s**

| Country | Period | Debt/GDP Ratio (in percent) | | | Contribution to Decrease (in percent) | | |
|---------|--------|----------|--------|----------|---------|----------|----------|
| | | Starting level | Ending level | Decrease | Primary balance | Growth-interest differential | Stock-flow adjustment |
| Canada | 1922–28 | 75.6 | 53.2 | 22.4 | 19.7 | 8.2 | –5.6 |
| France | 1921–29 | 237.0 | 138.6 | 98.4 | 24.7 | 118.2 | –44.5 |
| Italy | 1920–26 | 159.7 | 89.4 | 70.3 | 0.1 | 44.3 | 26.0 |
| Portugal | 1923–29 | 67.7 | 42.5 | 25.2 | 2.1 | 32.7 | –9.6 |
| United Kingdom | 1923–29 | 195.5 | 170.5 | 25.0 | 52.2 | –25.6 | –1.7 |
| United States | 1919–29 | 33.3 | 16.3 | 17.0 | 18.8 | –2.7 | 0.9 |
| **Simple average** | | 128.1 | 85.1 | 43.1 | 19.6 | 29.2 | –5.8 |
| **Weighted average** | | 82.4 | 51.9 | 30.5 | 21.1 | 11.7 | –2.3 |

*Sources:* IMF Historical Public Debt and Historical Public Finance Databases (IMF 2010, 2013) and authors' calculations.

Note: Episodes are identified based on debt reduction of at least 10 percentage points of GDP during 1919–29. Peak-to-trough episodes (years vary by each country). Initial dataset comprises nineteen advanced economies, including Australia, Austria, Belgium, Canada, Finland, France, Germany, Greece, Ireland, Italy, Japan, Netherlands, New Zealand, Portugal, Spain, Sweden, Switzerland, United Kingdom, and United States. The sample narrows by data gaps and the criteria used to identify the consolidation episodes. For instance, there are no data during (1919–29) for Greece, Ireland, and Switzerland. Debt ratios increased in Australia, Austria, Germany, Greece, Ireland, Japan, Netherlands, Spain, Sweden, Switzerland—with large data gaps in the cases of Germany, Greece, Ireland, and Sweden. Belgium is a special case: the decline in the debt ratio satisfies the criteria, but the debt ratio is available only for select years.

prewar exchange rate against the dollar was restored, and that Britain would experience chronic balance-of-payments difficulties. He lost the argument, but subsequent events proved him right, and the Bank of England was forced to keep interest rates high in order to prevent gold from draining abroad. Those high rates not only raised debt-service costs, but they depressed investment and, through that channel, growth.

That Britain nonetheless succeeded in reducing its debt-to-GDP ratio by more than 25 percentage points between 1923 and 1929 thus testifies to the overwhelming importance of budget surpluses. Debt service averaged 7 percent of GDP over the decade. With the overall budget in balance or slight surplus, this implied primary surpluses in that same amount.

Running large primary surpluses in a period of slow growth and chronic high unemployment was no mean feat. It helped that Conservative governments controlled British politics for most of the decade. The Conservative Party subordinated fiscal policy to maintenance of the sterling parity, which in turn was designed to restore Britain's position in international financial markets. To this end, the Conservatives included in the 1923 Finance Act a provision making annual budgetary contributions of £50 million to the sinking fund earmarked for debt retirement, up by a factor of ten from the prewar level.[20]

The short-lived Labour government of 1924 had a different political hue, but its fiscal and financial policies were the same. The overriding objective of this first-ever Labour government was demonstrating that it would govern responsibly, which in practice meant running primary surpluses.[21] Philip Snowden, the frosty chancellor, was known for his belief in balanced budgets more than for any progressive social values. Nevertheless, Snowden's 1924 budget lowered duties on imported tea, coffee, cocoa, chicory, and sugar, advancing the party's cherished ideal of the "free breakfast table." It extended unemployment benefits from twenty-six to forty-one weeks and increased eligibility for state pensions. However, Snowden achieved all of this within the existing budgetary envelope. Although the priorities of the Labour, Liberal, and Conservative Parties differed, it is hard to dispute that electoral politics were less polarized in Britain than in other European countries, which facilitated fiscal consolidation.[22]

This fact is further evident in the conclusions of the Colwyn Committee (formally, the Committee on National Debt and Taxation), which reported in 1927. Constituting this committee, with members from all parties, was a condition of the king for appointing a Labour government.[23] Its report concluded in favor of debt retirement and recommended raising contributions to the sinking fund in order to accelerate the process. Not even the minority report signed by four Labour members dissented from this recommendation.[24]

The most colorfully worded dissent came from John Maynard Keynes, who testified before the committee. Keynes objected to the committee's "pious ejaculations in favour of Sinking Funds" and criticized the report's two justifications for debt retirement.[25] To the observation that retiring debt would reduce the interest rate required of the government when it again needed to borrow, Keynes objected that interest rates were determined on world markets, not by British conditions. This objection was not very convincing; Keynes had not yet accustomed himself to a world where HM Government's credit was less than impeccable and the risk premium demanded by investors rose with the debt-to-GDP ratio. To the committee's argument that debt consolidation would make possible additional debt issuance in a future emergency, Keynes objected that "the difference between a large and very large internal debt should make a scarcely appreciable difference."[26] History would validate this second objection;

when that next emergency materialized, in the form of World War II, the government still had very considerable ability to borrow. It was actually able to borrow at lower rates during World War II than during World War I, despite having entered the second war more heavily indebted.

## The French Paradox

France, being more polarized politically, saw sharper disagreements over the budget. Contemporaries blamed those disputes for the alarming depreciation of the franc and pointed to budget deficits as the culprit.[27] However, reconstructions of the fiscal accounts, like those in Table 8.3, show the budget moving into primary surplus already in 1921. They then show primary surpluses for the remainder of the decade, excepting only 1923, when the budget net of debt service was balanced.[28] This fiscal rectitude reflected the extent to which members of the French intelligentsia, whether on the left or right, bought into the same ideology as their British counterparts—of restoring the gold standard and turning the clock back to the prewar golden age.

In fact, French debt and exchange rate dynamics were driven by divisions over means rather than goals. The parties of the left advocated higher business and wealth taxes to fund social programs—taxes that the parties of the right opposed. The question boiled down to whether a legislated haircut would be imposed on bondholders, allowing resources allocated to debt service to be redeployed. Whenever this so-called capital levy appeared likely—following an election that brought the left to power in 1924, for example—investors grew anxious about rolling over maturing short-term debt securities and subscribing longer-term issues.[29] The government was then forced to turn to the Bank of France for advances. The bank was more than accommodating; it provided the government with credit even when doing so meant exceeding the legal limit on advances and falsifying its accounts.[30]

The results predictably included currency depreciation and inflation, which rose to double-digits. During the "Waltz of the Portfolios" from April 1925 through July 1926, France saw six left and center-left governments and ten finance ministers, none of whom could definitively rule the capital levy in or out. In July 1926, with the bondholders on strike, the price level was rising at an alarming 13 percent monthly rate. In this climate, the fact that the budget was balanced was immaterial.

With prices racing out of control, the French public and its parliamentary representatives finally conceded that enough was enough. They unified behind a centrist coalition led by the wartime president, Raymond Poincaré. Formation of this government, with support from what was previously the right opposition

*Table 8.3* **French Budget Surplus and Components (Percent of National Income)**

| Year | Receipts | Expenditures | of which debt service[a] | Surplus[b] | Surplus net of debt service[b] |
|------|----------|--------------|--------------------------|------------|-------------------------------|
| 1920 | 20.5 | 36.0 | 9.2 | −15.5 | −6.4 |
| 1921 | 20.5 | 28.5 | 9.4 | −8.1 | 1.3 |
| 1922 | 29.7[c] | 38.0[c] | 10.4 | −8.2 | 2.2 |
| 1923 | 19.8 | 28.6 | 8.8 | −8.8 | 0.0 |
| 1924 | 22.8 | 27.4 | 8.0 | −4.6 | 3.4 |
| 1925 | 20.2 | 21.1 | 10.3 | −0.9 | 9.5 |
| 1926 | 20.7 | 20.2 | 10.8 | 0.5 | 11.3 |
| 1927 | 22.0 | 21.9 | 9.6 | 0.0 | 9.7 |
| 1928 | 21.2 | 19.5 | 8.7 | 1.7 | 10.4 |
| 1929[d] | 26.2 | 24.2 | 10.8 | 2.0 | 12.8 |

*Source:* Prati (1991).

*Note:*

a Debt service measure is an estimate.

b Minus sign (−) indicates a deficit.

c Unusually high receipts and expenditures reflect large outlays and revenues of the budget of recoverable expenses.

d 1929 data are for a fifteen-month budget.

but also portions of the left, signaled that the capital levy was finally off the table. In a matter of weeks, the exchange rate recovered, and prices stabilized.[31]

Ironically, fears of a capital levy actually hastened the process of debt consolidation, since double-digit inflation eroded the real value of that portion of the French government's debt that was long-term.[32] This was not the intent of policy, but it was the effect. Rising revenues and improved international competitiveness then sustained the decline in the French debt-to-GDP ratio through the end of the decade.

## Forced Conversion

Politics drove debt dynamics in Italy as well, though they took a different turn than in France and Britain.

The Italian electorate was riven between the Socialists and Communists on the left and the Fascists on the right, with a forlorn Catholic Party in the middle. As in France, the question was whose taxes would finance public programs, those of wage earners or the wealthy. The left, as in France, advocated a capital levy. It actually succeeded in pushing through a modest wealth tax following a general election in November 1919. But household wealth was self-reported, and those who paid the tax were allowed to do so in installments over twenty years. As a result, the levy raised little revenue while only inflaming public opinion. The consequences included inflation and political unrest, the collapse of parliamentary coalitions, and violence in the streets.

It was in these difficult circumstances that King Vittorio Emanuele took the fateful step of asking Benito Mussolini to form a government. From there, it was a slippery slope. A 1923 electoral law gave two-thirds of parliamentary seats to a party or coalition that won no more than 25 percent of the vote; Socialist members of Parliament walked out following the assassination of a prominent member; still more authoritarian laws followed; and in 1926 the prime minister was given sole authority to set Parliament's agenda. Mussolini was now able to reduce the budget deficit without resistance from veto players. Spending was cut, and public services such as telecommunications were handed over to the private sector.[33]

Although these measures eliminated the budget deficit, they did not contribute materially to debt reduction. Rather, as Table 8.2 shows, it was the growth-rate–interest-rate differential that did. Real GDP grew by 15 percent between 1922 and 1926 once Italy put immediate postwar turmoil behind it. In addition, Mussolini's early years were punctuated by a series of rollover crises, when investors hesitated to renew their maturing short-term obligations, leading to bursts of monetization and inflation like those in France. Inflation reduced the real value of government bonds, although it did not exactly enhance the enthusiasm of investors for holding the government's obligations going forward.

In 1924, the Treasury then offered to exchange short-term debt for long-term bonds but failed to find a market. Unable to arrange a voluntary exchange, Mussolini resorted to a forced conversion, in which government bonds with a maturity of less than seven years—about a third of total debt—were converted into a new, consolidated issue bearing an interest rate of 5 percent. No sooner was the conversion completed in 1926 than the new bond fell to 80 percent of its face value, indicative of the present-value haircut applied to investors.[34] This was the dictator's way of consolidating the debt—by *force majeure*.

Whether forced consolidation made for sustainable consolidation was another matter. Even once Italy returned to the gold standard in 1927, interest rates remained above those in France, which did not resort to involuntary measures.[35] The Italian government found it difficult to place Treasury notes, given its earlier treatment of debt holders. It therefore resorted to loans from banks and municipalities such as Milan and Rome, which charged a premium. The growth-rate–interest-rate differential turned against the government and, starting in 1927, the debt-to-GDP ratio began rising again.

## Debt Consolidation with a Vengeance

The extreme case was Germany, where hyperinflation liquidated the debt. This was the operation of growth-rate–interest-rate differential with a vengeance.[36]

The episode was a particularly dramatic illustration of the destabilizing fiscal consequences of political polarization. Fundamentally, Germany's hyperinflation was a product of disagreement between the left and right over who should bear the costs of social programs, superimposed on disagreement over who should bear the financial burden of reparations.[37] Successive German governments caught in this vice were unable to balance their budgets, and the resulting deficits were promptly and fully monetized.

As inflation spiraled upward, it became increasingly disruptive economically and financially. Finally, in late 1923, the country's warring political factions agreed to a compromise, in which industrialists conceded higher taxes and labor abandoned the more radical and costly elements of its social agenda. This compromise, together with the international loan (the Dawes Loan) in conjunction with which Germany's reparations were rescheduled, allowed the budget to be balanced, the exchange rate to be stabilized, and inflation to be brought to a halt.

Investors did not forget this history. They subsequently demanded a premium when lending to the German government, an even larger premium than on loans to Italy. And with interest rates higher than the growth rate of the economy, the debt ratio began rising again. That debt-to-GDP ratio may have been lower than in other European countries (compare Great Britain in Figure 8.3). But together

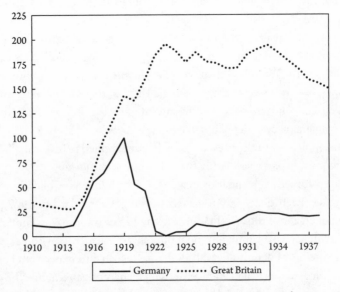

*Figure 8.3.* Public Debt Ratio in Germany and Great Britain, 1910–38 (percent of GDP)
Sources: IMF Historical Public Debt Database (IMF 2010) and authors' calculations.

with reparations, which being denominated in gold marks were impervious to erosion by inflation, it still confronted the German body politic with excruciatingly difficult policy choices when the economy turned down at the end of the 1920s.

## Roaring Twenties

A final contrasting case is the United States, where the federal government debt-to-GDP ratio was halved in the course of the 1920s. Political polarization, already low by European standards, declined further in the course of the decade (Figure 8.4). The resulting consensus made fiscal compromise and budget surpluses possible.

The United States experienced a recession in 1920–21, but otherwise enjoyed steady growth. Nonetheless, the growth-rate–interest-rate differential played no role in debt consolidation in the 1920s, with growth rates and interest rates both hovering in the low-to-mid-single digits. On balance, the differential actually contributed negatively to debt reduction, owing mainly to the impact of recession and deflation in 1920–21.[38]

Subsequently, real GDP growth averaged a robust 4.2 percent per annum, somewhat in excess of the real interest rate.[39] Given time, such vigorous economic growth would have reduced the debt ratio, assuming it was sustainable. However, growth in the 1920s was supported by a credit boom that inflated land prices (first in the corn-growing Midwest, then in Florida, and finally in New York and Detroit). Credit similarly fed the boom on Wall Street. This

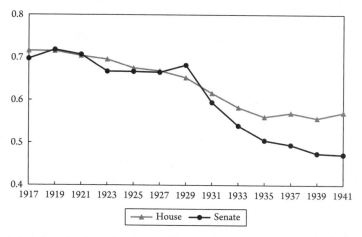

*Figure 8.4.* Political Polarization in the US House and Senate, 1917–41 (distance between party means)

Sources: Poole and Rosenthal (2007), with data from Voteview website, available at https://voteview.com/articles/party_polarization.

Note: Members of Congress are scored on a conservative/liberal scale that ranges from –1 to +1.

Vertical scale shows the average of the differences between each Democrat and Republican member.

private credit effectively substituted for public credit in supporting spending and fueling the economy's expansion.[40] Tax revenues were rising, and demands for public spending were muted because real wages were growing and unemployment was low. These factors made it possible to maintain primary budget surpluses and pursue debt consolidation, but only so long as the expansion fueled by the credit boom lasted.

The boom of course ended in 1929, dragging down GDP and causing the debt ratio to turn up again. At this point, policymakers were confronted with the unhappy choice of allowing the budget deficit to widen, which would raise the numerator of the debt-to-GDP ratio still further, or proactively seeking to balance the budget, which would only hasten the fall in the denominator. Under the Hoover administration, their budget-balancing instincts won out. Nominal GDP fell by more than 25 percent between 1929 and 1931 and the debt-to-GDP ratio rose sharply, reversing earlier gains. Franklin Delano Roosevelt, who assumed the presidency in 1933, was more tolerant of deficits, but more importantly oversaw a GDP recovery. The irony is that the deficit ratio rose faster and by more under Hoover than in Roosevelt's first term, reflecting the severity of the output and price collapse.[41]

The 1920s thus show that high debt can be reduced in a variety of ways. But lowering it sustainably requires building a stable political coalition in support of the requisite policies. In countries like Germany and France, the fallout from an extended period of political conflict and financial chaos permitted supportive coalitions to be cobbled together. But this didn't mean that such coalitions were stable.

Successful consolidation also required bringing indebtedness down in a manner consistent with maintaining economic and financial stability. The shortcuts and expedients of the 1920s—inflation, forced consolidation, and private credit expansion—did not meet these prerequisites. It followed that debt problems returned, and they did so in a matter of years.

## Foreign Lending Redux

As in the golden age of financial globalization before 1914, debt finance had an international dimension. However, the situation now differed in important respects.

First was the rise of New York as an international financial center. World War I brought foreign borrowers to the US market, which few had bothered to tap previously. America was transformed from a net foreign debtor to a net foreign creditor by the wartime liquidation of foreign investments in the United States and by America's accumulation of claims on other countries. In the 1920s, the current account of the balance of payments was in surplus (meaning that saving exceeded investment), enabling Americans to invest abroad without the Federal Reserve losing gold. The Fed could keep interest rates low without risking the stability of the dollar; those low interest rates in turn encouraged US investors to look overseas for yield. In 1927, when capital outflows from the United States were at their peak, the yield on long-term US government bonds was 3 percent, below the 4.5 percent yield on British consols and the 5 percent yield on French perpetual *rentes*, much less the 6 and 7 percent yields on Italian and German bonds.

Second, there was the role of the newly established League of Nations, which participated in long-term loans on behalf of Austria, Bulgaria, Danzig, Estonia, Greece, and Hungary.[42] The League planned their stabilizations and, through its association, lent credibility to their programs. It secured the support of the British for their governments to place bonds in London.[43] It monitored their use of loan proceeds. It placed trustees, permanent agents, and central bank advisors in the borrowing countries, in a more civilized variant of the prewar practice of foreign financial control.

Countries enlisting the League's help obtained financial-market access on more favorable terms than those shunning its assistance.[44] Although League loans totaling £90 million constituted only a fraction of total cross-border lending to European sovereigns in the 1920s, they provided incentives for economic and financial stabilization, which was necessary in order for trade to recover. Additional trade meant additional export receipts, further brightening the prospects for foreign borrowing. This kind of multilateral support for unseasoned borrowers had no precedent. It was another step in the globalization of the sovereign debt market.[45]

Third was the shift to foreign borrowing by countries such as Germany and France that previously had floated debt almost exclusively at home. They now joined Latin America and Eastern Europe in borrowing on the US market. Their reconstruction expenses exceeded their domestic savings, an imbalance that manifested itself in high interest rates and current account deficits financed by borrowing abroad. This was the flipside of the low interest rates and current account surpluses in the United States that created an incentive for American investors to look abroad for yield.

In Germany's case, the rules governing reparations payments, together with the stabilization loan extended under the Dawes Plan, created additional incentives for government borrowing. Commercial loans, including the bond subscriptions that funded the Dawes Loan itself, were senior to reparations. In effect, investors in the Dawes Loan and purchasers of other German bonds took precedence over governments owed reparations. Only if Germany had foreign exchange left over once interest was paid on its commercial debts would reparations transfers take place. This arrangement was justified as ensuring that the Dawes Loan, one such commercial obligation, would be adequately funded. But it was not incidental that the plan was drawn up by the same US bankers, such as Thomas Lamont of J. P. Morgan, with stakes in commercial lending. Be that as it may, the incentives for investors were clear: when contemplating a loan to the German government, it was safe to disregard reparations. The incentives for the German government were equally clear: the more it borrowed, the greater the likelihood that reparations would be rescheduled or abolished.[46]

Finally, there was the further democratization of the market. American banks sought to build on their experience selling Liberty Bonds by now marketing foreign government bonds to retail investors. National City Company, National City Bank's underwriting and brokerage affiliate, opened branch offices in fifty-one cities, many on the ground floor to encourage walk-in business.

Underwriting banks, when seeking to organize a loan, and retail investors, when deciding to subscribe, looked to whether governments new to the market adopted familiar institutional arrangements. They asked whether countries had established autonomous central banks and had gone onto the gold standard under the tutelage of specialist advisors such as Edwin Kemmerer of Princeton University or Otto Niemeyer of the Bank of England. They drew inferences from whether the issue was backed by a reputable investment bank such as J. P. Morgan or Kuhn, Loeb. These rules of thumb were far from fail-safe. Very far from fail-safe, as it turned out: come the 1930s, investors experienced catastrophic losses.[47]

## The Mother of All Sudden Stops

Together, these changes meant that the stability of sovereign debt markets hinged on the enthusiasm of American investors, which in turn rested on the low level of US interest rates. By implication, everything depended on the Federal Reserve, a new institution, and one new specifically to international finance.

By 1928, the Wall Street boom, by exciting expectations of capital gains, had reduced the incentive for American investors to search for yield abroad. US equities returned an impressive 38 percent in 1927 and were poised to return an even more remarkable 44 percent in 1928. In this environment, foreign government bonds, even when yielding 6 or 7 percent, held few attractions. At this point, the Federal Reserve's Open Market Investment Committee began selling US Treasury securities to drain cash from the market and rein in speculation. At the beginning of 1928, one Reserve Bank after another raised its discount rate. A second round of increases followed in April. The New York Fed, closest to Wall Street, tightened a third time in May. These steps were designed to make it more costly for investors to buy stocks on margin. They had the ancillary effect of pushing up rates on domestic bills and bonds, thereby rendering foreign government securities less attractive. This was confirmation that, when it came to Fed policy, managing international finance took a back seat.[48]

Predictably, US capital exports dropped from \$530 million in the second quarter of 1928 to \$120 million in the third. Borrowers such as Germany, where not just the federal government but also states, municipalities, and corporations relied on American credit, were forced to implement sharp spending cuts, causing economic activity to swoon.[49]

As the world economy followed Germany into recession, commodity prices collapsed. W. Arthur Lewis, the Saint Lucian economist who subsequently won the Nobel Prize for his work on development economics, described the litany of woes: "From 1929 to 1930 the average price of wheat fell by 19 per cent, cotton 27 per cent, wool 46 per cent, silk 30 per cent, rubber 42 per cent, sugar 20 per cent, coffee 43 per cent, copper 26 per cent, tin 29 per cent; the index of prices of commodities entering world trade fell from 1929 to 1932 by 56 per cent for raw materials, 48 per cent for foodstuffs. . . ."[50] In some cases, the consequences were calamitous. By 1932, the US dollar value of Chile's exports, almost entirely copper and nitrate, had fallen to a mere 12 percent of 1929 levels, leading the League of Nations to call Chile the country most badly damaged by the slump.[51]

The dollars needed to service foreign debts were nowhere to be found. Latin American countries relying on commodity exports thus had little choice but to suspend payments on their external debts. By 1934, fifteen Latin American governments were in default. In the words of the Haverford College economist Frank Whitson Fetter (whom we encountered in Chapter 4), "the fundamental background against which this default history took place was that the marketable public debt was almost all held abroad, and that the maintenance of full payments with the depression conditions of the 1930s would have involved a crushing burden on the economies of a number of Latin-American countries—a burden far greater than would have been the case had the bonds been held domestically, and the income on them subject to local taxation, and the income ex-taxes been available for domestic expenditures or reinvestment."[52]

The exception was Argentina, where provinces defaulted but the federal government continued to service its debt by drawing down its gold reserves.[53] Argentina had borrowed in London, reflecting historic links, and Britain was an important market for the country's beef and wheat. Policy was shaped by the ranchers and meatpackers who dominated beef export.[54] Federal officials foreswore interruptions to debt service to facilitate successful negotiation of the Roca-Runciman trading pact, which guaranteed Argentina a fixed share of the British meat market and eliminated tariffs on Argentine cereals. Economists have pointed to the threat of retaliation against a country's exports as one reason governments pay their debts.[55] Argentina in the 1930s makes the case.

Argentina also provides a test of whether maintaining debt service under these strained circumstances had benefits—equivalently, whether default had costs. A first glance suggests that other large and medium-sized Latin American economies (Brazil, Chile, Colombia, Mexico, and Peru) did better. GDP, industrial production, and even exports recovered more quickly in these other countries.[56] All else was not equal, of course; for example, there was the differential impact of the "commodity lottery" (how an economy did depended on what it exported). Accounting for these additional factors requires one to analyze a larger set of economies. Richard Portes, together with one of the present authors, considered some two dozen countries, divided into equal numbers of defaulters and nondefaulters. Adjusting for the commodity lottery, economic openness, and other factors, they found that the GDP growth rates of the defaulters were higher (Figure 8.5).[57]

This is not surprising. Credit-market access was worth little when credit markets were inactive. Export-market access was of limited value when governments around the world embraced protection and import substitution. In such circumstances, what mattered was not foreign market access but developments at home, as shaped by a country's fiscal, monetary, and exchange-rate policies. Relieved of having to transfer interest abroad, governments could support spending and investment. They could run more expansionary monetary policies.[58]

This is not to argue that default on a government's obligations necessarily pays. But it is most likely to pay when global commodity and credit markets are demoralized, since this is when the costs of losing market access are least.[59]

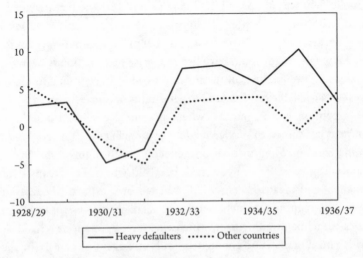

*Figure 8.5.* Change in Real GDP (annual, percent)
Source: Eichengreen (1991).

# Treatment of Domestic Debt

Politicians were more reluctant to default on domestic debts, since they would be defaulting on their own constituents.[60] When those bonds were held by local banks, they would be impairing the operation of the financial system. Servicing domestic debt was not as damaging to the economy as continuing to service external debt since, as Fetter observed, the recipient of the coupon payment had additional income to spend and taxes to pay. Servicing bonds denominated in local currency did not presuppose an ability to export; it did not depend as directly on global economic conditions. It required only enlisting the monetary authorities to provide the government with the currency needed to make payments, which the central bank could do by purchasing bonds. To be sure, monetizing debt could put upward pressure on prices, which was a concern in any country with a history of inflation. It might mean currency depreciation, an alarming prospect where there was a record of exchange-rate instability. Thus, even governments possessing the technical means to service domestic debts sometimes hesitated to use them.

Efforts to assess the frequency, much less the effects, of default on domestic debt are complicated by disagreement about what exactly constitutes a default: suspension of interest and amortization payments, or also buybacks of debt at a discount relative to par and repayment in depreciated currency.[61] In their classic book *This Time Is Different*, Carmen Reinhart and Kenneth Rogoff provide a catalog of domestic defaults that includes arrears, partial interest payments, suspensions of amortization, and forced conversions by China, Greece, Peru, Romania, and Spain in the 1930s.[62] China and Spain had little choice. The Spanish government went into arrears on its debt starting in 1936 due to the costs and disruptions of the country's civil war.[63] The Chinese debt consolidation of 1932, which extended the maturity and reduced the interest rate on outstanding domestic bonds, was undertaken in response to the crisis caused by Japan's annexation of Manchuria. Banks being the largest holders of China's domestic debt, this restructuring was deeply damaging to the financial system, which shows that the Chinese government resorted to it only in extremis.[64]

Reinhart and Rogoff also classify debt conversions undertaken by Australia and Britain in 1931–32 as defaults and restructurings. In the United Kingdom's 1932 debt-management operation, the UK Treasury bought back at par, in a manner consistent with their covenants, war bonds trading above par that were not voluntarily converted into new 3.5 percent annuities; this was exactly analogous to what Goschen had done in the 1880s.[65] The 1917 War Loan had been callable—that is, the original loan contract specified that it could be paid off in this way—since 1929. So there was nothing forced or irregular about this transaction. Similarly, in Australia's 1931 debt-management operation, outstanding bonds were voluntarily converted by businesses, banks, and small investors into new, lower-yielding bonds and bills.[66] Reinhart and Rogoff also categorize as a default the 1933 abrogation of gold clauses in US Treasury bonds, when the Treasury paid the bondholders in full, in current dollars rather than dollars of constant gold content. This is not a label with which everyone will agree; the prices of Treasury bonds actually rose on the decision, as if it rendered investors better off.[67]

As the Chinese and Spanish cases remind us, restructurings of domestic debts do occur, albeit under extreme circumstances. Another much later case in point is Greece, which restructured its domestic debt in 2012, as we describe in Chapter 12.[68] Greece, like China and Spain, had little choice. As a member of the Euro Area, it had to choose between abandoning the euro and reintroducing its own currency, which would have been messy and disruptive, and restructuring its domestic debt, despite nasty political consequences. The calculus is different for a country with its own currency and a central bank to backstop the bond market.

# The Legacy

The Great Depression had a mixed legacy for public debt. Debt burdens rose, but not as a result of countercyclical fiscal policies: in this pre-Keynesian era, governments largely adhered to the doctrine of balanced budgets.[69] They ran small primary surpluses in the 1930s; as shown in Table 8.4, the direct effect was to reduce the debt ratio.[70] But the indirect effect of those policies was to add to the collapse of gross domestic product, which constituted the denominator of the debt-to-GDP ratio. This is apparent in the dominant contribution of the interest-rate–growth-rate differential to the rise in debt ratios in the 1930s.[71] Evidently, maintaining a balanced budget in recessionary times is no virtue. Doing so does nothing to stabilize output. It doesn't even stabilize the debt.

Another legacy of the Great Depression was the further expansion of the welfare state. The Depression strengthened the argument for the state to provide insurance that individuals couldn't provide for themselves. Although actual increases in social spending were still limited in the 1930s, institutional changes such as federally funded unemployment insurance and the Social Security Act in the United States set the stage for more ambitious future increases. Transfer payments and social programs did not automatically mean larger deficits and debts. But they created the potential for deficits and debts according to the political-economy logic outlined at the start of this chapter.

Finally, the Depression brought to a close the first era when governments could place debt on international markets. The defaults of the 1930s highlighted

*Table 8.4* **Decomposition of Large Debt Accumulations, 1928–33**

| Country group | Debt/GDP ratio (percent) | | | Contribution to Increase (percent) | | |
|---|---|---|---|---|---|---|
| | Starting level | Ending level | Increase | Primary balance | Interest-growth differential | Stock-flow adjustment |
| **Advanced Economies** | | | | | | |
| Simple average | 61.4 | 83.7 | 22.4 | –3.5 | 26.9 | –1.0 |
| Weighted average | 46.7 | 69.3 | 22.6 | –2.5 | 23.1 | 2.0 |
| **Emerging Economies** | | | | | | |
| Simple average | 40.0 | 63.0 | 22.9 | –2.1 | 25.5 | –0.6 |
| Weighted average | 32.4 | 59.9 | 27.5 | –4.4 | 27.7 | 4.2 |

*Sources:* IMF's Historical Public Debt and Historical Public Finance Databases (IMF 2010, 2013) and authors' calculations.

*Note:* Episodes are identified based on debt increase of at least 10 percentage points of GDP. The debt increase is calculated using the exact years in the period, i.e., the change in the debt ratio between the start year (1928) and the end year (1933). Advanced economies included are Australia, Austria, Belgium, Canada, Finland, France, Germany, Greece, Ireland, Japan, Netherlands, New Zealand, Spain, Sweden, Switzerland, United Kingdom, and United States. Emerging economies included are Argentina, Brazil, India, Mexico, and South Africa.

the risks of investing in foreign government bonds. After World War II, investors displayed little appetite for such bonds. Legislators and regulators similarly came away critical of the operation of global bond markets. When governments again borrowed abroad, they instead turned to their fellow governments, to multilateral organizations such as the IMF and the World Bank, and, starting in the 1970s, to money-center banks. History would show that this, too, was a mixed blessing.

# Cycles of Debt

World War II and subsequent decades saw a debt cycle of enormous proportions. Public debts soared between 1939 and 1945 as governments mobilized for war. A period of consolidation, with debt burdens falling, followed once hostilities had passed.

Debts had also been consolidated after World War I, but those consolidations did not last. And debts now were even larger: debt-to-GDP ratios across the advanced economies were half again as high as after World War I. Yet, this time, debt consolidation continued for a quarter of a century. Advanced country debt-to-GDP ratios were reduced by a third between 1919 and 1929, from 90 percent to 60 percent. Between 1945 and 1970, in contrast, they fell by more than two-thirds, from nearly 140 percent to barely 40 percent.

This accomplishment was impressive. The question is how it was achieved.

The answer lies, in part, in economic growth that made for favorable growth-rate–interest-rate differentials and allowed governments to reconcile social spending with budget balance. This success at raising GDP reflected the scope that existed for catch-up growth. Capital formation was depressed in the 1930s, leaving productivity-enhancing investments on the table. In the United States, the adoption of modern mass-production methods had supported rapid productivity growth, but not so in Europe and Japan, where take-up of the electric motor and assembly line was slower.[1] In many countries, industrial production then fell below 1938 levels immediately after World War II.

But as a result of these very same developments, it was possible for growth to proceed rapidly once the immediate obstacles were removed.[2] The formula was freely available, and countries from Europe to North America and Japan were quick to apply it.

This superficial answer begs a deeper question, of course. How were countries now able to sustain high investment, implement new technologies, and shift resources from agriculture to industry when comparable adjustments had been frustrated after World War I? It was not as if circumstances now were uniformly more favorable. The post–World War II period saw housing shortages, foreign occupation, ethnic strife, and a tidal wave of displaced persons moving westward across East-Central Europe. It saw increases in military spending and disruptions to economic and political relations with the advent of the Cold War. These dislocations were extensive. Yet they failed to disrupt either postwar recovery or the subsequent process of catch-up growth.

No single factor explains the contrast, but an element worth highlighting, given the context, is debt management and fiscal policy. Forgiveness of debts owed to foreign governments allowed the new Federal Republic of Germany to increase social spending, ease its housing shortage, and assuage the anxieties of the displaced. This helped Germany avoid the labor disruptions and divisive politics that had hindered investment and growth after World War I. Debt reduction made German growth possible. In turn, German growth made European growth possible, given the dependence of European manufacturing on German capital goods. More generally, advanced-country governments successfully reconciled increases in spending on education, health, and other social programs with budget balance. Their fiscal policies thereby enhanced the prospects for growth.

All the while, interest rates remained below growth rates. Nominal GDP growth approached 10 percent per annum (6 percent growth plus 4 percent inflation), whereas annual debt service was only 3 percent of outstanding debt.

Investors held government bonds despite these low yields because they had few other choices. Interest rates on bank deposits were controlled.[3] Institutional investors who might have looked abroad, as they had in the 1920s, were constrained by capital controls.

It is fair to ask whether these policies of financial repression—for repressive they were—resulted in an inefficient allocation of resources. One view is that financial repression, by interfering with markets, is always and everywhere a drag on growth.[4] But another is that such costs were absent or even negative when there existed a technological backlog and decades-long investment shortfall to be made up. When the returns to physical capital were high and investments in upstream sectors had large positive spillovers for productivity in downstream sectors, and vice versa, capping interest rates on government debt was a way of forcing investors to search out these high-return opportunities. It was a way of encouraging capital formation in sectors where its social benefits exceeded private returns.[5] And even if those policies had costs, these did not prevent the advanced countries from achieving unprecedented growth and sustaining it for a quarter of a century.

Outside the advanced-country world, public debt ratios started out lower and rose modestly through the 1960s. The share of foreign debt remained stable at less than 15 percent of the total (Figure 9.1). Foreign finance did not play the same

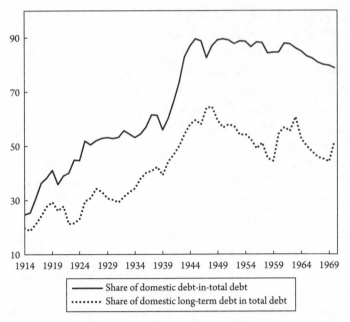

*Figure 9.1.* G-20 Emerging Economies Debt Structure (percent)
Source: Reinhart and Rogoff (2009).
Note: Domestic debt refers to debt issued internally. Long-term debt is defined as debt with maturity of
more than one year. Data on domestic debt cover select G-20 emerging economies, including Argentina,
Brazil, China, India, Indonesia, Mexico, Russia, and South Africa. Data on long-term domestic debt cover
only Argentina, Brazil, China, India, Mexico, and South Africa. Data are simple averages. Year coverage varies.

role as in the nineteenth century or the 1920s. Only a handful of foreign bonds
were traded in London and New York.[6] International capital markets had been
discredited by the defaults of the 1930s. Investors and governments were disinclined to trust the underwriting banks and rating agencies that had intermediated
foreign borrowing and lending in earlier periods. Regulators showed no more sympathy for rekindling this market; life insurance companies doing business in the
State of New York were prohibited from holding more than 1 percent of their assets
in foreign securities.[7] In Japan and Western Europe, controls prevented investors
from purchasing foreign government bonds, whether from emerging markets or
other countries. The United States used tax policies, such the Interest Equalization
Tax adopted in 1963, to discourage foreign portfolio investment. When emerging
and developing-country governments tapped foreign finance, they borrowed
mainly from advanced-country governments and multilateral institutions.

## Economic Consequences of the War

World War II was not limited to Europe and the Middle East, engulfing as it did
much of Africa and Asia. The combatants developed costly new weapons and

fighting machines, from advanced aircraft and radar to the atomic bomb, and enlisted extensive manufacturing capacity in military production.

Estimates of the direct costs of World War I for Germany, Britain, the United States, and Russia, cited in Chapter 8, can be compared with estimates of the share of national product mobilized for World War II. These suggest that the second war was twice as costly relative to GDP.[8] Over its course, government expenditure nearly doubled in Britain, more than doubled in Germany, and more than tripled in the United States.

As in the earlier war, only a fraction of this spending was covered by current receipts: 32 percent in Germany, 53 percent in Britain, and 46 percent in the United States.[9] And because the war was more expensive, financing the same revenue shortfall required even more debt. By 1945, the debt ratio had risen to 116 percent in the United States, 235 percent in the United Kingdom, and a staggering 300 percent in Germany.[10]

Germany's domestic debt was then wiped out by inflation and currency reform starting in 1945, just as it had been wiped out starting in 1919. This time, in addition, foreign obligations were written down by the London Debt Agreement of 1953.[11] The principal amount was reduced by half, and repayment was stretched out over thirty years.[12] Both the war-debt overhang that had slowed the reconstruction of trade and fiscal uncertainty that discouraged investment were avoided this time. By 1954, West Germany's debt-to-GDP ratio was just 21 percent, its interest payments as a share of GDP less than 1 percent.

A second difference was how the United States supported its allies. The Johnson Act, passed by Congress in 1934, barred foreign governments from negotiating loans in the United States until they settled their earlier debts, including the World War I debt, which had been defaulted on starting in 1932. This meant that friendly governments could purchase supplies in the United States only on a "cash and carry" basis. (They had to purchase materiel for *cash* and *carry* it home.) The Roosevelt administration, seeking to aid its friends, therefore had to find other ways of arranging assistance. Its solution was Lend-Lease, under which the United States provided the Allies with food, fuel, and materiel in return for leases on military bases.

The quid pro quo could also take the form of "joint action directed towards the creation of a liberalized international economic order in the postwar world."[13] In other words, debts could be discharged by cooperating in establishing the International Monetary Fund, the World Bank, and the other United Nations institutions constituting the global framework for growth. Trade had been stifled after World War I by disruptive international financial entanglements, whose consequences included refusal by the US Congress to ratify American participation in the League of Nations. An analogous morass was avoided this time.

## The Role of Central Banks

Governments employed the same tactics as in World War I for marketing bonds: publicity campaigns, appeals to patriotism, controls, and prohibitions on other investments. World War II being more expensive, hesitation about subordinating the central bank's balance sheet was less. Figure 9.2 shows how both central bank assets relative to GDP and government debt as a share of those assets far exceeded those in the earlier war.

The US case illustrates the point. Starting in April 1942, the Federal Reserve enforced a rate ceiling of 3/8 percent on Treasury bills and 2.5 percent on bonds by purchasing them in whatever amounts were needed to keep rates from rising.[14] In practice, this meant buying mainly bills. A patriotic public was prepared to subscribe to bonds yielding 2.5 percent, but bills yielding just 3/8 percent were another matter.[15] By the end of the war, short-term Treasury obligations therefore made up more than half the Fed's balance sheet.

As a result, the money supply rose even faster than in World War I.[16] Prices rose more slowly than the money stock, reflecting low interest rates conducive to holding cash balances, restrictions on the ability of households to finance purchases of consumer durables, and price controls.

The Bank of England similarly sought to keep borrowing costs low. John Maynard Keynes and career Treasury officials preferred a long-term interest

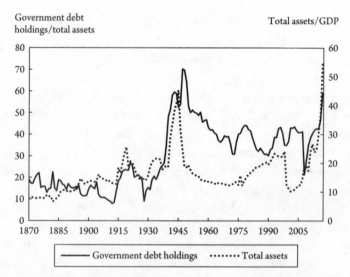

*Figure 9.2.* Central Bank Balance Sheets and Government Debt Holdings (percent)
Source: Ferguson, Schaab, and Schularick (2014).
Note: Government debt holdings are measured as a percent of total assets. Total assets are measured as a percent of GDP. Countries included are Australia, Belgium, Canada, France, Germany, Italy, Japan, Netherlands, Spain, Sweden, the United Kingdom, and the United States.

rate of 2.5 percent, as in the United States, but Montagu Norman and the Bank of England argued that investors would expect higher rates, perhaps 3 percent, given that a cash-strapped British government would be issuing massive amounts of debt.[17] Long-term yields were driven down from 3.7 percent in 1939 to 2.9 percent in 1945. To cap long-term rates at these levels, the Bank of England quintupled its loans to the government. By the end of the war, an extraordinary 98 percent of the bank's assets were in the form of government securities.[18] Nothing speaks more clearly to the role of the central bank in financing the war. This figure also puts twenty-first-century central bank bond purchase programs (discussed further in Chapters 13 and 14) in perspective.[19]

For the German Reichsbank, purchasing government securities was a red line, given the role of the central bank in the hyperinflation of the 1920s. Hjalmar Horace Greeley Schacht, in his dual roles as central bank president and acting head of the Economics Ministry, sparred with Hitler over this issue until 1939, when a new Reichsbank Act formally subordinated the central bank to the Führer and Schacht was dismissed.[20] After this, the share of government securities in the assets of the Reichsbank moved sharply higher, from 3 percent at the end of 1939 to 20 percent in 1941, 40 percent in 1943, and 70 percent in 1945.[21] These operations had as their counterpart an increase in currency circulation, from RM 11 billion at the outset of the war to RM 73 billion at its conclusion.[22] The cost of living rose over the same period by a more modest 11 percent.[23] This was indicative of comprehensive price controls and of the unlimited police powers backing them. But it also augured serious dislocations if controls were removed.

## Scaling Back

Equally remarkable is how central-bank balance sheets as a share of GDP fell back subsequently. Allied decrees rendered Reich debt non-negotiable, and the monetary reform effectively rendered it worthless. It therefore played no role when the Bank deutscher Länder, the first postwar German central bank, was established in the American and British occupation zones in 1948.

Elsewhere, balance was restored by growing GDP rather than selling off securities.[24] For the same twelve central banks included in Figure 9.2, the share of public debt in assets fell from 60 percent at the end of the war to 40 percent in the 1950s.[25] Still, domestic government debt accounted for twice the share of central bank assets as had been typical in earlier years.[26] This new higher fraction was a permanent change to central bank balance sheets; it persisted for the balance of the century.

Because central banks now held both bills and bonds, they could influence financial conditions by exchanging one for the other. They could use such operations to tilt the yield curve, as the Federal Reserve did in its 1961 "Operation Twist," when it purchased bonds and sold bills. Buying bonds pushed down long-term rates in order to reduce the cost of investment, while selling bills pushed up short rates and encouraged savers to shift into dollar deposits, strengthening the balance of payments.[27] The Fed followed a similar course in September 2011, when it announced a program of using $400 billion of proceeds from maturing Treasury bills and notes to purchase government bonds. Evidently, large central bank holdings of government securities have their uses.

In other instances, these large public debt holdings constrained monetary policy rather than facilitating it. Were the central bank to raise interest rates to tamp down inflation, bond prices would fall. The central bank would therefore be inflicting balance-sheet damage on itself and imposing losses on patriotic citizens who had purchased war bonds.[28] Raising rates would also make it more costly for the Treasury to issue new debt.[29] This caused a conflict in the United States. When the Federal Reserve first sought to lift its cap on long-term interest rates in the summer of 1947, the Treasury objected vehemently, and the Fed had to backtrack. This was a very visible instance of "fiscal dominance," of a central bank being pressured to subordinate monetary policy to debt-management considerations.

But by pegging rates on public debt, the Fed lost control of the price level. When the interest rates demanded by investors were above the central bank's ceiling on treasury rates, investors sold their treasuries for cash, fueling inflation. When the rates required by investors were below the Fed's target, as in the 1949 recession, investors engaged in the reverse operation, causing deflation. Consumer prices fluctuated wildly, increasing by 14 percent in 1947, falling by 1 percent in 1949, and again rising by 8 percent in 1951.

With the United States embroiled in the Korean War, but without the controls that suppressed bank lending to consumers during World War II, inflation grew increasingly worrisome. Yet the Fed was still hamstrung by its obligation to maintain the ceiling on Treasury notes. Contentious negotiations followed. On March 4, 1951, following a dispute between President Harry Truman and Fed Chairman Marriner Eccles, officials finally announced that they had reached "full accord" on policies to "assure the successful financing of the government's requirements and, at the same time, to minimize monetization of the public debt." The Fed agreed to support the price of five-year Treasury notes for several additional months, after which they would be left to float freely and the Treasury would be on its own.

With this Accord, as the agreement became known, the Federal Reserve was no longer in thrall to debt management, as it had been, in a sense, since Roosevelt took the United States off the gold standard and seized the monetary reins in 1933. That almost two full decades had to pass for the central bank to be freed from this indenture points to the prominence of public debt in engineering recovery from the Great Depression, in dealing with the financial consequences of World War II, and in managing the postwar transition.

European central banks were drawn into closer relations with governments not just for purposes of funding the public sector, but also as a way of channeling credit to strategic industries and sectors. Central banks and finance ministries regulated credit provision by commercial banks. Their objectives included those of conventional monetary policy, but extended also to industrial and trade policy by providing key sectors with preferential access to credit on favorable terms.[30] The most encompassing case was France, where the government's allocative ambitions were vast and the central bank orchestrated relations between public agencies and the private sector. It is argued that these policies encouraged investment in sectors where the social benefits exceeded private returns and helped in overcoming coordination problems, contributing thereby to economic growth and, by implication, to successful debt consolidation.[31]

## Foreign Finance

In the late 1940s and 1950s, as during the war, debt finance was homespun. In the first postwar decade (1946–55), total private loans to foreign governments worldwide averaged less than $500 million a year, the lion's share coming from the United States. This was a drop in the bucket, less than one-tenth of 1 percent of global GDP.[32] Intergovernmental flows, which were five times as large, also came mainly from the United States; these took the form of both grants and loans and went mainly to Europe and Japan. Between 1945 and 1949, US foreign aid then averaged $6 billion a year, or 2.5 percent of 1947 US GDP, first under the United Nations Relief and Rehabilitation Administration (UNRRA) and then the Marshall Plan. The fact that intergovernmental lending loomed so large relative to US GDP but small relative to the global economy is a reminder of how overwhelmingly dependent other countries were on American official lending.

Marshall aid was subject to macroeconomic policy conditions of the sort attached previously to League of Nations loans. Recipients were expected to balance their budgets and to place their debts on a sustainable footing. They could then stabilize the exchange rate, relax import and export controls, and restore current account convertibility, goals that American officials saw as in the interests of not only the aid recipients but also US exporters.

American aid was an inducement to move in this direction. By supplementing their budgets, Marshall aid reduced the amount of belt tightening required of governments. In doing so, it reduced the incentive for interest groups to engage in lengthy fights over cuts to favored programs. It thereby limited the wars of attrition that had made for instability after World War I.[33] A related requirement of the Marshall planners, that governments publish detailed budget accounts, helped to overcome the information asymmetries and confusion that had prolonged budgetary deadlocks after that earlier war.[34]

Multilateral finance played little role in the immediate postwar years. The United States discouraged IMF and World Bank lending, on the grounds that a competing source of finance would weaken the policy leverage exerted through the Marshall Plan. World Bank loans were small and limited initially to electric power, railway, and port rehabilitation projects.[35] They were extended at market rates for commercially viable projects only. World Bank lending to developing countries rose gradually in the 1950s, but not until the end of the decade did the Bank establish a soft loan window to provide finance on concessional terms.

Similarly, IMF lending was minimal in the second half of the 1940s and first half of the 1950s; it averaged a mere 0.06 percent of global imports between 1947 and 1955.[36] The war that erupted in 1956 following Egyptian President Gamal Abdel Nasser's nationalization of the Suez Canal, the Israeli occupation of Sinai, and French and British operations to take control of the canal, marked a turning point. The conflict dented confidence in the currencies of all four combatants. The hit to the British pound was alarming, given that sterling was widely held and used in international transactions, second only to the US dollar. Sterling had already been devalued once, in 1949. Another devaluation was seen as potentially constituting an existential threat to the Bretton Woods System agreed in 1944 and conceivably even to the IMF itself.

Sterling was vulnerable owing to large balances held outside the United Kingdom. These had been accumulated by Britain's wartime allies, principally members of the commonwealth and empire that had supplied it with commodities and war materiel and provided physical and financial support for British troops. The debts in question, being denominated in sterling, were known as "sterling balances." They provided Britain with as much wartime assistance as Lend-Lease. By the end of the war, the accumulated stock amounted to nearly seven times annual British exports.[37]

A significant fraction of these obligations was blocked, meaning that they couldn't be converted into merchandise or other assets. One-third were frozen through formal agreements between the United Kingdom and its creditors, while another third were held subject to understandings that amounted to de facto blocking. Either way, the creditors received only modest returns, on the order of 1 percent per annum.[38] This was debt sustainability supported by financial repression, tailored to British needs.

Not least among the holders was the Egyptian government itself, which responded to the 1956 invasion with financial retaliation, selling off its sterling holdings. The United Kingdom responded by freezing Egypt's sterling balances, which it could do since these were held in London. Not knowing where the escalation would stop and fearing either additional controls or further devaluation of the pound, more governments liquidated their sterling balances. This was a compelling, indeed an alarming, demonstration of the financial and political vulnerabilities that can arise when large amounts of government debt are held outside the issuing country.

The United States, opposed to foreign intervention in Egypt, initially blocked British access to IMF help, pressuring the United Kingdom to withdraw its troops. When the British government, left with no choice, acceded to US demands, the IMF extended its largest-ever loan to a member (an immediate $561 million drawing to replenish the UK's reserves, with an additional $739 million "stand-by" loan to be provided on an as-needed basis). Smaller loans were extended to France, Israel, and Egypt.

This response to the Suez crisis put the IMF on the map as an international lender. As more countries then relaxed their tariffs and quotas and allowed their currencies to be used more freely for trade-related transactions, balance-of-payments problems arose more frequently. IMF loans, conditioned on fiscal and balance-of-payments adjustments, became more common.

## Growth and Consolidation

It is tempting to infer—one might say to assume—that postwar debt consolidation was largely the result of financial repression. Carmen Reinhart and Belen Sbrancia write how "the World War II debt overhang was importantly liquidated via the combination of financial repression and inflation...."[39] In addition, however, budget surpluses played a more important role than is commonly assumed. Table 9.1 shows how the contribution of the primary balance after World War II, though smaller than after World War I, was substantial: it accounted for nearly four-tenths of the decrease in the debt ratio. The growth-rate–interest-rate differential that captures the effects of financial repression may have made the single largest contribution to debt consolidation after World War II, but it was not the entire story.

Similarly, the period of sharply negative real interest rates on government debt (when inflation exceeded nominal interest rates) ended in the mid-1950s (with the precise year depending on the country).[40] As Figure 9.3 shows, real rates (interest payments on the debt adjusted for inflation) remained positive until the late 1960s, after which inflation accelerated and real rates fell.

The contribution of the growth-rate–interest-rate differential, shown in Figure 9.4, reflects not just low interest rates but also rapid economic growth. Earlier we described how postwar growth reflected opportunities unexploited

*Table 9.1* **Decomposition of Large Post–World War II Debt Consolidations in Advanced Economies**

| | Debt-to-GDP Ratio (percent) | | | Contribution to Decrease (percent) | | |
|---|---|---|---|---|---|---|
| | Starting Level | Ending Level | Decrease | Primary Balance | Growth-Interest Differential | Stock-Flow Adjustment |
| Simple average | 95.5 | 22.4 | 73.1 | 22.6 | 82.6 | –32.2 |
| Weighted average | 112.0 | 26.2 | 85.8 | 33.3 | 80.2 | –27.7 |

*Sources:* IMF Historical Public Debt and Historical Public Finance Databases (IMF 2010, 2013) and authors' calculations.

*Note:* Episodes are identified based on debt reduction of at least 10 percentage points of GDP during 1945–75. Peak-to-trough episodes (years vary by each country). The countries (episodes) included are Australia (1946–75), Austria (1948–57), Belgium (1945–74), Canada (1945–74), Finland (1945–74), France (1946–69), Greece (1952–58), Ireland (1958–73), Italy (1945–47), Japan (1946–64), Netherlands (1946–74), New Zealand (1946–74), Portugal (1945–74), Spain (1945–75), Sweden (1945–66), Switzerland (1945–68), United Kingdom (1946–75), and United States (1946–74). Germany is excluded because the debt decline did not satisfy the criterion of at least 10 percentage points of GDP decline in the debt ratio during 1945–75.

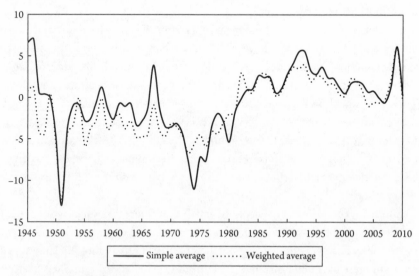

*Figure 9.3.* Real Interest Rate in G-20 Advanced Economies, 1945–2010 (percent)
Sources: Abbas et al. (2014a) and authors' calculations.
Note: Advanced economies included are Australia, Canada, France, Germany, Italy, the United Kingdom, and the United States.

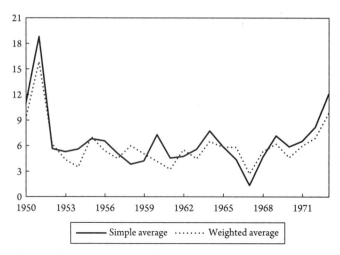

*Figure 9.4.* Nominal Growth Rate–Nominal Interest Rate Differential in Advanced Economies, 1950–73 (percent)

Sources: Jordà et al. (2018); Mitchell (2003); IMF *World Economic Outlook* (WEO); and authors' calculations.

Note: G-20 advanced economies are included, except Japan. Nominal GDP growth rates are calculated using WEO data, except for the following episodes: Finland (1958–60) and Switzerland (1963–65) for which the data are drawn from Jordà et al. (2018) database; and for Greece (1950–52, 1959–60) and Ireland (1950–60), for which the data are drawn from Mitchell (2003) database.

in the Great Depression and World War II that were now successfully pursued. There was nothing inevitable, however, about this process of catch-up growth, as experience after World War I had shown. Pursuing it after World War II required shifting resources into manufacturing and adopting mass-production methods, which entailed redefining tasks and jobs. In other times and places, workers pushed back against radical change with strikes, slowdowns, and machine breaking.[41] The post–World War II period was less contentious.[42] High unemployment in the 1930s had put a damper on labor militancy. The collaborative approach to labor-management relations adopted during wartime persisted into the peace.

Importantly, social programs reassured workers anxious about displacement. Increases in social spending were most rapid where there existed significant obstacles to labor mobility, and where workers consequently had the most reason to worry about losing jobs.[43] But the spending increase was general. Social spending in the United States doubled as a share of GNP between 1945 and 1950.[44] In the United Kingdom, the postwar Labour government adopted the National Insurance and National Assistance Acts.[45] Other countries saw similar developments.

Economic growth permitted governments to increase social spending within the existing budgetary envelope. Budget deficits in the advanced countries averaged less than 1 percent of GDP in the 1950s.[46] Even that modest average was disproportionately inflated by Greece, which had just concluded a debilitating civil war and whose deficit ratio ran into the double digits.[47] In the German case, debt consolidation under the London Debt Agreement freed up resources for social spending, as noted earlier. The growth of German public spending on health, education, and other social services per capita accelerated absolutely and relative to other European countries once debt was reduced in 1953, creating fiscal space.[48] It is hard to see how Germany could have massively shifted resources into manufacturing while at the same time addressing its citizens' demands for housing and other services absent this debt restructuring.[49]

In addition, it helped that there were few debt or banking crises. One catalog of banking crises in middle- and high-income countries identifies just one systematic banking crisis in the 1950s and 1960s.[50] Financial repression, evidently, had its advantages. That is to say, strict regulation of banks and financial markets, not limited to interest rate regulation, avoided the need for costly crisis-resolution measures.[51] Nor was there much active fiscal policy to add to debts, partly because recessions were few, and partly because the gospel of Keynesianism was not yet widely embraced.

Still, two consecutive decades of primary surpluses take some explaining, given the difficulty governments have had in running persistent surpluses at other times. The political economy theories of debts and deficits reviewed in Chapter 8 point to political polarization and fractionalization as making for deficit spending. It is thus relevant that the share of extreme parties on the left and right in the legislatures of the advanced economies reached twentieth-century lows in the 1950s and 1960s.[52] Those theories point to electoral uncertainty and to the temptation to raise spending on programs favored by supporters of the incumbent party before the political opposition gains power. Here it is relevant that the average margin of victory in legislative elections in the advanced economies in the 1950s and early 1960s was higher than it had been earlier and also higher than it became subsequently, limiting such uncertainty.[53]

## Lending Boom, Borrowing Binge

Advanced-country debt consolidation slowed and then stopped in the 1970s. Slower growth made for larger budget deficits and higher debts.[54] Although less growth meant that tax revenues would grow more slowly in the absence of policy action, the rise in spending did not slow commensurately. Politicians felt pressure to maintain social spending as real wages stagnated and unemployment rose. Legislatures needed time to agree on spending cuts, more so as political polarization and legislative fractionalization began to rise.[55]

This story is unsatisfactory insofar as the roots of the post-1973 growth and productivity slowdown remain obscure. It is incomplete in that these disturbing fiscal trends were already evident prior to the slowdown. Indeed, a rising ratio of government spending to GDP had been apparent in much of the OECD in the second half of the 1960s—that is, for nearly a decade prior to the growth slowdown.[56]

The United States is a case in point. In attempting to balance the needs of New Society programs, such as Medicare, Medicaid, and aid to education, with those of the Vietnam War, total outlays of all levels of government rose from 27 percent of GDP in 1965 to 31 percent in 1973. Similar increases in public spending ratios attributable to social programs were evident across the advanced-country world.[57] The increase was largest, rendering government spending highest, in Denmark, Sweden, and the Netherlands.[58] This heralded the development of what eventually became known as the Northern European or Scandinavian welfare state.[59]

Against this backdrop, the first oil-price increase from the Organization of Petroleum Exporting Countries (OPEC, founded in 1960) and the post-1973 growth slowdown were problematic. Governments had staked their popularity on new social programs. Believing the oil shock and productivity slowdown to be temporary, they chose to finance those programs, running what they understood to be temporary deficits. They adopted bridging policies, rather than adjusting. They pointed to their budget deficits as consistent with a commitment to full employment.[60] Even when it became apparent that the growth slowdown was persistent, it was still hard to adjust spending, especially in countries such as Belgium and Italy, where multiparty coalition governments complicated efforts to reach and sustain a consensus.

As inflation rose, real interest rates turned negative, as they had after World War II, encouraging governments to keep borrowing. Just why nominal interest rates didn't rise with inflation is something of a mystery even today. Lacking experience with a 1973-style oil-price shock and economic slowdown, investors may not have expected inflation to persist. Banks and markets were flush with petrodollar deposits that the oil-exporting countries had yet to spend.[61] We will turn next to the role of petrodollar recycling in lending to less-developed countries (LDCs) between 1973 and 1982. The point here is that those same funds financed the budget deficits of the advanced countries at rates favorable to the borrowers.

## Developing-Country Indebtedness

Developing-country indebtedness also began rising after 1973. As late as 1971–73, intergovernmental loans and aid, World Bank loans, and IMF programs provided nearly two-thirds of the total financing requirements of non-OPEC LDCs, commercial banks barely 20 percent. By 1974–76, commercial bank lending accounted for the majority, reflecting the boom in petrodollar recycling.

Bank lenders were organized into syndicates, often consisting of a hundred and more banks located in different countries. They attracted Eurodollars— that is, dollars deposited outside the United States—and extended "jumbo loans" which ran to the hundreds of millions of dollars.[62] Their loans bore variable interest rates and were repriced every three to six months. They were denominated in dollars, regardless of whether they were extended by US or foreign banks.[63]

In some respects, these arrangements resembled the earlier era of bond finance. A lead bank acted as syndicate manager, liaising with the borrower, structuring the loan, and placing it with syndicate partners. The difference now was that the entire loan was retained by the banks, retail investors in the bonds of LDCs being nowhere to be found. Since small banks took small bites, the resulting obligations were concentrated mainly on the balance sheets of money-center banks. This would make for very different political and economic dynamics than in, say, 1931, when retail investors were on the hook.[64]

Emerging markets and developing countries saw ample reason to borrow. When their growth accelerated in the 1960s, governments touted the arrival of an economic miracle.[65] As growth slowed, those same governments were reluctant to acknowledge reality, so they borrowed to delay the reckoning.

In addition, there was the argument that borrowing from banks was preferable to foreign direct investment because it did not require ceding the economy's commanding heights. As one economist put it, "Inflows of FDI in particular had a bad smell in the early 1970s: allowing foreign firms to own manufacturing capacity seemed like an affront to a developing country's sense of autonomy. . . . In contrast, borrowing from international banks seemed to imply no compromise at all of national autonomy. This idea was nicely reinforced by the fact that banks seemed happy to lend without asking too many questions about how funds were to be spent."[66]

The last part of this passage reminds us that it takes two to tango. Latin American debt, 80 percent of which was sovereign, couldn't have quadrupled between 1973 and 1979 without enthusiastic lenders. Having lost their large corporate customers to the commercial paper market, US money-center banks looked abroad for clients.[67] Moreover, when the members of a bank syndicate extended a loan to a developing-country sovereign, they didn't always take into account that other syndicates were doing likewise. As we saw in an earlier chapter, the gatekeeper function of lead banks had grown less effective over time. Now, without anyone to restrain them, the banks stampeded through the gates.

There were warnings of the risks of lending to Latin American sovereigns.[68] It was understood that loans to LDCs by US money-center banks amounted to two and more times the banks' capital, meaning that sovereign defaults could result in insolvency for systematically important financial institutions.[69]

But warnings to this effect went unheeded. Inexperience was partly to blame: syndicated bank lending to LDCs was a new phenomenon. The sovereign defaults of the 1930s were now half a century removed, and only the most geriatric bankers had experienced this episode at first hand. That there were few bank failures in the 1950s and 1960s allowed bank strategists to dismiss the risk of using short-term deposits to fund long-term loans. Policymakers, for their part, were mainly concerned with the adverse macroeconomic consequences of allowing petrodollars to sit idly on bank balance sheets, preferring that they fuel (as it were) US exports. As William Seidman, President Gerald Ford's economic advisor, put it, "The entire Ford administration, including me, told the large banks that the process of recycling petrodollars to the less developed countries was beneficial, and perhaps even a patriotic duty."[70]

Starting in 1979, with the second oil shock, and continuing through 1982, when the LDC debt crisis erupted, the banks and their LDC customers doubled down. The total debt of major LDC debtors doubled again as a share of GDP between 1978 and 1982.[71] Latin American countries had still larger balance-of-payments deficits to finance, some because of higher oil import bills, others because of higher US interest rates.[72] The banks were sitting on a second tranche of petrodollars, which they again recycled as LDC loans. Warnings against excessive bank commitments were issued, but they did not resonate. Bank profits remained strong, sustained by interest income on earlier loans and fee income on new loans—new loans that made possible payment of interest on earlier loans.

In hindsight, this was a house of cards, but this is not how financial markets saw it. Bank share prices held steady. The corporate bond ratings of the money-center banks remained stable into 1982, despite the banks' increasingly questionable commitments to Latin American sovereigns.

Table 9.2 shows the increase in sovereign indebtedness between 1973 and 1982. In both the median emerging market and the median advanced country, new borrowing financed mainly budget deficits. The contribution of primary budget deficits (net of interest payments) almost exactly matched the increase in debt as a share of GDP. Beyond that, the rise in indebtedness was slowed by the fact that nominal growth rates exceeded interest payments. This effect was almost exactly offset, however, by the positive impact on indebtedness of the stock-flow adjustment, which reflected currency depreciation and consequent increases in the burden of dollar debt. Given that these last two effects canceled

*Table 9.2* **Decomposition of Large Debt Accumulations, 1973–82**

| | Debt-to-GDP Ratio (percent) | | | Contribution to Increase (percent) | | |
|---|---|---|---|---|---|---|
| | Starting Level | Ending Level | Increase | Primary Balance | Interest-Growth Differential | Stock-Flow Adjustment |
| **Advanced Economies** | | | | | | |
| Simple average | 24.8 | 46.3 | 21.5 | 12.5 | −14.2 | 23.2 |
| Weighted average | 28.2 | 46.9 | 18.7 | 14.8 | −8.8 | 12.7 |
| **Emerging Economies** | | | | | | |
| Simple average | 23.1 | 38.2 | 15.1 | 10 | −48.5 | 53.6 |
| Weighted average | 25.4 | 38.0 | 12.6 | 9.5 | −42.1 | 45.2 |

*Sources:* IMF Historical Public Debt and Historical Public Finance Databases (IMF 2010, 2013) and authors' calculations.

*Note:* Episodes are identified based on debt increase of at least 10 percentage points of GDP during 1973–82. The debt increase is calculated using the exact years in the period, i.e., the change in the debt ratio between the start year (1973) and the end year (1982). Advanced economies included are Austria, Belgium, Denmark, Finland, France, Germany, Greece, Iceland, Ireland, Italy, Japan, Netherlands, New Zealand, Portugal, Spain, Sweden, Switzerland, and United States. Emerging economies included are Argentina, Brazil, India, Korea, Malaysia, Peru, Philippines, Thailand, and Turkey.

out, the table shows that the increase in sovereign indebtedness after 1973 was fiscally driven.

## Shaking the Markets

Mexican Finance Minister Jesús Silva Herzog's decision on August 12, 1982, to close his country's foreign-exchange market and his revealing that the Mexican government was unable to service its debts shook the markets. Argentina, Brazil, Venezuela, and another dozen Latin American countries followed with similar announcements. Their borrowed funds had been used for consumption rather than investment, and for financing imports rather than building up export capacity.[73] They had pegged their currencies to the dollar to make their economies appear less risky to foreign lenders. The result, in conjunction with inflation, was worsening international competitiveness.[74] But devaluing would have only increased the cost of debt service, given that debts were denominated in dollars, leading to inevitable arrears.[75]

Net lending to the governments of the crisis countries now fell from $60 bil-
lion in 1981 to near zero in 1983.[76] This sudden stop squeezed already cash-
strapped LDCs and threatened the money-center banks. If LDCs lapsed into
outright default, as opposed to just running interest arrears, advanced-country
regulators would require banks to classify their loans as nonperforming. This
would vaporize bank capital and force those regulatory authorities to step in, at
considerable cost to themselves.

Given this, it was tempting, indeed irresistible, to imagine that the crisis would
be fleeting, much as it had been tempting in 1973 to imagine that the oil shock
was fleeting. The hope was that troubled debtors would boost their exports as
soon as overvaluations were removed, enabling them to resume servicing their
debts and eliminating the threat to the banks.[77]

The first order of business was therefore to avert an outright default by the
Mexican government. Over the weekend following Silva Herzog's announcement, US negotiators arranged a $1.85 billion short-term loan, drawing on
the US Treasury's Exchange Stabilization Fund and, more creatively, on credit
guarantees through the US Department of Agriculture.[78] Two additional weeks
were then required to assemble another $925 million of credits from G10 cen-
tral banks.[79] These emergency measures provided a bridge to the final destination, namely an IMF program. On December 23, 1982, the IMF Executive
Board approved a three-year $3.75 billion loan, subject to a commitment by the
Mexican government to undertake comprehensive macroeconomic and structural reforms.

Assistance to other troubled countries followed the same template. By the
end of 1983, three-quarters of Latin countries had negotiated IMF programs.[80]
For their part, the banks agreed to push Mexico's principal repayments into the
future and granted similar concessions to other Latin American countries. The
IMF's managing director, Jacques de Larosière, insisted that their doing so was
a precondition for his institution providing official money. This was also a first
step by the Fund in the direction of its new policy of burden sharing, also known
as "bailing in the banks."

## Extend and Pretend

In this way, a global meltdown was averted. This is not the same, of course, as
saying that the outcome was a happy one. With their market access curtailed
and finance ministries under IMF tutelage, Latin American governments were
forced to implement deep cuts in public spending. Nor was it easy to substitute
external demand for the domestic demand that was lost. For Mexico to devalue
its currency and boost its exports was one thing, but for sixteen Latin American
countries to do so simultaneously was quite another, given that their exports

were almost all destined for the same markets. As the greenback now rose further, servicing dollar debts became still harder, and arrears to the banks continued to mount.

This was the period of extend and pretend: extend duration and capitalize arrears in the hope that the loans might somehow, someday, be repaid.[81] Operationalizing this approach required three things. First, continued regulatory forbearance was requisite so that the banks were not obliged to set aside reserves against impaired sovereign loans. In 1984, with their regulators in mind, the banks engaged in a new round of rescheduling talks.[82] These pushed payments as far as fourteen years into the future without reducing the overall obligation, allowing them to avoid acknowledging losses. Second, new money was required so that troubled countries could ramp up their repayments gradually, start growing again, and regain market access. In practice, new money meant money from the banks, since the IMF was now low on cash and governments complained of IMF stigma.[83] Third, there was more emphasis on structural reform; LDC debtors were asked to boost their exports and strengthen their finances.

This formula, announced by US Treasury Secretary James Baker at the 1985 IMF/World Bank meetings, was what came to be known as the Baker Plan. At last, it was acknowledged that the shock was more than temporary and that it would be necessary to finance an extended adjustment.

Forbearance was the easy part, especially in the United States, where regulators would have faced a costly bill, not to mention political flak, had they forced the banks to recapitalize.[84] Mobilizing new money was harder, since the banks questioned the borrowers' adjustment effort. The crisis had awakened them, as crises do, to the checkered history of sovereign lending and borrowing, and to the inability of governments to commit their successors to a course of action.[85] In addition, there was the familiar collective action problem, as each bank preferred that other banks provide the new money. Regional banks with small positions refused to contribute, burdening the large money-center banks. Thus, the same syndication practices that had facilitated loan placement now became an obstacle.

The resulting stasis lasted two years. Bank steering committees negotiated inconclusively with governments.[86] The IMF rolled over its stand-by loans. Debtors made progress on macroeconomic adjustment and structural reform. The banks worked to repair their balance sheets.

By 1987, Citibank was in a sufficiently strong capital position to acknowledge reality and set aside $3.3 billion as reserves in anticipation of future loses on its LDC loans. When no dire consequences followed—Citi's shares actually rose on the news—other banks followed. By the end of 1989, the money-center banks had set aside loan-loss provisions for half their LDC exposure.

## Back to Bonds

What these developments did not guarantee was that heavily indebted developing countries would regain market access and grow. These issues were finally addressed starting in 1989 by the Brady Plan, named after a subsequent US Treasury secretary, Nicholas Brady. Brady acknowledged that drawing a line under the crisis required not just provisioning for loans in arrears, but also removing nonperforming loans from the balance sheets of the banks and the national accounts of the borrowers. His formula was debt reduction for heavily indebted LDCs in return for structural adjustments to jump-start growth and enhance debt-servicing capacity. Whether growth would in fact be jump-started remained to be seen. After nearly a decade of crisis, it was at least worth trying.

LDC governments used funds raised from the IMF, the World Bank, and other donors to exchange their bank loans for bonds worth 50 to 70 cents on the dollar.[87] The banks went along because time had forced them to recognize that full repayment was unlikely, and because the new obligations seemed secure; the debtors used funds from the IMF and World Bank to purchase thirty-year zero-coupon US Treasury bonds, which were put aside to guarantee repayment in three decades.[88]

Mexico was the first country to take advantage of the Brady Plan, appropriately given that it had been the first to succumb to the crisis. Following, in alphabetical order, were Argentina, Brazil, Bulgaria, Costa Rica, the Dominican Republic, Ecuador, Ivory Coast, Jordan, Nigeria, Panama, Peru, the Philippines, Poland, Russia, Uruguay, Venezuela, and Vietnam. The length of this list is a reminder of the extent of the LDC debt crisis.

Wiping the slate clean, or at least wiping it clean of one-third of the debts of the eighteen Brady Plan countries, gave the participants a fresh start and restored their market access. Additionally, converting bank loans into securities raised the intriguing new possibility—also a very old possibility—of an international market in sovereign bonds.

The poorest countries, not having been on the receiving end of commercial loans, owed their debts instead to official creditors. Their intergovernmental debts were addressed, as they had been throughout the post–World War II era, by the Paris Club of creditor-country governments.[89] The Paris Club had restructured the debts of a series of developing-country sovereigns over the years. Now it was asked to restructure a large number all at once. Its initial concessions were criticized as inadequate, given the existence of a global debt crisis.[90] This led in 1988 to the "Toronto terms," providing for more generous debt reduction for the poorest countries.

In October 1988, Mali became the first country to restructure under the Toronto terms. Between 1989 and 1991, some twenty low-income countries then received Toronto-style debt reductions, averaging 33 percent of the inherited stock of debt.[91]

As for whether countries taking advantage of the Toronto terms would join their emerging market brethren in accessing the newly active international bond market, the world would find out soon enough.

# 10

# Oil and Water

It is tempting to think of the two decades ending with the Global Financial Crisis of 2008–9 as the calm before the storm. No advanced economy experienced serious debt and financial problems, in contrast to what happened next. But adopting this point of view would be to take a narrowly rich-country perspective. For emerging markets, it was more like the storm before the storm. From Mexico, Brazil, and Argentina to South Korea, Thailand, and Turkey, one country after another experienced serious debt-servicing problems, even crises, in these years.

This litany of woes encouraged the belief that sovereign debt and emerging markets were like oil and water. Emerging markets were "debt intolerant"; they could safely incur only limited amounts of debt.[1] They suffered from "original sin"; borrowing to fund public-sector deficits was risky because investors were reluctant to hold bonds denominated in emerging-market currencies.[2] It followed that instances where sovereign debt issuance was associated with successful state building and economic development were thin on the ground.

But just why emerging-market debt crises should have been so prevalent in the 1990s is not obvious. Debt was rising, to be sure, but so were exports and output (Figure 10.1). Public debt as a share of GDP actually trended downward in emerging markets and developing countries in the first half of the decade. It then remained broadly stable or only slightly rising in the decade's second half. The evolution of debt service as a share of exports was somewhat less favorable, but still far from disastrous.

In fact, the problem was not too much debt or some fundamental incompatibility of sovereign debt and emerging markets, but rather the failure of governments to adhere to some basic principles of prudent public debt management. Some of those principles were unfamiliar because they derived from relatively recent and still incompletely appreciated changes in the structure of finance, such as renewed activity in international bond markets. Others followed from equally recent changes in the policy environment, such as relaxation of

Debt-to-GDP ratio                                    Debt service-to-exports ratio

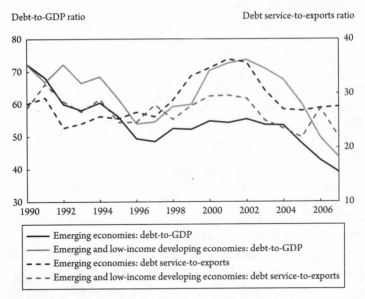

— Emerging economies: debt-to-GDP
— Emerging and low-income developing economies: debt-to-GDP
- - - Emerging economies: debt service-to-exports
- - - Emerging and low-income developing economies: debt service-to-exports

*Figure 10.1.* Debt-to-GDP and Debt Service-to-Export Ratios (percent)
Sources: IMF *World Economic Outlook* and authors' calculations.
Note: Simple averages for emerging and low-income developing economies. Country groups are based on IMF *World Economic Outlook* classifications.

capital controls. The principles in question were not entirely new and novel, since neither were the circumstances from which they flowed. They had precedents, in fact, in prior experience with sovereign finance. But they seemed new and novel to officials unschooled in this earlier history.

Though it may seem obvious, a short list of the principles in question would go like this. First, funding deficits with short-term debt is risky because the demand for debt securities can dry up abruptly. A government will then have to turn to the central bank to take up its new issuance, which will make for inflation and currency depreciation. This was a lesson learned by France and Italy in the 1920s, as we saw in Chapter 8. It was one that emerging-market policymakers did not now fully grasp because of the suddenness of the shift from syndicated bank loans, which were extended for as long as ten years, to intermediation by securities markets, where many of the securities in question matured in just thirty or ninety days.

Second, foreign-currency debt is risky. The sovereign's debt-servicing capacity will depend on its ability to generate foreign exchange receipts, which can fluctuate for reasons beyond its control. Neither was this observation entirely new: in the earlier era of bond finance, the vast majority of sovereigns, when seeking to borrow, had been forced to issue foreign-currency obligations and were exposed to the selfsame risks. Again, this was a lesson that emerging markets had to relearn from painful firsthand experience.

Three further corollaries flowed from these observations about the risks of short-term foreign-currency debt. First: a government that has foreign-currency-denominated liabilities should hold foreign-currency-denominated assets as a buffer stock. It should maintain foreign reserves sufficient to stay current on its debt-service obligations while also preserving the capacity to import essential goods and services in the worst-case scenario where its access to foreign finance is curtailed.

A standard rule of thumb suggests holding reserves sufficient to pay off all foreign debt scheduled to mature in the next twelve months and also to finance any ongoing current account deficit. This is known as "the Greenspan-Guidotti rule," following suggestions by Federal Reserve Chair Alan Greenspan and Argentine Treasury Minister Pablo Guidotti.[3] In practice, however, few emerging markets adhered to this guideline. Accumulating reserves required forgoing attractive consumption and investment opportunities. In addition, holding reserves was costly, since the yield on US Treasury bonds, the principal reserve asset, was lower than interest paid on the funds that governments borrowed.

Once they experienced the painful consequences of inadequate reserves—that is, after they experienced crises—emerging markets augmented their holdings (Figure 10.2). Better late than never, one might say. In some cases they augmented them so aggressively that the same critics who had previously cautioned against inadequate reserves now warned that reserve accumulation was excessive—that emerging markets were forgoing too many consumption and investment opportunities—and that they would be better off if they instead reduced their short-term foreign liabilities.[4]

Second, and closely related: governments should avoid volatile forms of debt, such as very short-term obligations that might have to be rolled over at much higher interest rates if market conditions change, or maybe that can't be rolled over at all. This point may seem straightforward, but its implementation was not. The temptation to load up on short-term debt was powerful when doing so offered immediate savings on borrowing costs. (It offered immediate savings because the yield curve typically slopes up; that is to say, investors require a higher interest rate if they must wait longer to get their principal back.)

Similarly, there could be pressure to sequence deregulation and capital account liberalization in ways that tilted the financial playing field toward more volatile forms of debt. One thinks of South Korea, where the authorities liberalized short-term capital flows because doing so favored the banks, which were then able to borrow from their foreign bank counterparts, in disregard of the fact that interbank lending is fickle.

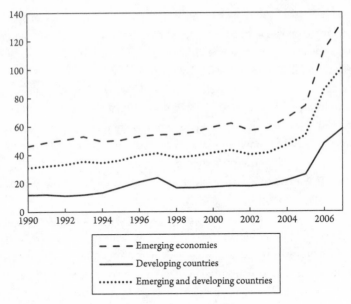

*Figure 10.2.* Foreign Reserves (percent of external debt)
Sources: World Bank *World Development Indicators* and authors' calculations.

Finally, governments should foster local markets in long-term debt securities. Some countries rely on foreign markets or short-term debt because they lack the reputation necessary to borrow long term at home. Others are compelled to issue foreign-currency debt because they lack the pension funds and insurance companies with domestic-currency-denominated liabilities for whom domestic-currency debt, which provides a matching income stream, is a natural investment. Still others lack the requisite brokers, dealers, and clearing and settlement systems. History shows that building deep and liquid secondary markets inhabited by a diverse population of individual and institutional investors, including locals, is a demanding task. And emerging market economies, with very few exceptions, started down this road only belatedly, in response to the crises of the 1990s.

A last point concerns local banks. When the bond market is shallow and borrowing is costly, it will be tempting to force-feed government bonds to the banks, requiring them to hold domestic debt securities to satisfy regulatory requirements. But when banks are required—or choose, in their wisdom—to hold domestic government bonds, anything that causes a fall in the prices of those bonds can threaten bank stability. In turn, this will worsen the condition of the economy and the government's own finances. Conversely, if banks encounter problems forcing them to engage in fire sales of government bonds, those sales will demoralize bond markets, while at the same time limiting the authorities' ability to backstop the financial system.

Eventually, these negative feedbacks became sufficiently notorious that they acquired their own name: following their devilish operation in the Euro Area debt crisis of 2008–10, they were dubbed the "diabolic loop."[5] Long before that, however, these dangerous connections were already evident in emerging markets, where the share of government bonds in commercial bank investment portfolios was more than double that in OECD countries, and where policymakers and regulators had ample opportunity to observe their destructive effects.[6] This point anticipates a more general lesson of the Global Financial Crisis and the Euro Area debt crisis, namely that what once were thought to be characteristic emerging-market debt problems were and are rather more general.

## Lessons in Debt Management

The 1994–95 Mexican crisis, also known as the "Tequila crisis," occupies a place of prominence in narratives of emerging-market crises of the 1990s, reflecting its precedence (Mexico was first), its evocative name (not every crisis is named after a country's national spirit), and how it encapsulated the debt-management problems also afflicting other countries.

The story has roots in the Mexican government's suspension of debt-service payments in 1982, the event that foreclosed capital market access for the better part of a decade.[7] For an economy that depended on petroleum exports, the 1986 collapse of world oil prices, noted in Chapter 9, was then a further blow. The peso fell sharply, causing import prices and, with them, wages to shoot up.

Faced with this crisis, the Mexican government negotiated an agreement with the representatives of labor, farm workers, and business, designed to re-balance the economy and spread the pain. As part of this Economic Solidarity Pact (*Pacto* in Spanish), monetary and fiscal policies were tightened to bring down inflation, and trade was liberalized in an effort to invigorate business. Labor for its part agreed to an incomes policy under which wages and prices were controlled. The plan worked in that inflation fell from 160 percent in 1987 to 20 percent in 1989. This stabilization and structural adjustment package allowed the country to qualify for its Brady Plan deal, restoring access to international financial markets.

But the *Pacto* contained a poison pill, namely the exchange-rate freeze that accompanied the wage and price freeze. (When wages and prices turned out to be incompletely frozen, the exchange-rate regime was later transformed into a crawling peg, under which the exchange rate crawled down against the dollar by roughly one peso a day.) Stabilizing the exchange rate was a useful expedient: it stopped the rise in import prices in its tracks and made domestic wage and price restraint easier to enforce. It broke the vicious spiral connecting currency depreciation to higher prices. By frontloading disinflation, it reassured financial markets. But it did not come with an exit strategy. It was not clear, in other words, whether the peg could be relaxed and greater exchange-rate flexibility could be reintroduced without also reintroducing questions about the authorities' commitment to disinflation.

This exchange-rate-based stabilization, like any exchange-rate-based stabilization, was fragile. The government had to subordinate monetary and fiscal policies to the imperative of stabilizing the exchange rate, disregarding other needs and the political pressure to pursue them. In addition, wages had to adjust, not only along with the exchange rate, but also in line with labor productivity. Specifically, the slower the growth of labor productivity, the slower the permissible rate of wage increase.

Mexico satisfied these conditions tolerably well through calendar year 1993. But starting in early 1994 the Mexican government began converting its peso-denominated debt, mainly in the form of *cetes* (medium-term Treasury certificates), into ninety-one-day dollar-linked *tesobonos*. Doing so was attractive to the government's debt managers because rates on *tesobonos* were only half those on *cetes*. This, then, was a classic instance of a government attempting to save on interest costs by giving in to the siren song of short-term foreign-currency debt. Investors in *tesobonos*, for their part, were protected from the possibility that the peso would depreciate and would get their money back in ninety-one days, assuming no untoward events. That said, the very fact that rates on dollar-indexed *tesobonos* were so much lower than those on nonindexed *cetes* suggested that currency depreciation was seen as a possibility and that the untoward was not inconceivable.

From negligible levels in early 1994, the stock of *tesobonos* rose to nearly $20 billion in August, at which point they exceeded the entirety of the Bank of Mexico's foreign exchange reserves. Whereas foreign investors at the end of 1993 had held mainly *cetes* and hardly any *tesobonos*, by late 1994 nearly 90 percent of their Mexican government debt holdings were in *tesobonos*.[8] This created an obvious pressure point: if foreign investors, for whatever reason, hesitated to buy new *tesobonos* when their existing holdings matured, the central bank would lack the reserves to provide the government with the resources to pay them off while also holding the exchange rate stable. Soon enough, this would provide a painful demonstration of the consequences of violating the Greenspan-Guidotti rule.[9]

Mexican officials, for the moment, adopted a "What, me worry?" attitude. They pointed to the fact that the public sector was running a primary budget surplus of 3.6 percent of GDP.[10] Public debt was just 30 percent of GDP, and the external debt ratio was less than 20 percent.[11] This is not to argue that all was copacetic; in particular, slow productivity growth was creating problems of international competitiveness.[12] But it is to argue that this was not a textbook crisis in which chronic budget deficits led to exploding debts.

In a sense, Mexico's problems were more political than economic; 1994 was an election year, which rendered the debt situation susceptible to political shocks. On January 1, the same day the North American Free Trade Agreement came into effect, the Zapatista movement launched an uprising in the state of Chiapas in the name of indigenous peoples and subsistence farmers. The candidate of the ruling Institutional Revolutionary Party (PRI), Luis Donaldo Colosio, was assassinated in March, possibly as a result of intraparty rivalry. This was followed by the assassination of a second prominent PRI member, José Francisco Ruiz Massieu, raising questions about the party's internal stability and ability to govern.

The political cycle also explains why the government's debt managers chose to shift from *cetes* to *tesobonos* at this time. Savings on interest costs that allowed additional resources to be diverted to other programs were a priority for a government facing an impending election.

As a result, Mexico had a big block of *tesobonos* maturing in the first quarter of 1995, reflecting the extent to which it relied on them in 1994. Investors had already begun moving assets out of the country in response to the Chiapas uprising and Colosio assassination, forcing the Bank of Mexico to buy pesos with dollars in order to prevent the exchange rate from weakening. Now, with the 1995 redemptions looming, investors asked, not unreasonably, whether the government had the dollars required to complete them while at the same time meeting other demands on its reserves.

The interregnum between an election and installation of a new government is always a period of heightened uncertainty—financially and otherwise. That interregnum now extended from August until December, during which time the central bank intervened extensively to prevent capital outflows from pushing up interest rates, reducing credit availability, and weakening the economy.[13] The Bank of Mexico used its dwindling dollar reserves to purchase peso-denominated securities, hoping to prevent their prices from falling and interest rates from rising (Figure 10.3).

This was the situation inherited by the new government of President Ernesto Zedillo, the Yale-educated economist who had replaced Colosio as PRI leader, on taking office on December 1. Two weeks later, the newly minted finance minister, Jaime Serra Puche (another Yale-educated economist), reiterated that the government would never devalue. Then, just five days after that, on being informed that the cupboard was bare, the cabinet conceded that devaluation was unavoidable. Investors were understandably led to question whether the new administration had a coherent strategy and whether it could be trusted to keep its promises. Panicked sales of pesos forced the central bank to commit half of

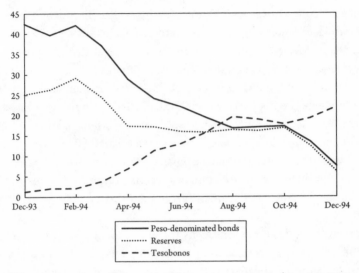

*Figure 10.3.* Mexican Foreign Reserves and Government Bonds (monthly, billions of US dollars)

Source: Secretaría de Hacienda y Crédito Público, as cited by Cole and Kehoe (1996).

its remaining reserves to supporting the exchange rate at its new lower level and then, this intervention not having worked, to float the currency.

Out of options, Mexican officials opened emergency negotiations with the US Treasury and the IMF. By the end of January 1995, Mexico was in receipt of $20 billion of emergency funding from the US Treasury, $18 billion from the IMF, $10 billion from the BIS, and $3 billion from commercial banks. A portion of this funding was used to pay off the maturing *tesobonos*. This alone was not enough to stem the flight out of other government securities or allow the exchange rate to recover, however. Distress now spread from the market in government securities to the banking system as the diabolic loop was activated. Mexican banks holding government bonds in order to satisfy their capital requirements saw the prices of those securities crater. Interest rates having risen and the exchange rate having fallen, bank borrowers fell into arrears.[14] Adding to the banks' woes, the weaker exchange rate rendered them unable to repay dollars they had borrowed abroad.[15]

An additional portion of the emergency loan from the IMF, BIS, and US Treasury therefore went to recapitalizing the banks, which were able to reimburse US financial institutions that had provided dollar funding. This was a happy outcome for the US banks, less so for their Mexican counterparts and the government south of the border. Recapitalizing and restructuring the banks cost Mexico 14 percent of its GDP, which in turn increased the public debt by half.[16] Mexican output, meanwhile, declined by 10 percent in the first half of 1995.

All this could have been avoided, or at least its impact could have been minimized, had government debt managers resisted the lure of short-term foreign-currency debt.

## Implicit Commitments

Nor did the next upheaval, the Asian crisis of 1997–98, fit the textbook model. The crisis erupted in Thailand in July 1997 and peaked with South Korea's critical funding problems at the end of the year.[17] Although Thailand's economic and financial weaknesses were no secret, the intensity of the crisis still came as a surprise. For Korea, with its seemingly robust export-oriented economy, the surprise was that there was a crisis at all.

On paper, the Thai and Korean governments were in strong fiscal shape. Thailand's budget, inclusive of interest payments, was in surplus to the tune of 3 percent of GDP in 1994–95 and 1 percent of GDP in 1996.[18] External debt was just 10 percent of GDP, while domestic debt was negligible. Korea's consolidated budget was in surplus throughout the 1994–96 period. Domestic public debt at the end of 1996 was just 8 percent of GDP, external debt just 6 percent. Inflation in both countries was moderate. Neither Thailand nor Korea had a recent history of sovereign debt problems.

Rather, these countries' difficulties centered on the private sector's excessive reliance on short-term, foreign-currency debt. Thus, even though the locus of the problem was different—unlike in Mexico, it originated in the private sector—its fundamental character, namely the mismatch between short-term liabilities and long-term investments, was the same. In any case, what started out in the private sector didn't stay in the private sector, since the public sector ended up socializing private debt. Asian governments had essentially guaranteed the investment activities, including loss-making investment activities, of banks and corporations that borrowed to carry out the government's development objectives. Those guarantees were, in essence, implicit or disguised fiscal costs that existed before the fact but materialized on the sovereign's balance sheet only when the crisis struck.[19]

In contrast to Mexico, which had placed its *tesobonos* with investors far and wide, Asian countries such as Thailand and South Korea relied on their banks as all-but-exclusive conduits for foreign borrowing. This difference reflected the heavily bank-based nature of Asian financial systems. The banks mobilized funding and lent to enterprises and sectors that their governments regarded as strategic—enterprises and sectors, it so happened, that were well connected politically. For many years, this economic development model was highly successful. The results weren't called the Asian miracle for nothing.

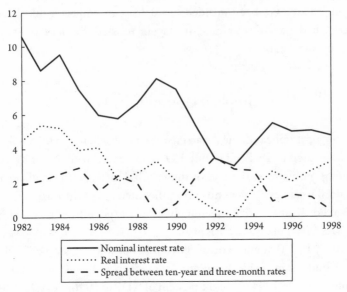

*Figure 10.4.* Interest rates in the United States, 1982–98 (percent)

Source: Bloomberg.

Note: Nominal interest rate is three-month rate. Real interest rate is three-month rate minus consumer-price inflation.

The banks obtained their funding on the wholesale market—that is to say, they borrowed large sums at short term from US, Japanese, and European banks. Interest rates in the United States and globally declined in the course of the 1990s (Figure 10.4), encouraging US banks in particular to look abroad to put their idle funds to work.[20] Thailand had eased restrictions on its banks' overseas borrowing starting in 1990. In 1993 it then established the Bangkok International Banking Facilities (BIBF), which all but eliminated remaining restrictions, with the goal of transforming Bangkok into an Asian financial center and its banks into regional leaders.[21] In Korea, the goal was not so much to transform Seoul into a regional financial center, although there was an element of this, as it was to give the country's large conglomerates, or *chaebol*, which conveniently owned the principal merchant banks, a ready source of funding without also requiring them to share control with foreign investors.

The resulting rise in short-term indebtedness was general: the ratio of short-term debt to reserves rose sharply across East Asia in the period ending in 1997. The share of short-term debt in total indebtedness rose from 20 percent in 1990 to 32 percent in 1996; as a share of foreign reserves, it rose from 124 percent in 1990 to 153 percent in 1996, and then to 214 percent in 1997.[22] Again, the rule that short-term indebtedness should not exceed central banks' reserve cover was observed only in the breach.

East Asian commercial and investment banks then turned around and lent the money they sourced abroad to corporations and real estate developers with which they were connected. It mattered little in what currency the loan was denominated. If access to foreign finance dried up and the local currency crashed, then the banks that had lent to local clients in baht or won would be unable to repay their borrowed dollars, since local-currency interest payments wouldn't cover the obligation. But if the banks lent dollars, then construction companies and other firms lacking dollar receivables would be unable to repay, and the banks' nonperforming loans would skyrocket.

Nor could the official sector help if things went wrong. The Bank of Thailand had committed a substantial portion of its foreign reserves to intervening in the foreign exchange market in support of the baht (intervention that proved futile when the currency collapsed). In fact, only the foreign investment banks that advised the central bank and booked its currency trades knew the true extent of these commitments. Rather than advertising the fact, or even alerting the Thai authorities of the risks, they sought to capitalize on their proprietary knowledge by shorting the baht.[23]

Korea's situation was little better. The Bank of Korea's usable reserves were less than $30 billion at the end of 1996, not even 40 percent of the short-term dollar debts of the corporate and banking sectors. As strains mounted, the central bank deposited dollars in the overseas branches of Korean banks so they could repay their dollar borrowings. In an attempt to reassure the markets, the Bank of Korea reported only its total reserves, including these deposits, and not also its usable reserves. Such information when withheld has an unfortunate tendency to leak. This effort to reassure investors only gave rise to rumors that the situation was even worse than it appeared.

## Debt in Service of the State

There is some disagreement about exactly what triggered the crisis. Precipitating factors included the property boom and bust (more than 40 percent of housing units in Bangkok built between 1992 and 1996 were unoccupied in 1997). They included a strengthening US dollar, which damaged Asian countries' export competitiveness (since Thailand pegged to the dollar, while Korea pegged to a basket in which the dollar had a heavy weight). They included weakness in the global market for semiconductors, an important Korean export and up-and-coming sector in Thailand.

At a deeper level, it could be argued that the problem was that the East Asian model had run its course. Governments were too slow to move from bank- to market-based financial systems and from growth based on capital investment to growth based on innovation. In this view, the crisis was the inevitable chickens coming home to roost.

Whatever the cause, the same financial capital that had flooded in now flooded out. Local banks that sourced finance on the wholesale interbank market were suddenly locked out, forcing their governments to intervene to prevent their collapse. Paying off the creditors and recapitalizing and restructuring the banks cost the South Korean and Thai governments dearly. More precisely, it cost them 24 percent and 35 percent of GDP, respectively.[24] That these amounts were multiples of earlier recapitalization costs in Mexico reflected the Asian economies' heavy reliance on bank finance.

In Korea, roughly a quarter of the public funds in question were used to settle deposit insurance obligations and provide liquidity to distressed financial institutions, thereby ensuring that the creditors got their money back. The rest went for recapitalization and purchases of nonperforming loans. Although Thailand didn't have a formal system of deposit insurance, the government, when suspending forty-two finance companies in August 1997, issued a blanket guarantee of all deposits and balances in banks and nonbank financial firms, since doing otherwise might have precipitated a panic. The Financial Institutions Development Fund (FIDF), an independent agency of the central bank, lent money to these troubled institutions to enable them to pay off their depositors.[25]

The challenge was doing all this quickly, in a manner that did not entail inflation and a collapsing currency. Issuing domestic debt was feasible only to a very limited extent, given the damaged balance sheets of domestic financial institutions and the shock to confidence. Even before getting there, there was the problem of paying off the banks' foreign creditors, since the Bank of Korea and Bank of Thailand lacked dollars, and the US and Japanese banks whose loans were maturing had every reason to cut and run.[26]

It followed that much of the new debt now incurred was debt to the IMF, which mobilized the largest rescue packages in its fifty-year history (Figure 10.5). South Korea's needs were so large that IMF funds were supplemented by the World Bank, the Asian Development Bank, and advanced-country governments that provided the so-called second line of defense. US and Japanese banks, responding to pressure from their governments, agreed to restructure a portion of their Korean clients' short-term debts, pushing maturities out into the future, albeit at punitive interest rates.

With their dollar debts addressed, governments could turn to recapitalizing and restructuring the banks. They did so by incurring yet additional debt. The Korea Asset Management Corporation (KAMCO), a government agency, purchased nonperforming loans from the banks in exchange for guaranteed bonds, giving the banks liquid assets with which to rebuild their balance sheets. Since KAMCO overpaid when making its purchases, this was not just liquidity

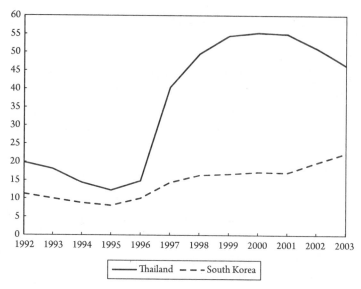

*Figure 10.5.* Debt-to-GDP Ratio for Thailand and South Korea (percent)
Source: IMF *World Economic Outlook* and authors' calculations.
Note: Annual data for general government debt.

support for the banks; it was stealth recapitalization, which helps to explain why public debt as a share of GDP soared.[27] The same scenario played out in Thailand, which established a Property Loan Management Organization to purchase problem real estate loans from banks and finance companies, supposedly at market but in many cases above prevailing prices, and which raised funds by issuing bonds backed by Ministry of Finance guarantees.

There was justifiable criticism of the two governments for having allowed these problems to arise, and much handwringing over the cost of the subsequent bank bailouts. There was criticism too of the IMF for demanding extensive restructuring of the corporate and financial sectors as a condition for its loans, despite the two economies' records of successful growth. The Korean and Thai economies contracted by 5 and 8 percent, respectively, in 1998, under the weight of these problems. But by 1999 both countries were growing again. That the authorities moved quickly to restructure the banking and financial sectors goes a long way toward explaining this early recovery.

No experience better illustrates the two aspects of debt. Excessive borrowing by the private sector, to advance its own aims but also those of the state, set the stage for these two countries' financial crises. Subsequently, the capacity to issue debt played a key role in enabling their governments to restore the health of the corporate and financial sectors so their economies could begin growing again. What debt took with one hand, it gave back with the other.

## Local Market Development as a Policy Response

The 1990s saw the reintegration of emerging markets into the global financial system. Latin American governments, building on their experience with Brady bonds, once more tapped international bond markets, while Asian countries, where financial systems were bank-based, accessed the global interbank market. Neither experience ended happily. Mexico, and eventually also Brazil and Argentina, saw the initial influx of foreign funding give way to capital flight. In Thailand, South Korea, and other Asian countries, what had been ready access to the interbank market dried up abruptly, bringing down the financial system and, with it, the economy.

These episodes were reminders that, even when its level is moderate, debt must be prudently managed. Maturities should be lengthened; short-term debt subject to rollover risk should be shunned. Foreign currency debt should be hedged, either naturally with exports or by holding adequate foreign reserves. Allowing banks to borrow offshore, short-term, in foreign currency is the riskiest practice of all, since it exposes the banks, and by implication the government and the economy, to a combination of vulnerabilities. In particular, bank debt exposes the government to large contingent liabilities insofar as the authorities can't allow the banking system to collapse, for the health of the economy and because the banks, in effect, are carrying out the government's bidding.

In the wake of these unhappy experiences, policymakers in Asia and Latin America made concerted efforts to develop local-currency bond markets as a way of supplementing foreign-currency borrowing and bank intermediation. Alan Greenspan, speaking metaphorically, referred to local-currency bond markets as a "spare tire." Asian officials took the metaphor to heart.[28] In 2002, the Association of Southeast Asian Nations, together with Korea, China, and Japan, launched an Asian Bond Market Initiative. This sought to develop local-currency bond markets in coordinated fashion, with harmonized regulation and integrated regional infrastructure. Latin America, Eastern Europe, Africa, and the Middle East moved more slowly and were less ambitious in attempting to harmonize regulation and infrastructure at the regional level, but they too made progress in developing the capacity to issue local-currency debt. In particular, better monetary policies and stronger central banks, which made inflation less of a threat, rendered local-currency denomination more attractive.

But issuing debt in local currency did not solve all problems. Where a diverse investor base was absent, secondary market liquidity (as measured by bid-ask spreads or turnover) was low. If a subset of investors sought to exit their positions, bond prices could move by a lot, with destabilizing consequences.

Where the local market was dominated by a single type of investor—banks in Turkey or nonbank firms in India, for example—members of that single class, all finding themselves in the same position, might seek to exit at the same time, again with destabilizing consequences. In countries where banks were the dominant investors in government bonds, the authorities had not actually freed themselves from their reliance on those banks as conduits for their borrowing. To the contrary, the problems of the banks could quickly become problems for the government, especially in circumstances where the banks were forced to pare down their portfolios in order to raise liquidity. Equally, problems with the debt could quickly become problems for the banks if the latter were heavily invested in government bonds.[29]

Nor had emerging-market governments, by developing local bond markets, freed themselves of foreign investors. Their debt securities might now be denominated in the local currency and sold on local markets, but the purchasers were still heavily, and in some cases almost entirely, foreign institutional investors, reflecting the continuing challenges of developing a domestic investor base. (Figure 10.6 shows the dominance, on the eve of the Global Financial Crisis, of foreign investors in the debt of a selection of emerging markets.) Policymakers had long been concerned that foreign investors, less than fully informed about the state of the economy, might attempt to infer its condition from the behavior of other investors, and that their herding would accentuate market volatility. Now that debts were denominated in the currencies of emerging market sovereigns, this problem was even worse. If anything went wrong, foreigners

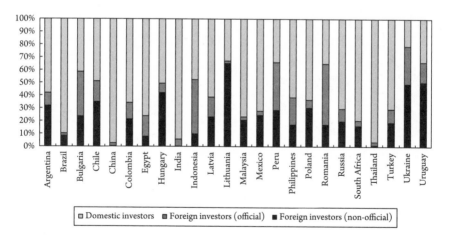

*Figure 10.6.* Investor Base of Emerging Market General Government Debt, End-2007Q4 (percent of total)

Source: IMF Sovereign Investor Base Dataset for Emerging Markets (IMF 2021).

were exposed to the double whammy of declining bond prices and, on top of that, a declining exchange rate.[30] By threatening to further reduce the value of their claims, that declining exchange rate only heightened their worries and their incentive to scramble out of the market at the first sign of trouble.

The implication was that shifting from foreign- to local-currency debt afforded less than the hoped-for protection. Governments were assured of safety only if they avoided worrisome economic and financial conditions in the first place, something that was easier said than done.

# Missed Opportunities

Compared to the spectacular series of crises in emerging markets, debt developments in the advanced economies were less sensational. Still, the decades spanning the turn of the century were remarkable when seen through the lens of public debt. In Japan, where the economy was mired in recession and deflation, central government debt shot up from below 50 percent of GDP in 1992 to nearly 140 percent in 2007.[1] Such a rapid run-up was astonishing in what was traditionally a low-debt economy. It was one of the largest percentage-point increases in the debt-to-GDP ratio witnessed anywhere, outside of wartime, in a span of fifteen years.[2] These new higher levels challenged Japanese debt managers. They challenged conventional notions of how much debt was sustainable.

Even while Japan was taking on unprecedented levels of debt, the United States was retiring its obligations. The federal government's debt-to-GDP ratio fell steadily between 1993 and 2001. However improbable it may now seem, the possibility that the debt might be extinguished and the market in US Treasury bonds would disappear was actively mooted. Participants in the Treasury market, the *New York Times* reported in April 2001, "are seeing the end of Treasuries—at least temporarily—as inevitable."[3] This, in turn, raised a number of thorny issues that pointed to the utility of public debt. Because Treasury bonds were the safe asset on whose basis corporate, agency, mortgage, and other asset-backed securities were priced, new benchmarks would have to be agreed for these markets. Hedging to reduce risk would have to be done with other securities. Investors would have to find another liquid asset to serve as a safe harbor in a storm.[4]

We now know that these anxieties were exaggerated, to put it mildly. After falling in the 1990s, the federal government's debt ratio turned around in 2001. But this development itself only raised further questions. Why were the same political economy forces that allowed steady reductions in the debt ratio no longer sustained after the turn of the century? For that matter, what exactly were the factors that had supported debt reduction in this earlier period? Did observed outcomes reflect a favorable political constellation leading to supportive policies, or simple good luck? And if the answer was supportive policies, what had changed?

In Europe, meanwhile, the 1990s were dominated by preparations for the euro. Among those preparations was reducing debts and deficits so that the newly created European Central Bank would not be subject to "fiscal dominance"—so that it would not feel pressure to keep interest rates low to help member states finance their deficits and service their debts. Debt and deficit reduction were therefore made prerequisites for any country qualifying for membership in Europe's monetary union. Membership being a valued political and economic objective, actual debt and deficit reduction followed. The question, however, was whether this trajectory, too, would be reversed after the turn of the century, once membership was achieved.

The period ending in 2007 may have lacked drama in the advanced economies, but it did not lack consequences. Economic expansion in the United States and Europe was sustained by substituting private debt for public debt. It followed that risks were not eliminated; all that changed was their locus. Specifically, if problems developed in financial markets, governments might come under pressure to socialize private debts, causing public debt levels to explode. The situation would then resemble that in East Asia in the 1990s. And this, of course, is just what happened in starting in 2008.

## Land of the Rising Debts

As its contribution to the Plaza Accord (the 1985 agreement between France, Germany, the United States, the United Kingdom, and Japan intended to rein in an overly strong dollar), the Japanese government agreed to intervene in the foreign exchange market to strengthen the yen.[5] It succeeded beyond its wildest dreams.

By the end of 1986, the yen had appreciated by nearly 50 percent against the greenback.[6] Predictably, this sharp appreciation interrupted the growth of exports and GDP. The Bank of Japan responded by cutting policy interest rates by 100 basis points and holding them at their new lower level.[7] To get the economy moving, it encouraged commercial banks to lend. It encouraged them to do so despite bank capital being lower than in other advanced countries and that a few loan losses could therefore undermine their solvency.[8] Such are the hazards of relying on the banking system for policy implementation, as other Asian countries also learned to their chagrin.

The result was an enormous credit and asset-price boom. The situation was not unlike the subsequent position of Mexico in 1994 or Thailand and South Korea in 1997, where the authorities also relied on cheap credit to keep an expansion going. But there was a twist. Once Japanese regulators relaxed restrictions on corporate bond issuance in the mid-1980s, the banks lost their lucrative corporate customers. Searching for new clients, they found them in homebuyers and real estate developers. Between 1985 and 1989, lending to the property sector rose twice as fast as the overall increase in bank credit to private borrowers. Land prices tripled, and other asset valuations rose in sympathy.

This was the "bubble economy" of which observers took note starting in 1988.[9] Among those observers were policymakers at the Bank of Japan, who reacted—some would say overreacted—by raising the bank's discount rate three times in 1989 and twice more in 1990. On cue, the bubble burst, compressing spending and causing bank loans to go bad. The Cabinet Office's Economic and Social Research Institute (ESRI) dated the subsequent recession as starting in February 1991.

Economic prospects would have been brighter had regulators promptly restructured and recapitalized the banks, which were in increasingly dire shape. But having worked hand-in-glove with the government in the years of "miracle growth," the country's well-connected bankers resisted being restructured out of business. Instead of being forced to acknowledge their losses and recapitalize, the banks were allowed to roll over (or "evergreen") their loans. As their weak balance sheets remained weak, they were then in no position to accommodate new borrowers.

To the extent that there was support for the economy, it came from fiscal policy. Earlier oscillations in monetary policy had not been helpful, and policymakers now feared that another round of monetary easing would fuel another bubble, followed by another crash. They worried that monetary stimulus, by causing the yen to depreciate, would reignite trade tensions with the United States; they had not forgotten that similar tensions led to the ill-fated Plaza Accord. So, instead, the Diet agreed to successive fiscal stimulus packages starting in 1993. By 1996 the general government budget, in balance as recently as 1992, had moved into deficit to the tune of 5 percent of GDP. Gross public debt as a share of GDP approached 100 percent.

At this point, the authorities grew anxious about the mounting debt. In response, they raised the consumption tax rate from 3 to 5 percent, which halted recovery in its tracks.[10] This experience foreshadowed the dynamic that would characterize the next quarter century of Japanese policy: crisis, fiscal stimulus, green shoots of growth, fiscal consolidation, and renewed crisis.[11] Rinse and repeat.

Budget deficits were responsible, in an accounting sense, for two-thirds of the increase in the debt ratio between 1991 and 2007, as shown in Table 11.1. Still, it was not so much excessive reliance on fiscal policy that caused Japan's debt-to-GDP ratio to explode but, rather, the reverse. Every time the economy showed

*Table 11.1* **Decomposition of Debt Accumulation in Japan, 1991–2007**

|  | Debt-to-GDP Ratio (percent) | | | Contribution to Increase (percent) | | |
|---|---|---|---|---|---|---|
|  | Starting Level | Ending Level | Increase | Primary Balance | Interest- Growth Differential | Stock-Flow Adjustment |
| Gross debt | 63.5 | 175.4 | 111.9 | 66.6 | 38.1 | 7.2 |
| Net debt | 17.6 | 97.6 | 80.0 | 66.6 | 13.5 | –0.2 |

*Sources:* IMF *World Economic Outlook* Database (IMF various years) and authors' calculations.

*Note:* Debt increase is calculated using the exact years in the period, i.e., the change in the debt ratio between the start year (1991) and end year (2007).

signs of recovering, the government closed the fiscal tap. Growth slumped, revenues cratered, and the deficit ratio rose.[12] Policymakers then put their collective feet back on the fiscal accelerator with even more force. At the end of the day, the debt ratio was higher than it would have been with a steadily expansionary fiscal policy.

The 1990s saw no alarming acceleration in the growth of government spending, consistent with this interpretation. The trend rate of increase of spending remained almost exactly unchanged from the preceding fifteen years.[13] What changed was the revenue side of the general government budget, which had been rising along with spending but now fell, growth having collapsed.[14]

Strikingly, even while the debt was rising, interest rates on Japanese government bonds (JGBs) were falling. This was exactly the opposite of what one would ordinarily expect when a country was running up historic levels of debt. JGB yields moved down from 7 percent in 1990 to 3 percent in 1994–95 and just 1.5 percent in 1997–98 before leveling off.[15] This fall in interest rates was what ensured the sustainability of Japan's now much heavier debt. It was, as Table 11.1 shows, why the interest-rate–growth-rate differential explained only a fraction of the increase in indebtedness between 1991 and 2007 despite the wholesale collapse of growth.[16]

The question is why interest rates weren't higher. Part of the answer lies in the distinction between gross and net debt (both shown in Figure 11.1). Institutional investors understood that the Japanese government held more than ¥200 trillion of securities (the equivalent of $2 trillion, or more than 40 percent of Japanese GDP).[17] It held ¥40 trillion of cash, along with real estate that could be sold or leased to help pay down debt.[18] The income on those assets explains the contrast, in Table 11.1, between the 120 percent rise in gross debt from 1991 to 2007 and the smaller 80 percent rise in net debt.[19]

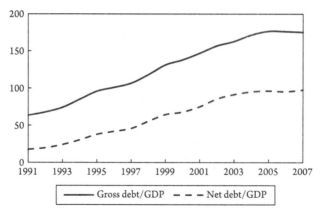

*Figure 11.1.* Gross and Net Debt-to-GDP Ratios in Japan, Annual, 1991–2007 (percent)
Source: IMF *World Economic Outlook.*

High savings further help to explain Japan's low interest rates. Although incomes rose more slowly in the 1990s than before, private spending rose more slowly still. The result was further expansion of the savings pool. The current account of the balance of payments, which measures the excess of saving over investment, widened after 1990.[20] Although household savings rates, traditionally high, trended gently downward, their decline was more than offset by rising corporate saving, as increasingly cautious corporate management responded to the slump by scaling back investment and building financial buffers.

As for where all this saving might go, the Nikkei 225, which lost more than 60 percent of its value between 1990 and 1999, was unattractive. Corporate bonds looked little better, given the difficulties of business. This left government bonds. More than 95 percent of the outstanding stock of JGBs was held domestically, by individuals who invested directly and through mutual funds and investment trusts, and by government-owned banks, public and private pension funds, and insurance companies with domestic-currency-denominated liabilities. The willingness of Japanese investors to hold their own government's bonds was also linked to the fact that the population, including the population of bondholders, was aged. Not only do the aged appreciate the predictability of the interest paid on fixed-interest securities, but they vote in disproportionate numbers. The implication was that the electorate would vote out of office a government that failed to preserve the value of their bonds. This echoes a pattern apparent in earlier chapters, that giving voice to the bondholders supports the market in sovereign debt.

In discussing the Great Depression, we saw how weak fiscal stimulus and on-again-off-again policies extended the slump and ended up raising debt ratios rather than reducing them. We saw how these policies produced the peculiar conjunction of rising debts and falling interest rates. Japan in the 1990s was another instance of the same phenomenon. These unsettling trends in indebtedness would persist and even accelerate. After the turn of the century, it was up, up, and away for debt, and down still further for interest rates, first in Japan and then in other countries.

## Rubinomics

Figure 11.2 displays general government debt as a share of GDP for the United States, together with debt service as a share of revenues. It shows the debt ratio rising in the 1970s and 1980s, peaking in 1993, and then heading back down. That ratio reached a modern low in 2000–2001, at levels not seen since 1984–85. This was the point where economists began discussing the financial implications of the disappearance of US Treasury debt.

That the 1993 peak in the debt ratio coincided with the inauguration of William Jefferson Clinton encourages the belief that credit goes to the budget-balancing instincts of President Clinton and his National Economic Council chair and subsequently Treasury secretary, Robert Rubin. In fact, concern with budget deficits had been mounting since the late 1960s, as explained in Chapter 9. Subsequent developments only heightened such worries. Medicare costs had risen further. The Social Security Trust Fund had deteriorated, reflecting the fact that virtually the entire population now reaching retirement age

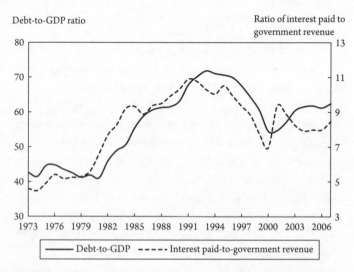

*Figure 11.2.* Debt and Interest Burden Indicators for the United States, Annual, 1973–2006 (percent)

Sources: IMF Historical Public Finance Database (IMF 2013) and authors' calculations.

had been covered by Social Security for all of its work history, making for higher benefits.[21] The Committee for a Responsible Federal Budget, an advocacy group focused on reining in debts and deficits, was established in 1981, giving voice to the growing sense of unease.

Notwithstanding pressure to act, President Ronald Reagan and his supporters refused to contemplate increases in taxation, while congressional Democrats resisted de-indexing Social Security, limiting Medicare benefits, and cutting other social spending. The Gramm-Rudman-Hollings Balanced Budget and Emergency Deficit Control Act of 1985 attempted to break this deadlock by requiring uniform reductions in spending if the two sides failed to agree on balancing the budget. It mandated across-the-board cuts ("budget sequestration") if discretionary fiscal appropriations exceeded allowable levels.[22] Sequestration was intended to be so distasteful as to force agreement between the parties on more nuanced cuts. Senator Warren Rudman referred to it as "a bad idea whose time has come."[23]

Initially, gimmicks such as overly optimistic assumptions about economic growth were used to circumvent Gramm-Rudman-Hollings's distasteful implications. As shown in Table 11.2, the debt-to-GDP ratio continued to rise between the act's adoption and Clinton's election in 1992. Primary deficits persisted, and interest rates continued to exceed growth rates. Both factors fed the rise in debt.

But with recession in 1990 and the ensuing collapse of revenues, gimmicks no longer sufficed. Across-the-board spending cuts remained unpalatable to Democrats, however, while higher taxes were anathema to Republicans. At this point sequestration, desired by neither side, threatened to kick in. President George H. W. Bush and congressional leaders therefore drew up a budget that combined limited spending reductions with limited tax increases (requiring

*Table 11.2* **Decomposition of Debt Accumulation in the United States, 1984–92**

| Period | Debt-to-GDP Ratio (percent) | | | Contribution to Increase (percent) | | |
|---|---|---|---|---|---|---|
| | Starting Level | Ending Level | Increase | Primary Balance | Interest-Growth Differential | Stock-Flow Adjustment |
| 1984–92 | 50.9 | 70.7 | 19.8 | 11.4 | 9.6 | −1.1 |

*Sources:* IMF *World Economic Outlook* Database (IMF various years) and authors' calculations.

*Note:* Debt increase is calculated using the exact years in the period, i.e., the change in the debt ratio between the start year (1984) and end year (1992).

Bush to abandon his campaign pledge of "Read my lips: no new taxes" and causing him, arguably, to lose the 1992 election to Clinton).

Conservative Republicans, led by Representative Newt Gingrich, opposed the tax increases, however, and defeated the bill. Lacking a budget, the federal government shut down in October. Faced with this crisis (a government on hiatus and a looming war in Iraq), the parties reached a compromise in November. The Republicans accepted additional taxes but only on high earners, while the Democrats agreed to spending restraint. Negotiators replaced current cuts in social programs, which would have been an embarrassing climb-down for the Democrats, with a commitment to future spending restraint. The latter entailed targets for the spending growth, where permissible levels rose more slowly than inflation. Further increases in spending were subject to "pay as you go rules" that required either additional taxes or compensatory reductions in other programs.

The 1990 Budget Enforcement Act worked better than Gramm-Rudman-Hollings. Instead of committing Congress to a set of headline numbers while allowing the details to be fiddled, the 1990 act specified rules to be followed and actions to be taken. It delegated responsibility for forecasting growth and the deficit to the nonpartisan Congressional Budget Office (CBO) and the Office of Management and Budget. The CBO projected that the 1990 act would reduce the federal deficit by $500 billion over five years, a forecast that proved broadly correct. The deficit reduction delivered by this act was thus an inheritance, not an achievement, of the Clinton administration.

## The New Economy

If the 1990 budget act helped to narrow the deficit in the first half of the 1990s, then faster productivity growth did so in its second. Economists Stephen Oliner and Daniel Sichel document how productivity growth accelerated after 1995.[24] Total factor productivity growth, they show, rose from 1.2 percent per annum in 1990–95 to 3.1 percent in 1995–99. Productivity accounted for more than three-quarters of the acceleration in GDP growth between the decade's first and second halves.[25] This was the so-called New Economy: efficiency improvements in sectors producing computers, other information-technology (IT) products, and to a lesser extent consumer durables. Efficiency gains were also realized in wholesale trade, retail trade, and financial services, which were among the first sectors to capitalize on these IT advances.

Budget deficits shrank further as faster growth arrived on the scene. Federal government revenues rose by 1.2 percent for every additional 1 percent of GDP growth.[26] Meanwhile, spending was still subject to the 1990 budget caps; it therefore grew more slowly than revenues. Much of the post-1996 improvement

in the fiscal position was attributable to this faster growth, along with a disproportionate share of income gains accruing to high earners who were subject to
high marginal tax rates.[27]

How much credit for this achievement should go to Clinton and Rubin?
"Rubinomics" involved trading fiscal consolidation for a more accommodating
Federal Reserve policy. This policy mix, it is argued in retrospective accounts,
including Robert Rubin's own, boosted investment in new technologies, stimulating growth and thereby reducing the debt-to-GDP ratio.[28] By this interpretation, the acceleration in productivity growth after 1995 was not fortuitous; it
was a byproduct of the Clinton-Rubin strategy of combining fiscal restraint with
investment-friendly interest rates.

Not all the evidence is consistent with this narrative. It is true that real interest
rates on Treasury securities were lower in the second Clinton term than in the
1980s. (The 1980s, recall, was a period of high interest rates, when Fed chair
Volcker was working to wring inflation out of the economy.) But the same is not
true of rates on corporate bonds that are relevant to private financing and investment decisions. In fact, there was only a limited uptick in investment, larger perhaps than the uptick at the comparable stage of the business cycle in the 1980s,
but smaller than at the same stage of the cycle in the 1970s.[29] As Table 11.3 shows,
the interest-rate–growth-rate differential that captures the effects of Rubinomics
(the effects of lower interest rates in encouraging investment and thereby growth)
contributed essentially nothing to fiscal consolidation in this period.

The one stretch when Clinton administration initiatives helped in narrowing
the budget deficit and slowing the growth of debt was between 1994 and 1996.
The administration's 1993 tax legislation raised the top marginal personal income tax rate from 31 percent to 42 percent and expanded the alternative minimum tax paid by high earners. As a result, the budget deficit realized in 1996
was $200 billion (2.5 percent of GDP) less than forecast by the CBO in January

*Table 11.3* **Decomposition of Debt Consolidation in the United States,
1993–2001**

| Period | Debt-to-GDP Ratio (percent) | | | Contribution to Decrease (percent) | | |
|---|---|---|---|---|---|---|
| | Starting Level | Ending Level | Decrease | Primary Balance | Growth-Interest Differential | Stock-Flow Adjustment |
| 1993–2001 | 72.4 | 54.7 | 17.7 | 15.6 | −3.3 | 5.4 |

*Sources:* IMF *World Economic Outlook* Database (IMF various years) and authors' calculations.

*Note:* Debt decline is calculated using the exact years in the period, i.e., the change in the debt ratio
between the start year (1993) and end year (2001).

1993.[30] In subsequent revisions, the CBO attributed the majority of that improvement to the 1993 budget act.

## Starve the Beast

In hindsight, worries that these developments would lead to extinction of US government debt seem almost quaint. Starting in 2001, federal government debt started rising again, and sharply, reaching 62 percent of GDP in 2007. The George W. Bush administration passed three major pieces of debt-augmenting tax legislation in its first three years. The 2001 tax cut phased in reductions in income tax rates, reduced and ultimately repealed the estate tax, and added tax breaks for saving, education, families with children, and married couples. The 2002 act cut taxes on new business investment, while the 2003 tax cut reduced the taxation of dividends and capital gains.[31]

On the spending side, fiscal years 2002–5 saw a 19 percent increase in real outlays.[32] Although entitlement spending contributed in a minor way, more important was discretionary spending, which rose by a cumulative 28 percent, more rapidly than in any presidency since that of Lyndon Baines Johnson. Defense spending rose faster than under any president back to and including LBJ, who had occupied the White House during the Vietnam War.[33] Nondefense discretionary spending rose by 21 percent; comparable figures had not been seen since the Nixon administration. This was a sharp change from Clinton, in whose two terms nondefense discretionary spending had been flat.[34]

The Bush administration's reductions in top income and estate tax rates were consistent with constituent self-interest. The Republicans held a ten-point advantage in party identification among individuals in the top 20 percent of the income distribution.[35] The idea that tax cuts would pay for themselves was deeply ingrained in the party's DNA. Specifically, it was deeply ingrained in the Bush administration's DNA. Vice President Dick Cheney and Defense Secretary Donald Rumsfeld were both present at the 1974 dinner at the Two Continents Hotel in Washington, DC, where the economist Arthur Laffer had sketched his eponymous curve.

Finally, tax cuts ratcheted up pressure on Congress to limit spending. According to Google's Ngram Viewer, references to the phrase *starve the beast*, as this strategy was known, fluctuated at low levels in the 1980s and 1990s before rising sharply in 2001, coincident with the beginning of Bush's term in office.[36] This strategy, evidently, was very much in the air, if not also on policymakers' lips. This is different, of course, from saying that it delivered the expected results.[37]

Why discretionary spending rose so strongly is harder to explain. It may be that the party in power favored different forms of discretionary spending (Republicans favoring defense, Democrats social programs) and rushed to get it while the getting was good. Political polarization, indicative of differences in the two parties' inclinations, continued to rise, as it had since the 1970s (Figure 11.3). We know that the greater the difference in policy preferences, the greater is the incentive to ramp up spending on one's favored programs now and leave the consequences for another day.[38] This fact played its part in the rise in US indebtedness in the early twenty-first century.

## Maastricht's Tight Trousers

In Europe, debt-to-GDP ratios had been trending up since the 1970s, as governments responded to pressure for social programs even while revenue growth fell off. There were then scattered efforts in the 1980s at fiscal consolidation, some more successful than others. The most successful, in Denmark in 1982 and Ireland in 1987, reduced debt and deficit ratios without interrupting growth.

These positive experiences consequently gave rise to a theory of expansionary fiscal consolidation, which ran as follows. If spending is out of control, then expenditure cuts will enhance confidence and encourage investment. The positive impact of this confidence channel may so overwhelm the direct negative effect of less government spending that no economic contraction will ensue. Cutting the deficit, it follows, will be painless from a macroeconomic point of view.[39]

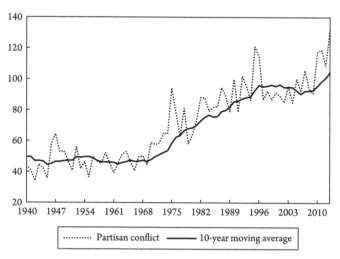

*Figure 11.3.* Political Polarization in the United States (normalized to 100 in 1990)
Source: Federal Reserve Bank of Philadelphia (2021).
Note: Political polarization is measured by the partisan conflict index. It is constructed as the number of articles in major US newspapers mentioning partisan conflict, relative to total articles in those same newspapers. Available at http://marina-azzimonti.com/datasets/

If so, then it is peculiar that more European countries failed to partake of this free lunch. It may be that the domestic political preconditions for forcing through spending cuts were absent, even if those cuts were costless from a macroeconomic standpoint. Workers, pensioners, and business owners all defended their preferred spending programs without acknowledging that the sum total of their demands raised indebtedness and, in so doing, depressed growth.[40] We know that it is difficult to agree on spending cuts in a fragmented political system with many veto players and when government is by coalition, this being the situation in several European countries.[41]

In addition, Europe's fiscal problem was not always and everywhere excessive public spending. The effects of cutting spending would not have been favorable if governments were cutting muscle rather than fat. Or it may be that the theory—that the positive confidence effects induced by fiscal consolidation will swamp its negative aggregate demand effects—itself was flawed.

In the event, debts remained uncomfortably high in too many European countries. In Italy, debt as a share of GDP in 1989 was 96 percent and rising. In Belgium, Europe's debt champion, it was 131 percent. These countries' debts were worrisome compared to the United States, where the debt-to-GDP ratio was a much lower 54 percent, and even compared to Japan, where the debt-to-GDP ratio at this time was still only 69 percent.[42]

In fact, Europe's problem was less fiscal profligacy than slow growth, which yielded an unfavorable growth-rate–interest-rate differential. Belgium, the country with the highest debt, was actually running primary budget surpluses. Even Italy had reduced its primary deficit to 1.5 percent of GDP by the late 1980s. But GDP growth between 1981 and 1989 averaged just 1.9 percent in Belgium and 2.3 percent in Italy. By comparison, the United States grew half again as fast, by 3.5 percent per annum, over the period.

As something needed to be done, Europe responded with the Single Market Act. To be implemented by 1992, the Single Market was designed to enhance the continent's international competitiveness. Forcing companies to compete on a Europe-wide playing field required them to boost efficiency in order to survive.[43] To be sure, there were political as well as economic motivations for the Single Market.[44] But so went the theory.

The Single Market in turn created pressure for a single currency. Firms and governments would not feel the full blast of competition's chill winds if they could devalue their way out. Moreover, if some EU member states were seen as manipulating their exchange rates, others would be reluctant to extend them the full privileges of the Single Market. Devaluations might be met by tariffs, or if tariffs were prohibited they might be met by regulatory barriers. The European Union's prohibition on subsidies and state aids would be meaningless if the exchange rate could be manipulated in their stead. Again, more than just economics motivated the authors of the Delors Report, which laid out the blueprint for a monetary union to complement Europe's economic union.[45] But this logic linking economic union to monetary union was a critical element.

In turn, the prospect of a Single Currency (now that it was a thing, it was written in caps) applied pressure for fiscal consolidation. The European Union's more debt- and inflation-averse members (read: Germany) hesitated to give up their national currencies, fearing that a single European currency and a European central bank would become engines of inflation. They feared specifically that other more heavily indebted member states would pressure the central bank to purchase their debts. They worried that a European central bank might be pressed to backstop the debt markets of weak members, not just in exceptional circumstances, but routinely.

As a condition for moving ahead with monetary union, Germany and other member states sharing its perspective therefore demanded that candidates for monetary union demonstrate their inflation and deficit-spending bona fides (more precisely, their *anti*-inflation and *anti*-deficit bona fides). They wrote into the Maastricht Treaty on Economic and Monetary Union what came to be known as the Convergence Criteria. Aspiring members were expected to keep their exchange rates stable. They were expected to keep their interest rates and inflation rates low. Most consequentially, they were expected to keep their budget deficits below 3 percent of GDP and bring their public debts down to no more than 60 percent of GDP, and to do so by the end of 1997, when the decision on membership would be reached.[46]

These targets or, in EU-speak, reference values of 3 and 60 percent were intended to filter out countries insufficiently committed to fiscal stability. They provided a template for the rules and procedures that would govern debts and deficits once the euro came into being. This idea of extending the Convergence Criteria into the period of monetary union itself came, not surprisingly, from Germany; it was proposed by German Finance Minister Theo Waigel in 1995. Under the Waigel-inspired Stability Pact, the European Commission would monitor member states' compliance with those requirements. On detecting violations, it would recommend sanctions and fines. Whether sanctions and fines were in fact possible in the collegial atmosphere of the European Union was another matter, since countries voting for fines one year might be at risk of falling afoul of the rules in another.[47]

The 3 and 60 percent reference values might seem arbitrary—which of course they were; 60 percent just happened to be the EU-wide debt ratio when the Maastricht Treaty was signed. Three percent was the deficit consistent with keeping that debt ratio stable, given prevailing, again arbitrary, assumptions about growth rates and inflation rates.[48]

The consequences are apparent in Figure 11.4, which shows the cyclically adjusted budget balance relative to GDP (with business cycle effects removed from both the numerator and denominator), for the eleven founding members

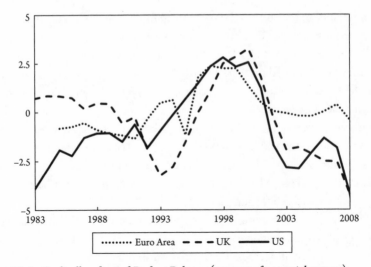

*Figure 11.4.* Cyclically-adjusted Budget Balance (percent of potential output)
Source: *OECD Economic Outlook* 2019, no. 106, November 2019.
Note: Euro Area data are calculated as 2007 PPP adjusted GDP-weighted average for Austria, Belgium,
Finland, France, Germany, Ireland, Italy, Luxembourg, Netherlands, Portugal, and Spain.

of the Euro Area, with the United Kingdom and the United States for comparison. Starting in 1993, immediately after ratification of the Maastricht Treaty, the cyclically adjusted budgets of the Euro Area aspirants began improving. Although that improvement wasn't quite as strong as in the United States, where the budget was benefiting from the 1990 Budget Enforcement Act, Rubinomics, and the New Economy, it came close.[49] Budgets continued strengthening through 1997, at which point the decision was made of who qualified for membership in the Euro Area. Table 11.4 shows that debt consolidation in this period was achieved mainly by policies of austerity. Only in Ireland, where fiscal adjustment was initiated already in the 1980s, did the debt ratio also fall with help from economic growth.

Like a man who has gained weight but still fancies an old set of trousers, European governments had sucked in their bellies in order to fit into the tight waistband of the Maastricht Treaty. But once they gained admission to the monetary union, they let out their collective breath to accommodate spending pressures. The deterioration in the cyclically adjusted budget balance after the turn of the century was not as dramatic as in the United States, but it was there. Desultory discussion of fines and sanctions against member states that violated the hopefully renamed Stability and Growth Pact yielded little in the way of concrete action, since two big, politically powerful countries, France and Germany, were among the violators.

*Table 11.4* **Decomposition of Debt Consolidations in the Run-Up to the Euro**

| Country | Period | Debt-to-GDP Ratio (percent) | | | Contribution to Decrease (percent) | | |
|---|---|---|---|---|---|---|---|
| | | Starting Level | Ending Level | Decrease | Primary Balance | Growth- Interest Differential | Stock-Flow Adjustment |
| Austria | 1996–97 | 68.4 | 64.4 | 4.0 | 1.2 | –2.3 | 5.1 |
| Belgium | 1993–99 | 134.1 | 113.8 | 20.3 | 28.5 | –18.6 | 10.3 |
| Finland | 1994–99 | 57.7 | 46.6 | 11.1 | –1.1 | –0.2 | 12.4 |
| France | 1998–99 | 59.4 | 58.9 | 0.6 | 1.0 | –1.1 | 0.6 |
| Ireland | 1993–99 | 94.1 | 48.5 | 45.6 | 25.4 | 27.7 | –7.5 |
| Italy | 1994–99 | 121.8 | 113.7 | 8.1 | 22.6 | –15.7 | 1.2 |
| Luxembourg | 1996–99 | 8.6 | 7.1 | 1.5 | 7.2 | 0.4 | –6.0 |
| Netherlands | 1993–99 | 78.5 | 61.1 | 17.4 | 8.4 | –5.0 | 14.0 |
| Portugal | 1995–98 | 59.2 | 50.4 | 8.8 | 0.2 | 1.6 | 6.9 |
| Spain | 1996–99 | 67.4 | 62.3 | 5.1 | 3.2 | 1.3 | 0.6 |
| **Simple average** (all countries) | | 74.9 | 62.7 | 12.2 | 9.7 | –1.2 | 3.8 |
| **Weighted average** (all countries) | | 82.6 | 75 | 7.6 | 9.5 | –4.8 | 2.9 |
| **Simple average** (4 countries)* | | 91.1 | 67.5 | 23.6 | 15.3 | 1.0 | 7.3 |
| **Weighted average** (4 countries)* | | 92.8 | 71.7 | 21.1 | 14.8 | –3.7 | 9.9 |

*Sources:* IMF *World Economic Outlook* Database (IMF various years) and authors'

*Note:* Peak-to-trough episodes (years vary by country).

\* The four countries in shaded gray exhibited largest debt reduction during the period. Germany was excluded as its debt ratio increased during this period.

The upshot is that there was neither enough fiscal consolidation nor enough growth to reduce debt-to-GDP ratios between 1999 and 2008 (see Figure 11.5).

## Conclusion

With hindsight, it's clear that the signal fiscal and debt-management failure of the decades leading up to the Global Financial Crisis was the inability of

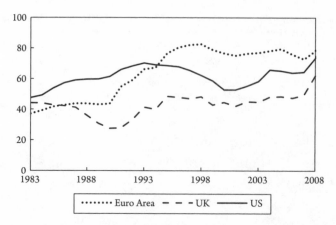

*Figure 11.5.* Gross Government Debt (percent of GDP)
Source: *OECD Economic Outlook* 2019, no. 106, November 2019.
Note: Euro Area data are calculated as 2007 PPP adjusted GDP-weighted average for Austria, Belgium, Finland, France, Germany, Ireland, Italy, Luxembourg, Netherlands, Portugal, and Spain.

policymakers to keep their powder dry. In the United States, the period starting around 1995 was one of relatively rapid productivity growth. In Europe, it was a period of economic and financial stability, compared to both what had come before and what came after. Common sense dictates that governments should run budget surpluses and retire debt in good times so they can run deficits and issue debt when the need arises. Consequently, the decades immediately preceding the Global Financial Crisis should have been a period of surpluses and debt consolidation. This was, in fact, the case in most advanced economies in the second half of the 1990s. The United States reaped the fiscal benefits of the 1990 Budget Act and the New Economy. European countries ran surpluses and reduced their debts in order to gain admission to the Euro Area.

It didn't last. A new US administration cut taxes and ramped up defense spending in the wake of 9/11. Having qualified for monetary union, European governments were able to relax and indulge popular pressures for spending. When economic expansion resumed following the brief 2001 recession, it was no longer accompanied by debt reduction. Quite the contrary.

As a result, debts were uncomfortably high when the Global Financial Crisis struck. They rose still higher when governments met the emergency by ratcheting up public spending. This confronted countries with uncomfortable choices—choices that grew even less comfortable when another crisis erupted a bit more than a decade later.

Hindsight is 20/20. But if history tells us one thing, it is that crises happen. There will always be economic and financial emergencies. Keeping one's fiscal powder dry is prudent under the circumstances. It's just easier said than done.

# ‖ 12 ‖

# Debt to the Rescue

Throughout history, states have issued debt to address economic, financial, and existential needs that can't be met by current revenues alone. Earlier chapters showed how public debt soared in wars, economic disasters, and financial crises, when governments struggled with exceptional events. Debt issuance in such circumstances was a matter not just of state building but, fundamentally, of state survival.[1] Revealingly, the two twentieth-century instances when debts rose most dramatically were the world wars. Other instances when governments resorted to large-scale debt issuance were similarly justified as circumstances tantamount to war.[2]

Not everyone agrees, of course, on what circumstances are tantamount to war. Nor do they agree that the actions made possible by debt issuance justify the costs. They worry about crowding out investment and weakening the public finances. They worry about hobbling the ability of government and society to meet even more serious threats. They fret that debt issuance, if it succeeds in papering over problems, relieves society of the need to confront their source. They complain of the distributional consequences of policies that transfer income and resources from taxpayers, whose payments service the debt, to beneficiaries of public programs. They observe that debt is a burden that current generations pass on to the unborn. They suspect that those who invoke a crisis as justifying debt issuance are using events as a pretext for pursuing self-interested political agendas and distributional goals. Some reason by way of analogy with the household balance sheet: just as a household must live within its means, so too should a government. They view debt accumulation in moral terms. That the German word for debt—*Schuld*—is also the word for guilt shows that this instinct is deeply ingrained.

Never was this morality play more intense and policy debate more heated than in the twenty-first century, when countries suffered through the Global Financial Crisis, the Euro Area crisis, and the COVID-19 crisis. These were the most serious peacetime economic and financial crises since the 1930s. They were met by issuing debt, as governments invoked macroeconomic, financial-stability, and humanitarian imperatives for ramping up spending. But this response, taken in the heat of battle, unleashed a reaction once that heat died down. Critics warned that debt accumulation heightened the fragility of the public finances, distorted incentives, and was fundamentally immoral, justifying and indeed requiring an early return to austerity.

Thus, in the wake of the 2009 "Obama stimulus" adopted in response to the Global Financial Crisis, the Republican Party regained control of the US House of Representatives. The newly installed Speaker, John Boehner, took the opportunity to put the point the following way:

> Here we must speak the truth. Yes, this level of debt is unsustainable. It is also immoral. Yes, this debt is a mortal threat to our country. It is also a moral threat. It is immoral to bind our children to as leeching and destructive a force as debt. It is immoral to rob our children's future and make them beholden to China. No society is worthy that treats its children so shabbily. "A good man leaves an inheritance for his children's children," Proverbs reminds us. For too long, Washington has been ignoring this time-honored principle. As part of the designs of unrestrained government, Washington uses our people, our most plentiful resource, as its prime revenue source. Through more taxes and more regulations, money and freedom is drained from the people and transferred to Washington, which then redistributes these resources.[3]

Yet there was also another view, in which debt was viewed in economic rather than moralistic terms, and where its issuance was seen as a solution to problems, not as their source.

## Originate and Distribute

The 2008–9 episode was widely hailed (if that's the right word) as the worst financial crisis since the 1930s. That it did not culminate in an economic crisis as severe as that of the 1930s reflected the fact that advanced-country governments had policy space and were prepared to use it.[4]

As we saw in Chapter 11, fiscal positions had deteriorated in the run-up to the crisis. US deficits widened with the 2002–3 tax cuts and increases in defense and nonentitlement spending. European governments that had limited their spending in order to meet the conditions for adopting the euro felt able, following its inception, to relax. But the deterioration was limited because GDP growth made for rising receipts. In the Euro Area, budget deficits rose to more than 3 percent of GDP in 2003, when growth slowed, before falling to roughly half that level as the expansion reaccelerated.[5] US deficits, at more than 4.5 percent of GDP in 2003 and 2.5 percent in 2005–6, were roughly half again as large. The situation was the same in the United Kingdom, except that there was essentially no decline in the budget deficit as a share of GDP between 2003 and 2006 despite GDP growth that never dipped below 2 percent.[6]

Behind the headline numbers, however, all was not well. Lax supervision and regulation combined with excessive risk taking to accentuate imbalances in financial markets. Financial institutions took on leverage and created off-balance-sheet subsidiaries to evade rules requiring them to maintain adequate capital buffers. The Federal Reserve loosened in response to 9/11, encouraging investors to search for yield in dark corners of financial markets. Low interest rates and loose lending standards fed housing demands, linking the fortunes of regional and even entire national economies to a volatile construction sector.

For multiple reasons, then, it was uncertain whether the economic growth buoying the fiscal accounts was sustainable. By implication, governments should have been running surpluses during what, in retrospect, would be seen as the "good times." They should have been keeping their fiscal powder dry so they would be in a position to cut taxes and boost spending in the event of a shock and to maintain that fiscal support for as long as necessary without exciting bondholders or political critics.

At the outset, the American part of the story attracted the most attention. The United States had pioneered the most notorious financial practices and then experienced the most spectacular financial failures when home prices faltered and problems surfaced in the markets in which residential mortgages were securitized.[7] Difficulties surfaced first in the spring of 2007 among subprime lenders that had extended loans to homebuyers whose only hope of repaying was by realizing capital gains courtesy of ever-increasing house prices. When home prices stopped rising, these lenders found themselves unable to package and market their loans to other investors.[8]

By summer, distress had spread to the hedge funds and investment banks that had loaded up on earlier subprime securities, starting with two in-house funds operated by the investment bank Bear Stearns & Co., which suspended redemptions in June, and three funds operated by BNP Paribas, suspended in August. The situation exploded in March 2008, when Bear Stearns had to be rescued by the Federal Reserve and was acquired at knock-down prices by J. P. Morgan Chase.[9] The crisis came to a head in September 2008, when the investment bank Lehman Bros. filed for bankruptcy, unleashing a systemic crisis. In response, the Fed and Treasury undertook a series of unprecedented interventions, starting with rescue of the insurance giant American International Group (AIG).

The United States officially entered recession in December 2007. By late 2008, downward pressure on the economy was intense, highlighting the need for a fiscal response.

## A Transatlantic Crisis

That response was not limited to the United States, however, because neither was the crisis. The problems at BNP Paribas were an early indication that what was initially understood as a US financial crisis was in fact a transatlantic crisis.[10] Europe, like the United States, had frothy housing markets. Ireland, Spain, and the United Kingdom experienced housing booms and busts that matched and in some cases exceeded in intensity that in the United States.[11] Spain, Portugal, Ireland, and Greece experienced credit booms that surpassed that in America. This reflected the sharp decline in bank funding costs following their adoption of the euro, when investors bet that interest rates would converge across the currency area. European banks, for their part, engaged in many of the same dodgy mortgage-lending practices as their American counterparts. Spanish banks offered home loans of more than 100 percent of the purchase price and repayment terms of 50 years.[12] Northern Rock, the doomed British building society cum bank, offered "Together Loans" allowing homeowners to borrow 125 percent of the value of their homes.[13]

Moreover, European banks were even more leveraged than their American counterparts. Whereas bank assets in the United States exceeded bank capital by a multiple of 12, European banks' investments were fully 20 times their capital. European banks obtained their leverage by borrowing on the wholesale money market, often in the United States. These practices were enabled by the US Securities and Exchange Commission, which enlarged the class of securities allowed as collateral for repurchase agreements (or repos).[14] Specifically, European banks were able to borrow in the United States by pledging as collateral their governments' sovereign bonds, which they held in abundance.[15] Those same banks then turned around and invested their borrowed funds in mortgage-backed securities and in the derivatives known as collateralized debt obligations (CDOs), again in the United States. We have seen repeatedly how the availability of public debt as collateral can facilitate transactions in other riskier securities and foster financial development. Here we have a reminder that financial development is not always and everywhere good.

Some of the CDOs in question were produced by US financial institutions expressly for sale to hapless European banks, such as the semipublic Bank for German Industry Obligations (*Bank für deutsche Industrieobligationen,* or IDB), which like other once-staid financial institutions plunged into new and novel investments. In some instances, CDOs were originated by the US securities affiliates of European banks themselves, with the goal of distributing them more widely. However, with turmoil in financial markets, distributing mortgage-backed securities was easier said than done, and banks ended up warehousing them on their balance sheets.[16]

The other destinations of funds sourced by European banks were Greece, Ireland, Italy, Portugal, and Spain, collectively known as the GIIPS. Once the euro eliminated exchange-rate risk, or at least perceived exchange-rate risk, what had been a modest financial flow became a flood. It appears to have escaped the attention of investors that removing currency risk did not also automatically remove credit risk (the risk of a default). In Spain and Ireland, foreign money helped to finance housing excesses. In Greece, it financed budget deficits. In Portugal, it did both. Typically, the money flowed through local banks (there's that interbank market again) before reaching its destination. Consequently, if the flow was interrupted or, worse, turned around, it would bring down not only the ultimate borrower—the construction sector, the housing market, or the government—but the banks themselves.

This was dry tinder requiring only a spark.[17] That spark turned out to be the collapse of the wholesale money market following the failure of Lehman Bros. Unsure of who was solvent, banks stopped lending to one another. Institutions that had relied on the wholesale market found themselves unable to raise funds to pay off their creditors and unable to sell off their assets. Their governments were forced to step in, recapitalizing the banks, purchasing their nonperforming assets, and guaranteeing their deposits (and, in some cases, their other liabilities).

The direct fiscal costs approached 10 percent of GDP in Belgium, 20 percent in the Netherlands, and 40 percent in Ireland.[18] These enormous bills reflected the extent to which very large, highly leveraged banks had been built on the platforms of small economies. Expensive as it was, however, preserving economic and financial stability required no less.[19]

## Mixed Response

From this point, the fiscal policy response unfolded in stages. First, revenues fell and deficits widened, causing automatic stabilizers to kick in. With growth collapsing, previously favorable growth-rate–interest-rate differentials turned unfavorable, and debt ratios rose even faster than deficits. America having entered recession first, the swing in federal government budget was especially large, from a 2.9 percent of GDP deficit in 2007 to 6.6 percent in 2008. The comparable swing in the United Kingdom was slightly smaller, from 2.7 to 5.1 percent. The Euro Area and Japan moved in the same direction, though more modestly.[20]

In the second stage (late 2008 through early 2009), governments launched major new spending initiatives. The United States adopted the $787 billion American Recovery and Reinvestment Act (ARRA), with the House of Representatives voting along party lines and Republicans objecting that the package augured a dangerous increase in debt. (The US had already passed a smaller $152 billion stimulus in early 2008, reflecting the relatively early onset of recession, and for some members of Congress this was enough.) The United Kingdom cut value-added tax (VAT) and income taxes while bringing forward public investment.[21] Deficits rose in calendar year 2009 by an additional 4 percent of GDP in the Euro Area, 5.5 percent of GDP in the United Kingdom, and 6.5 percent of GDP in the United States. Japan, which entered the crisis with heavy debts (Figure 12.1), increased its deficit by an additional 5.5 percent of GDP.

The cyclically adjusted primary budget balance as a percentage of GDP, in Table 12.1, provides a measure of this discretionary component, removing the impact of the business cycle from the ratio's numerator and denominator. It shows that the majority of the change in deficit ratios in 2009 was due to discretionary action.[22]

In fact, it was China and not these advanced economies that launched the single largest package. China's stimulus amounted to some 12.5 percent of the country's 2008 GDP, spent over twenty-seven months. About a quarter of the total was central government spending, while the remainder was spending by local governments and credit for construction and related projects from state-owned and -directed banks.[23] This was more than twice the size of the ARRA similarly scaled (5.4 percent of GDP spread over twenty-four months).

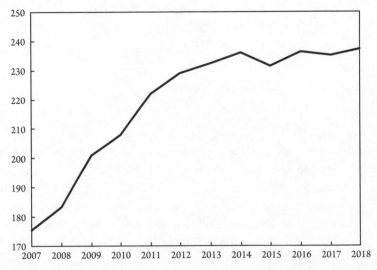

*Figure 12.1.* General Government Gross Debt in Japan, 2007–18 (percent of GDP)
Source: IMF *World Economic Outlook.*

*Table 12.1* **Cyclically Adjusted Government Primary Budget Balance, 2007–14 (percent of potential GDP)**

|  | 2007 | 2008 | 2009 | 2010 | 2011 | 2012 | 2013 | 2014 | Change 2010–14 |
|---|---|---|---|---|---|---|---|---|---|
| France | −1.51 | −1.2 | −3.3 | −3.42 | −2.2 | −1.48 | −0.74 | −0.5 | 2.92 |
| Germany | 1.38 | 1.27 | 1.31 | −1.21 | 0.82 | 1.73 | 1.58 | 1.65 | 2.87 |
| Greece | −5.93 | −9.08 | −12.26 | −5.45 | 0.21 | 2.24 | −1.42 | 6.02 | 11.47 |
| Ireland | −2.51 | −6.95 | −10.13 | −27.81 | −8.28 | −2.02 | 0.7 | 0.02 | 27.83 |
| Italy | 1.77 | 1.45 | 1.09 | 1.18 | 1.66 | 4.23 | 4.55 | 3.97 | 2.79 |
| Portugal | −1.4 | −1.7 | −5.89 | −8.13 | −2.25 | 1.69 | 3.09 | 0.5 | 8.63 |
| Spain | 0.1 | −5.35 | −8.07 | −5.44 | −4.03 | −2.02 | 2.96 | 3.34 | 8.78 |
| **Euro Area (16 countries)** | **0.19** | **−0.7** | **−2.06** | **−2.57** | **−0.85** | **0.59** | **1.5** | **1.57** | **4.14** |
| Japan | −3.29 | −3.75 | −6.74 | −7.67 | −7.18 | −6.75 | −6.88 | −4.62 | 3.04 |
| United Kingdom | −2.67 | −3.6 | −6.18 | −4.72 | −2.85 | −3.91 | −1.84 | −2.71 | 2 |
| United States | −2.26 | −4.62 | −7.67 | −7.31 | −5.69 | −4.27 | −1.63 | −1.03 | 6.28 |

*Source:* OECD estimates, reproduced from Alesina, Favero, and Giavazzi (2019).

How could China launch such a large stimulus, when emerging markets are typically constrained in their ability to borrow? It helped that the combined debt of state, local, and provincial governments in 2008 was just 27 percent of GDP. To be sure, corporate debt was heavier, at some 100 percent of GDP. And a substantial portion of this was debt of state-owned and -connected enterprises, which were too important to fail. These were implicit liabilities of the government, in other words.

What mattered for initiating such a large stimulus was that, like Japan before it, China was a high-saving economy. Household and corporate savings flowed into state-controlled banks, which used those resources to purchase the central government's bonds and lend to local and provincial authorities. Savings flowed into the banks, and thereby into the bond market, because capital controls limited the range of alternative assets on offer. They limited the danger that deficit spending and aggressive liquidity creation would precipitate capital flight and cause the currency to crash.

As China recovered, with GDP growing by nearly 9 percent in 2009, the country's energy and commodity imports recovered with it. This was different from previous global downturns and recoveries, when policy support had come almost exclusively from advanced-country governments.[24] Admittedly, there were worries about longer-term structural consequences of this spending, which heightened China's dependence on the construction and heavy industrial sectors, from which planners were seeking to wean the economy. Still, China's stimulus was an important part of the explanation for why the 2008–9 crisis did not produce a more severe global downturn.

In all, these national cases display differences as well as common features. Those differences reflect variations in the severity of the crisis (the magnitude of the earlier property and financialization booms and of the problems they bequeathed), whether inherited debts were high or low, and attitudes toward deficits and debts. Ireland, for example, saw an enormous increase in its debt ratio. It incurred massive costs when recapitalizing its banks and suffered a deep recession, but also inherited a debt of just 25 percent of GDP, providing fiscal space. At the other extreme, Italy limited the increase in the deficit as a share of GDP to half the Euro Area average because its inherited debt was heavy and it feared that adding more would provoke an adverse market reaction. Germany too was reluctant to see debt rise because of fears that deficit spending portended inflation.

## Dueling Multipliers

The extent to which fiscal stimulus helped to mitigate the downturn is disputed. In the US case, for example, estimates of the fiscal policy multiplier (the percentage point increase in GDP for every percentage point increase in fiscal stimulus) range from zero to two—that is, from zilch to very substantial. Economic analysis, evidently, remains less than a science.

Estimates at the lower end of this range derived from misapplication of the theory of Ricardian equivalence and from wishful thinking that households needing credit were unconstrained. Ricardian equivalence is the idea that if the government increases its spending, even temporarily, and finances that increase by borrowing, then households will be obliged to reduce their spending over time in order to pay the taxes needed to service the debt. The resulting shifts in public and private spending will offset one another.[25] There will then be no visible impact on economic activity.

The misapplication entered via neglect of the proviso that households will reduce their spending *over time*. In other words, although the positive effect of additional government spending is felt on impact, which in the present context meant in 2009, the reduction in household spending could be spread over many years, matching the time profile of the debt service.[26] Thus, even though there may be some immediate offset to public spending from reduced private spending, that offset will be less than complete.

Similarly, those who denied that government transfers to households affected consumption posited that individuals "used the money to shore up depleted bank accounts or pay off overextended credit card bills."[27] Their assumption was that people who wanted to spend could do so because they had either savings or access to credit. Government borrowing to finance rebate checks was just "taking a bucket of water from the deep end of a pool and dumping it into the shallow end."[28] These skeptics similarly questioned the effect of federal transfers to the states, arguing that state governments simply reduced their borrowing accordingly.

This assumes, of course, that state governments were able to borrow—that they too were not credit-constrained. In fact, forty-nine of the fifty states have balanced-budget laws or constitutional provisions of one sort or another.[29] Since some had rainy-day funds to tap, transfers from the federal government could in fact have replaced some drawdown of these funds. However, rainy-day funds were limited in all but a handful of cases.[30] Studies of the actual behavior of states and localities, across which the value of federal transfers differed, point to an aggregate deficit-spending multiplier of "about 1.7 or above."[31] A discretionary stimulus consisting of direct government spending and transfers to state governments of 0.9 percent a year in 2009–10, combined with a multiplier of 1.7, implies that GDP would have been 1.5 percent lower in the absence of fiscal action.

This exercise assumes no rise in interest rates owing to expectations of increased inflation and no monetary response. These assumptions work to increase one's estimate of the fiscal multiplier, since they eliminate any crowding out of other spending due to higher interest rates. But this is precisely the point. In 2009–10, interest rates were low and were destined to stay there as a result of economic weakness and Fed policy. These were precisely the circumstances when the multiplier was large—and when fiscal action was most valuable because interest rates couldn't go any lower.

Payments to households have been analyzed using the University of Michigan's Survey of Consumers and the Nielsen Consumer Panel. The 2008 stimulus allows the cleanest analysis because of a quirk of timing. The Internal Revenue Service could process only so many checks a week, and the week in which a check was deposited to a household's bank depended, randomly, on the second-to-last digit of the taxpayer's Social Security number. Leveraging this administrative detail, economists Christian Broda and Jonathan Parker found that the average household raised its spending by 10 percent the week the payment arrived, and that its spending remained high for three subsequent months.[32] This response was concentrated among households with low wealth and low past income. It occurred when the payment arrived, not when the household learned it was coming. All this is consistent with the existence of credit constraints and with the idea that stimulus mattered.

## The Geography of Deficit Spending

In Europe, in comparison, the impact of government borrowing and spending was more limited. To start, there was less stimulus. Tax cuts and discretionary spending increases were only half as large as in the United States.[33] This reflected debt aversion in some countries, limited fiscal space in others, and delayed recognition that economic and financial dislocations were not just a US problem.

Other factors dampened the effects of such stimulus as was applied. The European Central Bank raised interest rates in 2008 and 2011 and was slower than the Fed to embrace quantitative easing.[34] As a result, there was some crowding out of interest-rate-sensitive private-sector spending. The ECB had been created as a bulwark against inflation and found it hard to shake that preoccupation, even in deflationary times.

In addition, Europe entered the crisis with more public debt. When inherited debt is large, the government's credit may be downgraded and interest rates will rise more quickly with additional spending.[35] As a result, higher levels of debt are associated with smaller fiscal multipliers.[36] Some went so far as to argue that there comes a point where additional deficit spending and a higher debt ratio actually cause the multiplier to turn negative.[37] They suggested that Europe's most heavily indebted countries were close to or even past this threshold.

Finally, countries with the most economic slack, where one would normally expect the multiplier to be largest, were often those with the least fiscal capacity. Where fiscal space was most valuable it did not exist, and where it existed it was least valuable. And unlike in the United States, there was no federal fiscal system at the level of the continent to transfer resources to the most financially constrained states and regions.

## Contractionary Fiscal Contraction

Starting in 2010, concerns over market access combined with ideology and political pressure to prompt a shift toward austerity. In a detailed study of the question, Christina and David Romer single out Spain, Portugal, Italy, and Greece as countries where problems of market access compelled governments to pursue fiscal consolidation, and the United Kingdom, France, Denmark, and Austria as countries where, instead, ideological and political pressures prompted the shift.[38]

Some theorists argued that fiscal consolidation would be expansionary in Europe's circumstances.[39] If Europe was on the portion of the debt-growth relationship where more debt meant slower growth, then it followed that less debt, made possible by fiscal consolidation, should have meant faster growth. If Europe, or at least a subset of European countries, was on an unsustainable path that, uncorrected, would lead to a disruptive default, then an orderly correction might bolster confidence and in so doing encourage investment. Intuitively, if European governments were hurtling toward a fiscal cliff, then tapping the brakes would enhance confidence. And if the problem causing excessive deficits was a bloated state, then cutting spending rather than raising taxes was the best way forward.

That was the theory, anyway, and one that gained considerable currency in policy circles.[40] Unfortunately, testing it is not easy. The decision to cut public spending may in fact have a positive impact on economic activity even in the short run, as posited by the apostles of expansionary fiscal consolidation. Equally, however, a third factor that affects economic activity positively may simultaneously reduce the deficit by boosting revenues and reducing spending on, inter alia, support for the unemployed. In this case, the decline in the deficit will be the result, not the cause, of the improvement in economic conditions.[41]

One way of distinguishing cause from effect is the so-called narrative approach, which uses budget speeches and documents to separate fiscal changes motivated by the desire to narrow the deficit from changes responding to economic conditions.[42] A study conducted in house by the IMF drew on central bank, OECD, and IMF country reports and on budget announcements by finance ministers to identify 173 exogenous fiscal adjustments (fiscal changes motivated by the desire to narrow the deficit) in seventeen OECD countries. It found that fiscal consolidation is contractionary, more often than not, and significantly so.[43] This suggests that tapering stimulus in the United States and the turn to austerity in Europe depressed consumption, investment, and growth.

The contractionary effects of fiscal consolidation were most pronounced in countries with fixed exchange rates. Such countries were not able to depreciate their currencies to crowd in exports and substitute foreign for domestic demand. Similarly, the contractionary effects were larger where the central bank was slow to cut interest rates in order to crowd in spending.

These were precisely the conditions confronting the Southern European countries that implemented the largest deficit reductions starting in 2010. As members of the Euro Area, they had no national currency to devalue. And that multiple European countries turned simultaneously to fiscal consolidation made finding export markets (substituting external for domestic demand) even harder.[44] Their national central banks were subsidiaries of the ECB, which embarked in 2011 on a policy of interest-rate increases, not reductions, and which was reluctant to support their bond markets, given statutory prohibitions against financing budget deficits. The fragility of their banking systems and reluctance of their banks to lend meant that firms had little ability to borrow and invest as a way of taking up the slack created by the reduction in public spending. The result for these countries was a double-dip recession, as the recovery initiated in mid-2009 was aborted in 2011.

## The Greater Depression

None of this would have surprised the Greek in the street. Starting in 2010, the Hellenic Republic suffered a downturn of Great Depression–like proportions. Real GDP fell by 28 percent. Unemployment similarly reached 28 percent, surpassing even the United States in the 1930s. By 2013, GDP per capita in Greece was lower than when the country adopted the euro in 2002.

Like other countries of the Euro Area periphery, Greece experienced an enormous credit boom in the run-up to its crisis. Enjoying the credibility bequeathed by the euro, its banks borrowed on the interbank market and on-lent to households and firms. House prices in Athens doubled between 2001 and 2008, in only the most visible manifestation of the more general process. The government meanwhile was able to finance its deficits by placing its bonds with institutional investors, including French and German banks.

Things unraveled in 2008 when housing prices started falling. Shortly after the failure of Lehman Bros., the Conservative Karamanlis government was forced to commit €28 billion, or 12 percent of GDP, to bailing out the banks. The crisis then exploded in late 2009 when the new Socialist prime minister, George Papandreou, revealed that the debt and deficit were larger than acknowledged by his predecessor. Public debt was actually an alarming 110 percent of GDP (Figure 12.2). The deficit, at 13 percent of GDP, was far above the 3 percent ceiling prescribed by the European Union's Excessive Deficit Procedure.[45] This was not the first time the fiscal books were cooked, but this latest burst of disguised spending, which occurred in the run-up to a hotly contested election, was especially large.

Spending cuts and tax increases were the textbook remedy prescribed by the International Monetary Fund, the European Commission, and the ECB— the Troika that came to Greece's rescue, as it were. There were echoes of how the European powers in the 1920s had called in the League of Nations to arrange stabilization loans for troubled countries.[46] Then as now, creditor-country governments were reluctant to demand stringent conditions of a sovereign nation, preferring to outsource the task to an international organization with a claim to technocratic impartiality. In both cases—the League of Nations in the

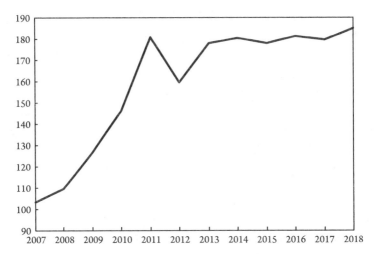

*Figure 12.2.* General Government Gross Debt in Greece, 2007–18 (percent of GDP)
Source: IMF *World Economic Outlook.*

1920s, the IMF now—the international organization in question put up only a sliver of money, which should have raised alarms about whether it could face down the other creditors when they sought to advance their claims.

In May 2010, European governments and the IMF provided Greece with a €110 billion emergency loan to be paid out over three years.[47] At this stage, there was little discussion of the possibility of restructuring Greek debt. The hope was that the loan would suffice to keep the banks and debt afloat until the economy revived. For its part, the Greek government agreed to €30 billion of spending cuts and tax increases. It raised VAT rates and increased taxes on fuel, alcohol, cigarettes, and luxury goods. It used Google Earth to crack down on undeclared swimming pools and other untaxed real estate. It reduced holiday bonuses, cut pensions, and scaled back unemployment benefits. These austerity measures reduced the deficit excluding interest payments by half between 2009 and 2010 and then by another third (to 3.4 percent of GDP) in 2011.[48]

If ever the conditions were in place for a confidence-inspired increase in private consumption and investment, this was it. The debt and deficit were on an unsustainable path. Remedying this should have boosted confidence and, if confidence was sufficient for economic growth, bolstered the economy. Much public spending was unproductive, as evidenced by a significant portion having been hidden. Public sector wages had risen by 50 percent between 1999 and 2007, far faster than in other Eurozone countries. The government had squandered nearly 5 percent of GDP on the 2004 Olympic Games alone.

This earlier public spending binge fueled investment as well as consumption by creating the appearance of a boom. Between 2000 and 2007, real GDP per capita rose by nearly 4 percent per annum—rapidly, by European standards. This veneer of growth was yet another reason, besides the euro, Greece was able to place debt at modest interest rates. But when the Global Financial Crisis struck and the extent of the deficit was revealed, these brittle foundations crumbled. Of such ingredients, crises are made.

Cutting fat and cracking down on tax avoidance, under these circumstances, should have boosted confidence and stimulated private spending, according to the expansionary-fiscal-contraction doctrine. They should have affected growth positively, or at least minimized any recessionary effects. In fact, consumption and investment responded negatively, not positively. The IMF's 2010 forecast saw the Greek economy shrinking by 4 percent that year and by a further 2.6 percent in 2011 before returning to growth in 2012. The actual contraction was 4.9 percent in 2010, 7.1 percent in 2011, 6.4 percent in 2012, and 4.2 percent in 2013. As Table 12.2 shows, not only did Greece have far and away the largest increase in debt between 2007 and 2013, but that increase was entirely accounted for by the collapse of growth and rise in interest rates.[49]

Although 60 percent of the deficit-closing measures in the initial program were spending cuts, the balance of them were tax increases.[50] It might be argued on these grounds that the policy mix was wrong. But insofar as the problem in Greece was a culture of tax evasion, cracking down on evasion should have been every bit as confidence-inspiring as cutting spending. The IMF's own contemporaneous study of fiscal effort concluded that Greece was able to raise only 80 percent of the revenues mobilized by other countries with its per capita income and other economic characteristics.[51]

Another potential objection is that Greece, or more precisely the Troika, erred by cutting social programs that disproportionately benefited the poor. This violated fairness norms and provoked a political reaction. It fueled the rise and electoral victory in 2015 of Syriza, a left-wing, anti-austerity party. It was far from clear that Syriza would remain committed to the country's Troika program. Even before 2015, there was reason to ask whether the Greek government was prepared to stay the course and whether the electorate would let it. This uncertainty weakened confidence premised on the notion of durable deficit reduction. It did not encourage investment.

Eventually, the IMF, chastened by this experience, acknowledged that, to be politically sustainable, adjustment programs had to protect the poor.[52] But this turnabout came too late for Greece.

## Lessons

What, then, are the lessons for debt management and sustainability? First, debts should be restructured when they are unsustainable. The Greek sovereign debt

*Table 12.2*  **Decomposition of Large Debt Accumulations during the Great Recession, 2007–13**

| Country | Debt-to-GDP Ratio (percent) | | | Contribution to Increase (percent) | | |
|---|---|---|---|---|---|---|
| | Starting Level | Ending Level | Increase | Primary Balance | Interest-Growth Differential | Stock-Flow Adjustment |
| Australia | 9.7 | 30.5 | 20.8 | 19.6 | 0.5 | 0.7 |
| Austria | 64.7 | 81.0 | 16.3 | 5.0 | 6.5 | 4.7 |
| Belgium | 87.0 | 105.5 | 18.4 | 2.5 | 8.9 | 7.0 |
| Canada | 66.9 | 86.2 | 19.4 | 11.7 | 5.9 | 1.7 |
| Finland | 34.0 | 56.5 | 22.5 | 7.3 | 3.7 | 11.4 |
| France | 64.5 | 93.4 | 28.9 | 17.3 | 8.1 | 3.4 |
| Germany | 64.0 | 78.6 | 14.6 | –3.7 | 4.9 | 13.4 |
| Greece | 103.1 | 177.9 | 74.8 | 24.9 | 75.9 | –25.9 |
| Ireland | 23.9 | 120.0 | 96.1 | 66.0 | 17.3 | 12.8 |
| Italy | 99.8 | 129.0 | 29.2 | –5.6 | 28.7 | 6.1 |
| Japan | 175.4 | 232.5 | 57.0 | 44.4 | 23.5 | –10.9 |
| Netherlands | 42.0 | 67.8 | 25.9 | 13.1 | 8.5 | 4.2 |
| New Zealand | 16.3 | 34.6 | 18.3 | 10.9 | 3.6 | 3.8 |
| Portugal | 68.4 | 128.9 | 60.4 | 22.2 | 26.8 | 11.5 |
| Spain | 35.5 | 95.5 | 59.9 | 40.5 | 18.2 | 1.3 |
| United Kingdom | 41.7 | 85.2 | 43.4 | 33.1 | 5.4 | 4.8 |
| United States | 64.6 | 104.8 | 40.1 | 40.7 | 1.8 | –2.4 |
| **Simple average** | 62.5 | 100.5 | 38.0 | 20.6 | 14.6 | 2.8 |
| **Weighted average** | 77.2 | 115.8 | 38.6 | 29.9 | 8.9 | –0.2 |

*Sources:* IMF *World Economic Outlook* Database (IMF various years) and authors' calculations.

*Note:* Episodes are identified based on debt increase of at least 10 percentage points of GDP. Debt increase is calculated using the exact years of the period, i.e., the change in the debt ratio between the start year (2007) and end year (2013).

crisis was lengthy and disruptive because the principals denied the need for re-structuring. The Greek government was forced to impose larger cuts in social programs, pensions, and unemployment benefits because of its failure to obtain a significant reduction in debt-servicing costs. And those cuts provoked a political reaction that undermined support for adjustment and, ultimately, the confidence of investors.

Why this reluctance to restructure? There was the belief, not well informed by history, that advanced economies don't restructure. Greek leaders were anxious to preserve their country's mantle as an advanced economy. They hesitated to impose losses on domestic investors, who were also voters, and worried about destabilizing the banks. European leaders similarly had their reasons. German and French banks were heavily invested in Greek government bonds. French banks had more than €60 billion of exposure to Greece, German banks over €35 billion.[53] Moreover, the president of the ECB, Jean-Claude Trichet, feared that one restructuring might lead to another, causing debt runs on Spain and Ireland.[54] The IMF deferred to the other members of the Troika, European governments having put up the majority of rescue funds.

By 2012, there was overwhelming evidence that Greece's debt was unsustainable and that lending without also reprofiling its debt would be throwing good money after bad. The bondholders therefore accepted reductions in interest rates and some lengthening of maturities, equivalent to a 60–75 percent writedown of their claims. Extending the maturity of bonds governed by Greek law was straightforward: the Greek Parliament simply passed legislation changing the terms. Replacing bonds issued in foreign markets and governed by foreign laws was more difficult. Fortunately, most of these bonds included collective action clauses enabling a qualified majority of bondholders to cram down the exchange on holdouts.[55]

The obstacles to restructuring, evidently, were more political than technical. So what changed between 2010, when restructuring was dismissed as beyond the pale, and 2012, when it was successfully concluded? Domestically, working-class households had suffered enormous pain, and the idea that bondholders should be spared was no longer tenable. Internationally, French and German banks had reduced their exposures to Greece and strengthened their balance sheets, enabling them to absorb the blow.

This points to a second lesson of the crisis, namely the importance of dismantling the diabolic loop connecting banks with sovereign debt distress.[56] When financial institutions are encouraged to hold a government's bonds, whether as a way of keeping down debt-servicing costs or for other reasons, policymakers will hesitate to restructure. Moreover, anything that raises questions about a government's ability to service its debts will create problems for the banks. Depositors will run, and wholesale markets will curtail their funding. The government will have to inject capital, extend guarantees, and take nonperforming loans off bank balance sheets, in operations that further weaken the public finances. With investors doubting the capacity of the government to finance such measures, the funding crisis will intensify. Such feedbacks are why this diabolic process is known as a loop.

We saw in Chapter 9 how, in circumstances tantamount to war, it becomes tempting to draft the central bank into service and instruct it to do whatever it takes to prevent interest rates from rising. We will see this again when we come to the response to the COVID-19 pandemic, widely perceived as a crisis akin to war. But this temptation is also why, in normal times, prudent supervisors and regulators prohibit banks from holding concentrations of government bonds. It is why the most recent iteration of the agreement setting capital standards for internationally active banks (Basel III) sought to eliminate the zero capital charge that incentivizes banks to hold their government's bonds.[57] Distinguishing normal from abnormal times is not easy in a highly charged environment when politicians are pushing for all the help they can get in marketing debt. For this reason, the European Union's decision in 2013 to create a single supervisor not beholden to national governments to oversee its systemically important banks was an important step.

A third lesson was the need for a central bank to backstop the debt market. Volatility can spike when the debt-to-GDP ratio, the budget, or the growth-rate–interest-rate differential develops unfavorably. But volatility can also be triggered by a simple loss of confidence, as happened in France in the 1920s (see Chapter 8) and Asia in the 1990s (see Chapter 10). The government will then be left unable to roll over its maturing debts. Seeing bond prices plummet, investors will flee the market. Panics happen when investors are uncertain of the intentions of the authorities and of one another. In this situation, the role of the central bank is to act as liquidity provider and bond buyer of last resort until conditions normalize, at which point it can sell its bond holdings back into the market.

Until 2012, the ECB denied this responsibility. The central bank saw itself as targeting inflation, pure and simple.[58] Trichet insisted that was not the role of the ECB to backstop the bond market. Instead, governments were obliged to manage their affairs "individually and collectively, to ensure financial stability. [This] is the way Europe has been constructed and it is the way, it seems to all of us, we must proceed. If it is not done by governments, it will not be credible. . . . On the concept of last-resort lending . . . [w]e don't intervene for financial stability reasons. We consider that is the responsibility of governments."[59]

This changed with the 2012 pledge by Mario Draghi, in his early days as Trichet's successor, to "do whatever it takes" to preserve the integrity of the Eurozone—where in this case integrity meant preventing debt runs. The ECB board authorized the bank's traders to purchase the bonds of troubled countries outright.[60] Testifying to the power of intention, mere announcement of the

ECB's readiness to backstop the markets was enough to stabilize prices; the bank didn't have to make actual purchases.

The ability to issue and manage public debt is a matter of state building and even state survival, as we've emphasized throughout this book. But the Greek government was hamstrung by the mismatch between the capacity to issue debt, which resided at the national level, and the capacity to backstop the market, which rested with an institution, the ECB, run collectively by nineteen countries. The crisis made clear that the interests of the Greek government and the ECB were not aligned, at least prior to 2012. The consequences for the Greek state extended to an unprecedented slump, riots, and the rise of far-right political movements. There were real questions about whether Greek democracy in its current form would survive and whether Greece would remain a member in good standing of the European Union.[61]

In the early years of the euro, leaders sought to square this circle by limiting governments' ability to issue debt, creating the European Union's Excessive Deficit Procedure and a debt target of 60 percent of GDP. In this way, the same level of government, namely the European Union, was charged with both deciding what debt levels were acceptable and providing the financial backstop. (The European Commission, the EU's executive branch, was responsible for the first task, the ECB for the second.) But this reconciliation worked poorly. In particular, the Excessive Deficit Procedure proved easier to write than enforce, while the ECB was reluctant to act as a lender of last resort.

The other way of squaring the circle would have been for the European Union to issue bonds, so that both the entity issuing the debt and the one backstopping the market would be agencies of and therefore answerable to Europe. In this way, the incentives of the issuer and the central bank would have been aligned. But this option, known as "debt mutualization," was a bridge too far for more debt-averse EU members. The proposal was immediately quashed. It would take an even more serious crisis in 2020 to breathe new life into the idea.

# COVID-19

The COVID-19 pandemic unleashed a tsunami of debt issuance. By September 2020, with the crisis still barely six months old, G20 governments had already deployed as much as $15 trillion in fiscal resources: $7 trillion of direct budgetary support and an additional $8 trillion of public-sector loans and equity injections into corporations (Figure 13.1).[1] This $15 trillion was nearly 14 percent of global GDP. It demonstrated the essential role of debt issuance in allowing governments to address pressing societal needs and provide critical public services at a time of national emergency. But it also raised troubling questions about debt sustainability and, if there were going to be sustainability problems, about how these would be solved.

The fiscal response was striking for its scale and speed. A lesson had been learned in 2008–9, namely that the longer the delay, the higher the eventual bill. In 2008–9, few if any policymakers had firsthand experience with a full-blown crisis. This led to a period of indecision while officials debated the best way forward. In 2020, there was no such delay. Memories of events a decade earlier were still fresh. Policymakers could dust off the relevant chapters of their financial crisis playbook. It helped that no debt apocalypse or inflationary explosion followed the fiscal actions taken in 2008–9.

In the United States, it was commonplace already by May 2020 to observe that the virus had claimed more American lives than the Vietnam and Korean Wars combined.[2] Extraordinary circumstances, in this respect tantamount to war, justified and indeed required extraordinary action. If acting created fiscal risks, then these could wait. That the pandemic was no fault of the households and firms that suffered its economic and financial effects meant there were few moral-hazard worries to give leaders pause.

Initially, governments were able to issue these very substantial amounts of debt without placing upward pressure on interest rates. Central bank bond purchases, obviously, were an important part of the story. Later in this chapter we will consider the role of the European Central Bank in stabilizing bond

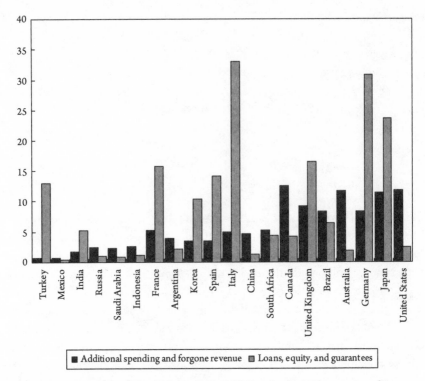

*Figure 13.1.* Summary of Fiscal Measures in G-20 Economies in Response to the COVID-19 Pandemic (percent of GDP)

Sources: IMF *Fiscal Monitor*, October (IMF 2020a) (estimates as of Sep. 11, 2020).

Note: G-20 aggregates are calculated using PPP-adjusted GDP weights. Estimates focus on government discretionary measures that supplement existing automatic stabilizers, which differ across countries in their breadth and scope.

markets. But the Federal Reserve moved even faster and more aggressively than other central banks, including the ECB. In addition to keeping interest rates low for an extended period, its intervention was critical for the stability of the financial system, and specifically for markets in public debt. Because of their liquidity, US Treasury bonds are widely held as reserves by central banks and corporate treasuries. When the COVID crisis hit, many such holders, scrambling for cash, sold off a portion of those reserves. Treasury yields jumped, wrong-footing hedge funds that had bet that yields would remain low.[3] This created the prospect of large losses on the trade, leading to margin calls that might force hedge funds and others to liquidate yet additional Treasury holdings. In the worst case, the prices of Treasuries could have cratered, not only creating liquidity problems, but also tarnishing the reputation of US Treasury bonds as a safe asset and conceivably even leaving the government unable to fund itself.

Thus, by pushing Treasury yields back down and restoring orderly conditions, the Fed's intervention was critical for financial stability and also for investors' perceptions of US debt securities.[4] It was a reminder that markets in public debt, when disturbed, do not automatically right themselves. Markets need a backstop in the form of a liquidity provider of last resort. Without this, the collateral value of even high-quality sovereign debt securities can be lost. Worse still, the repo market through which banks provide one another with short-term liquidity, taking Treasury bonds as collateral, could cease to function. Bank lending and the economy might grind to a halt.

Instead, the dominant role of the dollar and US Treasury securities in global financial markets was preserved and, if anything, reinforced, by the Federal Reserve's timely intervention. This was the case because the Fed understood the importance of backstopping the market and, informed by that understanding, took concerted action.

## Fiscal Contrasts

Several additional facts, besides the sheer size of debt issuance, jump out of Figure 13.1. Most obviously, advanced countries organized larger fiscal packages than emerging markets. This was not because emerging markets were forecast to sidestep the pandemic and recession. To the contrary, more than $100 billion of portfolio capital hemorrhaged out of emerging markets already in the early months of 2020, three times as much as in the early months of the Global Financial Crisis. Remittances fell by an additional $100 billion.[5] Global trade was on course to fall even faster than in 2009. The crisis may have been slow to reach the emerging and developing world, but there was no question that it was coming.

Brazil, Turkey, and South Africa, three hard-hit emerging markets, ran larger primary budget deficits in 2020 than during the Global Financial Crisis. Yet even their stimulus packages were small by the standards of advanced economies. And other emerging markets, such as India, Indonesia, and Mexico, did considerably less. This reflected these countries' more limited fiscal space and greater financial stability concerns. In a few cases, such as Guatemala and Peru, emerging markets were able to issue new foreign currency debt in the early stages of the crisis.[6] More often than not, however, they were forced to rely on domestic issuance and local investors. Emerging markets like, once again, Brazil, Turkey, and South Africa succeeded in issuing additional domestic debt in the first half of 2020, but subject to sharply rising interest costs, since debt loads looked increasingly perilous with the decline in GDP. With few exceptions, interest-rate spreads were even wider than during the Global Financial Crisis. Credit rating agencies downgraded emerging markets even more quickly than in that earlier crisis. Already by the summer of 2020, as the virus reached a growing number of emerging markets, forbidding questions were asked about the sustainability of their debts and how quickly they would be compelled to turn back in the direction of austerity.

The response of the international policy community bore an unnerving resemblance to its response to the Latin American debt crisis of the 1980s, which was not reassuring. Recall how it took seven years from the onset of the crisis to the inauguration of the Brady Plan, under which problem debts were finally restructured.[7] In the interim, advanced-country governments encouraged banks to roll over their commitments rather than recognizing losses and therefore impairing their balance sheets. This approach limited bank recapitalization costs for advanced-country governments, but for Latin America it meant little new money, little debt restructuring, a debt overhang, and a lost decade.

In April 2020, G20 governments acknowledged the plight of the poorest countries and offered a temporary moratorium on their bilateral (government-to-government) debts.[8] The IMF provided grants to fund interest payments on monies lent previously to its low-income members.[9] This, at least, was something, although the threat by one major rating agency that it would downgrade any government availing itself of this facility rendered countries reluctant to participate.

In contrast, there was no moratorium on low-income countries' debt to the private sector, and no help for middle-income countries. The G20 outsourced these problems to private lenders. Specifically, it delegated organizing negotiations to the Institute of International Finance (IIF), the trade group of the creditors.[10]

This approach had something of a fox-in-the-henhouse quality. Guidance from the Institute of International Finance read as if it had been written by the hedge funds, mutual funds, and sundry and assorted institutional investors that held the debt—which, of course, it had. The institute cautioned governments that restructuring might jeopardize market access, not just for themselves but also for their peers. It warned that the fiduciary responsibility of institutional investors was to their clients, not to governments or the global community. It emphasized the need to proceed on a case-by-case basis.

There was at least a plausible argument that the advanced countries seeing sharp increases in their public debt burdens as a result of the COVID-19 emergency could manage those heavier debts. They might be able to work them down as a share of GDP, albeit gradually over a substantial period of years, through a combination of primary budget surpluses, moderate inflation, and successful economic growth. For emerging markets, any such argument was more tenuous. Inflation and interest rates were higher, the political capacity to run budget surpluses was more limited, and growth prospects were even more severely damaged by the pandemic and its byproducts of recession and deglobalization.

Hence, lack of acknowledgment that the existing ad hoc machinery for dealing with defaults and restructurings was unable to cope with an impending wave of emerging market debt crises was deeply troubling. Perhaps the problem looked less threatening to advanced-country governments because debts were no longer concentrated in the hands of a few large money-center banks. But this fact did not make the problem any less threatening to emerging markets themselves. A couple of isolated basket cases, Argentina and Ecuador, were able to restructure their debts in the midst of the pandemic. In both cases, their bonds contained collective action clauses requiring only a qualified majority of bondholders to agree on restructuring terms and preventing a handful of vulture funds from holding the process hostage. But even these negotiations were complex and extended. And whether the same institutional investors could handle a tidal wave of restructuring negotiations was more dubious.[11] Given all this, the absence of forceful official intervention to organize the process did not bode well for the outcome.[12]

## Fish Out of Water

Recall that in 2009, China had implemented the largest stimulus of any economy.[13] Although that stimulus brought a quick end to the country's slump, it was criticized for bequeathing inefficient infrastructure projects, encouraging investment in sectors where China had excess capacity, supporting state-owned enterprises (SOEs) at the expense of the private sector, and allowing heavily indebted companies to gorge on credit.[14] The Politburo had previously sought to rebalance the economy away from heavy industry and construction in favor of high tech. It had taken steps to shift the composition of spending from investment to consumption. It had attempted to reduce the economy's dependence on bank credit. From all these angles, the 2009 stimulus worked in the wrong direction.

In addition, although China's public debt load was moderate (at the end of 2019, central government debt was a bit more than 40 percent of GDP, while general government debt, including provincial and municipal debts, was some 50 percent of GDP), the nonfinancial corporate sector was indebted to the tune of 160 percent of GDP. Taken together, these debts were nearly twice the level, relative to GDP, at which China had entered the Global Financial Crisis. SOEs, and for that matter other nonfinancial corporations, remained an important source of employment, notwithstanding efforts to grow the private sector. They provided social services to their employees and communities, despite efforts underway since the global financial crisis to shift this responsibility to local governments. With the outbreak of COVID-19, they were instructed to provide rent holidays for business tenants, such as retail stores. It followed that if SOEs ran into trouble, the central and local governments would be loath to let them fail. The price of public-sector support might be that a portion of SOE debt would end up on governments' balance sheets.

These were reasons to proceed cautiously. In 2020, as the world descended into recession, the Chinese authorities assembled a rescue package of 5 percent of GDP.[15] This was considerably less than in 2009.[16] As Premier Li Keqiang remarked, "We are now providing water so that the fish can survive—fish will die without enough water, but there will be bubbles if we provide too much water."[17]

The other fish out of water were the low-income countries that had borrowed from China, many as part of its Belt & Road Initiative. In all, China had provided loans and signed memoranda with 138 countries. As of 2020, debt payments owed by the governments of low-income countries to the Chinese government and its state-owned lenders exceeded total repayments owed to all other bilateral creditors, reflecting not just the size of the loans, but also that many of them had been extended at market-based commercial, not concessional, interest rates. The loans in question were for infrastructure projects along six land and sea corridors linking China to other regions and for sundry mining and manufacturing projects. As we saw in earlier chapters, there is a long history of countries borrowing to finance railways, ports, and telecommunication systems, three purposes to which Belt & Road loans were put. But we also saw how such investments didn't always generate the revenues needed to repay, in which case the loans in question had to be restructured.

China already had some experience with restructuring intergovernmental debts. Between 2007 and 2016, its Export-Import Bank, an arm of the government, had extended several rounds of loans to the government of Sri Lanka to construct a deep-water port at Hambantota. When the port failed to generate traffic and revenue sufficient to repay the debt, Sri Lanka leased Hambantota port and 15,000 surrounding acres to a Chinese company, China Merchants Port Holdings, for a period of ninety-nine years, receiving in return exactly the amount of money it needed to pay off the Export-Import Bank. One might think of this as debt restructuring by another name, or perhaps as a kind of debt-for-equity (debt-for-national-patrimony?) swap. Similarly, in 2020, Laos's state-owned Electricité du Laos sold off majority control of its electric grid to the China Southern Power Grid Co., in return for forbearance on interest payments owed by the Lao government and state-owned enterprises to the Chinese government and its policy banks on debt incurred to build dams and hydroelectric projects. (Exact terms of the deal were not disclosed.) In all, there were more than two dozen debt restructurings and credit events (delays in payment) since 2011 on China's loans to developing countries.[18]

All of which is to say, the Chinese government was intimately familiar with what it was now being asked to do. But although China was party to the G20 communiqué announcing a moratorium on the bilateral debts of the poorest countries, it sent conflicting signals about whether that moratorium would apply to its Belt & Road loans, and specifically to loans provided by the

China Development Bank, another of the country's policy banks.[19] A further problem was that the exact amount of these loans was not known outside of official Chinese circles.[20] China was not a member of the Paris Club, the organization of creditor-country governments that restructures bilateral debts to governments and other official entities, freeing it from the club's standard disclosure agreements.[21]

Exactly how much debt relief countries needed, consequently, was uncertain. Other governments were reluctant to forgive the bilateral loans they had extended to poor countries, not knowing whether China would go along and worried that their contribution to debt forgiveness might end up paying off Chinese creditors. So interest and principal payments were deferred temporarily, not forgiven. This gap in the international financial architecture, much like China's undersized quota at the IMF, reflected the country's very recent emergence as an international lender. It now left official bodies poorly placed to deal with emerging debt problems.

## Releasing the Debt Brake

Figure 13.1 also shows that some countries traditionally averse, even phobic, about debt finance were prepared to throw caution to the wind. In March 2020, the German government suspended its constitutionally enshrined Debt Brake, which limited federal government budget deficits to 0.35 percent of GDP, and implemented a very large spending package. This was in contrast to 2009, when discretionary stimulus was just 1.6 percent of GDP. That the pandemic was an exceptional emergency was part of the explanation. The crisis also satisfied the "not of the state's own making" proviso in the escape clause from the Debt Brake, meaning that there were few concerns about moral hazard. Again, it helped that there had been no eruption of inflation following the fiscal stimulus of 2008–9. Moreover, a social commitment to the welfare state and the view that government had a responsibility to limit unemployment and company failures created broad political support for additional spending in response to a societywide pandemic. In all, this was a reminder that what is fiscally unthinkable in normal times can become entirely thinkable in a crisis.

Finally, Figure 13.1 points up the very different composition of fiscal and quasi-fiscal measures across Europe. Italy applied barely a third of the spending and revenue measures of Germany, reflecting high inherited debt and tenuous investor confidence. The Italian government was forced to concentrate its efforts elsewhere: policy initiatives were skewed toward loans to the private sector, which the government could claim would be paid back, and toward equity injections, which, it argued, would pay for themselves once that equity was sold.

Yet spreads on Italian government bonds rose less in the first half of 2020 than during the Global Financial Crisis or even when the populist Lega-5Star government was formed in 2018. This was despite the fact that the Italian government entered 2020 with a debt-to-GDP of more than 130 percent, nearly a third higher than in 2008 and the highest of any advanced country other than Greece.

The paradox dissolves when one observes that the ECB responded to the pandemic by ramping up purchases of Eurozone government bonds, including those of Italy. The central bank's newly installed president, Christine Lagarde, committed an early faux pas, remarking that the ECB was "not here to close [bond] spreads; this is not the function or the mission of the ECB." These remarks contradicted or at least watered down the implications of Draghi's 2012 do-what-ever-it-takes pledge and more generally disregarded episodes throughout history when central banks had played a role in backstopping sovereign debt markets. They predictably provoked an Italian bond selloff and worries about the euro.

Lagarde's advisors quickly reminded her of this 2012 history. Within days, the ECB reversed course, announcing a Pandemic Emergency Purchase Program (PEPP) under which it purchased the bonds of all European sovereigns so as to reduce "fragmentation" in European bond markets (read: bring down spreads on bonds such as those of the Italian government). PEPP was large relative to the ECB's earlier quantitative easing. In addition, unlike earlier programs, the composition of bond purchases was not constrained to match the share of a country in the ECB's capital, allowing it to purchase as many Italian bonds as it wished.

The spread between ten-year Italian bonds and German Bunds immediately fell by 100 basis points (Figure 13.2). Again, this highlighted the role of the central bank as a liquidity provider of last resort and its ability to backstop the market in sovereign bonds when the authorities' continuing ability to issue debt was literally a matter of survival.

## A Hamiltonian Moment, or Just the Broadway Version?

The ECB's action also highlighted the mismatch between nineteen national treasuries and a single central bank. It rekindled worries that the ECB's exceptional measures might become unexceptional, with inflationary consequences in the future, even if there were no such consequences now. Not only did this tap into historically grounded fears, but it had troubling distributional implications. Although the inflation tax would be paid by the residents of all Eurozone countries, the subsidy it financed would accrue only to the residents of countries whose bond markets received ECB support.

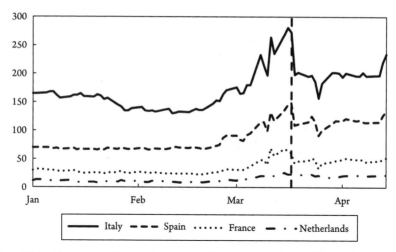

*Figure 13.2.* 10-year spreads over German Bunds, January-April 2020 (daily, in basis points)
Source: Haver Analytics. http://haver.com/
Note: The vertical dashed line marks announcement of the PEPP by the ECB on Mar. 18, 2020.

The criticism, at root, was that the ECB was engaging in quasi-fiscal policies with first-order distributional consequences. If there were going to be transfers between member states, the argument ran, then these should be decided by national leaders and parliaments. They should be undertaken by national treasuries in conjunction with the European Union.

Ultimately, this mismatch turned out to be midwife to a fiscal breakthrough, namely authorization for the European Union to issue bonds. Controversy over the need for an EU fiscal capacity was of long standing, as we have seen. This debate now took a turn. In May 2020, in the midst of the pandemic, President Emmanuel Macron of France and Chancellor Angela Merkel of Germany proposed that the European Union should issue €500 billion of bonds. Other governments, such as Spain's, tabled their own plans, with price tags up to €1 trillion. The European Commission split the difference, proposing €750 billion of bonds, the proceeds from which would finance loans and grants to member states. This was very different from the relatively miserly €20 billion of additional spending with which the European Union had responded to the Global Financial Crisis.[22] The prices of Italian and other peripheral Euro Area bonds again rallied on the news.

The Macron-Merkel proposal was a game changer, coming as it did from France and Germany, the dual engines of European integration. It was widely portrayed as Europe's Hamiltonian moment. (Recall from Chapter 3 Alexander Hamilton's 1790 proposal that the US federal government should assume the obligations of the states and consolidate them into a new federal debt.) But whether this was in fact a turning point on Europe's road to fiscal union—toward creating a single European Treasury to complement its Single Currency and central bank—remained uncertain. The €750 billion total was less than 6 percent of EU GDP.[23] Transfers to the member states would be spread over several years, with just 10 percent of the total to be paid out in 2021. Only half took the form of grants (the balance was in the form of loans that had to be repaid, meaning that they added to the debt burden of the recipients). In any case, a precedent set in a once-in-a-century pandemic might not be seen as carrying over to ordinary circumstances.

A critical element of Hamilton's plan had been to match the new obligations with revenues from customs duties and tariffs that accrued directly to the federal government, ensuring that the latter would have the capacity to service its newly created debt. Initially, the European Commission did not specify how interest payments on EU bonds would be financed, although there were vague allusions to an increase in "own resources"—to new taxes on financial transactions, perhaps, or on digital platforms, the proceeds from which would accrue directly to the European Union. For the moment, however, leaders agreed only on a largely symbolic tax on nonrecycled plastic waste and punted remaining decisions into the future.

Ultimately, the extent of own resources would tell the tale. The US Congress established the Customs Service in 1789, creating the basis for a stream of federal revenues that expanded along with the economy, and allowing the government to service a larger debt. Revenues from an EU digital tax or financial-transaction tax that did not compete with national taxes could similarly grow over time. Collection of these taxes would be a permanent competence of the European Union. But if the EU relied on resources transferred from national treasuries when servicing its bonds, resources that would be decided in the context of periodic budget negotiations, then there could be no certainty that these would rise over time or become permanent. In this case, Europe's fiscal union would be frozen in amber.

## The Legacy

These crises left a mixed legacy. It was reassuring that governments could incur large debts when necessary without seeing interest rates shoot up. They may have been able to do so only with support from their central banks, but no untoward consequences followed. Private spending remained sufficiently subdued that governments could ramp up their borrowing and spending and central banks could ramp up their support without triggering runaway inflation.

The question was what would happen when private spending recovered and it came time to stabilize and reduce the debt. The historical episodes reviewed here suggest that the heavy debts with which governments and societies emerge from wars, financial crises, and other emergencies are best stabilized through a combination of approaches: by running primary surpluses, tolerating moderate inflation, and encouraging economic growth. But when societies rely entirely on inflation or imagine that they can sustain very large primary surpluses for extended periods, things turn out badly. High inflation tends to erode support for the government and confidence in the economy. Political and economic circumstances get in the way of efforts to maintain primary surpluses. In post–World War I Germany, relying entirely on inflation helped to seal the fate of Weimar democracy. In twenty-first-century Greece, relying entirely on primary surpluses came close to producing the same catastrophic result.

These two cases are also a reminder that durable debt consolidation requires shared sacrifice and social consensus. There must be political support at home. In both Germany and Greece, requirements for how to manage sovereign debt were imposed from outside. In neither case was this a setting conducive to building a political consensus.

Running primary surpluses, engineering moderate inflation, and fostering faster economic growth will not be easy under post-COVID conditions. Population aging in advanced economies and an increasing number of emerging markets will slow the growth of GDP. Spain and Italy will have to run cyclically adjusted primary budget surpluses of about 7 percent annually, year after year, to return their debt ratios to pre-COVID levels within a decade. Maintaining such large primary budget surpluses is difficult under the best of circumstances. It is especially difficult in polarized societies that are likely to be even more polarized in the wake of a global pandemic whose effects fall most heavily on the poor, that lays bare the extent of inequality, and that creates demands for the public sector to provide additional social services.

Paying for these additional services with higher taxes on the wealthy is problematic when high earners and their financial assets can move. The history of capital levies, recounted in Chapter 8, is not encouraging. There may be some increase in taxes on high earners, given the inequality and the societal fault lines exposed by the pandemic. But don't hold your breath that the revenue so generated will make a significant dent in the debt.[24]

A burst of inflation that liquidates debt burdens similarly seems unlikely. The "stability culture" that has enabled central banks to keep inflation and interest rates in check is deeply ingrained. Central banks may have purchased a significant share of the bonds issued by governments, but those bonds are also held by households, commercial banks, and pension funds. These creditors would not take well to policies that significantly erode the value of their savings.

Central banks may choose to overshoot their target rates of inflation for a time, given that recent crises have bequeathed heavy debts and that inflation has undershot for an extended period. This would not be a disaster. Moderate inflation can help bring down debt burdens for prudent governments that have lengthened the duration of their debts. The danger is that moderate inflation can turn into rapid inflation if not accompanied by primary budget surpluses. But the will to run primary budget surpluses does not last forever. Sooner or later, austerity fatigue sets in. Memories of the exceptional events now said to justify shared fiscal sacrifice will begin to dim. This is why growth is important. Without growth, other debt-consolidation strategies simply take too long.

As always, there is the alternative of debt restructuring. Debt restructuring, it is tempting to assert, is inconceivable in a G20 country. But pause before saying that. Argentina, recall, is a G20 country.

# 14

# Conclusion

When we started writing this book, it felt as if we were pushing a boulder up a hill. It would be hard, we feared, convincing readers accustomed to thinking about spendthrift governments and dangerous debt overhangs that public debt does good and not only harm. Then the COVID-19 pandemic made the case for us. Public debt provided precious fiscal space for governments struggling to meet a public health emergency and economic crisis. Through the programs it financed, it offered a lifeline to people unable to work, parents unable to feed their children, and businesses unable to make payroll. The crisis would have been infinitely worse had governments not resorted to debt issuance. This is evident in the contrast between advanced-country governments that were able to borrow freely, and low-income countries that lacked well-developed bond markets and were constrained in responding.

This pandemic-induced surge of debt issuance is the most recent instance of a pattern that has recurred throughout history. Time and again, governments have borrowed to meet wars, natural disasters, financial crises, and economic downturns, when the public-policy response requires more resources than can be mobilized using current revenues alone. But borrowers need willing lenders. Those lenders in turn demand protections in order to make a market in public debt. Such protections include checks on arbitrary action by the sovereign, in the form of a power-sharing arrangement. They include a liquid secondary market so that investors can diversify their holdings and exit as needed. They include a central bank to backstop the market, ensuring its liquidity when liquidity is at risk. They include a monetary rule, such as a target for inflation or the exchange rate, to assure investors that their claims won't be inflated away.

Forward-looking governments have been known to put these requisites in place before they are needed. In other cases, such as during England's Glorious Revolution, the sovereign has been forced to concede them in the midst of a crisis, when borrowing is urgent and the state's survival hangs in the balance. But, either way, it's not hard to see connections between the prerequisites for public debt issuance and broader economic, financial, social, and political changes, including strengthening political checks and balances, the development of markets, and the emergence of market-supporting institutions. It's not hard, in other words, to see connections with what social scientists refer to as "modernization"—a process with economic, financial, social, and political dimensions.

The implication is that sovereign debt has been integral to modern economic growth. (There's that word *modern* again.[1]) Modern economic growth is fundamentally about nonlinearities—about a sharp acceleration relative to an earlier rate of growth resulting from positive feedback.[2] The link from public debt and its role in financial development to faster growth, and from faster growth back to financial deepening and economic development, is just such a feedback.

This is not a static story, of course. History has seen significant changes in the purposes to which sovereigns and states put their borrowed funds. As we have described, borrowing by sovereigns first occurred with regularity in the early centuries of the second millennium CE. This timing coincided with changes in military technology that increased the cost of offensive and defensive wars. European sovereigns were prominent in this transition, owing to Europe's Commercial Revolution and a physical and political geography that made for recurrent conflict.

Sovereigns borrowed to finance military adventures but also to repel threats. Thus, the capacity to issue debt was central to state building. It was a matter of state survival. Sovereigns seeking access to credit might grant privileges in order to secure the cooperation of their creditors. As those creditors obtained checks on absolutist rulers and created representative assemblies to approve the taxes needed to pay interest and principal, sovereign debt contributed to the broader process of political development. Similarly, the sovereign's creditors might seek to establish a secondary market on which to trade their claims, diversify their holdings, and manage their risk. Claims traded there functioned as collateral for other financial transactions, and their prices served as benchmarks for pricing riskier credits. Sovereign debt thereby contributed to financial development. A seminal question in economic history is why Europe was "first." How did it differ from other continents financially and politically, and why was it early in completing the transition to modern economic growth? Herein lies part of the answer.

As incomes rose, the focus of public finance then shifted toward providing public goods and services. Because the nation's security is an essential public good, large-scale debt issuance remained, and remains today, concentrated in times of war and other national emergencies. Increasingly, however, governments also borrowed to finance public infrastructure: water and sewer works, urban lighting, and transportation systems. Using debt to finance these projects fit their profile, since the increase in economic activity and associated revenues materialized only later. It's hard to imagine the transition to modern economic growth without railways to knit together national and international markets and urban agglomerations to act as hotbeds of innovation. And it's hard to imagine those railways and cities without debt finance.[3]

Increasingly, this developmental model was pursued not just by the nineteenth century's pioneering industrializers, but also by follower states that sought to emulate their example. These followers had not yet put in place the prerequisites for well-functioning debt markets. They therefore piggybacked on countries that had, borrowing in international financial centers where investment banks acted as gatekeepers and organized exchanges regulated the market. Investors in those financial centers adapted their practices to accommodate the global character of the market, creating specialized services for assembling and disseminating information on far-flung regions, and committees to represent the lenders.

By the end of the nineteenth century, the market in sovereign debt was significantly globalized. It was globalized in the sense that debt was issued by governments in every part of the world. It was globalized in that debts were regularly traded across borders.

Not all investment projects were well conceived and executed, of course. And sovereign loans supported public consumption as well as public investment. Although the information environment had improved, this did not mean that such behaviors were easy to detect. And when a foreign sovereign had problems, bondholders were reminded of their limited recourse. They could enlist the help of their government, although some governments were more accommodating than others. They could bar a defaulting debtor from their market, although that debtor might still be able to tap alternative venues. The main thing they could do was demand a risk premium sufficient to compensate for repayment interruptions, and diversify their holdings so as to avoid putting all their eggs in one basket. These strategies worked imperfectly. But they worked well enough that by the end of the nineteenth century they supported an active and expanding global market in public debt.

The two world wars transformed this landscape. The nineteenth century was less than peaceful, but the two twentieth-century world wars vastly exceeded, in destructiveness and cost, what had come before. With this expense, wartime governments ran up very large debts. Following the return of peace, these burdens were managed with varying degrees of success. In some cases, mainly after World War I, governments paid down their debts by running primary budget surpluses. In others, mainly after World War II, countries outgrew their debt burdens. Investors in some countries were expropriated by inflation and interest-rate ceilings that reduced the value of their claims.

A less immediate but no less consequential legacy was the impetus provided by the two world wars for development of the welfare state. Some countries had taken modest steps in the direction of social insurance already before World War I. Bismarck's Germany provided health and injury insurance. Asquith's Britain created the nucleus of state-run unemployment insurance. Among their motivations was heading off social unrest among an urban, industrial labor force questioning the legitimacy of states that enforced private property rights while neglecting the needs of the working class. World War I heightened these pressures, since governments sending men off to fight in the trenches were compelled to extend them the franchise on their return, if those governments were to preserve what limited legitimacy they still possessed. Returning soldiers who had served as cannon fodder in a purposeless war were understandably disaffected, as evidenced by the Bolshevik Revolution in Russia, the Sparticist Uprising in Germany, the *biennio rosso* (two red years) in Italy, and other proto-revolutionary movements. Governments sought to reassert their authority by addressing their citizens' legitimate concerns. They did so by expanding access to social benefits.

The Great Depression worked in the same direction. It led publics to question whether governments were making good on their promises. In response, those governments sought to reassure their constituents by establishing public programs intended to deliver on their commitments, as in the United States, where the New Deal led to increased provision of unemployment insurance, old-age pensions, and other forms of social security. World War II then lent additional impetus to the process, and governments responded to popular calls by expanding existing programs and supplementing them with state support for health, education, and housing.

The result, by the mid-twentieth century, was bigger government, together with demands for the state to do still more. Starting in the second half of the 1960s, there then developed a visible tendency for spending to run ahead of revenues and for governments to issue debt to make up the difference. So when growth in the advanced countries slowed in the 1970s, public debts shot up. Governments made fumbling efforts to address the problem, a few successfully, many not.

The 1970s were also when developing countries, in Latin America and elsewhere, re-entered the sovereign debt market, having been shut out since the 1930s. With productivity and GDP growth slowing, the timing was not propitious. Slower growth of their principal export markets did not make servicing debts any easier. More debt did not automatically translate into more investment, as politicians currying favor with voters plowed borrowed funds into consumption. Even where there was more investment, the latter did not always translate into faster growth. Meanwhile, the money-center banks providing the finance, which might have cautioned against excesses, looked the other way. They received their comeuppance when the Volcker shock (the sharp increases in US interest rates occurring on Paul Volcker's watch) brought the Latin American debt crisis to a head.

One lesson of this episode was that it was risky to organize sovereign lending through bank syndicates, since problems experienced by developing-country borrowers could quickly become problems for money-center banks, and by implication for their governments. It followed that when the Latin American debt crisis was finally laid to rest in the 1990s, and lending resumed, the conduit for cross-border transfers, as in the nineteenth century, once more became the bond market. This allowed the risk of lending to be spread more widely, reducing—if not eliminating—the danger of systemic instability on the creditor side.

Another widely touted lesson, known as the "Lawson doctrine," eponymously named after the UK Treasury official who championed it, was that money should be lent to countries that prioritized investment over consumption, since they were apt to grow and be best able to repay.[4] This inference was more problematic. Lending to finance investment made sense only when investment was productive, not so much when it financed empty office towers, inefficient nickel smelters, and the other white elephants of which governments everywhere are so fond. Even when plans were well conceived, moreover, events beyond the borrower's control might interrupt their execution and, given the long gestation period of investment projects, prevent the payoff from materializing.

Among the countries with the highest investment rates were the Asian "Tigers" (South Korea, Taiwan, Hong Kong, and Singapore) and other regional economies that followed their example. Given their high investment rates and records of successful growth, creditors were more than willing to accommodate them, and their governments took full advantage. But when growth failed to accelerate, lenders were reminded that not all investments are productive. Borrowers first experienced greater difficulty in accessing external finance, then capital flight, and finally financial crisis. This was not a uniquely Asian phenomenon, of course; there was no dearth of crises in other emerging markets—in Mexico, Brazil, Ecuador, Argentina, and Turkey, to name a few.

The first decade of the twenty-first century then saw countries in Latin America, Asia, and elsewhere continuing to grapple with these problems. Governments in middle-income countries sought to reduce their dependence on external funds. They strengthened their fiscal positions and otherwise retrenched in order to move the current account of the balance of payments into surplus. Surpluses reduced their dependence on external finance and helped them accumulate foreign reserves as a cushion. Officials sought to develop markets on which local-currency bonds could be bought and sold so that the financial position would no longer be subject to the whims of the foreign exchange market and they would not be at the mercy of foreign investors.

They half succeeded. More emerging markets successfully marketed public debt denominated in their own currencies. They were less successful, however, in marketing it at home. Local demand being limited, a significant share of their local-currency debt was purchased by foreign investors attracted by high interest rates. These securities were still subject to sharp selloffs since, when things went wrong, foreign investors were now hit by both declining bond prices and a declining exchange rate. Shifting from foreign- to local-currency debt was no panacea, in other words.

There was, if anything, even less progress in the advanced-country world. The United States came under scrutiny for its twin budget and current-account deficits. Critics warned that relying on foreign investors to finance those deficits exposed the country to a disorderly correction if the foreign appetite for debt securities dried up. European governments resumed running budget deficits following the period of austerity required to qualify for the euro. Japan, fighting a chronic slump, outdid everyone by running budget deficits in the high single digits year after year and accumulating mountains of debt.

Then came the Global Financial Crisis and COVID-19. Notwithstanding earlier problems, public debt was an indispensable ally in the fight against each. During the Global Financial Crisis, debt was issued to prevent spending from collapsing, to keep banks from going under, and to support auto companies and other large employers. To be sure, there was hesitation to resort to debt finance on moral-hazard grounds. Critics warned that using borrowed funds to bail out banks whose excesses had set the stage for the crisis only rewarded bad behavior. Policymakers worried that additional debt issuance would push up inflation and interest rates and depress investment. Still, public debt played a key role in managing the crisis, much as it had in managing crises through the ages. By preventing events from spinning out of control, it preserved the legitimacy of the state.

There was no little criticism of the response, much of it valid. Fiscal initiatives were underpowered. Governments favored Wall Street over Main Street. They did too little to aid homeowners faced with foreclosure. In some places, fiscal support was withdrawn prematurely. The response was less than ideal, in these and other respects. But imagine how much more intense this criticism would have been were there no fiscal response at all.

When COVID-19 struck, there was less hesitation about ramping up public spending and issuing debt. In the same way that a state will use all available resources, including the financial, to defend against a foreign military threat, governments used all available resources, including debt, to defend against this life-threatening viral invasion. Moral hazard was a nonissue in a crisis touched off by a viral mutation. In any case, the Global Financial Crisis had shown that additional debt did not automatically lead to inflation, high interest rates, and fiscal crisis, contrary to earlier fears.

The situation also differed in other respects from that twelve years before. Most obviously, inherited debts were heavier. The United States, for example, entered the COVID crisis with federal government debt held by the private sector of 80 percent of GDP, twice that in 2008.[5] Nonetheless, its fiscal response was even more dramatic in size and speed. The Congressional Budget Office estimated that debt held by the public would rise, as a result of the crisis and measures taken in response, to 100 percent of GDP by the end of 2020, less than a year into the crisis, and 102 percent by the end of 2021.[6] It would approach 105 percent of GDP by 2030 and would continue to rise from there.[7]

Stein's Law says that if something can't go on forever, it will stop. The question is when and how. It could be that debt can keep rising, at least for a while, without causing major disruptions. Japan's experience is consistent with this view: as a result of the COVID crisis and fiscal measures taken in response, the Japanese government's gross debt reached 250 percent of GDP in 2020. Net debt, a better measure of the fiscal position, was poised to move above 170 percent of GDP, less astronomical but still far above US levels.[8] Yet no untoward financial consequences followed. Interest rates on Japanese government bonds didn't spike. The yen didn't collapse. The Nikkei performed better than other major indices. To be sure, the Bank of Japan's asset purchases and cap on bond yields had a lot to do with this stability. But neither was there a cost in the form of inflation, which dyed-in-the-wool monetarists warned would be an unavoidable consequence of central bank bond purchases.

Still, even if servicing such a high debt is possible for Japan, it may not be possible for other countries. As a result of three decades of deflation fighting, the Bank of Japan holds a larger share of the national debt, on the order of 50 percent, than any other advanced-country central bank. It is not clear that the Fed's political masters would let it to go there. Japanese households are high savers and plow their savings into government bonds. Corporate governance entrenches conservative management, which makes for limited ambition and limited investment—investment that is further dampened by deflation and unfavorable demographics. All this makes a large pool of savings available to the government bond market.

One might argue that ample household savings and conservative corporate management are not exactly hallmarks of the United States. Yet the fact is that the US private sector has displayed a growing excess of saving over investment for the better part of two decades. This is evident in the behavior of real interest rates (nominal rates adjusted for inflation), which have fallen steadily in order to bring saving and investment into line. Just why real rates have fallen, in the United States and globally, is disputed. Some say that the explanation is the high savings of Germany, Saudi Arabia, and fast-growing emerging markets such as China. In an integrated global market, their ample savings depress interest rates around the world. Demography works in the same direction. Life expectancy in the advanced economies has risen by nearly five years over the last three decades. Living longer and looking ahead to more years of retirement leads people to sock away more savings while working. Still other observers suggest that interest rates have fallen because the need for physical investment has declined with the shift from manufacturing to services and from physical platforms to digital platforms.[9] Whatever the cause, the result has been to confront more saving supply with less investment demand, resulting in lower interest rates.

Those lower rates in turn mean that US and other advanced-country governments are actually devoting a smaller fraction of GDP to interest payments, despite their now carrying more debt. In the United States, federal government debt service cost just 2 percent of GDP in 2020, virtually unchanged from 2001, when the debt-to-GDP ratio was barely half as high. Given current low interest rates, there is no immediate crisis of debt sustainability, in other words.

Indeed, with nominal interest rates hovering just above zero, attempting to reduce the debt now could be a recipe for disaster. Normally, reducing public spending would cause interest rates to fall, encouraging private spending. But rates can't fall significantly when they are already near zero. Under these circumstances, shifting the budget toward surplus and borrowing less could so depress aggregate demand as to actually raise debt-to-GDP ratios, as in Japan in the 1990s and 2000s.[10] Some will argue that central banks can take up the slack by purchasing bonds and substituting monetary support for fiscal support. But we know that by keeping a lid on the return on safe assets, such central bank policies encourage savers to herd into riskier investments, in stock markets for example, in a desperate search for yield. There was plenty of evidence of those behaviors in 2020–21. Such policies risk creating asset bubbles, resulting in financial distress and dislocations when they burst. They only substitute private-sector financial vulnerabilities for public-sector weaknesses.

There's no guarantee, of course, that interest rates will remain at rock-bottom levels. The savings rates of oil-exporting economies could fall as the demand for their petroleum dries up. Consumption in China could rise to levels more customary for a middle-income country as the government builds out the social safety net. The additional deficit spending undertaken by the Biden Administration and the US Congress could supercharge demand so much as to put upward pressure on interest rates. But even if these things happen and interest rates do rise, disaster need not follow. If debt managers are savvy, they can sell very-long-term bonds and lock in low interest rates.

If they aren't so savvy, higher interest rates will create the need to reduce debt-to-GDP ratios. The obvious way is by running primary budget surpluses. In recent times, a small number of countries have succeeded in running large primary surpluses, for extended periods, on the scale that will be required for countries like Spain and Italy to reduce their debt ratios to pre-COVID levels.[11] One recent study identifies just three countries that have been able to run primary surpluses averaging 5 percent of GDP for as long as ten years: Singapore after 1990, Belgium after 1995, and Norway after 1999.[12] These cases are special. Norway's surpluses were associated with windfall revenues from North Sea oil, which were on stream for a few years and that the government paid into its Petroleum Fund for the benefit of future generations. Singapore enjoyed no such windfall but had a strong, technocratic government insulated from popular pressures and concerned to build up a reserve against contingencies. It therefore paid current revenues into its sovereign wealth funds, Temasek Holdings and the Government Investment Corporation.[13]

In 1995, Belgium had the highest debt-to-GDP ratio of any European country, which it had to reduce to convince its European partners that it would be a reliable member of the Eurozone. It was in the fortunate position of having instituted budgetary reforms a decade earlier, widening the tax base, constraining regional government spending, and empowering its National Finance Council to monitor federal and regional fiscal policies. Now that its adoption of the euro hung in the balance, it was able to move the budget into surplus and keep it there. Still, that it took the better part of a decade for those reforms to translate into substantial budget surpluses is sobering.

Evidently, large, persistent primary surpluses of the sort needed to bring down high post-COVID public debts are rare, barring special circumstances. The ability to run such surpluses is especially limited in a polarized political environment, as explained in Chapter 8. When political parties are far apart on necessary and desirable reforms, the compromise needed to sustain reforms is elusive. Thus, dealing with post-COVID debt is likely to be especially challenging for a country like the United States where political polarization has been rising since the 1960s and where COVID-19 has only elevated it further. The United States will surely experience demands for additional public spending on healthcare, childcare, eldercare, and other social needs, the COVID crisis having laid bare gaps in the safety net. Nor has the crisis done anything to moderate longstanding opposition to the higher taxes needed to finance such services. In the spring of 2021, when President Biden proposed an increase in capital gains taxes to pay for additional spending on children and families, Republicans in Congress were quick to voice their opposition.

Crises have a way of overcoming such opposition. Pitt the Younger secured Parliament's assent to an income tax in response to the crisis of the Napoleonic Wars. The United States adopted its first income tax in 1862 in response to the exceptional demands of the Civil War. Income-tax rates were raised to unprecedented heights, in the United States and elsewhere, to meet the pressing needs of World War I and World War II. COVID, conceivably, could do the same.[14]

But even if taxes are raised to pay for the additional social services demanded by post-COVID publics, they will have to be raised even further, or entirely new revenue sources will have to be found, to generate the large, ongoing primary surpluses needed to pay down debts. Invoking the analogy with war, some observers have recommended levying an annual wealth tax, a one-time COVID solidarity tax, or a digital tax to address the fiscal legacy of COVID-19.[15] But the political feasibility of such proposals is questionable. To again invoke the analogy with war, it is not clear that widespread popular support for those much higher taxes can be sustained once the emergency of the pandemic has passed.[16]

A sharp rise in interest rates is one possible trigger for a crisis that brings about overdue adjustments.[17] Higher interest rates will mean higher costs when maturing obligations are rolled over. Higher interest rates will similarly make for higher costs on any additional bonds issued to finance ongoing deficits. And if the appetite for fiscal consolidation is weak, deficits will persist.

In response, central banks can purchase Treasury securities in whatever numbers are needed to cap interest rates, as the Federal Reserve did after World War II. But the result then was that the Fed lost control of the price level, as described in Chapter 9. The question is whether the same could happen now. When the fiscal costs of the COVID crisis became apparent in the spring of 2020, central banks ramped up their bond-purchase programs to prevent Treasury prices from falling and yields from rising. Yet despite this, at the end of 2020, nearly a year into the COVID crisis, financial market participants still anticipated that the Fed, the ECB, and the Bank of Japan would undershoot their 2 percent inflation targets and that they would continue doing so for as long as a decade.[18]

Evidently, investors believed that private spending would remain sufficiently subdued that the increase in public spending, however financed, would not cause inflation to overshoot, in contrast to 1946–48 and 1951. Those earlier bursts of inflation were the result of sharp shifts in private and public spending, reflecting demobilization, termination of wartime price controls, and the Korean conflict.[19] In contrast, investors apparently anticipated no comparably dramatic post-COVID shocks and no sustained burst of private spending.[20]

We know that wars, pandemics, and crises can have permanent impacts on saving and investment behavior and other economic decisions.[21] Having been reminded of the inadequacy of their financial reserves, households may respond to COVID-19 by raising their precautionary saving and maintaining that more cautious stance. This suggests American households, post-COVID, will look and act more like Japanese households. The implications are not entirely happy, but one implication is that the United States will be able to sustain higher levels of debt without experiencing significant inflationary pressures. At least this appeared to be what investors were betting in late 2020 and early 2021.[22]

Investors have been wrong before. What if, instead, private spending rises sharply and remains elevated?[23] To continue with the US example, the Federal Reserve can allow inflation to accelerate. This will cause the growth of nominal GDP to rise relative to the nominal interest rate the government pays on its debt, since some of that debt is long-term and its interest rate is fixed to maturity.[24] A favorable nominal-growth-rate–nominal-interest-rate differential is one way that governments, in the past, have worked down heavy debts. With enough inflation, it could happen again.

The question is how long it will take for investors to shift to short-maturity debt—equivalently, how long before they demand a larger term premium—at which point the nominal interest rate will catch up with the nominal growth rate.[25] The only thing we can say for sure is that this shift will occur. By implication, in order to engineer sizable reductions in their debts this way, central banks will have to be prepared to see inflation rise significantly. They will have to be prepared to see it rise much faster than expected by investors.[26]

So will the Fed and other central banks in its position be prepared to contrive much higher inflation, and will their political overlords and constituents approve? COVID-19 changes everything, it is said. Still, we are skeptical that it will create a tolerance for much higher inflation. An inflation rate marginally above 2 percent for some period, perhaps, as the Fed itself has proposed.[27] But not more. By running inflation at significantly higher levels, central banks would be inflicting financial losses on the pension funds, insurance companies, and banks that hold government bonds—not to mention on individual investors. The American population is aging. Older people dislike inflation for self-interested financial reasons, including that they invest in bonds. And they vote in disproportionate numbers.

Others see inflation rising in short order to "more than 5 per cent, or even on the order of 10 per cent . . ." as debts are inflated away.[28] They argue that the debtors' lobby of nonfinancial corporations and governments is more powerful than the savers' lobby of pension funds, insurance companies, and retirees who invest in fixed-income securities. They suggest that central banks will allow inflation to run at these higher levels for however many years, even decades, are required to bring debt ratios down to more comfortable levels. Time will tell if they are right.

The alternative is for central banks to raise interest rates to tamp down inflation, regardless of the implications for debt service. In this case, the growth-rate–interest-rate differential will be less favorable. Depending on the maturity structure of the debt and on how the economy responds to tighter monetary conditions, the interest rate may rise above the growth rate. Or not. In 1952–53, after regaining its policy autonomy, the Fed took action against inflation. It raised its discount rate and allowed Treasury bill rates to rise. In that instance, there was no crisis of debt sustainability. The growth-rate–interest-rate differential remained favorable, given the growth-enabling environment of the third quarter of the twentieth century and the limited alternatives available to investors. It was just less favorable than before.

But it is unlikely that this Goldilocks-style outcome can be replicated. Advanced-country governments are contemplating, and in some cases implementing, very large programs of ongoing fiscal stimulus as their economies recover from the COVID-19 pandemic. In the US, for example, the resulting increase in debt is large even by the standards of Korean War-era deficits to which the Fed was responding in 1952–53. Policy makers hope that they can "run the economy hot" without precipitating significant inflation and requiring sharp increases in interest rates. If they are wrong, Goldilocks will be nowhere to be found.[29]

Compared to the post–World War II period, moreover, investors today have a rich menu of alternatives to Treasury bonds. Some analysts speak of financial repression as a way of reducing sovereign debt, but that would require significantly restricting investment options, which is hard to imagine. It is hard to imagine prohibitions preventing US investors from investing abroad, or imposition of a new Investment Equalization Tax like that adopted in 1963 to make it less profitable for Americans to undertake such investments.[30] Or it may just be that we lack imagination.

And compared to the postwar golden age, growth prospects today are less rosy. Demography is less favorable. Economic dynamism, as measured by rates of firm entry and exit, has declined, and follower firms show less ability to close the productivity gap vis-à-vis the technological leaders. Educational attainment is rising more slowly, necessarily now that such attainment has already reached relatively high levels. Faster economic growth, as always, would be the painless way of bringing down debt-to-GDP ratios. Alas, we lack a magic elixir to produce faster growth.

This is not to deny that it would be nice to have less debt rather than more. The heavier the debt and the higher the interest rates, the less scope there will be for borrowing to meet the next emergency. COVID-19, like the Global Financial Crisis, is a warning that such "fat-tail events," as they are known in the parlance of finance, may be more frequent than thought previously—which places a premium on borrowing capacity. That said, it is also important to recall what Keynes told the Colwyn Committee in 1927 (as recounted in Chapter 8), namely that a large versus a very large internal debt makes little difference in the ability of a government to respond to an all-hands-on-deck emergency. The United States already had a large internal debt as a result of the Global Financial Crisis, yet this did not prevent it from ramping up fiscal policy and debt issuance in response to COVID-19.

In addition, the heavier the debt and the higher the level of interest rates, the greater will be the temptation to force-feed government debt securities to banks and other financial firms, with destabilizing consequences for the financial system in the event of a fall in bond prices. Still, this is not justification for forsaking those productive public investments or for shifting prematurely, in ways that are both economically and politically unsustainable, to fiscal consolidation.

All this is to say that there are no simple solutions, which is also the note on which we ended Chapter 13. To repeat what was said there: countries that have successfully addressed problems of debt sustainability without major economic, financial, and political dislocations have done so by maintaining stable financial conditions, turning to fiscal restraint when the time was right (not before), and growing their economies. Failing to address the problem from all three angles is a recipe for disaster.

This caution is an appropriate note on which to end. But it is important not to lose sight of how we got here. Sovereigns and states have resorted to public debt to finance battles against military rivals, economic and financial crises, and pandemics. The massive debts incurred in the battle against COVID-19 are a case in point. Protecting the health and welfare of the citizenry against such threats is a legitimate, indeed an essential, role of the state. Political regimes that fail to mobilize all available resources to contain and repel such dangers will not retain popular support.

Enduring states are those that cultivate and, where necessary, restore their capacity to use debt finance, and that have the foresight to do so in advance of when it is needed. They will need to do some restoring now.

# ACKNOWLEDGMENTS

This project started in 2018 with a commission from Ali Abbas, Alex Pienkowski, and Ken Rogoff to contribute a historical chapter to a conference and volume on sovereign debt; that chapter turned into Eichengreen, El-Ganainy, Esteves, and Mitchener (2020). Without this commission and encouragement, we probably wouldn't have started down this road. In scholarship as in life, however, one thing leads to another. The coronavirus pandemic interrupted our progress, making library and archival materials temporarily inaccessible. But it also brought urgency to our efforts to complete the manuscript, given how the public-policy response to the pandemic entailed levels of debt issuance unprecedented in peacetime. Placing that public-policy response in historical context is important, we would argue, for understanding governments' choices, both retrospectively and going forward.

For comments on the manuscript, we thank Zamid Aligishiev, Mark De Broeck, Jan de Vries, Mark Dincecco, Vitor Gaspar, Richard Grossman, Takuma Hisanaga, Rick Holman, Takatoshi Ito, Ken Kashiwase, Trevor Lessard, Peter Lindler, Debin Ma, Moustapha Mbohou Mama, Giovanni Melina, Nobuki Mochida, Masahiro Nozaki, Şevket Pamuk, Hong The Pham, Mia Pineda, David Stasavage, Larry Summers, John Tang, Peter Temin, Christoph Trebesch, Ted Truman, Ali Coşkun Tunçer, Francis Vitek, Eugene White, and two anonymous referees for Oxford University Press. Ekkerhard Koehler and Andreas Schaab kindly shared data. Julieta Mariana Contreras and Jaime Andres Sarmiento Monroy assisted with graphics and computations, and Fatma Ibrahim helped with manuscript preparation. Andrew Wylie helped with placing the manuscript, Dave McBride provided valuable editorial guidance, and Amy Whitmer ably coordinated production. We thank also Dorothy Bauhoff and Thomas Finnegan for excellent copyediting.

Given one current and one past affiliation among the coauthors with the International Monetary Fund, we hasten to add that nothing here necessarily represents the views of that organization or its members. Views expressed, it should be understood, are those of the authors alone.

But you knew that.

# NOTES

## Chapter 1

1. The full speech can be found in *The Hill* (Dec. 21, 2020, 5:00 pm EST), https://the.hill.com/blogs/congress-blog/economy-budget/531173-debt-is-not-a-sustainable-policy-decision.
2. Foreigners enjoy the least legal protection because, according to the doctrine of sovereign immunity, a state can be sued only in its own national courts, which will be disinclined to hear a case on behalf of foreign litigants.
3. An analysis that puts Smith's concern with public debt in perspective is Phillipson (2010).
4. Smith (1904[1776]), vol. II, p. 396.
5. Peterson, a businessman and investment banker who served as Commerce Secretary under President Richard Nixon, created the Peter G. Peterson Foundation in 2008 to promote public awareness of fiscal-sustainability issues in the United States.
6. Smith (1904[1776]), op. cit. Smith's own preference, it should be noted, was for the resulting obligations to be discharged by levying user fees rather than through direct taxation.
7. In contrast, responsibility for repayment of debts of state governments, local governments, and parastatals can be and sometimes is assumed by the national government. This makes the debts of state and local governments different. It also creates ambiguity for precisely defining and measuring the central or national government's obligations. We attempt to include under the heading of the debts of national governments those state and local government debts that are assumed by the national authorities, while excluding other state and local debts. In practice, of course, it can be difficult to draw the line. The line between public and private debt, similarly, can be hard to draw, as when governments, in times of crisis, assume the obligations of banks and other private-sector entities. Graeber (2011) is concerned with the ambiguous relationship between public and private debts.
8. A few twentieth-century sovereigns voluntarily subjected themselves to the jurisdiction of a court in their contracts with creditors, in particular foreign creditors, as a way of enhancing their ability to borrow. As alluded to in our second footnote, these instances are exceptions to the rule.
9. We see here a further complication, namely that the nature of sovereignty has changed over time. Prior to the emergence of the modern nation-state, sovereignty, defined as supreme power, generally over a territory and its inhabitants, was vested in a king or monarch, making sovereign debt a personal obligation. Subsequently, sovereignty came to be associated with the powers of the highest level of government, and sovereign debt was understood as an obligation of the state rather than of its leader. See Walker (2003). We discuss this "depersonalization" of sovereign debt in Chapters 2 and 3.
10. Another distinction is between debt defined as an obligation of the sovereign, state, or public sector, on the one hand, and debt defined as obligations held by the public, on the other. For those who adopt the second definition, the existence of secondary markets on which

investors trade debt obligations is the defining characteristic of public debt. In this view, prior to the establishment of secondary markets in the early modern period there was no such thing as public debt. We prefer the first definition. As we show in Chapter 2, sovereigns and states borrowed before the early modern period for many of the same purposes for which they borrow today, and they borrowed before secondary markets were established. Hence, we adopt a more expansive definition of public debt and consider a longer period.

11. Evidence of a positive correlation between foreign borrowing and economic growth is weaker for the twentieth century. The two periods are compared by Schularick and Steger (2010), to whom we will return. Admittedly, this positive correlation was less than universal, another fact we will revisit.

12. This is Karl Polanyi's famous formulation (1944) of the relationship between state and market.

## Chapter 2

1. Graeber (2011) describes an even earlier history of debt-related transactions of states, sovereigns, and religious foundations. He argues that debt arose out of the obligations of citizens to rulers and that it preceded money. But whereas these obligations (taxes and tributes) were debts of citizens to the sovereign, we are concerned with the obverse.

2. Aristotle (1920), 1349b.

3. An account of this episode is Bogaert (1968).

4. Readers can find the text at https://www.atticinscriptions.com/inscription/AIUK3/3.

5. Winkler (1933) asserts that the final result was default. His interpretation may be erroneous, however, since other elements of his account are questionable. He argues that borrowing was by an alliance of Greek city-states headed by Athens that formed the Second Athenian League, and that they borrowed from the temple to mount a counter-campaign against the Spartan general Sphodrias after he attacked the Athenian port of Piraeus. We are aware of no evidence analogous to the Fitzwilliam marble that this was the actual circumstance of the loans.

6. That this was a functioning credit market is evident from the fact that loans could be assigned; they could be bought and sold.

7. In addition, *societates* could not issue tradable shares. See Sosin (2001) and Harris (2006). In contrast, *societates publicanorum* could issue traded limited-liability shares.

8. See the discussion in von Reden (2013).

9. This is discussed by Kessler and Temin (2008) and Temin (2012).

10. Keeping its capital intact was an appropriate policy for an institution that saw itself as infinitely lived, not unlike a university endowment today.

11. See Tacitus (1931) *Histories* IV:47; Frederiksen (1966); and Lo Cascio (2006). Municipal authorities, in contrast, borrowed regularly, mostly to fund public works. The central government was sufficiently worried about the prospect of municipal defaults that it banned borrowing on the security of future municipal revenues (Temin 2012).

12. On the modern German view, see Tooze (2015). We return to the *schwarze Null* and its exceptions in Chapter 13.

13. As described by Kent (1920).

14. Stasavage (2011) compares interest rates on these loans with the rate of return implied by land rents (his measure of the risk-free rate) and finds them to be considerably higher.

15. See Tracy (2003) and von Glahn (2013). They sometimes did incur implicit debts by delaying payment of their bills. Tracy describes how merchants who provisioned Ming Dynasty troops were paid in salt contracts convertible into actual salt only with delay, sometimes as long as thirty years.

16. On the Ottoman case, see Pamuk (2013) and Chapter 5 in this volume.

17. Scheidel (2019) ascribes the collapse of the Carolingian Empire to the lack of primogeniture in royal succession, resulting in feuding among Charlemagne's sons and grandsons and ultimately in "intense fragmentation of power" (p. 240), as lords, lesser nobles, and church leaders all set up their own castles.

18. As Dincecco and Onorato (2018) note, the Carolingian Empire, not unlike the Roman Empire, was an exception to the general European condition of political fragmentation.

19. In Tilly (1992). Or as he famously summarized elsewhere, "War made the state, and the state made war" (1975, p. 42). Why Japan, which was also politically and geographically fragmented, did not borrow more is an interesting question. Explanations include less commercial and financial development, lower per capita income and therefore less ability to invest in gunpowder technology, and exclusion of foreigners from the country.

20. This is described by Ehrenberg (1928) and Hoffman (2015).

21. China's geography (the existence of a great Central Plain) made for greater centralization and less political factionalism. Scheidel (2019, p. 245) emphasizes how geography favored cavalry over infantry, concentrating military power. In addition, the Great Wall protected the regime from military threats from outside. The result was a lower level of military spending than in Europe as late as the nineteenth century (Hoffman, Postel-Vinay, and Rosenthal 2007). Hoffman (2015) emphasizes how distinctive political histories in Europe and China led to different attitudes toward warfare and subservience to the state. They led also to political cultures that undermined and supported imperial survival, respectively, and that therefore created different incentives to invest in the technology of war. All this changed, finally, with the Taiping Rebellion of 1851–64. Putting down the rebellion was sufficiently costly that for the first time in dynastic history the state resorted to deficit finance, with consequences that we detail in Chapter 5.

22. Peter's pence was an annual tax of a penny from every English householder with land of a certain minimum value. Dating from Anglo-Saxon times, it was discontinued in 1534 following King Henry VIII's break with Rome.

23. These being the city-states of the Lombard League.

24. As Padgett (2009, p. 4) puts it, "Religion bridged state and market through war."

25. These transactions were typically settled at the Champagne fairs that functioned as a European clearinghouse (Neal 2015).

26. Since the interest rate could be hidden when calculating the exchange rate used in these international payments, bills of exchange were conveniently exempt from the usury restrictions of the Church. See Denzel (2006) and Goldthwaite (2009).

27. A discussion is Del Punta (2010).

28. Goldthwaite (2009, p. 246) explains that the popes favored the Florentines because the latter supported the papacy's opposition to the heirs of imperial Ghibellinism, whereas the Sienese, the Florentines' financial rivals, were on the other side.

29. See Sapori (1970). Note, however, that Padgett (2009) challenges some of the specifics of Sapori's account.

30. This observation is emphasized by Epstein (2000) and Stasavage (2011).

31. As Mueller (1997, p. 455) puts it, cities "were more creditworthy than royal governments, for an urban patriciate guaranteed continuity, whereas a new king might well not honor the debts of his predecessors."

32. Blockmans (1997) emphasizes this point.

33. In 1407–08, the Casa di San Giorgio, a public bank in which all *compere* received shares, was chosen to manage Genoa's debt. Shares paid 7 percent annually. They were transferable, allowing *compere* to sell them to other investors. The securities in question were held and traded widely among citizens. The Republic handed over governance of Corsica and other possessions to the Casa, giving it and, by implication, the creditors first claim on income from those properties. The model had legs: a similar approach to consolidating and servicing government debt was undertaken in Britain some three centuries later when the Bank of England was formed. We describe this in Chapter 4.

34. The first loan was raised to finance a fleet to battle the Byzantine emperor Manuel Komnenos.

35. See Tracy (2003). Alfani and Tullio (2019) describe how taxation differed between Venice proper and the Republic's outlying provinces. Here we focus on the former.

36. Not incidentally, the Grand Council itself was also established in 1172, the date of the inaugural loan.

37. IMF (2018), p. v.

38. See, for example, our discussion of bondholder committees in Chapter 6 and of the Paris Club in Chapter 9.

39. Again, see Tracy (2003).

40. See, for example, Stasavage (2003).
41. Higher nominal yields may have also reflected inflation caused by the negative supply shock of the Black Death. In constructing Figure 2.1 we adjust for a uniform 5 percent coupon.
42. Already in 1442, when passing a new tax law, the Senate criticized "insolent, bold and presumptuous" persons who refused to subscribe to their forced loans and, more provocatively, who incited others to resist (Mueller 1997, pp. 505–506).
43. The rate varied with the maturity of the loans, ranging from 14 percent for life annuities to 5 percent for five-year deposits (Pezzolo 1990).
44. Goldthwaite (2009), p. 495.
45. Najemy (2006), p. 121. In Paris, the raising of the *taille* (a wealth tax) was similarly delegated to the city's quarters and administered by local assessors. The tax rolls were made public and residents could contest their peers' tax assessment if they thought it unfair. This made truth telling an equilibrium (Slivinski and Sussman 2019).
46. Becker (1965), p. 443.
47. The quotation is from Najemy (2006), p. 118.
48. This indicated that the economy was on the downward-sloping portion of the consumption-tax Laffer Curve (the parabolic relationship between the tax rate and total tax revenue, after the eponymous economist who purportedly drew it on a napkin during a 1974 dinner meeting at the Two Continents Restaurant in Washington, DC). We revisit this meeting in Chapter 11.
49. Economists will recognize this as the source of the backward-bending supply-of-credit curve that makes for credit rationing (Jaffee and Russell 1976).
50. The Bardi and Peruzzi were to experience even more damaging shocks two years later, as we describe in the next section.
51. Claims on this *monte* could be transferred to another party on instruction of the current holder. In these respects (reduced interest rate and securitization), the restructuring and creation of the *Monte Comune* were like the 1989 Brady Plan, in which troubled bank loans were written down and converted into negotiable securities. On the Brady Plan, see Chapter 9.
52. It stabilized them for a while, anyway. By the end of the fifteenth century, the state was delaying repayment of invested dowry funds and forcing their owners to accept other bonds in settlement of their accounts (Marks 1954). Prices reacted accordingly.
53. By one estimate (Pezzolo 2003), as late as 1641 only a seventh of Venice's consolidated debt was owned by foreigners.
54. As Slater (2018, p. 20) puts it, "a monarch was unlikely to survive the revulsion of public opinion at the loss of such valuable symbols of a country's prestige and heritage, so a financier who could get his hands on such assets as collateral was unlikely to be bilked."
55. In addition, the Florentine bankers to the English kings received a monopoly concession to trade the most important English export: wool.
56. Unlike the republican city-states of the Italian peninsula, these towns were not autonomous political entities. But kings and princes could grant them the privilege of legal personality, which allowed them to own assets, raise taxes, and sign contracts as a collectivity. But what the king giveth, the king could also take away, which remained a problem.
57. Life annuities, in contrast, expired with the death of the original purchaser, rendering them less liquid. There were also two-lives annuities, which could be bequeathed one time to an assignee and continued to pay until the death of the inheritor.
58. Munro (2013) describes how in the 1330s Barcelona issued perpetual annuities with a yield of 7.2 percent and "two-lives" (see the immediately preceding footnote) at 14.3 percent.
59. Although there was some dispute of the point, a final theological settlement was reached in the fifteenth century. This added further conditions for the legitimacy of perpetual annuities, but these were easier to circumvent than the initial prohibition of interest on loans. See Munro (2013).
60. In contrast, short-term loans to cities and sovereigns were not exempt from religious interdiction against usury. Not only did this limit the adjustment of interest rates, but it was not uncommon for cities to seek ecclesiastic authority in order to renege on these "usurious debts."
61. It is uncertain when sovereign bonds were first used as collateral. However, De Luca (2008) documents that such bonds were preferred as pledges in collateralized loans (*censi*

*consegnativi*) in Milan in the late sixteenth century. By the eighteenth century, claims on sovereigns had become the dominant form of collateral for short-term credit.

62. For a discussion of the role of collateral in financial development, see Singh (2013).

63. Additional mechanisms for surety were developed, namely the joint-liability rule binding together all parties involved in a bill of exchange (De Roover 1953; Santarosa 2015).

64. Neal (2015) elaborates this argument.

## Chapter 3

1. In the words of van Zanden and van Reil (2004, p. 35), the ruling elite "had to a large extent invested their personal wealth in public debt. . . ." Consequently, that elite "completely committed itself to ensuring that interest on the national debt continued to be paid."

2. The tariff was adopted in 1582. Of the five admiralties, three were in Holland, with one each in Zeeland and Friesland.

3. de Vries and van der Woude (1997), p. 97.

4. The richest province, Holland, contributed between 60 and 70 percent (de Vries and van der Woude 1997).

5. Israel (1995), p. 285.

6. Lefevre Pontalis (1885) describes the evolution of this body.

7. See Gelderblom and Jonker (2011).

8. The councilor pensionary was also the de facto chief executive in the States-General. Decisions there required not merely a qualified majority but unanimity, making such coalition building indispensable.

9. His calculations led him to conclude that life annuities were the better investment, although, according to Rowen (1986, p. 61), "the general public outside found the explanation in the treatise, which was published, to be beyond its understanding and it continued to prefer redemption bonds."

10. See Gelderblom and Jonker (2006), Figure 2.

11. As usual, to get at real interest rates we need to subtract inflation. We use methods introduced by Engle (1982) to impute expected inflation one period ahead. Since prices in this period were very volatile, we model not only average inflation but also its variance. For the interested reader, the model is an ARMA(1,1) GARCH(4,1).

12. de Vries and van der Woude (1997), p. 116.

13. They collected it also in the adjoining regions.

14. In addition, collecting less strengthened the argument, voiced by provincial representatives, that their own province's quota, inherited from Spanish days, should now be reduced.

15. de Vries and van der Woude (1997), p. 123. Or, as van Zanden and van Riel (2004, p. 40) put it, characterizing the late eighteenth century, "The falling creditworthiness of the Republic left it defenseless, so that French troops, almost without resistance, but with the assistance of the freezing rivers, brought the Republic to its knees."

16. See North and Weingast (1989).

17. Sacks (1994), p. 18.

18. Cox (2016) emphasizes the comprehensive nature of these reforms.

19. Recall the discussion in Chapter 2 of borrowing by the Republic of Florence in the fourteenth century.

20. The phrase quoted is from Drelichman and Voth (2014, p. 274), from which much of the rest of our account of this case is drawn.

21. Drelichman and Voth (2014) estimate that real returns on their short-term loans exceeded 10 percent.

22. Álvarez-Nogal and Chamley (2014, 2016) dispute this interpretation of Philip's experience, arguing that events were driven by the resistance of the Spanish parliament (Cortes) to borrowing by the king. The key to Philip's ability to borrow was not the Genoese cartel, they argue, but rather the expectation that the king's short-term debt (*asientos*) to his Genoese bankers would be converted into long-term *juros* guaranteed by the revenues of cities represented in the Cortes. One such instance was in 1575, when the king stopped paying on the *asientos* held by his Genoese bankers. Despite doing so, he did not touch the service of long-term *juros*. The

source of the problem was that cities might refuse to assent to the tax increase needed to retire the stock of *asientos*. This disrupted not just the king's finances, but also the commercial credit market. The king and the cities then played a game of chicken until the ongoing commercial crisis forced the cities to concede. In effect, the finances of Philip II resembled periodic government shutdowns in the United States because of the need for congressional approval to raise the debt ceiling, rather than the repeated defaults of debt-intolerant states.

23. See van Zanden, Buringh, and Bosker (2012). Whereas the Castilian Cortes met in more than fifty years per century until the seventeenth century, in France the maximum frequency was 19 percent of potential years in the fifteenth century and still less subsequently. According to Ormrod (1995), this was partly due to the greater wealth of the king's own domain, which postponed the need to introduce direct taxation until the disastrous battle of Poitiers, when John II was taken prisoner by the English and was returned only against payment of a ransom of 4 million *écus*.

24. Other courts also possessed the same privilege of registering the king's acts and were referred to as *cours souveraines*, indicative of their constitutional function. But *parlements* were the most formidable.

25. They did so on the grounds that only the Estates General had the legitimacy to create new imposts.

26. In a similar moment of exasperation, his successor, Louis XV, abolished the *parlements* in 1771. This constitutional coup (as it was described by the aggrieved magistrates) lasted three years. When the king died in 1774, his successor, Louis XVI, reestablished the old magistracies in a gesture of goodwill. The latter did not repay the kindness, however, and continued to oppose the fiscal initiatives of the new monarch, leaving him with little alternative but to appeal to the nation, as represented in the Estates General. Ironically, the same elite magistrates who saw themselves as the ultimate protectors of freedom against arbitrary power were among the first to lose their positions following the French Revolution (Ford 1953).

27. This was a "mosaic" fiscal state, in the characterization of Strayer (1970).

28. The idea of a centralized syndicate (*fermes générales*) reporting to the Royal Council was the brainchild of Jean-Baptiste Colbert, who assumed responsibility for the royal finances in 1661.

29. Entry barriers were high, to put the point in economic terms.

30. Finally, in the 1780s, desperate for revenues, finance ministers started imposing revenue-sharing rules on the contractors, ignoring the discomfort of income fluctuations. Yet another way that the king could have increased his tax take was by hiring salaried officials to do the collecting. But this would presuppose an ability to verify that those officials were making good-faith efforts to collect what was due. Colbert canceled the farms on some taxes and took over their collection, but his example was not taken up by his successors, since this left the Crown even more exposed to income fluctuations and even more dependent on borrowing to smooth its spending (White 2004).

31. The Church, however, contributed to the king's budget with a "voluntary gift" (*don gratuit*). Originally, this was offered to fund the war against the Huguenots and other Protestant states, but French kings made a habit of requesting it annually. The amount had to be negotiated, however, and was ultimately at the discretion of the Church.

32. In the words of White (2001, p. 95), "Privilege shaped French society and privilege shaped the fiscal system."

33. The only point of agreement between the two states was their aversion to raising funds through seigniorage. Committed to a monetary regime based on gold and silver, the French government's ability to raise real resources through inflation was limited, although debasement was still possible. Debasement was popular with French kings in the Middle Ages but less so in the early modern period. Louis XIV debased the currency when under pressure to fund his Europe-wide wars, but his successors avoided this, with the exception of his immediate successor, the regent, who allowed the Scottish adventurer John Law to issue paper money to prop up the market for public debt. The failure of this system, described later in the chapter, reinforced the attachment of the French authorities to sound metal-based money, holding back development of fractional reserve banking until the nineteenth century.

34. The argument is analogous to that for demand deposits as a disciplining device on banks (e.g., Calomiris and Kahn 1991), since investors can run if they see problems. The analogy with banks thus suggests that short-term debt as a device for disciplining the sovereign worked imperfectly—since it worked imperfectly for banks. For details, see Velde (2008).

35. This is similar to the Spanish king's funding of long-term *juros* with revenues from municipal taxes, described earlier.

36. Stasavage (2011) characterizes its role as analogous to that of a representative assembly in a city-state.

37. See Vam Malle (2008) and Slater (2018). Despite this rocky start, *rentes* remained one of the main sources of extraordinary funding of the French monarchy until the Revolution.

38. Offices were popular, in addition, because the income they offered was stable and secure compared to that obtained through trade and manufacturing, and because they conferred prestige (Doyle 1984).

39. The sale of offices was politically unpopular, however, a fact reflected in the modern meaning of the contemporary name for the practice: venality (Descimon 2006). Although the French Revolution effectively terminated the practice, it reappeared in the early nineteenth century in a limited number of cases.

40. "Mémoire sur l'état actuel des offices tant casuels qu'à survivance," Bibliothèque Nationale de France BNF Ms Fr. 11440, authors' translation.

41. The more attractive (and expensive) offices also gave their holders entry into nobility. This was prized not just for its prestige but also for its many tax exemptions, which reduced the tax base further.

42. See Weir (1989) and Velde and Weir (1992).

43. Wilson (2016), p. 405.

44. Wilson and Schaich (2011), p. 4.

45. Technically, the territory so mortgaged remained the property of the imperial realm, but its subjects were required to take an oath of allegiance to their new temporary lord (Fryde and Fryde 1963, pp. 508–509).

46. Isenmann (1999), p. 253. By the mid-fifteenth century, as a result, the emperor was reduced to living on customary taxes on imperial cities and levies on the Jewish population.

47. This according to the calculations of Drelichman and Voth (2014).

48. The province of Holland began to tap international capital markets already in the period of Habsburg rule, and other provinces then leveraged this capacity by borrowing in Holland. See Tracy (1985) and Gelderblom (2009).

49. In contrast, the land tax had to be renegotiated continuously with landowners. Another problem prior to establishing a professional tax commission was that assessments were made by local justices of the peace. "Notoriously, faced with the pressure of local expectations, their valuations of their neighbour's wealth became less and less accurate" (Braddick 2000, p. 236). Reinforcing a point made earlier, Coffman (2013b) shows that the growth of excise revenues and the practice of assigning income from specific excises to servicing specific debt instruments already had been developed under the Long Parliament (1640–60)—that is, even before the Glorious Revolution.

50. See Boynton (1967). Development of a standing navy was more advanced. Having previously relied on mobilizing armed merchant ships, the navy by 1520 had built thirty dedicated ships. But the practice of paying a subsidy to merchants who built ships that were also serviceable in war persisted into the early eighteenth century.

51. This was somewhat smaller after the restoration of King Charles II in 1660 than before.

52. We follow Dincecco's definition (2009, p. 52): "Fiscal centralization was completed the year that the national government began to secure revenues by way of a tax system with uniform rates throughout the country." According to this author and others (inter alia Brewer 1988), the English monarchy had been centralized since the Norman Conquest of 1066, whereas other European states achieved this only as a consequence of the French wars.

53. Braddick (2000), p. 9.

54. Brewer (1988), p. xvii.

55. As Coffman (2013a, p. 84) puts it, "A robust money market grew up around this system."

56. British governments resorted to similar operations to fund their wars as late as the nineteenth century. In return for placing more debt on the bank's balance sheet, they granted repeated extensions of the bank's charter and privileges.

57. The effects were not unlike how the European Central Bank's (ECB's) asset purchases stabilized the prices of euro-denominated securities starting in 2013. On the comparison with ECB asset purchases, see Hammermann et al. (2019) and Chapter 13 in this volume.

58. See O'Brien and Palma (2020).

59. Exactly how much private investment was crowded out by government borrowing is disputed. See Williamson (1984), Heim and Mirowski (1987), and Temin and Voth (2005) for the flavor of the debate.

60. This conversion of debt into equity was similar to that undertaken by the Casa di San Giorgio in 1408 when it consolidated the Genoese debt and provided shares in the bank in return (see Chapter 2).

61. Technically, the company bought up the government's bonds, agreeing to accept a reduced interest rate and thereby rendering the transaction agreeable to the sovereign. It financed the purchases by issuing shares, funding dividends out of those same reduced interest payments and earnings on the South American trade. See Neal (1990).

62. It turned out that King George was among those who had taken advantage of the opportunity to put down only 20 percent. For subsequent share issues, the down payment was reduced further to 10 percent.

63. See Roberds and Velde (2016); Ugolini (2018).

64. This episode became known as Shays' Rebellion.

65. The Constitution then came into operation one year later.

66. Sylla (2011), p. 67.

67. One of Duer's biographers describes him as tainted "by an imputation of rashness, over-sanguineness, and a slightly unpleasant odor . . ." (Davis 1917, p. 280).

## Chapter 4

1. Ahsan, Panza, and Song (2019) document the decline in interstate conflict. The French Wars starting in 1792, when Britain, Prussia, Austria, Russia, and others engaged in extended conflict with Revolutionary France, were a notable exception. Consistent with this observation, Sargent and Velde (1995) and Sonenscher (2007) have linked the Revolution, whose regime was attacked by foreign powers to prevent it from spreading, to the weakness of France's fiscal system and the efforts of Louis XVI to impose a new tax system with fewer exemptions and privileges, which we described in Chapter 3. The aftermath of the French and Napoleonic Wars then saw the Congress of Vienna, which cemented the stability of the state system.

2. See for example the model of Acemoglu (2005).

3. Grafe and Irigoin (2006) discuss the literature, asking whether this incapacity was a legacy of Spanish colonialism and the weak fiscal systems bequeathed by colonial rule.

4. The central bank can purchase government bonds on the secondary market to the extent that it possesses foreign exchange reserves. But reserves are costly to accumulate and hold and therefore tend to be limited, as we discuss later.

5. On the treatment by the market of seasoned and new sovereigns, see Tomz (2007).

6. As described in Landes (1958), European nations frequently relied on the services of amateur consuls. These men were business types operating in emerging nations seeking to issue bonds in Europe. They sometimes abused their diplomatic status for personal gain in exchange for extending their support for the funding operations of governments.

7. Byron (1823), Canto XII, verse 6.

8. This in the words of Fetter (1947, p. 143), in his classic account of this episode.

9. The Poyais loan is conventionally characterized as the "biggest fraud in history" (in the words of the December 22, 2012, edition of *The Economist*). Clavel (2019) has recently sought to recast the episode as a failed attempt to establish a personal colony in Central America rather than an outright fraud. Be this as it may, in the last days of the Spanish American empire, sovereignty was fluid, and many entrepreneurs sought to get ahead by dealing with poorly defined authorities in resource-rich Latin America (Flandreau 2016).

10. Fetter (1947), p. 144.
11. Neal (1998) refers to these interventions as expansionary open-market operations. In addition, the Treasury exchanged still-outstanding long-term bonds for lower-yielding securities. This too encouraged investors searching for yield to take up Latin American bonds. This debt exchange also resembled the much later "Operation Twist" in the United States, when in 1961 the Federal Reserve sold short-term debt while buying long bonds, with the dual goals of attracting short-term capital inflows while encouraging long-term fixed investment. We discuss this episode in Chapter 8. The Fed again attempted something similar in 2011 in response to the global financial crisis (Chapter 12).
12. Jenks (1927), pp. 57–58.
13. The banker's adage "It's not speed that kills, it's the sudden stop" was popularized by Dornbusch, Goldfajn, and Valdés (1995).
14. This being the title of the chapter on this period in Marichal (1989). Similarly, the 1820s through 1850s are referred to in the literature as Latin America's "lost decades."
15. Bignon et al. (2015) argue that there was positive feedback between the fiscal space of Latin American governments, on the one hand, and railway investment and trade, on the other. More trade led to more revenue from the customs house, which in turn allowed governments to subsidize or guarantee new railway links and encourage additional trade.
16. This figure draws on Obstfeld and Taylor (2004), who combine Woodruff's estimates (1967) of the stock of foreign assets owned by European nations and the United States with Maddison's figures (2001) for world GDP.
17. This according to the estimates of Edelstein (1982).
18. This figure counts Britain's own colonies and those of other European nations.
19. This is according to data from Stone (1999) and Bent and Esteves (2016).
20. See Davis and Huttenback (1986) and Accominotti et al. (2010).
21. This figure, for stocks and bonds alike, is from Michie (1999).
22. See Tomz and Wright (2013). Domestic government debt, by comparison, accounted for 14 percent of all securities quoted in London in 1913.
23. The different estimates of net capital inflows in the literature are discussed by Jackson (1977), p. 72.
24. We return to this crisis shortly.
25. See Fitz-Gibbon and Gizycki (2001).
26. Whether they were unwilling or unable is debatable. McLean (2013) provides discussion.
27. The Australian colonies also faced coordination problems in the absence of a single government to reorganize their debts. Had colonial governments formed a united front, they might have gotten further in negotiations with their London banks. This experience played no little role in the decision to federate in 1901.
28. The Supreme Court ruled in 1793, for example, that US states did not enjoy sovereign immunity. This decision was then superseded by the Eleventh Amendment to the US Constitution. Even then, however, the Supreme Court ruled that Congress could abrogate state immunity under powers vested in it by the Fourteenth Amendment.
29. Hillhouse (1936), pp. 169–70.
30. Davis and Cull (1994) estimate that 41 percent of end-of-period borrowing went to funding banks, while 44 percent was for transport improvements (25 percent canals, 15 percent railroads, and 4 percent roads).
31. The timing is explained by expiration of charter of the Second Bank of the United States in 1836 (President Andrew Jackson having vetoed renewal). The bank had previously been an important source of working capital. In response, state legislatures issued bonds (or guaranteed bonds issued by banks themselves) to help capitalize successor institutions (McGrane 1935, p. 6).
32. This is according to the calculations of English (1996).
33. Gayer, Rostow, and Schwartz (1953), p. 297.
34. The Europeans' sudden lack of appetite for US bonds was also attributable to low cotton prices. Low prices for staple exports often coincide with sudden stops in capital flows to emerging markets, as we discuss elsewhere.

35. Although these bonds were denominated in dollars, those marketed to British and Dutch investors came with prespecified exchange rates for converting interest payments from dollars into sterling and guilders (what financiers refer to as exchange or gold clauses), meaning that currency depreciation wouldn't have helped.

36. It is sometimes argued that this refusal to assume state debts reflected moral hazard concerns—the belief that assuming state debts in 1790 led the states to anticipate that the practice would be repeated and encouraged them to overborrow. In fact, moral hazard does not appear to have figured prominently in the congressional debate.

37. The *Floridian*, cited in McGrane (1935), pp. 39–40.

38. Thus, federal government debt never scaled the same height in the first half of the nineteenth century. It had risen to $127 million in the wake of the costly War of 1812. However, it never exceeded $64 million thereafter, representing less than a third of the accumulated state debt of the 1840s.

39. The Province of Buenos Aires, having meanwhile defaulted and then settled up with its creditors, returned to the market for a new loan in 1870.

40. Platt (1983), p. 40.

41. Baring Brothers had held on to a portion of its now-questionable Argentine bond issues, something that was standard practice in the investment-banking business, as we explain in the following. Given its systemic importance, the bank was not allowed to fail for fear that its troubles would spill over to other financial institutions. It was saved by a lifeboat operation co-ordinated by the Bank of England and survived to see another century (White 2018). Twice unlucky, its time came in 1995, when fraudulent transactions by one of its traders brought the bank down, this time without a rescue operation.

42. Williams (1920), pp. 98–99.

43. Diplomatic tensions between Argentina and Chile ratcheted up in 1891 when, in response to the *Baltimore* Crisis (the stabbing of two US navy sailors in Valparaiso), Argentina offered the province of Salta to the United States as a base from which to launch a military attack against Chile, and in return requested US support in its boundary dispute with Chile. This obviously increased the perceived urgency of maintaining market access. Large budget deficits owing to appropriations for military expenditures in 1896 and 1898 were attributable to the boundary dispute and were financed by three short-term foreign bank loans (Shepherd 1933, p. 45).

44. Ferns (1992), p. 263.

45. For details, see della Paolera and Taylor (2001).

46. Figures are from Bent and Esteves (2016).

47. *Journal of Commerce*, Jan. 31, 1905, quoted in Best (1972), p. 322.

48. These loans were extended for noneconomic as much as economic reasons, as in the case of loans to Japan, which were arranged by US investors critical of Russia's social policies and seeking, by supporting its enemy, to foment a change in regime. See Chapter 5. Russia too sought to tap the New York market, its efforts extending to having the czar gift a silver vase to the New York Stock Exchange, but its bonds did not sell.

49. Committee on Banking, Finance and Urban Affairs (1980), p. 502.

50. Specifically, they were not able to augment that capital by taking deposits. These firms re-sold limited numbers of bonds issued by governments of countries such as Great Britain to US investors; we return to this practice in Chapter 8.

51. The actual number of countries varies, as we consider only independent nations. In the last period, we add three new sovereigns (Australia, New Zealand, and South Africa) and subtract one (Egypt, for reasons described in Chapter 6). The total number of sovereigns (including self-governing British dominions) rose from thirty-six to forty-four over the same period.

52. The total world stock of sovereign debt (domestic and foreign-owned) was remarkably stable as a fraction of GDP. According to figures in Nash (1874, 1883), it stood at 17 percent of global GDP in 1873 and 16 percent in 1883.

53. Again, see Nash (1883). On a per capita basis, four of the top five debtors were Australian colonies, followed by France. The other top European borrowers by this measure were Britain, Portugal, Spain, and Belgium.

54. The table averages data for twelve European nations: Belgium, Denmark, Finland, France, Germany, Italy, the Netherlands, Norway, Portugal, Spain, Sweden, and the United Kingdom.

55. We return to this development in Chapter 8.
56. See Fishlow (1985) and Davis and Huttenback (1986).
57. For evidence, see Schularick and Steger (2010).
58. This has been a theme of economic historians from Feis (1930) to Fishlow (1985). There were exceptions, as we will see; a balanced presentation will mean also analyzing these cases.
59. The 1873 crisis in Europe is best understood as the collapse of a credit and property boom, in which banks had overlent for development of formerly agricultural land on the periphery of the continent's growing cities. The precipitating event was the weakness of grain prices, and hence a fall in the value of agricultural land, owing to the "grain invasion" from the United States. Difficulties associated with borrowing for railway development in South-Central Europe and, by coincidence, the United States were an additional factor.
60. A summary of this modern view is Crafts and Harley (1992), updated by Crafts (2019).
61. This is if the heroic estimates of Maddison (2001, p. 126) are believed.
62. The Chinese case, the Boxer Rebellion, is discussed in Chapter 5.
63. Considerable heterogeneity hides behind this average, with costs falling sharply for trade within Asia and between Asia and Europe, and less so in the cases of intra-European and intra-American trade. This is partly because the Suez Canal opened for navigation in 1869, whereas the Panama Canal had to wait until 1914. Other authors (e.g., North 1958; Harley 1988) have compiled evidence of comparable reductions in international (maritime) trade costs in the first two-thirds of the nineteenth century.
64. This tendency is documented by López-Córdova and Meissner (2003).
65. For evidence, see Mitchener and Weidenmier (2015).
66. The London Stock Exchange absorbed the Foreign Stock Market in 1832 after Latin American defaults essentially eliminated trading. Hence, when trading resumed, it was on the London Exchange.
67. On the governance of the London Exchange, see Neal and Davis (2006) and Flandreau (2013). Some of these innovations are analyzed further in Chapter 6, where we focus on defaults and restructurings.
68. The standard description is Jenks (1927), p. 47.
69. In periods when business was booming and many banks were competing for clients, the solicitation might be in the other direction.
70. The quote is from Suzuki (1994), p. 25.
71. For the details of this reputational equilibrium, see Flandreau and Flores (2009).
72. More than a century later, starting in 1973, syndicated bank lending to emerging markets reappeared, when money-center banks began recycling the petrodollars of oil-exporting countries as sovereign loans to emerging markets. This perspective from the 1860s suggests that there was nothing new or novel about the practice.
73. This account follows Suzuki (1994), pp. 28–29. Syndication sometimes had less savory aspects: it was a way of limiting competition for business among banking houses and of thereby driving up commissions.
74. We describe in Chapter 5 how Hongkong and Shanghai Bank provided this function for Qing China's bonds. There is also a less flattering interpretation, that the bankers manipulated bond prices at the expense of other investors; see Marichal (1989, pp. 38–39) on the Latin American case.
75. Banks extracted steep compensation for lending their reputations. This generated what economists refer to as a separating equilibrium, in which only countries able to pay the commissions of top underwriters issued debt at moderate yields, whereas more speculative nations were brought to market by lesser (and cheaper) banks but had to float their bonds at larger discounts. For the sovereign, the option of hiring an expensive underwriter did not always pay (after commission).
76. On the press, see Poovey (2002) and Schefferes and Roberts (2014).
77. Investors on the Continent were able to access similar information thanks to publications patterned after the English. Reference publications in France included *Le Rentier* (since 1868) and *L'économiste français* (1873), while German investors consulted *Den Deutschen Ökonomist* (1882) and *Die Bank* (1908). The main handbooks in these languages were Courtois's *Manuel des fonds publics* (published since 1855), the *Annuaire des valeurs admises*

*à la cote officielle* (1881) and the *Salings Börsen-Papiere* (1884). Last to arrive in this crowded market, since the US was last to emerge as a lender, were the publications of American rating agencies, such as the *Fitch Record of Government Finances*, with annual issues from 1916.

78. Then as now, not all published information was trustworthy, since certain newspapers were prepared to tailor their editorial line about foreign sovereigns in exchange for publicity income or even outright bribes (Bignon and Flandreau 2011).

79. Hyde Clarke (1878), p. 306. The author then goes on: "Whereas formerly only a few houses of stability were engaged in loan transactions: of late, all kinds of persons have been so occupied, not to the public benefit." Hyde Clarke, it should be noted, was founding secretary of the Corporation of Foreign Bondholders, discussed in Chapter 6.

80. Flandreau et al. (2010) make the comparison explicit.

81. By our count, 107 in London, 61 in Paris and Berlin.

82. Figures are from Esteves and Flandreau (2019).

83. For details, see Hutson (2005), Rouwenhorst (2005), and Chabot and Kurz (2012).

84. The Foreign and Colonial continues to trade to this day under the same structure, i.e., a closed-end fund (Chambers and Esteves 2014). An earlier, more specialized fund had been established in Aberdeen in 1837 to promote investments in Illinois real estate by a Scottish financier, Alexander Anderson, and a business associate, George Smith, who immigrated to Chicago some years earlier in the midst of a property boom.

85. A contemporary demonstration is Lowenfeld (1910).

86. This is according to the enumeration of Scratchley (1875).

87. Hutson (2005, p. 448) discusses various estimates of their number. The United States did not establish its investment trust industry until the late 1920s, reflecting its late emergence as a foreign creditor (Bullock 1959).

88. See Chabot and Kurz (2012).

## Chapter 5

1. MacClintock (1911), p. 216.

2. Flandreau and Flores (2012) compare the returns on loans floated by Bischoffsheim & Goldschmidt unfavorably with those of other more reputable names. They describe the investment bank as having been widely regarded as "the villain in this boom-bust cycle" (p. 363).

3. An issue price of 60 means that a bond with a face value of £100 was sold to the initial purchaser for £60. Since 10 percent interest was paid on the £100, the effective return to the investor—assuming no subsequent difficulties—was significantly above 10 percent.

4. Quoted in House of Commons Select Committee Proceedings (House of Commons 1875, p. lxiv).

5. To cement Bischoffsheim & Goldschmidt's popular association with the loan, Honduras's representative, Don Carlos Gutierrez, purchased two shipments of mahogany and had them conspicuously delivered to Bischoffsheim & Goldschmidt for sale in London (see Miranda 2017).

6. Like other borrowers lacking a track record, the new government of unified Italy was forced to offer investors higher yields than the earlier fragmented Italian states (Collet 2012).

7. There are parallels here with the Tuscan bankers discussed in Chapter 2.

8. Details may be found in Pamuk (2018).

9. Cottrell (2008), p. 65.

10. Clay (2001), p. 26.

11. An earlier loan underwritten by the Rothschilds on purely commercial terms failed to find a market.

12. On the Egyptian case, see Chapter 6. When the Ottoman debt was restructured and the British occupied Egypt in the 1880s, this annual tribute was forwarded directly from Egypt to London.

13. The Ottoman government was known in Europe as the "Sublime Porte" in a reference to the main gate of the sultan's palace in Istanbul.

14. Anderson (1964), p. 58.

15. Later capitulations were extended under duress. A contemporary account is Angell (1901).

16. Cottrell (2008), p. 69. However, the author then continues, "Nevertheless, members of the Greek and Jewish commercial and financial diasporas were to continue to play a part through either staffing the institutions controlled by Western bankers or directly establishing corporate banks with the backing of Western capital." We return to the continuing role of the Galata bankers later in this chapter.

17. Tunçer (2015) p. 56.

18. There was also a director general in Constantinople, with a handful of local assistants, responsible for day-to-day relations with the Ottoman government, but he reported to the French and British boards.

19. We noted this event earlier, in Chapter 4.

20. It also absorbed another institution, the Austro-Ottoman Bank.

21. These figures are 1876 dollars and pounds sterling.

22. The remainder of the sentence then read, "although it is seldom recognized as such." Clay (2001), p. 1.

23. Tunçsiper and Abdioğlu (2018), p. 9.

24. The reduction of principal reflected agreement that the Porte should be required to repay no more than it had actually received from its lenders. This meant reducing the debt, depending on whom you asked, to 59.5 percent of its par value, this being the average price at which the bonds had been sold to investors, or to 42 percent, the share of par actually received by the government. The two sides ended up splitting the difference, reducing the nominal obligation by half.

25. Pamuk (2018) estimates that the administration in fact controlled as much as a third of the state's revenues. In this the Ottoman Empire was not alone. For example, Egypt also defaulted on its external debt in 1876 and accepted Franco-British control similar to the Ottoman Debt Administration, as we discuss later. Foreign control was first applied in Tunisia in 1869 and was copied for other default cases, notably in Serbia (1881), Greece (1898), and in a sense China (1911). We analyze some of these experiences later in this chapter and in Chapter 6.

26. Tunçsiper and Abdioğlu (2018), p. 11.

27. This is according to Thomson (2019). Sexton (2005, pp. 129–30) discusses alternative estimates.

28. There had been a dearth of marketable federal debt previously, as noted in Chapter 4.

29. As also already noted in Chapter 4.

30. European investors had various incentives for supporting this speculative issue by a new government. Some British investors were motivated by their economy's dependence on cotton exported by the American South and were inclined to support its campaign in the hope of avoiding a cotton embargo (Sexton 2005). Blackett (2001) argues, in addition, that the British aristocracy and upper middle class identified with the conservative, "gentlemanly" Confederacy. It is revealing that the Union government had greater success at borrowing in Continental Europe than in Britain. The estimate of a 12 percent effective interest rate follows the calculations of Grossman and Han (1996).

31. This was the case starting in 1862.

32. Hall (1998), p. 149.

33. Todd (1954), p. 49.

34. See Gentry (1970).

35. This is in the words of the *New York Times* (Nov. 9, 1865), p. 4.

36. This was the Taiping Rebellion mentioned in Chapter 2, which opened the door to dynastic borrowing from local merchants and ultimately abroad.

37. Three-quarters of this debt, issued at progressively lower interest rates, was sold to British investors. The decline in yields was even larger than the fall in coupon rates, from 10.4 percent in 1875 to 6.3 percent in 1885, 5.1 percent in 1896, and 5.2 percent in 1899.

38. The United States applied a portion of its share to educating Chinese students in the US and another portion to constructing Tsinghua University.

39. There were good reasons China was slow to transition to gold. It was the historic center of trade in Asia, and there were network effects of nearby economies being on silver. See Mitchener and Voth (2011) for discussion.

40. See Goetzmann, Ukhov, and Zhu (2007) for a complete list of taxes pledged as backing for foreign loans. In addition, the Customs Service took on other responsibilities, such as postal delivery, lighthouse maintenance, and policing trade routes, again paralleling the activities of the Ottomans' Public Debt Administration.

41. As German trade with China increased, HSBC opened an additional branch in the port city of Hamburg in 1889, followed by offices in San Francisco, New York, and Lyon.

42. The other third was denominated in silver (King 1987, pp. 549–50). Sometimes HSBC managed the risk of issuing a loan in gold in London while taking payments from the Chinese government in silver by contracting another firm (typically the German firm Telge & Co., based in Shanghai) to assume the exchange risk in return for a 5 percent commission.

43. The banking crisis had roots in a commodity boom, which led to speculation on the Shanghai Stock Exchange. When the bubble burst, local banks were rendered insolvent, forcing provincial officials to turn to foreign banks for support (King 1988, p. 458).

44. It qualifies as the first central bank, unless one wishes to count the short-lived Bank of the Board of Revenue (also known as Daqing Bank and the Great Qing Government Bank), active from 1905 to 1911.

45. In response, British banking interests teamed up with German partners to organize the Anglo-German loans of 1896 and 1898. These bore coupons of 5 and 4.5 percent, respectively, although they were issued at discounts of 10 percent relative to face value, rendering the return to investors correspondingly higher.

46. King (1988), pp. 482–90.

47. See, for example, Ma (2019).

48. A portion was then redeposited in other foreign banks in Shanghai.

49. Cited in Van de Ven (2014), p. 163.

50. Internal turmoil and then war with Japan eventually forced the government to suspend payment, partially in 1932 and completely after 1938 (Lee 1997; Ho and Li 2014). We return to this Chinese debt consolidation in Chapter 8. In 1987, the Thatcher government was then able to secure partial repayment for British investors as part of the negotiation for handing over Hong Kong and giving China access to the London capital market. This led a group of American bondholders to argue that selective payment (as they didn't receive the same treatment) was tantamount to default. They later attempted to enlist the Trump administration, as part of its trade war with China, to enforce their claims.

51. It can be argued that the causality was actually the opposite: that it made sense to disburse the bonds to the samurai only after the secondary market existed and their securities could be traded. Jha, Mitchener, and Takashima (2015) discuss the connections.

52. Japan Securities Research Institute (2014), p. 15.

53. Asakura (1970, p. 278) describes how government bonds quickly "became, along with land, excellent security for credit, and consequently receiving credit became extraordinarily easy in comparison with the past."

54. The government sought to interest the US financier Jay Cooke in underwriting an American tranche, sending a delegation to his home. Cooke was more interested in financing the Northern Pacific Railroad, the project that led to his bankruptcy and the Panic of 1873.

55. There was no more foreign borrowing until the 1890s, that is (see later discussion).

56. For some years, the government remained unable to establish a nationwide tax system and was forced to rely on merchants, who had employees and networks that could be enlisted to collect taxes in return for a cut. Taxes were paid initially in rice, and after 1873 in monetary form.

57. The quotation is from Suzuki (1994), p. 64.

58. "Original sin," the term used in this context by Eichengreen and Hausmann (1999), refers to the inability of governments to place long-term domestic-currency-denominated debt with foreign investors.

59. The yield was 4.4 percent, to be precise.

60. Sussman and Yafeh (2000) argue that going onto the gold standard in 1897 also enhanced market access and compressed yields. In fact, the yield differential between the 1897 and 1899 bonds was minimal, as shown in Table 5.1. Mitchener, Shizume, and Weidenmier

(2010) conclude that the gold standard made relatively little difference, since the authorities were guaranteeing the value in foreign currency of the bonds.

61. This episode is recounted by Best (1972) and Smethurst (2007).

62. These additional syndicate members were backed by John D. Rockefeller and J. P. Morgan, respectively.

63. Foreign investors absorbed more than 80 percent of this domestic issue (Best 1972, pp. 316–17).

64. Bordo, Meissner, and Redish (2005) consider this same transition in the United States and five British dominions. They conclude that it took until the mid-twentieth century for these economies to match Japan's achievement.

## Chapter 6

1. Figure 6.1 displays decennial averages. The number of sovereign nations rose over the century to forty-seven on the eve of World War I. We create frequencies by scaling the number of defaults by the number of independent countries in each year.

2. This represents more than three-quarters of all Latin American nations. Probability of default means the likelihood of observing a randomly selected country in default in a given year.

3. Again, the 2.5 percent per annum figure counts new but not ongoing defaults.

4. We described the spillover of the Argentina-Baring Crisis to Australia in Chapter 4. Mitchener and Weidenmier (2008) analyze contagion to other Latin American countries.

5. This according to Suter (1992).

6. See, for example, Feis (1930), Reinhart and Rogoff (2009), and Tomz and Wright (2013).

7. Here see Flandreau and Zumer (2004) and Flores (2011).

8. A classic discussion that conveys how contemporaries saw this state of affairs is Hyde Clarke (1878).

9. See Lindert and Morton (1989). Tomz (2007), among others, provides evidence to the contrary. We return to this later in the chapter.

10. In addition, there was the occasional debt-for-equity swap, in which coupons were forgiven or defaulted bonds were extinguished in return for farmland, a railway line, or (in the case of Peru) guano.

11. War-of-attrition models in which delay is driven by uncertainty about the preferences of the other party have been developed in the context of unions and strikes (Kennan and Wilson 1988), unions and central banks (Backus and Driffill 1985), and governments and taxpayers (Alesina and Drazen 1991).

12. Unity could also be difficult to maintain when one set of creditors had easier access to the collateral guaranteeing the loans. The Turkish default of 1875 illustrates the point. The owners of two "tribute loans" were able to settle their bonds earlier than other foreign bondholders (in 1877 instead of 1881) and with a smaller haircut (see Borchard and Wynne 1951 and Esteves 2013). These loans were secured by the annual tribute paid by Egypt in return for its political autonomy from the Porte. As described in what follows, Egypt defaulted six months after Turkey but settled earlier, in late 1876, releasing the payments that secured the tribute loans. The owners of other Turkish bonds had to wait until 1881 for less generous settlement of their claims.

13. Their position presumably reflected the English sovereign's own substantial debts, as described in Chapter 7. An analysis of nineteenth-century legal doctrine toward sovereigns is Waibel (2011).

14. See Billyou (1948). Chabot and Gulati (2014) found an even earlier case of an 1843 Mexican bond that included a clause similar in spirit if not in letter, although its precedent was not followed. The *pari passu* clause lives on; see Buchheit and Gulati (2017).

15. For details see Sraffa (1955) and Flandreau (2013).

16. These difficulties should not be exaggerated. As Flandreau (2013) observes, the same subset of bondholders often served on committees dedicated to the debts of different countries. Although retail investors regularly plunged into sovereign bonds in boom periods, they tended to cut their losses in the aftermath of a default by selling out to professional investors, many of whom knew one another (Jenks 1927, p. 121).

17. Thus, the same Jacob (Jack) Ricardo who chaired the first Greek bondholder committee was also a member of the London Stock Exchange.

18. The precedent-setting case was an application in 1831 to float a new loan on behalf of the Portuguese government, which had been in default on its bonds since 1828.

19. George's father, as founder of the firm, objected to these loans as putting his patrimony at risk. Anxious to expand the family business, George and his brother Charles disagreed. On the Egyptian bonds, see Jenks (1927), pp. 284–91. The family disagreement is the subject of Spinner (1973), pp. 8–9.

20. Nonprofit status was intended to eliminate the temptation for the corporation's staff and officers to press for early agreements in order to earn a commission on a subsequent bond exchange or funding loan. Fees paid to officers and members of country-specific committees were kept low for similar reasons.

21. *Economist* (1897) no. 55, p. 1624, cited in Esteves (2013), p. 392. Flores (2020) documents this tendency for issuing houses, at least some of them, to settle prematurely in anticipation of new business and suggests that this contributed to the problem of serial default.

22. From this date the Council had twenty-one members, six appointed by the British Bankers Association, six appointed by the London Chamber of Commerce, and nine other "certificate holders."

23. By 1913, its library held eighteen volumes of newspaper clippings on Brazil, for example, and more than five hundred volumes overall (Mauro and Yafeh 2003, p. 13).

24. The same concern was raised at the inaugural meeting of the Corporation of Foreign Bondholders. As the highest-ranking politician in the room, it again fell to Goschen to argue against excessively close relations between the corporation and Whitehall on the grounds that it would be "dangerous to have the idea go forth that when an Englishman lends his money to a foreign Government he is creating a national obligation, guaranteed by the full weight of the English government" (cited in Jenks 1927, p. 291).

25. Critics complained that these default-specific committees were costly to operate. Their arguments, if not also criticisms of bank dominance, resonated with George Siemens, the head of Deutsche Bank, who on three occasions sought to marshal support for a German bondholder association. But in a country where financial business was dominated by a handful of big banks, these could resist pressure to dilute their control, even when doing so would have created a more efficient and representative creditors' organization. There was also rivalry among the principal financial institutions. Thus, Siemens's project stumbled over opposition from the Disconto Gesellschaft and S. Bleichröder, which feared an organization headed by Deutsche (Barth 1995).

26. Examples are given by Mauro and Yafeh (2003), p. 20.

27. It finally settled in 1913, giving in to threats of British military intervention (see our discussion of gunboat diplomacy later in this chapter).

28. Kelly (1998), pp. 34, 42.

29. Esteves (2013) reports evidence to this effect.

30. This statement holds when the post-settlement rate of return is compared with pre-default returns. Returns were also 7 percent higher when negotiated by a standing committee with a representative, post-1899 Corporation of Foreign Bondholders structure. Evidently, investors benefited from the administrative and informational efficiencies of standing committees, but also from governance in which there was a counterweight to underwriting banks.

31. In 1987 some thirty-seven hundred British holders of czarist bonds, in a deal brokered by the British Foreign Office, received partial payment, in the amount of 10 percent of the bonds' original face value. In return the Foreign Office agreed to free up Russian money frozen in London since 1917. A similar agreement was reached with France a few years later (Oosterlinck 2016). Compare the contemporaneous deal brokered by the United Kingdom with the Chinese government (cited in Chapter 5).

32. This was the tribute used by the Porte to collateralize its external loans in 1854–55 (as described in Chapter 5).

33. However, since Egyptian taxes were levied under the Ottoman sultan's authority, future Egyptian loans were subject to the sultan's permission.

34. The Comptoir had been established in response to lobbying from publishers to provide credit to booksellers and their customers. It thus was an example of how public intervention in financial markets could have unintended consequences.

35. The impact of the cotton famine resulting from the US Civil War was noted in Chapter 5.

36. Debt figures are from Tunçer (2015). We backcast Egyptian GDP from the estimates of Yousef (2002), assuming that GDP grew at the same rate as exports.

37. As we have seen, the Ottoman Empire and Egypt were separate fiscal states, but this did not prevent investors from fearing that what happened in Istanbul wouldn't stay in Istanbul.

38. The transfer took place in 1876. Italian and Austrian creditors were also involved.

39. Goschen had previously offered his services to the Corporation of Foreign Bondholders and had been appointed its representative in future negotiations at a general assembly of Egyptian bondholders. Individual investors disregarded the conflict of interest, evidently appreciating Goschen's connections to the Conservative government (Spinner 1973, pp. 50–51). Goschen's report on his Egyptian adventure was published as *Council of Foreign Bondholders* (1876).

40. An earlier intervention, different in its particulars, was in 1868 following default by the Tunisian Regency (Tunçer 2015).

41. The British and French governments obtained dual control over the remaining Egyptian finances by securing the right to appoint two controllers-general, one for revenues and the other for audit and debt, with powers to collect the revenues and administer the expenditures of the Egyptian state.

42. Debt service remained unsustainable, however, until a reduction of the coupon three years later, to 4 percent.

43. The earlier dual control of French and British commissioners was replaced by a solely British administration. This was despite that the French held two-thirds of the debt (Feis 1930).

44. In addition, the earlier Ottoman capitulations had extended extraterritorial rights to all European powers. British military intervention solved this problem, from the British point of view anyway, by effectively terminating the extraterritorial rights of other powers.

45. Esteves and Tunçer (2016) provide details.

46. See Tunçer (2015). Even though revenues grew, they did so more slowly than in Turkey, Serbia, and Greece, other countries also under international financial control.

47. This is Mitchener and Weidenmier (2010).

48. They were settled twice as quickly, according to Mitchener and Weidenmier's calculations. Esteves (2013) reports similar results.

49. As Platt (1968, pp. 346–47) puts it (perhaps too strongly): the "tradition of laissez-faire and non-intervention was at its harshest when applied to the bondholders, and their complaint was not simply that they were normally unsuccessful in persuading the Foreign Office to take up their cause, but that even when they were entitled to official support they received less than their due."

50. Borchard and Wynne (1951), vol. 2, p. 239. In Palmerston's words (cited in Tomz 2007, p. 144), "no doubt an expression of the intention of the British Government authoritatively to interfere on behalf of the bondholders might be useful to them; but such a declaration would be at variance with the fixed rule of the British Government in regard to all such cases."

51. The quote, from 1856, is cited in Steele (1991), p. 357. Investors sought to build the political case in a variety of ways. In 1875 they induced Parliament to open an official inquiry, the Select Committee on Loans to Foreign States, which concluded that lenders had shown "reckless disregard for the borrower, misuse of the loan proceeds, commissions so usurious that no honest borrower would submit to them, collusion between government representatives and issuers, and falsification of the market to dispose of the bonds" (Feis 1930, pp. 105–6). The Palmerston Doctrine, as this nonintervention presumption came to be known, was not embraced with equal enthusiasm elsewhere. Some Continental European governments encouraged the foreign financial adventures of domestic investors as a way of cementing diplomatic alliances and consequently felt an obligation to intervene on their behalf when things went wrong.

52. In a subsequent amendment to the agreement, Germany and Britain were given an additional payment of 30 percent over and above the claims from other countries on the grounds that they had footed the military bill.

53. *New York Times*, "The President's Annual Message," Dec. 7, 1904, p. 4.
54. It went on, "they bear the endorsement of the 'big stick,' so to speak." *New York Times*, "Mr. President Roosevelt as a Stock Boomer," May 5, 1905, as cited in Corporation of Foreign Bondholders (1905), p. 186. Mitchener and Weidenmier (2005) analyze the behavior of bond prices in this episode.
55. The pioneering article adopting this approach is Romer and Romer (1989).
56. The average responses for both groups are surrounded by their respective 95 percent confidence bands.
57. These ten countries together accounted for more than 90 percent of debt issued by emerging-market sovereigns between 1880 and 1913. On the eve of World War I, the foreign debt of the same countries represented 64 percent of the world's foreign debt stock, according to the sources in Table 4.2. For each loan, Lindert and Morton (1989) calculate the internal rate of return (the discount rate at which the value of the cash flow from the investment is zero).
58. This is a reminder that the influence of creditor-country governments can cut both ways. It is also a reminder that, when computing rates of return on pre-1914 investments, it may be necessary to track the performance of bonds into the post–World War I period in cases where those bonds had not been retired.
59. In addition, its financial needs happened to be concentrated in years when interest rates on British consols, which dictated borrowing costs, were relatively high.
60. Returns on these were 2.5 percent in those same years.
61. Total returns add coupon payments to capital gains accruing during the year. This method has the advantage of allowing one to compare the average return with its volatility.
62. Chabot and Kurz (2010) is the complete analysis.
63. This conclusion reflects that the standard deviation of the prices of foreign government bonds stood at 1.8 percent, which was only moderately above the comparable figure for British bonds of 1.2 percent. Meyer, Reinhart, and Trebesch (2019) analyze a longer period and reach the same conclusion.
64. This last point is documented by Goetzmann and Ukhov (2006). For related perspectives, see Cairncross (1953) and Kennedy (1987).
65. Mitchener and Pina (2020) document the pattern for the classical gold standard period.
66. Resident investors did little better insofar as a corollary of currency depreciation was inflation, which also eroded the real value of interest income.
67. This is according to the calculations of Mitchener and Weidenmier (2015), who consider the domestic currency debts of seventeen emerging markets in the period before 1914, and compare their borrowing costs with those of core gold standard countries, such as France and Germany. Note that 220 basis points means 2.2 percent.
68. See Flandreau and Sussman (2005).
69. Because of its size, this loan was marketed not just at home but also in London and therefore included an exchange clause guaranteeing payment at a constant sterling exchange rate.
70. So did China, as described in Chapter 5.
71. It would be nice to know what share of domestic currency bonds ended up in the hands of foreign investors, but there exists little evidence on this question. Our suspicion is that these issues were heavily but not exclusively held by domestic residents.
72. The evidence we cite here is from Mitchener and Weidenmier (2008).

## Chapter 7

1. A complete list would include also Canada and Italy, whose cases we touch on later.
2. We return to this question in the context of COVID-19 in Chapter 14.
3. Khan (2020, pp. 202–3) refers the Civil War as a "watershed" in technology and a "more capital-intensive approach to armed conflict" than what had come before. Details are found in Bacon (1997).
4. Formal treatments are Barro (1987, 1989).
5. The Fed did likewise in the COVID-19 pandemic, purchasing commercial paper, municipal bonds, and other securities to keep markets functioning. Antipa and Chamley (2017) emphasize the Bank of England's role in ensuring the smooth operation of the payment system. Data

on the Bank of England's balance sheet are from "Research datasets" on the bank's website (https://www.bankofengland.co.uk/statistics/research-datasets).

6. There was no formal deadline by which debt would have to be retired, since most of the government's obligations took the form of the consols (perpetuities) described earlier.

7. Setting aside funds for debt retirement by establishing a sinking fund was yet another financial innovation pioneered by Italian city-states in the fourteenth century. In Britain, an earlier sinking fund was established by Robert Walpole in 1716 and operated effectively for a couple of decades (Hargreaves 1967).

8. Bordo and White (1991) cite the government's failure to rebut criticism of the Bank of England in the 1810 Bullion Report as indicating of its intention to restore convertibility at the prewar rate.

9. This again is consistent with the theory of optimal tax smoothing. By 1815, Pitt's tax contributed nearly 20 percent of total tax revenues. The tax was abolished in 1816, after Waterloo brought the war to a decisive end and signaled that the need for tax finance would be correspondingly less. It was later reinstated by Peel in 1841.

10. Pitt's 3 percent consols were issued at an average price of 60 percent of face value. As interest rates fell after the war, consol prices rose, reaching 90 percent of par in 1824 and 100 percent in the 1840s. Hutchinson and Dowd (2018) argue that these capital gains for investors were an important source of income that helped to finance the British Industrial Revolution.

11. The price level here is Gayer, Rostow, and Schwartz's index (1953) of prices of domestic and imported commodities.

12. The fluctuation of bond prices and the price level suggests that the contingent nature of the bargain was understood. Antipa (2015) shows that battlefield reversals led to declines in bond prices and rises in the price level, as investors shifted out of government debt, forcing the Bank of England to purchase more bonds, with inflationary consequences, whereas battlefield success had the opposite effect.

13. Pollack (2014) describes how attitudes toward income tax shifted as the war dragged on.

14. Prices here are the Warren and Pearson (1933) index for all commodities.

15. In Giffen ([1872] 1904).

16. The five-times estimate is from O'Brien (1989). GDP estimates are from Lévy-Leboyer and Bourguignon (1985) for France, and from Goldin and Lewis (1975) for the United States.

17. A contemporary analysis is Hozier (1872).

18. Total wartime borrowing was 4.5 billion francs, half again as much as the direct costs of the war, as estimated by Giffen, since the government also had to make up for the wartime shortfall in revenues. Treasury notes were retired gradually over the subsequent decade.

19. There also were suggestions that the bank's directors, residing in Paris, feared for their safety (Liesse 1909, p. 141).

20. The bank also sought to undercut the revolution by paying out funds to the Commune as slowly as possible (Jellnick 2008). And following the example of the Bank of England in the Napoleonic period, the bank increased its discounts of private bills to keep the private credit machinery operating, although it limited its discounts to high-quality paper.

21. White (2001), Table 5.

22. A significant share was floated in London, as noted in Chapter 6. A portion of the latter was then repurchased by French investors once their financial situation normalized. Machlup (1976) infers this from the swing in the current account of the balance of payments, which was even larger than needed to complete the transfer to Germany.

23. Liesse (1909), pp. 152–53. The second loan was then even more successful.

24. This interest-rate–growth-rate differential is then multiplied by the lagged debt-to-GDP ratio, since the magnitude of this effect depends on the level of inherited debt (as described in the appendix to this chapter). We refer to the interest-rate–growth-rate differential in episodes when the debt ratio is rising, since in this case an excess of the interest rate over the growth rate causes the debt to rise; in contrast, we refer to the growth-rate–interest-rate differential in episodes when the debt ratio is falling, since in this case an excess of the growth rate over the interest rate causes the debt to fall. With this convention, a positive differential contributes positively to the outcome of interest in both cases.

25. Put another way, it is the adjustment needed to reconcile the flow of new debt issued to finance current government spending with the increase in the reported stock of debt.

26. The appendix to this chapter explains the makeup of this term in more detail.

27. This is as good a place as any to acknowledge the uncertainty surrounding historical estimates of national income, which are generated by estimating growth rates in earlier periods and backcasting starting from modern levels of GDP. In the case of the United Kingdom, those growth rates have been revised downward by recent scholars, resulting in upward revisions of the level of GDP in, say, 1822, the starting point of our UK series. We use the most recent estimates, combining the values for Great Britain from Broadberry et al. (2015) with those of Andersson and Lennard (2018) for Ireland.

28. Pace is important for these decompositions. For example, while Table 7.1 shows that although the excess of the interest rate over the growth rate was larger for France than for the United States, the negative contribution of the growth-rate–interest-rate differential to overall debt reduction was smaller, since there were fewer years for that differential to impact.

29. Mehrotra (2017) argues the opposite—that the interest rate was below the growth rate for portions of the nineteenth century. His finding appears to hinge on the deflators he uses to transform nominal rates into real rates: his sources employ the GDP deflator to deflate nominal GDP, while using the change in the consumer price index to convert nominal interest rates into real interest rates. Mauro and Zhou (2020) avoid this problem, as do we, by comparing nominal interest rates with nominal growth rates; in their sample of countries, interest rates were above growth rates on average between 1800 and 1938, not unlike here. A second difference is that Mehrotra uses a three-year moving average of past inflation rather than current inflation to capture inflation expectations. Substituting this measure has little impact on the decompositions in this chapter.

30. As a result, our perspective differs from that of Slater (2018), who emphasizes the sixfold increase in British GDP between 1815 and 1914 as explaining the decline in the country's debt-to-GDP ratio.

31. Although the difference between the average growth rate and average interest rate was small in the United States, the growth-rate–interest-rate differential still makes a relatively large (negative) contribution to debt reduction. The growth-rate–interest-rate differential was mostly positive in the first twenty years of consolidation; it was more frequently negative later, when the debt stock was smaller. Thus, the positive differential in the early period more than offset the negative differential in the later period, leaving a relatively large (negative) contribution to debt consolidation, even though the average growth-rate–interest-rate differential was small.

32. We noted this in Chapter 6. To be sure, more than official suasion mattered: Parent and Rault (2004) argue that French capital exports reacted to economic and financial motivations as well as to political pressure. For more on the connections between foreign investment and alliance politics, see Feis (1930) and Cameron (1961).

33. This is a theme of Campbell (2004).

34. The website of the British National Archives (https://www.nationalarchives.gov.uk/currency-converter/#) tells us that 40 shillings in 1800 equaled the wages of a skilled tradesman for twelve days, so not all these individuals were large landholders.

35. Antipa and Chamley (2017), p. 5.

36. The quote is from MacDonald (2003), p. 351.

37. The nature of this implicit bargain is elaborated by Daunton (2001) and Maloney (1998).

38. This is argued by Lindert (1994).

39. See Bloch (1940). An income tax was passed only in 1914 and implemented in 1916, in conjunction with the World War I experience described in Chapter 8.

40. This is emphasized by Dyson (2014).

41. Recall that we discussed the history of this problem in Chapter 3.

42. The primary surplus as a share of GDP and the annual percentage point reduction in the debt ratio, which both averaged 2.5 percent, were the same because the initial debt ratio was close to 100 percent. Analysis of modern data (e.g., Eichengreen and Panizza 2016) suggests that this is the political limit of the primary surpluses that can be sustained over long periods (we return to this in Chapter 14). By comparison, the pace of debt reduction was 1.8 percent per annum for Britain and 0.8 percent for the United States.

43. In addition to consols, there were small amounts of fixed-term 3 percent debt ("Reduced Threes" and "New Threes").

44. In Italy, the debt-to-GDP ratio fell from 125 percent in 1894 to 77 percent in 1913, due almost entirely to primary surpluses (the growth-rate–interest-rate differential again contributed negatively to debt reduction). In Canada, the debt ratio fell from 42 to 21 percent over the same period. In this case, both primary surpluses and the growth-rate–interest-rate differential contributed, as Canada experienced a substantial influx of immigrants. The two countries' consolidation experiences are discussed in Bartoletto and Marzano (2012) and Di Matteo (2017), respectively.

45. $i_t$ is sometimes referred to as the implicit interest rate, rather than simply the interest rate, to reflect that it captures interest rates on a mixture of financial obligations.

46. Put differently, it depends on the initial stock of debt. Mauro and Zilinsky (2016) discuss an extended decomposition designed to address how high (low) growth rates could ease (complicate) the political constraints surrounding developments in the primary balance. Their approach requires strong assumptions about how fiscal variables respond to growth in order to quantify the additional indirect impact of growth on changes in debt through its impact on the fiscal variables. For this reason, we do not pursue it here.

47. This distinction between gross and net government debt will figure importantly in Chapter 11.

48. For details, see European Central Bank (2015a) and Maurer and Grussenmeyer (2015).

49. See the discussion in Abbas et al. (2011) and Weber (2012).

## Chapter 8

1. Meltzer and Richard (1981) develop this argument. Acemoglu and Robinson (2000) and Aidt and Jensen (2014) suggest that extending the franchise was seen by the political elite as heading off social unrest and revolution by making credible the future commitment to welfare-state redistribution.

2. It follows that growth of the welfare state was associated with aging populations, as advanced countries underwent the demographic transition to lower fertility and some, such as the United States, shut their doors to immigration. Limiting immigration may have also reduced perceived social distance and opposition to transfers on the grounds that these were extended to groups different from one's own.

3. Abrams and Settle (1999) argue that in contexts where women shoulder a heavy share of the caregiving burden, they are the primary beneficiaries of more caregiving by the public sector and vote accordingly. Miller's finding (2008) that enfranchisement of women in the United States inclined representatives to support greater spending on public-health programs targeted at children is consistent with this view.

4. Even the elderly could contribute to and derive sustenance from the farm. It followed that France, which remained relatively rural and agricultural, established its first noncontributory state pension system only in 1956.

5. The Organisation for Economic Co-operation and Development (OECD; 1985) provides statistics for nineteen advanced countries. Subsequent OECD publications show the ratio rising further to 18 percent in 2000 and to more than 20 percent in 2018, as noted. These last figures are depressed, moreover, by new members (South Korea, Chile, Mexico, and Turkey) with relatively low social spending ratios acceding to the OECD.

6. Wagner's Law (1883), developed to explain these trends, argues that social programs are a luxury good, demands for which rise even faster than incomes.

7. Yared (2019) provides an overview of the political economy literature in which these ideas are developed. Aidt and Mooney (2014) offer evidence consistent with these theories, analyzing spending in Britain before and after the 1918 extension of the franchise.

8. Of course, this figure did not yet include reparations, which were settled later.

9. In contrast, the comparable figure for Britain was just 20 percent. Statistics here are from Ferguson (1999), p. 326.

10. The risks of short-term debt also feature prominently in Chapter 10, when we come to the Mexican crisis of 1994 and the Asian financial crisis of 1997–98.

11. It helped that the United States had a well-developed entertainment industry: a successful advertising campaign, with specially commissioned posters and rallies featuring movie stars such as Douglas Fairbanks and Mary Pickford, is credited with fanning enthusiasm for Liberty Loans (Sutch 2015).

12. Brown (1940), pp. 122–23, describes the mechanisms.

13. Strachan (2004), p. 145.

14. Germany, in contrast, enjoyed only very limited access to the US market even prior to America's entry into the war. National City Bank expressed an interest in funding German as well as British imports but withdrew when the UK government threatened to blacklist banks in neutral countries doing business with Germany.

15. Britain used its access to the US market to funnel financial resources to other Allied powers, underwriting their purchases of materiel in the United Kingdom and neutral nations. The French government, in turn, lent a portion of this finance to other countries, such as Russia, Belgium, Serbia, and Greece, although it required that they use the funds for purchases of French commodities and merchandise. These included $5.7 billion of British and French loans to Russia on which the new Bolshevik government defaulted in 1918.

16. In addition, life insurance companies had significant holdings of government bonds at the end of World War I, in the United Kingdom for example, where they were required to sell their US and Canadian securities, repatriate the proceeds, and invest in government bonds. See Morecroft (2017), p. 145.

17. This refers to the broad (M3) money supply. Figures are from Holtfrerich (1986).

18. Fisk (1922), p. 14.

19. The calculations in Table 8.2 do not include Germany, which is an extreme case that would dominate the results were it included—while only reinforcing the importance of the growth-rate–interest-rate point in the text.

20. More precisely, the annual figures were £40 million in 1923–24, £45 million in 1924–25, and £50 million thereafter.

21. In addition, Labour, as a minority government, required the support of the centrist Liberal Party in Parliament.

22. This is the conclusion of Alesina (1988), p. 63 and passim.

23. Oakley (2011), p. 84.

24. One signatory, in a reservation, advocated significantly higher taxes to fund even faster debt retirement, along with additional social spending.

25. The phrase is from Keynes's published review of the Colwyn Report (Keynes 1927, p. 212).

26. Keynes (1927), p. 210.

27. See, for example, the account of the franc's depreciation in Dulles (1929), pp. 125, 152, and passim.

28. Indeed, that the budget including interest payments was balanced was recognized at the time, as Prati (1991) observes.

29. It didn't help that officials fixed the interest rate on short-term debt below rates prevailing in the market, causing such debt to sell at a discount, if at all (Makinen and Woodward 1989). This was a continuation of the wartime attempt to place debt at artificially low interest rates.

30. This subterfuge was achieved by having the Treasury sell bills to the banks on the understanding that the central bank would rediscount them.

31. In addition, Poincaré allowed the interest rate on short-term debt to rise, which eliminated the problem noted above.

32. This inflation and the associated currency depreciation account for the negative contribution of the stock-flow adjustment in Table 8.2. France had incurred significant amounts of dollar-denominated debt during the war. Currency depreciation increased the burden of that debt; this shows up as a negative stock-flow adjustment and increase in the debt ratio. Working in the other direction was the reduction in the present value of intergovernmental debts under the London debt accord of 1926 and related agreements. European countries received maturity extensions and modest reductions in interest rates, but no reduction in principal. This changed in 1932–33, when European countries other than Finland repudiated their war debts to the United States. These repudiations followed the Hoover Moratorium of June 1931 and the Lausanne Conference of 1932, which effectively ended German reparations.

33. Details are in Zamagni (1993), pp. 244–46. Table 8.2 shows that the primary budget deficits of the previous period and the surpluses of the subsequent period canceled one another out.

34. The large contribution of the stock-flow adjustment for Italy in Table 8.2 indicates the same thing.

35. This was true of Italy's short- and long-term interest rates alike.

36. In other words, the rate of growth of nominal GDP vastly exceeded the nominal interest rate, which adjusted with a lag.

37. A classic account is Maier (1975). Alesina and Drazen (1991) provide a model of the process. Austria, Hungary, and Poland all suffered from similar problems. In addition to the dispute over reparations and the burden of taxation, there were disagreements over apportionment of the Austro-Hungarian debt, as well as ongoing border disputes that made fiscal burdens even less certain (Lopez and Mitchener 2021).

38. Nominal GDP growth averaged 3 percent between 1920 and 1929, the effective interest rate 4 percent.

39. The 4.2 percent figure is again for 1920–29.

40. The credit-boom interpretation of this episode goes back to Hayek and Mises, as described by Eichengreen and Mitchener (2004).

41. Jacobson, Leeper, and Preston (2019) make the same point.

42. In Bulgaria and Greece, League loans also helped governments deal with the expense of managing refugee inflows.

43. The United States not being a League member, no such permission was obtained from the US government.

44. This pattern is documented by Flores and Decorzant (2016).

45. In addition, it created the template for lending by the International Monetary Fund after World War II, which we will discuss later.

46. This implication was understood in German government circles, according to Ritschl (2012). This logic also may have been understood by the US government, which, unlike European governments, was not owed reparations. This is one explanation for why the US Commerce and State Departments registered few objections to US lending to Germany in the 1920s (Eichengreen 1989).

47. That said, Mintz (1951) shows that relying on reputable investment banks made a difference: losses on loans underwritten by these banks were less than those on loans backed by new operators.

48. Some historians argue that the Fed was better attuned to these needs prior to the death in 1928 of Benjamin Strong, the founding governor of the Federal Reserve Bank of New York. They point to the Long Island meeting of central bankers from Germany, France, the United Kingdom, and the United States in 1927, a product of which was a cut in the discount rate of the New York Fed designed to keep capital flowing to Europe. On Strong, see Friedman and Schwartz (1963). On the Long Island meeting, see Clarke (1967).

49. Contemporary sources date the business cycle peak as mid-1928 for Germany, Australia, and Brazil, and early 1929 in Poland, Canada, and Argentina—all economies that depended on foreign, and specifically US, finance.

50. Lewis (1949), p. 56.

51. Cited in Palma (2000), p. 65. The League noted that the peso value of production had fallen by 30 percent, on top of a depreciation of the currency by 50 percent. In Argentina, Brazil, and Peru, the fall in the dollar value of exports was less, but still on the order of 30–40 percent (Abreu 2006, p. 105).

52. Fetter (1947), p. 147.

53. The Dominican Republic, Guatemala, Haiti, and Honduras were other Latin American countries that did not default, although in several cases their governments delayed making payments. Venezuela didn't default because it had no foreign government debt.

54. In contrast, wheat farmers were often tenants and didn't vote (Solberg 1987, pp. 226, 229 and passim).

55. See, Bulow and Rogoff (1989). On the evidence see Rose and Spiegel (2004) and Rose (2005).

56. See Campa (1990) for the comparison.

57. See Eichengreen and Portes (1989). The modifier "heavy" defaulters in Figure 8.5 means that the authors chose not to include countries that only delayed interest payments for short periods.
58. These patterns are documented in Eichengreen (1991), pp. 157–58 and passim.
59. Contrast the analysis in Chapter 6 of defaults before World War I, an earlier period when global commodity and credit markets were buoyant. There we found that default had significant output costs.
60. In continuing the passage quoted earlier, Fetter notes this while also observing that the Latin American situation was complex: "This situation was undoubtedly complicated by an understandable decrease in the will to pay when creditors were foreigners. It seems evident, however, that even if the will to pay had been equally great as regards foreign and domestic creditors of Latin-American governments, there were institutional features of the public debt situation of Latin-American countries that go far to explain the almost unparalleled record of default in the 1930s on the foreign-held public debt" (Fetter 1947, p. 147).
61. We encountered this controversy in Chapter 7 when we considered Goschen's conversion of British government debt in 1888.
62. See Reinhart and Rogoff (2011). They include also Mexico's arrears of payment on civil and military pensions.
63. Grossman and van Huyck (1988) would term this an "excusable default," occurring for reasons not of the government's own making and therefore not causing reputational damage.
64. Ho and Li (2014), p. 413.
65. As described in Chapter 7, Reinhart and Rogoff are consistent: they classify Goschen's loan conversion as a domestic default.
66. Schedvin (1970, pp. 201–2) emphasizes the voluntary nature of the conversion and highlights the role of patriotism and propaganda, not unlike during the loan funding drives of World War I.
67. See Kroszner (1998) on bond prices. For another view, see Edwards (2018).
68. And we similarly described, in Chapter 2, the much earlier domestic debt restructurings of the Venetian and Florentine authorities.
69. Germany was different after the Nazis came to power. Another exception was Japan. The Finance Ministry under Takahashi (whom we encountered in Chapter 5) ramped up military spending and provided an emergency relief program for rural areas starting in 1932; the budget swung sharply into deficit, which the Bank of Japan financed by purchasing government bonds. The US federal government ran primary budget deficits, financing infrastructure projects, public relief, and other social spending under the New Deal. Sweden also ran primary budget deficits after forming a Social Democratic government in 1932. It borrowed for investments in electric power generation, transportation, and communications. Such examples notwithstanding, deficit spending was not the general practice.
70. Country case studies conclude the same thing. For example, Crafts and Mills (2015) consider the United Kingdom, which ran primary surpluses of more than 5 percent of GDP until the late 1930s, when rearmament spending took over. They confirm that the direct effect was to put downward pressure on the debt-to-GDP ratio.
71. This is similarly evident in the substantial literature attributing the depth of the Great Depression in part to failures of fiscal policy (Brown 1956).

## Chapter 9

1. The role of organizational change and technology in productivity growth in this period is the focus of Field (2012).
2. Abramovitz (1986) and Temin (2002) argue that the subsequent acceleration of growth can be entirely explained by the shift of resources from low-productivity agriculture to high-productivity manufacturing and by widespread adoption of modern mass-production methods. Temin does not include Japan in his sample, but his point applies equally to that country. See Ohkawa and Rosovsky (1973) and Maddison (1969), p. 52 et seq. The explanation applies least well to the United States since it was the technological leader and the shift out of agriculture was relatively limited (two related points).

3. Demand deposits, like cash, paid no interest, while time deposit rates were subject to ceilings.

4. See Jafarov, Maino, and Pani (2019) for this view.

5. By this interpretation, interest-rate caps were a form of industrial policy motivated by strategic complementarities and coordination problems (as in Eichengreen 1996). Wyplosz (2001) frames the issue more narrowly but provides systematic support for the view.

6. Meyer, Reinhart, and Trebesch (2019) count just seventy-three newly issued sovereign bonds between 1950 and 1990, most on behalf of European borrowers, not developing countries.

7. See Cooper and Truman (1971) for details.

8. See Broadberry and Harrison (1998). This refers to wartime expenditure relative to immediate prewar levels.

9. These national figures are for fiscal years 1942, 1944, and 1945, respectively, from Lindholm (1947), p. 122.

10. The estimate for Germany is as a share of 1938 GDP, from Ritschl (2012), GDP estimates for 1944–45 being unreliable.

11. Those debts included both unpaid Dawes Loan obligations and clearing debt. Clearing debt refers to accounts that the German central bank had set up with Central and Eastern European countries, as well as with countries like Italy, Norway, and Denmark, for financing the Reich's wartime imports. This was a device for circumventing the Reich's inability to borrow abroad, a problem from which it also suffered during World War I. These other countries nominally accumulated claims on Germany when transferring commodities and materiel. In practice, their claims were inaccessible; they were frozen by the Reichsbank. By the end of the war, these blocked balances amounted to perhaps 40 percent of German GDP when valued at the exchange rates the Reichsbank attached to its transactions. At more realistic exchange rates, they might have amounted to twice as much. Had these additional obligations been included as part of Germany's public debt, the debt burden, at some 400 percent of prewar GDP, would have been heavier even than after World War I, when domestic debt was 100 percent of GDP and reparations added another 250 percent. The reparations calculation includes so-called A, B, and C bonds, as in Ritschl (2013), Table 1.

12. In addition, Germany's transfer was capped at 3 percent of export earnings.

13. Cited in Office of the Historian (n.d.).

14. Thus, its operations in support of the war differed from those in World War I. Then it had lent through the discount window to banks that offered Treasury securities as collateral. Having since developed open market operations, the Fed now purchased Treasury securities from investors. Starting in February 1942, the Fed also purchased new issues directly from the Treasury, overriding a provision of the Banking Act of 1935 that limited Fed purchases to the secondary market.

15. The bill rate was kept lower because this had been customary in the 1930s, when high liquidity preference and depressed economic conditions pushed the short rate toward zero.

16. Meltzer (2003), Table 7.1, reports that the M1 money supply rose by 10.2 and 16.9 percent during the first and second wars, respectively.

17. More debt, that is, relative to GDP. Officials referred to this as a "three percent war" to distinguish it from America's 2.5 percent.

18. This was up from less than 50 percent in the final prewar year. These are holdings of British government debt as a share of the consolidated balance sheet, as reported in https://www.bankofengland.co.uk/statistics/research-datasets.

19. The closest comparison is the modern-day Bank of Japan, for which Japanese government bonds accounted for some 70 percent of assets, circa 2020. Although high, this doesn't begin to approach the Bank of England's 98 percent.

20. Schacht had resigned as economics minister earlier, in 1937, in protest against actions taken by Hitler's planning commissioner, Hermann Göring.

21. These are data underlying Ferguson, Schaab, and Schularick (2014). We thank the authors for providing them.

22. James (1999), p. 42.

23. The period in question being from 1939 to 1944.

24. There were minor exceptions, such as Federal Reserve sales of government bonds in 1949, when interest rates fell due to recession. Such open market sales of securities (contractionary open market operations) are not exactly what one would desire under recessionary conditions.

25. The additional assets were made up of domestic securities, purchased as central banks accommodated the need of their growing economies for additional credit, and additional gold and foreign exchange, as they rebuilt their international reserves.

26. Again, the German case was special; the share of government securities in central bank assets hovered around 9 percent throughout the 1950s.

27. In effect, this was an effort to stimulate investment without jeopardizing the dollar's peg to gold. Swanson (2011) estimates that Operation Twist reduced long-term yields by 15 basis points.

28. Of course, this was a bookkeeping loss rather than an economic loss for institutions such as the Bank of England and the Bank of France, which were now fully nationalized; it was a reduction in the market value of the government's debt to itself.

29. Macroeconomists refer to this as "fiscal dominance." We return to it in our concluding chapter.

30. In some cases, those objectives extended also to financial stability (insofar as credit policies were designed to prevent asset-price booms and busts) and to furthering social aims (such as enhancing access to housing).

31. Reviews of this experience and associated controversies include Hackett and Hackett (1964), Zysman (1977), Estrin and Holmes (1990), Loriaux et al. (1997), and Monnet (2018).

32. Avramovic (1958), pp. 12–13.

33. This argument for the Marshall Plan as a solution to the budgetary war of attrition is from Casella and Eichengreen (1996). The analogous post–World War I war of attrition was described in Chapter 8.

34. As they recovered, European economies similarly provided transfers to their now former colonies in Africa and Asia. By 1960, France's foreign aid, directed heavily toward Africa and Indochina, was larger than that of the United States as a share of GDP, while the shares of the United Kingdom and Germany were about the same as America's.

35. The World Bank did in fact loan some $500 million in 1947—that is to say, prior to the Marshall Plan—to France, Denmark, the Netherlands, and Luxembourg for reconstruction needs. Its efforts were then superseded by the much larger US grant-in-aid program. The Bank made its first loan to a developing country, $2.6 million for a power and irrigation project in Chile, in 1948.

36. This according to the calculations of Boughton (2000), p. 4.

37. This figure included even re-exports, goods that Britain had to purchase abroad in order to export, meaning that the stock of debt relative to Britain's capacity to earn net export revenues was even higher.

38. Countries had their own reasons for agreeing to these modest terms. Some relied on Britain's defense and security umbrella. Others saw value in sterling's role in the international monetary and financial system and worried that this might be jeopardized by the abrupt liquidation of sterling claims. Britain's colonies had no say in the matter. Some countries holding sterling balances obtained exchange or gold clauses protecting them from relatively high British inflation, but not others, such as still-dependent India, the single most important holder of sterling after World War II.

39. See Reinhart and Sbrancia (2015).

40. The date varies also depending on precisely how one defines "sharply."

41. Frey (2019) recounts the relevant history.

42. This is not to deny the prevalence of strikes for higher wages, which were another matter. For perspectives, see Barbash (1976) and Ebbinghaus and Visser (2000).

43. This is one of the conclusions of Wilensky (1975), p. 55 et seq. We return to the determinants of these rising levels of social spending in the next section.

44. Figures are for federal, state, and local entities combined, from Merriam (1955).

45. As a result, spending on health, labor, and insurance doubled between 1944 and 1948.

46. 0.8 percent of GDP to be exact.

47. Even the Greek government's deficit declined in the latter part of the decade.

48. This is the principal finding of Galofré-Vilà et al. (2019).

49. Vonyó (2018) analyzes these points, emphasizing the housing aspect.

50. The catalog in question is Eichengreen and Bordo (2003).

51. Currency crises were more frequent, as anticipated by earlier mention of the 1956 sterling crisis. These are discussed by Eichengreen and Bordo (2003) for the advanced countries and Edwards and Santaella (1993) for emerging markets and developing countries. But even these were less costly and disruptive than later crises, reflecting the extent to which cross-border portfolio capital flows and foreign-currency positions were limited by controls.

52. Legislative fractionalization, as measured by the probability that two members of the lower chamber are from different political parties, also reached a century-long low in this period (Yared 2019, p. 126).

53. Ten-year moving averages are from Funke, Schularick, and Trebesch (2016) and Yared (2019).

54. See, e.g., Roubini and Sachs (1989) and Tujula and Wolswijk (2004) on this association.

55. Empirical studies of this period find that the elasticity of the budget balance/GDP ratio with respect to growth for Europe was 0.5; that is, the deficit ratio increased by 0.5 percent for every 1 percent deceleration in the rate of GDP growth. That elasticity was smaller in the United States and Japan, but still significant at 0.25 percent. See Van den Noord (2000) for a summary of estimates.

56. In the OECD as a whole, total general government outlays as a share of GDP rose from 29.5 percent in 1965 to 33 percent in 1973. See Roubini and Sachs (1989) for documentation.

57. France and Finland were the only exceptions among OECD members. France already had the highest ratio of public spending to GDP in the OECD. Bank of Finland (1989) comments on the slow rate of growth of public services through the 1960s and points to the importance of small-scale agriculture in explaining the limited demand for transfers, consistent with arguments in Chapter 8.

58. The trend in these countries was associated with the decline of traditional agriculture and the relative insecurity of employment in the manufacturing and service sectors. It coincided with the rising labor force participation of women, which created demands for spending on childcare and eldercare.

59. Lindbeck (1997, p. 1275) concludes of Sweden that "it was not until the mid-1960s and early 1970s that Sweden diverged from other Western countries [in terms of government spending rates and labor regulations] to the extent that it was appropriate to talk about a special Swedish model." Hendriksen (n.d., n.p.) observes that "the most conspicuous feature of the Danish economy during Golden Age [of economic growth] was the steep increase in welfare-related costs from the mid-1970s and not least the corresponding increases in number of public employees. Although the seeds of the modern Scandinavian welfare state were sown earlier, the 1960s was when public expenditure as a share of GDP first exceeded that of most other countries." Similarly, the Netherlands by the mid-1960s already had the largest and most costly welfare state of any European country (Wilensky 1975, pp. 11–12; Cox 1993, pp. 3–4).

60. This reflected the increased currency of Keynesian arguments for countercyclical fiscal policy. Google Ngrams shows a sharp increase in references to "Keynesianism" in books starting in 1969. Richard Nixon's comment that "We are all Keynesians now" dates from 1971.

61. That in some countries, such as Saudi Arabia, the initial current account surplus was fully 50 percent of GDP renders this unsurprising.

62. The Eurodollar market was born in the 1950s when the Soviet Union deposited its dollar earnings in London rather than New York in order to keep them away from US regulators. US banks then entered the Eurodollar market when inflation accelerated and regulation prevented onshore interest rates from rising.

63. Indeed, the distinction between US and foreign banks could be nebulous, as when Citibank established an investment bank subsidiary, Citicorp International Banking Ltd., in London. Citi was the first US bank to move into cross-border lending to sovereigns as a strategy for expanding more rapidly than was possible domestically (Friedman 1977; Cleveland and Heurtas 1985).

64. A qualification is that American and British banks had extended significant amounts of commercial credit to German exporters and importers, so that Germany's moratorium and default in 1931–32 (see Chapter 6) damaged their balance sheets. On these cases, see Ritschl and Sarferaz (2014) and Accominotti (2012).

65. A good example was Brazil, whose *milagre econômico* was much commented on (Veloso, Villela, and Giambiagi 2008).
66. Lubin (2015), p. 27.
67. The growth of the commercial paper market had been encouraged by a provision in US securities law exempting short-term (270 day or less) debt securities from more demanding Securities and Exchange Commission registration requirements, as following a 1970 judicial decision.
68. For a retrospective, see Seidman (1993).
69. The UK situation was not dissimilar: the LDC exposure of large British banks was on the order of 250 percent of capital (Dicks 1991). The exposures of French, German, Swiss, and Japanese banks were smaller but only somewhat.
70. Seidman (1993), p. 38.
71. Avery (1990), p. 506.
72. Following the Volcker interest-rate shock in October 1979, the London Interbank Offer Rate (LIBOR, the benchmark interest rate for international financial transactions) rose from 10 percent in 1980 to 16 percent in 1981–82. In addition, there was growing capital flight from Latin American countries (see Cumby and Levich 1987).
73. This is discussed by, inter alia, Cline (1995).
74. In addition, Mexico had a problem of falling oil prices owing to the global recession in 1981–82. The country had held a presidential election a month earlier, prior to which monetary and fiscal policies were relaxed. So there was plenty of blame to go around.
75. This was the case for both sovereigns and other borrowers whose revenues were denominated in their home currencies.
76. Dicks (1991), p. 500.
77. In the language of debt sustainability, the expectation was that this was a liquidity problem, not a solvency or sustainability problem.
78. These arrangements were announced on Sunday, August 15, while the markets were still closed. Nine days later, the United States provided Mexico an additional $1 billion as advance payment for oil imports at a price favorable to the US Strategic Petroleum Reserve.
79. These credits, in which Switzerland and Spain also participated, were channeled through the Bank for International Settlements (BIS).
80. In some cases, IMF loans were supplemented by adjustment loans from the World Bank and regional development banks and by further credits from official bilateral lenders.
81. Following the Mexican precedent, between the end of 1982 and 1984 the banks rescheduled, pushing into the future, the obligations of an additional thirty-one countries.
82. These were the so-called multiyear restructuring negotiations.
83. The IMF expected that its bridge loans would be repaid when new money was secured from other sources. Net LDC drawings from the IMF fell to zero in 1985 and remained negative every year through 1989—this despite creation of the Structural Adjustment Facility in 1986. Pastor (1989) describes the backlash against IMF policy advice in Latin America.
84. Seidman (1993) and Eisenbeis and Horvitz (1993) estimate that as many as eight of the ten largest US banks would have been rendered insolvent by recognition of their loan losses in the first half of the 1980s.
85. Additionally, there was the Mexico City earthquake in September 1985, which caused financial and physical damage, rendering Mexico a less attractive destination for new money. On top of that, the weakness of non-oil commodity prices and collapse of oil prices starting in 1986 dimmed developing countries' prospects. In all, a bit more than half of the new money envisaged by the Baker Plan was delivered (Cline 1995), much from multilateral development banks as opposed to private financial institutions. In the event, this was not enough to restore growth.
86. These committees had been established already in August 1982, when the crisis erupted, and continued up through the Brady Plan period (see later discussion). They were known as the London Club, reflecting the role of the Eurodollar market in LDC lending, although physical negotiations took place in New York, where the principal banks were headquartered.
87. These were known, for self-evident reasons, as "discount bonds." In some cases, where interest payments and not the size of the principal were the pressing issue, governments issued "par

bonds" in the full amount of their bank debts that bore submarket interest rates. This was in order to expand the menu of options to accommodate various bank accounting and regulatory constraints.

88. To qualify, governments had to get the IMF's seal of approval for their reforms.

89. This is called the Paris Club because its meetings are in Paris, because the French Treasury provides a secretariat, and because a French official serves as chair.

90. Criticism came from the Group of 77 developing countries, whose members pushed for an International Debt Commission under United Nations aegis to replace the ad hoc machinery of the Paris Club. The response of the G7 governments that dominated the Paris Club was more generous restructuring terms, about to be described, as well as rendering the operating principles of the Paris Club more transparent and inviting the United Nations Conference on Trade and Development (UNCTAD) to send an observer to deliberations.

91. These principal reductions averaged 33 percent in present value terms. They were achieved through partial write-offs of overdue debt service, longer maturity periods, and concessional interest rates. In contrast to the Brady Plan, however, poor countries were offered no principal reduction, G7 governments arguing that they lacked legal authority to restructure development loans (Daseking and Powell 1999, p. 17).

## Chapter 10

1. The term "debt intolerance" was coined by Reinhart, Rogoff, and Savastano (2003).

2. We encountered "original sin," in the context of Japanese financial development, in Chapter 5.

3. See Greenspan (1999a) and Guidotti (1999). Strictly speaking, this is the extended version of the rule, where the original focused on the twelve months of maturing debt but not on the current account deficit. There are also other more sophisticated metrics, such as those of Jeanne and Rancière (2006).

4. See, for example, Rodrik (2006) for arguments to this effect.

5. The term first appears in Google's Ngram Viewer in 2008, coincident with development of serious debt problems in Europe, after which mentions rise exponentially.

6. Gennaioli, Martin, and Rossi (2018) use data from Bankscope for 191 countries in the period 1998–2012, finding that banks in emerging markets typically hold nearly 13 percent of their assets in government bonds, compared to 5 percent in OECD countries.

7. We described the events of 1982 in Chapter 9.

8. Lustig (1995), p. 13.

9. The rule, as we have seen, was articulated only later, but it was understood at the time. Calvo (1994, p. 302) warned in the first half of the year that "Mexico's ratio of short-term highly liquid government cum banks' liabilities to net international reserves is the highest in Latin America, by a wide margin. In 1993, cetes held by the public represented close to 100 percent of net international reserves . . . a more comprehensive measure of short-term government cum banks' obligations like M3 (which includes cetes) was six times larger than net international reserves. Much of M3 could quickly turn around and head for Miami."

10. The overall deficit, including interest payments, was barely 2 percent of GDP. This was in 1993, just prior to tesobono-related financial manipulations.

11. Again, this was as of the end of 1993. Even those who characterize emerging markets as intrinsically debt intolerant would have little trouble with such figures. Reinhart, Rogoff, and Savastano (2003) point to an external debt-to-GDP ratio of 35 percent as the threshold above which emerging market debt becomes a problem.

12. Those problems of external competitiveness are also one reason Mexico's foreign exchange reserves were low. The country's competitiveness problems were highlighted before the crisis by Dornbusch and Werner (1994). That said, these and other authors may have exaggerated the extent of the problem by focusing on relative Mexico-US price levels. In fact, the dollar had depreciated against other major currencies, meaning that Mexico's loss of competitiveness was less when measured globally and not just against the United States.

13. In technical terms, the central bank "sterilized" the capital outflow.

14. The weaker exchange rate mattered here because foreign currency loans were about a third of all loans made by Mexican banks, and many were extended to firms without foreign-currency income (Krueger and Tornell 1999).

15. Mexican banks had funded approximately 20 percent of their loan portfolios with interbank loans, predominantly from foreign banks and denominated in dollars (Haber 2005).
16. Recapitalization costs here are as estimated by Caprio and Klingebiel (1996).
17. Our capsule account focuses on these two countries because their cases are different and because in timing they bookended the crisis. More comprehensive accounts of the Asian crisis that focus on finance and political economy include Goldstein (1998) and Haggard (2000).
18. These figures, as well as aspects of the argument, are from Burnside, Eichenbaum, and Rebelo (2000).
19. Again, a clear statement of this view is Burnside, Eichenbaum, and Rebelo (2000).
20. Dasgupta et al. (2000), p. 337.
21. Remarkably, BIBF banks were not subject to capital requirements. This regulatory subsidy eventually turned into a fiscal subsidy when the government was forced to take their nonperforming loans off their books (see later discussion).
22. Dasgupta et al. (2000), p. 327.
23. Effectively they were front-running their client.
24. Our standard decomposition indicates that the increase in debt ratios between 1996 and 2000 in the two countries was almost entirely driven by the stock-flow adjustment, which captures these operations.
25. In 1998, when the FIDF issued government-guaranteed bonds replenish its coffers and the government converted the FIDF's earlier loans into equity stakes in the banks, it became clear that this was at root a fiscal operation—it was the socialization of private debts. Ten years later, the FIDF was still paying off the resulting debt.
26. Defaults by local intermediaries on those loans would not have inspired confidence and, in addition, might have seriously damaged a major US or Japanese commercial bank (Blustein 2001; Copelovitch 2010).
27. In September 1998, KAMCO moved to a system where it paid prices closer to the current market value of the loans (Chopra et al. 2002).
28. The reference was in Greenspan (1999b).
29. Again, this was the diabolic loop that would feature prominently in the Global Financial Crisis and the Euro Area debt crisis.
30. Another way of thinking about this is that foreign investors have liabilities in dollars but assets in foreign currency, so depreciation of the foreign currency triggers losses and fire sales as they seek to restore their liquidity. This problem is the focus of Hofmann, Shim, and Shin (2020). The authors document that foreign ownership of local currency sovereign bonds of emerging markets remains in the 25–30 percent range even today, while for some countries, Colombia and Peru for example, it approaches 50 percent.

## Chapter 11

1. The contemporaneous increase for the general government, including also state and local authorities, was even more striking, from 68 to 175 percent.
2. It was exceeded only by Belgium in the fifteen years ending in 1993, a case to which we return later, and by Greece in the last two decades of the nineteenth century, a case that ended in default in 1893.
3. Fuerbringer (2001).
4. See Schinasi, Smith, and Kramer (2001) for contemporary discussion of this problem.
5. It was known as the Plaza Accord because it was negotiated at the Plaza Hotel in New York City.
6. The currency appreciated by 46 percent to be precise. The yen also appreciated by 30 percent in real effective terms—that is, even adjusting for inflation and movements in other currencies.
7. The bank held them there for three years.
8. This refers to their Tier 1, or core, capital, made up mainly of common stock and retained earnings.
9. A book search using Google's Ngram Viewer shows references to "bubble economy" shooting up in 1988 and peaking in 2000.
10. Economic growth declined by 3 percent over the subsequent ten quarters.

11. This sequence is sometimes referred to as the CRIC cycle, where CRIC stands for crisis, response, improvement, complacency (and repeat) (after Feldman 2003).

12. Ito (2003) finds that a 1 percentage point decline in the growth rate induced an increase in the deficit ratio of 2.4 percentage points relative to the previous year.

13. This is according to data in OECD (2010).

14. To be sure, other factors compounded the problem. Deflation heightened the difficulty of maintaining growth and debt sustainability. This deflation problem was related to the concurrent rise in public debt, insofar as Bank of Japan officials worried that debt issuance had inflationary consequences, leading them to withdraw monetary support. In addition, the country's demographics turned against it. But the authorities' stop-go stimulus aggravated the situation.

15. The ex post real rate (adjusted for the actual change in the GDP deflator) fell as well, from 4.2 percent in 1990 to 2.4 percent in 1998. Estimates of ex ante real interest rates based on expected rather than actual inflation show the same pattern. There is no universally agreed way, of course, of imputing these expectations. Ito (2003) estimates a model of ex ante real interest rates, modeling inflation expectations as a function of current observable variables. He finds that ex post and ex ante real rates tracked one another through 1995. After that, the decline in ex ante rates lagged the decline in ex post rates, as if deflation were not fully anticipated. None of this changes the fact that real rates fell sharply at the same time that debt ratios were rising.

16. We will see something similar in Chapter 12, where we consider the increase in indebtedness in other advanced economies following the Global Financial Crisis.

17. This included government bonds and commercial paper purchased by the Bank of Japan starting in 1997. Whether one should count government bonds held by the central bank as public-sector assets depends on whether one thinks that those bonds will be held indefinitely or sold. That is, it depends on one's forecast of future monetary policy. Central bank holdings are not subtracted from gross debt in the figures shown here.

18. Figures in this paragraph are for the end of the 1990s.

19. Although not all land was readily leased, and not all securities could be sold, the contrast between net and gross debt is nonetheless part of the story. There is a further contrast in the relative importance of the growth-rate–interest-rate differential and the stock-flow adjustment when one considers gross versus net debt. This is because when decomposing the increase in net debt we subtract interest income and interest payments from both total revenue and total expenditure when computing the primary balance.

20. The only exception was in 1996, when spending rose as a result of the 1995 fiscal stimulus.

21. These higher benefits were now guaranteed by automatic cost-of-living adjustments.

22. The path for the latter was calibrated to eliminate the deficit by fiscal year 1991. A limited set of defense programs, Social Security payments, and eight programs for the poor and veterans was exempted from across-the-board cuts.

23. Quoted in Meyers (1998).

24. See Oliner and Sichel (2000) and, for a longer period, Fernald and Wang (2015).

25. Growth meanwhile accelerated from 2.5 to 5.1 percent (according to Basu, Fernald, and Shapiro 2001). The authors adjust for factor utilization, factor accumulation, and returns to scale when constructing their estimates.

26. This is according to the estimates of Cohen and Follette (2000).

27. See Auerbach (2001). Closely related, there were also increases in capital gains tax revenues due to a surging stock market.

28. See Rubin (2003), pp. 124–211.

29. Baker (2005) compares the decades.

30. The CBO forecast was predicated on unchanged legislation and consequently included the effect of the 1990 budget act. These CBO projections are described and analyzed by Elmendorf, Liebman, and Wilcox (2002).

31. These cuts took place against the backdrop of the 2001 recession, typically dated as starting in March and lasting through November, which would have reduced revenues in any case.

32. Figures in this paragraph are from de Rugy (2009).

33. Defense spending rose by a cumulative 36 percent in real terms over Bush's first term.

34. De Rugy's figures show defense spending declining by 8.0 percent in Clinton's first term and rising by 8.9 percent in his second.
35. The difference was 37 percent versus 27 percent as of 2000 (Pew Research Center 2009, p. 24).
36. A historical exegesis of the starve-the-beast idea is Bartlett (2007).
37. Romer and Romer (2009) test and reject the starve-the-beast hypothesis on post–World War II data for the United States.
38. See McCarty, Poole, and Rosenthal (2016) on polarization generally and Yared (2019), referred to already in Chapter 8, for the application to debts and deficits. Alesina and Tabellini (1990) present a model in which deficit spending increases with political polarization and disagreements over the composition of spending.
39. See, for example, Alesina and Perotti (1996). We consider the subsequent evidence for and against this theory in Chapter 13.
40. This common-pool problem is the explanation emphasized by Roubini and Sachs (1989), cited in Chapter 9, in their analysis of deficits in Europe. A more general treatment is Pavlović and Xefteris (2020).
41. Tsebelis (2002) is a classic analysis of fiscal adjustment with veto players. Alesina, Perotti, and Tavares (1998) and Persson, Roland, and Tabellini (2007) analyze adjustment when government is by coalition.
42. These figures are for gross public debt as a share of GDP, from the OECD. Recall, however, the earlier caveat about the distinction between Japan's gross and net debt (which reinforces the point).
43. The playing field would be leveled by, among other things, limiting state aids and subsidies for domestic firms.
44. In particular, the Single Market was sometimes seen as a stage in the process running from the customs union through the Single Market to monetary union, all with the goal of creating a political federation that would bind Germany peacefully into Europe. As German Chancellor Helmut Kohl put it in 1991, "It is absurd to expect in the long run that you can maintain economic and monetary union without political union" (Spolaore 2016, p. 442).
45. Formally, the Delors Committee was the Committee for the Study of Economic and Monetary Union (1989).
46. Precisely, the deficit had to be no more than 3 percent or only slightly above that limit but declining "substantially and continuously before reaching the level close to the 3 percent limit" or else be above that limit because of "exceptional circumstances ... [of] a temporary nature." Similarly, if the debt ratio was above 60 percent, it had to be "sufficiently diminished" and "approaching the reference value at a satisfactory pace."
47. In addition to the fact that the politics would make it difficult for governments to punish one another, levying fines would perversely weaken already weak budgets still further (Eichengreen and Wyplosz 1998). Fines that fanned disputes within the monetary union might also raise doubts about the survival of the project. For these same reasons, threats to expel a member were not credible.
48. Since the Maastricht criteria referred to the overall budget deficit (not the primary deficit), inflation, not the interest rate, was relevant for how the debt ratio evolved. Another rationale for the 3 percent deficit ratio was that 3 percent was the public investment share of GDP, and public investment that pays for itself might be thought of as harmless from the standpoint of debt dynamics. For the flaws in this logic, see Buiter, Corsetti, and Roubini (1993).
49. The United Kingdom was different, as also shown in Figure 11.4, because it never wished to adopt the euro and obtained an opt-out from the process.

## Chapter 12

1. Survival in this context can mean reelection or continuation in office, but it can also mean something more.
2. This was specifically the case in the COVID-19 crisis, for example in the quotation attributed to Harvard University professor Ken Rogoff by Detrixhe (2020).
3. Reported by James (2011).

4. Here we are paraphrasing Brown (1956, pp. 863–64): "Fiscal policy, then, seems to have been an unsuccessful recovery device in the thirties—not because it did not work, but because it was not tried." Fiscal policy, to be sure, is only part of the explanation for the contrast between crises. In addition, there was the very different monetary-policy response (Bordo and Sinha 2016). And this time one of the three largest economies, China, which was only partly open financially, resumed its strong growth and pulled other emerging markets along with it (Zheng and Tong 2010; see also later discussion).

5. Figures for net borrowing by all levels of government are from the April 2020 edition of the IMF's *World Economic Outlook* database. Additional deficit figures cited in this chapter are from the same source unless indicated otherwise.

6. That is to say, it never dipped below 2 percent on an annual basis.

7. In addition, the fact that home prices started falling two years earlier in the United States than the Euro Area (Europe's turned down only in the fourth quarter of 2008, according to European Central Bank 2015b) trained attention on the United States. This timing flowed from the level of interest rates in Europe's periphery. These reflected not just central bank policy (as the Fed's tightening put a damper on US home prices) but also the decline in real interest rates owing to adoption there of the euro. They reflected real interest rates being lowest at the Euro Area periphery because inflation rates there were highest (Walters 1986, 1990), something that bought these economies and their housing markets additional time.

8. Federal Deposit Insurance Corporation (2009) describes how a growing number of privately securitized mortgage originations were nontraditional (so-called affordability) mortgages. These included negative-amortization loans (where the mortgage principal grew over time), balloon payment loans (with large lump-sum payments at the end), and interest-only loans (where amortization was not required in the first years of the loan).

9. The Federal Reserve Bank of New York first agreed to provide Bear Stearns with $25 billion of liquidity, collateralized by the bank's holdings of housing-related securities. Informed by its lawyers that it was not empowered to lend to a nonmember bank, the Fed created a special-purpose vehicle, later named Maiden Lane LLC, which purchased $30 billion of Bear's assets.

10. The transatlantic scope of the crisis is a theme of Bayoumi (2017).

11. The US housing boom was concentrated in certain states and regions, above all the so-called sand states of Arizona, California, Florida, and Nevada. Thus, the fact that the housing bubble infected some parts of Europe more than others was not distinctive to that continent.

12. Hopkin (2020), p. 189.

13. Northern Rock expanded aggressively during the boom, but with problems in US financial markets, it found itself unable to securitize and sell off its loans. Delays in obtaining liquidity support from the Bank of England led to a depositor run (the first in the UK in 150 years), a Treasury-backed guarantee of the institution's deposits, and nationalization (Walters 2008).

14. The SEC adopted this new regulation in 2003.

15. Repos are one of the main instruments for borrowing short term, whereby the borrower (typically a bank) lends a safe asset with an agreement to repurchase it later. The change in SEC regulation was driven by lobbying from US broker-dealers who complained that the repo market was being constrained by a limited supply of collateral, namely, US Treasuries (Bayoumi 2017, pp. 74ff.). Recall that this was shortly after financial-market participants had grown anxious about the disappearance of US government debt (see Chapter 11).

16. A detailed treatment is McCauley (2018).

17. An important question is how European regulators allowed this situation to develop. Answers include that European financial systems were heavily bank-based, rendering their economies bank-dependent, which in turn encouraged regulators to cut the banks slack; that universal banks could claim safety owing to the diversity of their business lines; and that a number of banks had links to regional or national governments and assumed that they enjoyed implicit guarantees. In addition, a significant share of assets was hidden in affiliates and off-balance-sheet vehicles and therefore out of sight of regulators.

18. Estimates of direct fiscal costs of these bank rescues are from Amaglobeli et al. (2015). The European Central Bank's own estimates (2015a) are slightly more flattering to the governments involved.

19. This is not to deny that more adept policymakers might have found ways of reducing fiscal costs. An egregious case was Ireland, where the government paid off, at taxpayer expense, not just retail deposits but also banks' wholesale borrowings from bondholders and others (Donovan and Murphy 2013).

20. In Europe, the budget deficit-to-GDP ratio rose from 0.6 percent in 2007 to 2.2 percent in 2008, in Japan from 3.2 percent to 4.5 percent.

21. European Union stimulus packages were mainly at the national level, reflecting the EU's limited own resources, but there was also €20 billion of additional EU spending.

22. This highlights, moreover, the very large increases in deficits in Ireland and Spain in 2008–9, as these countries continued to grapple with banking and property crises.

23. As is always the case with China, it is hard to draw a line between public and private sectors and therefore to know what precisely to count. By some estimates (e.g., Wong 2011), total stimulus including the increase in credit to the economy was even larger, as much as 27 percent of GDP. Other authors tallying only central government spending make it smaller.

24. China had implemented a fiscal stimulus in 1998 in response to the Asian financial crisis (see Chapter 10). Although that stimulus was credited with helping China stave off the crisis, it did less for the rest of the world. In that earlier episode, China accounted for a smaller share of global GDP, and the earlier stimulus was smaller, government revenues being only two-thirds as large as in 2008 and the public finances being more fragile.

25. The theory was originally proposed by the English political economist David Ricardo in 1820, following the British government's heavy wartime accumulation of public debt, discussed in Chapter 7. Ricardo's essay is reprinted in McCulloch (1888). His brother Jack is featured in Chapter 6.

26. This assumes that the maturity of the debt issued to fund the burst in public spending is longer than the stimulus itself, as suggested by theories of optimal tax smoothing (e.g., Barro 1979).

27. The quotation is from Cogan and Taylor (2011), p. 24.

28. This quote is from Roberts (2008).

29. Many of these were adopted in the wake of the defaults on state debts in the 1840s discussed in Chapter 6.

30. Rainy-day funds averaged just 4.8 percent of annual general fund spending in 2008 (Edwards 2020).

31. Chodorow-Reich (2019), p. 3. There are now multiple such studies, as surveyed in this same article. They adopt a variety of approaches to the problem that regional variations in stimulus spending are not exogenous. Some use the seniority of a region's representatives in Congress as an instrument for stimulus receipts, whereas others relate the relative size of transfers to the demographic characteristics of the region. They reach broadly similar conclusions.

32. They report the findings in Broda and Parker (2014).

33. This is as a share of 2008 GDP.

34. In technical terms, the assumption of no monetary offset did not apply.

35. If the rating downgrade and interest rate increase create doubts about the government's capacity to service its debt, there may be a debt run in response, forcing the fiscal authority to reverse course, and this anticipated reversal will further dampen spending. This risk is greatest when the central bank is reluctant to backstop the market, as in Europe before 2012.

36. See Nickel and Tudyka (2013).

37. In addition to the just-cited paper by Nickel and Tudyka, see also Reinhart and Rogoff (2010) and Cecchetti, Mohanty, and Zampolli (2011).

38. See Romer and Romer (2019).

39. Alesina and Ardagna (2010, 2013) were the leading exponents of this view.

40. As HM Treasury put it in the UK's 2010 Budget, "These [effects of fiscal consolidation] will tend to boost demand growth, could improve the underlying performance of the economy and could even be sufficiently strong to outweigh the negative effects" (HM Treasury 2010, p. 19).

41. Policymakers may even withdraw fiscal stimulus in advance of the improvement in the economy, anticipating that such support is no longer needed. The decline in the deficit may be the result of improved economic conditions, in other words, even before the improvement becomes visible. Efforts to finesse this problem by focusing on "nonpolicy" changes in the

budget—improvements in the fiscal balance owing to a boom in the stock market and capital-gains-related revenues, for example—founder on the fact that the exogenous improvement is probably not exogenous. The stock market may just be reacting to an expected future improvement in economic conditions, for example, that will also favorably affect consumption and investment. The correlation of fiscal consolidation, private spending, and economic growth will then be biased in positive directions.

42. We did something similar in Chapter 6 to identify the effect of defaults on subsequent economic outcomes.

43. See Guajardo, Leigh, and Pescatori (2014). In fairness, we should note that Alesina, Favero, and Giavazzi (2019) adopt a version of this same approach and, consistent with their priors, find that fiscal consolidations emphasizing spending cuts are expansionary, whereas consolidations based on tax increases are not. For completeness, we should mention that another widely used approach, synthetic control, which involves matching countries initiating sharp fiscal consolidations with other countries sharing their economic characteristics, also points to the conclusion that contractionary fiscal initiatives are contractionary. See Rayl (2020).

44. We flagged the same problem in Chapter 9 when we discussed the difficulty of boosting exports when multiple Latin American countries simultaneously succumbed to crisis in the 1980s.

45. The deficit of 13 percent of GDP was eventually revised upward again to 15 percent of GDP, the debt of 110 percent of GDP to 127 percent of GDP, according to subsequent figures from the OECD.

46. See Chapter 8.

47. The initial agreement was serially renegotiated and extended. By the end of 2013, total official assistance to Greece from the IMF and European governments totaled €283 billion, 150 percent of the country's GDP. Assistance amounts are from Independent Evaluation Office (2016), p. 4.

48. The overall deficit fell more slowly, reflecting the country's growing indebtedness and corresponding interest payments. The two Troika programs in fact had even more ambitious projections (read: targets) for the deficit, which in the event were not achieved.

49. Greece also ran primary budget deficits, to be sure, but their consequences for the debt were almost exactly restructured away. Other patterns that emerge from the table include that the US and Japan took more forceful action than the Euro Area, and that the other crisis countries suffered the consequences, like Greece, of collapsing growth-rate–interest-rate differentials.

50. This is according to the calculations of Alesina, Favero, and Giavazzi (2019), p. 154.

51. See Fenochietto and Pessino (2013).

52. IMF (2019) is an example.

53. See Bastasin (2015), Chapter 13.

54. A detailed account is Blustein (2016).

55. Recall our discussion of the early origins of these provisions in Chapter 6. There was a renewed push to include such clauses in European sovereign bonds in the early twenty-first century.

56. We already encountered this diabolic loop in Chapter 10.

57. Zero capital charge means that no capital need be held by banks when they invest in government bonds. A good source on this is Meyland and Schäfer (2017).

58. Formally, the ECB had a two-pillar strategy, where it targeted inflation and monetary aggregates (this last target being an inheritance from the German Bundesbank). For an early warning of the need for a central bank that does more than follow a monetary rule, see Folkerts-Landau and Garber (1992).

59. Quoted from Trichet testimony before European Parliament (2011).

60. The program in question was known as Outright Monetary Transactions, or OMT.

61. Before accusing us of exaggeration, consider Anastasakis (2012, n.p.): "Greek parliamentary practices are operating under emergency procedures, a government has been overturned overnight and constitutional practices are being bypassed. The national parliament, the symbol of representative and competitive democracy in Greece, has become purely symbolic and procedural in the way it votes for its austerity laws. External pressures to impose a Special

Commissioner to run the country's finances and recommendations regarding the date of national elections—and the most desirable outcome—are all attacking the heart of Greece's democracy, its sovereignty."

## Chapter 13

1. Not all loans on offer were fully paid out at this stage. In addition, some loans were financed by central banks in the first instance but subject to Treasury guarantees. In the latter case, loan losses and related costs were likely to end up on the public-sector balance sheet eventually.
2. By September 2020 this became "more American lives than World War I and II combined."
3. Technically, the fund managers in question had borrowed in the short-term repo market on the expectation that current yields would converge to futures prices, where current yields now diverged instead. Borrowing in the short-term repo market means that investors borrowed Treasury bonds at their current prices and committed to selling them back at tomorrow's prices, which they expected to be higher, as indicated by the higher prices of futures. This last expectation was one that now threatened to be disappointed by events. Recall also our discussion of the repo market during the Global Financial Crisis in Chapter 12.
4. In addition to purchasing Treasury bonds, the Fed activated swap lines with foreign central banks, enabling the latter to satisfy their own clients' demands for dollar liquidity and limiting distress sales of US Treasuries outside the United States. The Fed's liberal provision of dollar swaps was also critical for solidifying the safe-asset status and collateral value of US Treasury securities.
5. This was the World Bank's estimate (2020) for calendar year 2020, as of April.
6. Advanced-country central banks like the Fed were supporting the prices of a range of other risk assets, but not emerging-market bonds. As the crisis wore on, there was then positive spillover from the Fed's ongoing security purchases to emerging markets, as advanced-country investors stretching for yield moved into emerging-market debt.
7. Recall further how actual restructuring dates varied by country, with some restructuring occurring only five and more years after announcement of the Brady Plan.
8. Initially set to expire on December 31, 2020, the suspension was eventually extended through the end of 2021.
9. The IMF used its Post-Catastrophe Debt Relief Trust (renamed the Catastrophe Containment and Relief Trust) to fund these grants, which covered interest payments potentially for as long as two years. These calisthenics were necessary because the rules governing IMF lending did not permit the Fund to simply cancel payments.
10. The IIF had been created in 1983 in response to the Latin American debt crisis, much as the Committee of Greek Bondholders was created in 1826 in response to an earlier Greek debt crisis (see Chapter 6).
11. Indicative of this fact, four additional countries—Lebanon, Suriname, Belize, and Zambia—also defaulted in 2020, but without making much progress on restructuring.
12. As for what specifically the multilaterals led by the IMF might do, Hagen (2020) points to the desirability of incentives to maximize creditor participation in debt-restructuring operations. These include measures like a UK law to prevent holdout creditors from suing sovereigns that secure debt relief in the context of IMF programs, and a US Executive Order to prevent litigation in the context of restructurings. These are the sort of measures that the United States and the United Kingdom, home to the leading global financial centers, would be reluctant to implement on their own but would be more likely to adopt with multilateral pressure. Relatedly, Bolton, Gulati, and Panizza (2020) have suggested adoption of a United Nations Security Council resolution shielding the assets of impacted countries from litigation and attachment.
13. That is, it had implemented the largest stimulus as a share of GDP. Again, depending on what one counts, estimates of the size of the Chinese stimulus differ. We sum central government spending, local government spending, and bank lending taken at state direction.
14. See, for example, Wong (2011); Huang, Pagano, and Panizza (2020); and Cong et al. (2019).
15. This included central government spending and off-budget debts (both special issuance of Treasury bills and support for local government to issue additional bonds). See Huang and Lardy (2020).

16. Some observers prefer to add in the quasi-fiscal credit expansion from state banks and others, which amounted to another 8.5 percent of GDP, bringing the total fiscal impulse to roughly 13.5 percent of GDP. This doesn't change the essential point: 13.5 percent of GDP was just half the 27 percent of GDP impulse, calculated on the same basis, applied during the Global Financial Crisis (as explained in Chapter 12).

17. Quoted in Tang, Mai, and Zheng (2020).

18. This is according to the estimates of Horn, Reinhart, and Trebesch (2019).

19. In November 2020, six months after the rollout of the Debt Service Suspension Initiative, the China Development Bank announced on its website that it had signed rescheduling agreements with unspecified DSSI beneficiaries involving $748 million of debt service payments, but without providing specifics.

20. Nor does China participate in the OECD's Creditor Reporting System. Horn, Reinhart, and Trebesch (2019) and IMF (2020b) do their best to enumerate China's official lending.

21. China has observer status, however. On the Paris Club more generally, see Chapter 9.

22. As described in Chapter 12.

23. There was a further €100 billion of loans under the Support to Mitigate Unemployment Risks (SURE) program, which were designed to enable member states to continue to subsidize employment on a temporary basis—although this doesn't change the essential point.

24. The top-end revenue estimates are from Saez and Zucman (2019). For an entry on the more skeptical side, see Gleckman (2019).

## Chapter 14

1. The term *modern economic growth* is associated with the economist Simon Kuznets, in a book of the same name (Kuznets 1966). He used it to denote nineteenth- and twentieth-century national cases where growth was rapid, sustained, and marked by significant structural change.

2. We mention this at the outset of Chapter 3. Economists have developed formal models of these nonlinearities and feedbacks affecting the economic growth process. Azariadis and Drazen (1990) is an influential formulation. A survey of the literature is Cohen-Cole, Durlauf, and Rondina (2012).

3. Some of this borrowing was by private companies, reflecting the mix of private and public returns flowing from such investments. But much of that private borrowing was possible only with state guarantees, given the scope of the investments.

4. This was Nigel Lawson, UK Chancellor of the Exchequer in 1983–89. The Lawson doctrine is devastatingly critiqued by Reisen (1998).

5. The figure for the eve of the COVID crisis is as of September 30, 2019 (the end of fiscal year 2019), according to Congressional Budget Office (2020). Additional figures in this paragraph, also for the end of the fiscal year, are from Congressional Budget Office (2021).

6. This was assuming no further discretionary fiscal action, and expiry of emergency spending measures implemented since March 2020. These figures did not include, for example, any impact on the debt of the $1.9 trillion COVID relief bill signed by President Joe Biden in March 2021, which the CBO had not yet costed when this book went to press. Note that these ratios include debt held by the Federal Reserve, presumably on the assumption that the Fed will shrink its balance sheet and sell these holdings back into the market. Debt held by the public net of Federal Reserve holdings was projected to be roughly 70 percent of GDP at the end of 2020.

7. This again was on the assumption of no changes in the laws governing revenues and spending. Such projections depend also on the CBO's estimates of the growth of total factor productivity and GDP, which are not easy to forecast ten and more years ahead. For the appropriate cautions, see Shackleton (2018). The path of debt also depends on future interest rates, which are similarly uncertain. CBO projected rates on ten-year Treasury bonds as recovering to historically typical levels—which meant that it saw them as more than tripling between 2020 and 2030. But if households are made newly aware of the riskiness of the economic environment by recent experience, they may increase their precautionary savings; in this case demand, inflation, and interest rates will remain lower. If those households grow more risk-averse, they will hold more safe assets in their investment portfolios, where US Treasury bonds are safe

assets par excellence, the implication again being downward pressure on the relevant interest rates. We return to these points later in the chapter.

8. The importance of distinguishing between gross and net debt, especially for Japan, was emphasized in Chapter 11.

9. These are the "savings glut" and "secular stagnation" hypotheses of Bernanke (2005) and Summers (2014).

10. See Chapter 11 for details.

11. Not everyone will agree that this is the appropriate thought experiment. Some will object that we have learned from recent events that governments can safely manage higher debt levels than assumed previously. Others will object, to the contrary, that heavy indebtedness was already creating problems prior to COVID-19. As a point of departure for thinking about the challenges, it makes sense to split the difference and contemplate what it would take to reverse out the impact of the latest crisis. At the same time, it is important to emphasize, as we have in this book, that there is no single optimal target level for debt.

12. The reference is to Eichengreen and Panizza (2016).

13. Those contingencies were associated with the high volatility of the pharmaceutical and financial sectors on which the economy relied and with the country's sometimes prickly relations with Malaysia, its neighbor to the north. Krishmadas (2013) discusses the role of Singapore's sovereign wealth funds in its national defense strategy.

14. More generally, Alesina, Ardagna, and Trebbi (2006) document the tendency for crises to catalyze needed fiscal adjustments.

15. See, for example, Landais, Saez, and Zucman (2020) and Bloomberg Tax (2020). International Monetary Fund staff have similarly considered a personal income tax surcharge, perhaps restricted to the highest income levels, or a tax on excess corporate profits as a COVID-19 "recovery contribution." See Klemm et al. (2021).

16. The outlook is especially bleak when one observes that fiscal adjustments are least sustainable when governments are weak and divided, which is the case in polarized political environments like today's. The association between fiscal adjustment and government strength is analyzed by Alesina, Ardagna, and Trebbi (2006).

17. This is documented by Mauro and Zhou (2020).

18. These expectations can be imputed from Treasury yields, actual inflation, inflation swaps, and survey-based measures, following the methodology in Federal Reserve Bank of Cleveland (2020). Alternatively, they can be inferred from the difference between the yields on a nominal Treasury bond and an inflation-indexed bond of the same maturity (the so-called Treasury break-even inflation rate). In early 2021, when this manuscript went to the publisher, the US Treasury ten-year break-even inflation rate had moved slightly above 2 percent. In the Euro Area and Japan, the analogous five- and ten-year break-even rates remained below their respective central banks' inflation targets.

19. Another way of thinking about this is that equating saving and investment required sharp changes in the real interest rate, given these oscillations in spending. Since nominal rates were pegged, these could be realized only through changes in actual and expected inflation (McCallum 1986; Barro 1989).

20. The modifier *sustained* is important here. There were plenty of suggestions that there might be a temporary burst of spending when COVID lockdowns were lifted, vaccination was widespread, and activities such as dining out became safe again. But central bankers vowed to "look through" any transitory inflation that resulted. See for example Powell (2021).

21. See Malmendier and Nagel (2011) and Giuliano and Spilimbergo (2014).

22. In addition, there is the possibility that the COVID-19 crisis will further raise the demand for safe assets by central bank reserve managers and corporate treasurers, where US Treasury bonds are the main form of safe assets. This reservoir of additional demand, it is said, will keep US Treasury yields low for even longer than otherwise. However, that yields on European bonds, which do not play the same role in reserve portfolios, were even lower than yields on US bonds during the COVID crisis suggests this factor is not of first-order importance. In any case, the experience of earlier reserve currencies, such as the British pound after World War II, suggests that this "exorbitant privilege," even if of long standing, can be lost.

23. Some observers point to a "K-shaped" recession and recovery in which low-income households hit hard by the crisis increase their precautionary saving, but high-income households, whose wealth increased during the COVID-19 recession, do the opposite. Thus, Remes and Kohli (2021) "expect spending by middle- and high-income cohorts in the US to bounce back to pre-pandemic levels in 2021–22, while spending by low-income groups could drop below pre-pandemic levels once stimulus measures end." Hannon (2021) observes that older and richer people, who accrued most of the increase in wealth and income during the pandemic, have a high propensity to save, which points to a relatively subdued recovery of spending.

24. This ignores the relatively small share of five-, ten-, and thirty-year Treasury bonds that are inflation-protected.

25. The term premium is the extra compensation investors demand in order to hold long-term debt.

26. To put it another way, they succeeded only when they allowed the nominal-growth-rate–nominal-interest-rate differential to widen substantially before investors responded by demanding a higher term premium.

27. The reference is to the Federal Reserve's "average inflation targeting approach" announced in the fall of 2020, which indicates a willingness to accommodate inflation rates above 2 percent in order to make up for earlier periods of below-target inflation, and in order to drive unemployment down to lower levels so long as pressure on unit labor costs remains subdued.

28. Goodhart and Pradhan (2020), p. 214. Their case in point is the United Kingdom, but the argument is more general.

29. This is not an argument for an early return to austerity. The question, rather, is how much deficit spending is too much, given the economy's finite productive capacity. The answer turns in part on the level of private spending, whose prospective strength is uncertain, as argued above.

30. As described in Chapter 9.

# REFERENCES

Abbas, S. M. Ali, Nazim Belhocine, Asmaa El-Ganainy, and Mark Horton. 2011. "Historical Patterns and Dynamics of Public Debt—Evidence from a New Database," *IMF Economic Review* 59: 717–42.

Abbas, S. M. Ali, Nazim Belhocine, Asmaa El-Ganainy, and Andreas Weber. 2014a. "Current Crisis in Historical Perspective," in Carlo Cottarelli, Philip Gerson, and Abdelhak Senhadji eds., *Post-Crisis Fiscal Policy*. Cambridge, MA: MIT Press, pp. 161–91.

Abbas, S. M. Ali, Laura Blattner, Mark De Broeck, Asmaa El-Ganainy, and Malin Hu. 2014b. "Sovereign Debt Composition in Advanced Economies: A Historical Perspective," IMF Working Paper no. 14/162 (September).

Abramovitz, Moses. 1986. "Catch Up, Forging Ahead, and Falling Behind," *Journal of Economic History* 46: 385–406.

Abrams, Burton, and Russell Settle. 1999. "Women's Suffrage and the Growth of the Welfare State," *Public Choice* 100: 289–300.

Abreu, Marcelo de Paiva. 2006. "The External Context," in Victor Bulmer-Thomas, John Coatsworth, and Roberto Cortés Conde, eds., *The Cambridge Economic History of Latin America*, Vol. II: *The Long Twentieth Century*. Cambridge: Cambridge University Press, pp. 101–34.

Accominotti, Olivier. 2012. "London Merchant Banks, the Central European Panic, and the Sterling Crisis of 1931," *Economic History Review* 64: 385–407.

Accominotti, Olivier, Marc Flandreau, Riad Rezzik, and Frederic Zumer. 2010. "Black Man's Burden, White Man's Welfare: Control, Devolution and Development in the British Empire, 1880–1914," *European Review of Economic History* 14: 47–70.

Acemoglu, Daron. 2005. "Politics and Economics in Weak and Strong States," *Journal of Monetary Economics* 52: 1199–1226.

Acemoglu, Daron, and James Robinson. 2000. "Why Did the West Extend the Franchise? Democracy, Inequality and Growth in Historical Perspective," *Quarterly Journal of Economics* 115: 1167–99.

Ahsan, Reshad, Laura Panza, and Yong Song. 2019. "Atlantic Trade and the Decline of Conflict in Europe," CEPR Discussion Paper no. 14206 (December).

Aidt, Toke, and Peter Jensen. 2014. "Workers of the World, Unite! Franchise Extensions and the Threat of Revolution in Europe, 1820–1938," unpublished manuscript, University of Cambridge and University of Southern Denmark (August).

Aidt, Toke, and Graham Mooney. 2014. "Voting Suffrage and the Political Budget Cycle: Evidence from the London Metropolitan Boroughs 1902–1937," *Journal of Public Economics* 112: 53–71.

Alesina, Alberto. 1988. "The End of Large Public Debts," in Francesco Giavazzi and Luigi Spaventa, eds., *High Public Debt: The Italian Experience*. Cambridge: Cambridge University Press, pp. 34–79.

Alesina, Alberto, and Silvia Ardagna. 2010. "Large Changes in Fiscal Policy: Taxes versus Spending," *Tax Policy and the Economy* 24: 35–68.

Alesina, Alberto, and Silvia Ardagna. 2013. "The Design of Fiscal Adjustments," *Tax Policy and the Economy* 27: 19–67.

Alesina, Alberto, Silvia Ardagna, and Francesco Trebbi. 2006. "Who Adjusts and When? On the Political Economy of Reforms," *IMF Staff Papers* 53: 1–49.

Alesina, Alberto, and Allan Drazen. 1991. "Why Are Stabilizations Delayed?" *American Economic Review* 81: 1170–88.

Alesina, Alberto, Carlo Favero, and Francesco Giavazzi. 2019. *Austerity: When It Works and When It Doesn't*. Princeton, NJ: Princeton University Press.

Alesina, Alberto, and Roberto Perotti. 1996. "Reducing Budget Deficits," *Swedish Economic Policy Review* 3: 113–34.

Alesina, Alberto, Roberto Perotti, and José Tavares. 1998. "The Political Economy of Fiscal Consolidations," *Brookings Papers on Economic Activity* 1: 197–248.

Alesina, Alberto, and Guido Tabellini. 1990. "A Positive Theory of Fiscal Deficits and Government Debt," *Review of Economic Studies* 57: 403–14.

Alfani, Guido, and Matteo Di Tullio. 2019. *The Lion's Share: Inequality and the Rise of the Fiscal State in Preindustrial Europe*. Cambridge: Cambridge University Press.

Álvarez-Nogal, Carlos, and Christophe Chamley. 2014. "Debt Policy under Constraints: Philip II, the Cortes and Genoese Bankers," *Economic History Review* 67: 192–213.

Álvarez-Nogal, Carlos, and Christophe Chamley. 2016. "Philip II against the Cortes and the Credit Freeze of 1575–1577," *Revista de Historia Económica* 34: 351–82.

Amaglobeli, David, Nicolas End, Mariusz Jarmuzek, and Geremia Palomba. 2015. "From Systemic Banking Crises to Fiscal Costs: Risk Factors," IMF Working Paper 15/166 (July).

Anastasakis, Othon. 2012. "Has Greece's Democracy Regressed?" *CNN* (Mar. 1), https://edition. cnn.com/2012/03/01/opinion/greece-democracy/index.html

Anderson, Olive. 1964. "Great Britain and the Beginnings of the Ottoman Public Debt, 1854–55," *Historical Journal* 7: 47–63.

Andersson, Fredrik, and Jason Lennard. 2019. "Irish GDP between the Famine and the First World War: Estimates Based on a Dynamic Factor Model," *European Review of Economic History* 23: 50–71.

Angell, James. 1901. "The Turkish Capitulations," *American Historical Review* 6: 254–59.

Antipa, Pamfili. 2015. "How Fiscal Policy Affects the Price Level: Britain's First Experience with Paper Money," unpublished manuscript, Banque de France (May).

Antipa, Pamfili, and Christophe Chamley. 2017. "Monetary and Fiscal Policy in England during the French Wars (1793–1821)," unpublished manuscript, Banque de France and Boston University.

Aristotle, and Edward Seymour Forster, trans. 1920. *Oeconomica*. Oxford: Clarendon Press.

Arslanalp, Serkan, and Takahiro Tsuda. 2014. "Tracking the Global Demand for Emerging Market Sovereign Debt," IMF Working Paper 14/39 (March).

Asakura, Kokichi. 1970. "The Characteristics of Finance in the Meiji Period," *Developing Economies* 5: 274–300.

Auerbach, Alan. 2001. "U.S. Fiscal Policy in a (Brief?) Era of Surpluses," *Japan and the World Economy* 13: 371–86.

Avery, William. 1990. "The Origins of Debt Accumulation among LDCs in the World Political Economy," *Journal of Developing Areas* 24: 502–33.

Avramovic, Dragoslav. 1958. *Debt Servicing Capacity and Postwar Growth in International Indebtedness*. Baltimore: Johns Hopkins University Press.

Azariadis, Costas, and Allen Drazen. 1990. "Threshold Externalities in Economic Development," *Quarterly Journal of Economics* 105: 501–26.

Backus, David, and John Driffill. 1985. "Inflation and Reputation," *American Economic Review* 75: 530–38.

Bacon, Benjamin. 1997. *Sinews of War: How Technology, Industry and Transportation Won the Civil War.* Novato, CA: Presidio Press.

Baker, Dean. 2005. "Short-Term Gain for Long-Term Pain: The Real Story of Rubinomics," unpublished manuscript, Center for Economic and Policy Research (November).

Bank of England. 2017. "A Millennium of Macroeconomic Data for the UK." Version 3.1. London: Bank of England, https://www.bankofengland.co.uk/statistics/research-datasets/

Bank of Finland. 1989. *The Finnish Economy 1860–1985: Growth and Structural Change.* Helsinki: Bank of Finland.

Barbash, Jack. 1976. "The Labor Movement after World War II," *Monthly Labor Review* 99: 34–37.

Barro, Robert. 1979. "On the Determination of the Public Debt," *Journal of Political Economy* 87: 940–71.

Barro, Robert. 1987. "Government Spending, Interest Rates, Prices, and Budget Deficits in the United Kingdom, 1701–1918," *Journal of Monetary Economics* 20: 221–47.

Barro, Robert. 1989. "Interest Rate Targeting," *Journal of Monetary Economics* 23: 3–30.

Barth, Boris. 1995. *Die deutsche Hochfinanz und die Imperialismen. Banken und Außenpolitik vor 1914.* Stuttgart: Franz Steiner.

Bartlett, Bruce. 2007. "'Starve the Beast': Origins and Development of a Budgetary Metaphor," *Independent Review* 12: 5–26.

Bartoletto, Silvana, and Elisabetta Marzano. 2012. "The Sustainability of Fiscal Policy in Italy: A Long-Term Perspective," unpublished manuscript, Parthenope University of Naples (May).

Bastasin, Carlo. 2015. *Saving Europe: Anatomy of a Dream.* Washington, DC: Brookings Institution Press.

Basu, Susanto, John Fernald, and Matthew Shapiro. 2001. "Productivity Growth in the 1990s: Technology, Utilization and Adjustment," *Carnegie-Rochester Conference Series on Public Policy* 55: 117–65.

Bayoumi, Tamim. 2017. *Unfinished Business: The Unexplored Causes of the Financial Crisis and the Lessons Yet to Be Learned.* New Haven, CT: Yale University Press.

Becker, Marvin. 1965. "Problemi della finanza pubblica fiorentina della seconda metà del trecento e dei primi del quattrocento," *Archivio Storico Italiano* 133: 433–66.

Bent, Peter, and Rui Esteves. 2016. "Capital Pull Factors at the Turn of the 20th Century: A Sectoral Analysis," unpublished manuscript, University of Oxford.

Bernanke, Ben. 2005. "The Global Saving Glut and the U.S. Current Account Deficit." Speech presented at the Federal Reserve Bank of St. Louis, *Homer Jones Lecture,* Apr. 14, www.federalreserve.gov/boarddocs/speeches/2005/20050414/default.htm

Best, Gary Dean. 1972. "Financing a Foreign War: Jacob H. Schiff and Japan, 1904–05," *American Jewish Historical Quarterly* 61: 313–24.

Bignon, Vincent, and Marc Flandreau. 2011. "The Economics of Badmouthing: Libel Law and the Underworld of the Financial Press in France Before World War I," *Journal of Economic History* 71: 616–53.

Bignon, Vincent, Alfonso Herranz-Loncán, and Rui Esteves. 2015. "Big Push or Big Grab? Railways, Government Activism and Export Growth in Latin America, 1865–1913," *Economic History Review* 68: 1277–1305.

Billyou, De Forest. 1948. "Corporate Mortgage Bonds and Majority Clauses," *Yale Law Journal* 57: 595–612.

Blackett, R. J. M. 2001. *Divided Hearts: Britain and the American Civil War.* Baton Rouge: Louisiana State University Press.

Bloch, Henri-Simon. 1940. "The Evolution of French Taxation: An Historical Sketch," *Bulletin of the National Tax Association* 25: 266–73.

Blockmans, Wim. 1997. *A History of Power in Europe: Peoples, Markets, States.* Brussels: Fonds Mercator of the Banque Paribas.

Bloomberg Tax. 2020. "Digital Tax Even More Important in Pandemic: France's Le Maire," *Bloomberg Tax* (May 4), https://news.bloombergtax.com/daily-tax-report-international/digital-tax-even-more-important-in-pandemic-frances-le-maire

Blustein, Paul. 2001. *The Chastening: Inside the Crisis That Rocked the Global Financial System and Humbled the IMF.* New York: Public Affairs.

Blustein, Paul. 2016. *Laid Low: Inside the Crisis That Overwhelmed Europe and the IMF.* Waterloo, ON: CIGI Press.

Bogaert, Raymond. 1968. *Banques et banquiers dans les cités grecques.* Leiden: A. J. Sijthoff.

Bolt, Jutta, Robert Inklaar, Herman de Jong, and Jan Luiten van Zanden. 2018. "'Rebasing Maddison': New Income Comparisons and the Shape of Long-Run Economic Development," Maddison Project Working Paper no. 10. Groningen: University of Groningen.

Bolton, Patrick, Mitu Gulati, and Ugo Panizza. 2020. "Legal Air Cover," Duke Law School Public Law & Legal Series, No. 2020-63 (October).

Borchard, Edwin, and William Wynne. 1951. *State Insolvency and Foreign Bondholders,* 2 vols. New Haven, CT: Yale University Press.

Bordo, Michael, Christopher Meissner, and Angela Redish. 2005. "How Original Sin Was Overcome: The Evolution of External Debt Denominated in Domestic Currencies in the United States and the British Dominions, 1800–2000," in Barry Eichengreen and Ricardo Hausmann, eds., *Other People's Money: Debt Denomination and Financial Instability in Emerging Market Economies.* Chicago: University of Chicago Press, pp. 122–53.

Bordo, Michael, and Arunima Sinha. 2016. "A Lesson from the Great Depression That the Fed Might Have Learned: A Comparison of the 1932 Open Market Purchases with Quantitative Easing," NBER Working Paper no. 22581 (August).

Bordo, Michael, and Eugene White. 1991. "A Tale of Two Currencies: British and French War Finance during the Napoleonic Wars," *Journal of Economic History* 51: 303–16.

Boughton, James. 2000. "Northwest of Suez: The 1956 Crisis and the IMF," IMF Working Paper no. 00/192 (December).

Boynton, Lindsay. 1967. *The Elizabethan Militia, 1558–1638.* Toronto, ON: University of Toronto Press.

Braddick, Michael. 2000. *State Formation in Early Modern England, c. 1550–1700.* Cambridge: Cambridge University Press.

Brewer, John. 1988. *The Sinews of Power: War, Money and the English State, 1688–1783.* New York: Alfred A. Knopf.

Broadberry, Stephen, Bruce Campbell, Alexander Klein, Bas van Leeuwen, and Mark Overton. 2015. *British Economic Growth 1270–1870.* Cambridge: Cambridge University Press.

Broadberry, Stephen, and Mark Harrison, eds. 1998. *The Economics of World War II: Six Great Powers in International Comparison.* Cambridge: Cambridge University Press.

Broda, Christian, and Jonathan Parker. 2014. "The Economic Stimulus Payments of 2008 and the Aggregate Demand for Consumption," *Journal of Monetary Economics* 68: S20–S36.

Brown, E. Cary. 1956. "Fiscal Policy in the Thirties: A Reappraisal," *American Economic Review* 46: 857–79.

Brown, William Adams. 1940. *The International Gold Standard Reinterpreted, 1914–1934,* 2 vols. New York: National Bureau of Economic Research.

Buchheit, Lee, and Mitu Gulati. 2017. "Restructuring Sovereign Debt after NML v. Argentina," *Capital Markets Law Journal* 12: 224–38.

Buiter, Willem, Giancarlo Corsetti, and Nouriel Roubini. 1993. "Excessive Deficits: Sense and Nonsense in the Treaty of Maastricht," *Economic Policy* 8: 57–100.

Bullock, Hugh. 1959. *The Story of Investment Companies.* New York: Columbia University Press.

Bulow, Jeremy, and Kenneth Rogoff. 1989. "Sovereign Debt: Is to Forgive to Forget?" *American Economic Review* 79: 43–50.

Burnside, Craig, Martin Eichenbaum, and Sergio Rebelo. 2000. "Understanding the Korean and Thai Currency Crises," in *Economic Perspectives.* Chicago: Federal Reserve Bank of Chicago, pp. 45–60.

Byron, Lord George Gordon. 1823. *Don Juan*, 1973 ed., T. G. Steffan, E. Steffan, and W. W. Pratt eds. Harmondsworth: Penguin.

Cairncross, A. K. 1953. *Home and Foreign Investment*. Cambridge: Cambridge University Press.

Calomiris, Charles, and Charles Kahn. 1991. "The Role of Demandable Debt in Structuring Optimal Banking Arrangements," *American Economic Review* 81: 497–513.

Calvo, Guillermo. 1994. "Comment on Dornbusch and Werner," *Brookings Papers on Economic Activity* 1: 298–303.

Cameron, Rondo. 1961. *France and the Economic Development of Europe 1800–1914*. Princeton, NJ: Princeton University Press.

Campa, José. 1990. "Exchange Rates and Economic Recovery in the 1930s: An Extension to Latin America," *Journal of Economic History* 50: 677–82.

Campbell, Todd. 2004. "Sound Finance: Gladstone and British Government Finance, 1880–1895," unpublished Ph.D. dissertation, London School of Economics.

Caprio, Gerard, and Daniela Klingebiel. 1996. "Bank Insolvencies: Cross Country Experience," World Bank Policy Research Working Paper no. 1620 (July).

Carreras, Albert, and Xavier Tafunell, coords. 2005. *Estadísticas históricas de España. Siglos XIX–XX*. Bilbao: Fundación BBVA.

Carter, Susan, Scott Sigmund Gartner, Michael R. Haines, Alan Olmstead, Richard Sutch, and Gavin Wright, eds. 2006. *Historical Statistics of the United States: Earliest Times to the Present*. New York: Cambridge University Press.

Casella, Alessandra, and Barry Eichengreen. 1996. "Can Foreign Aid Accelerate Stabilisation?" *Economic Journal* 106: 605–19.

Cecchetti, Stephen, Madhusudan Mohanty, and Fabrizio Zampolli. 2011. "The Real Effects of Debt," BIS Working Paper no. 352 (September).

Chabot, Benjamin, and Mitu Gulati. 2014. "Santa Anna and His Black Eagle: The Origins of Pari Passu?" *Capital Markets Law Journal* 9: 216–41.

Chabot, Benjamin, and Christopher Kurz. 2010. "That's Where the Money Was: Foreign Bias and English Investment Abroad, 1866–1907," *Economic Journal* 120: 1056–79.

Chabot, Benjamin, and Christopher Kurz. 2012. "British Investment Trusts: The Precursors of Modern Structured Finance," mimeo.

Chambers, David, and Rui Esteves. 2014. "The First Global Emerging Markets Investor: Foreign & Colonial Investment Trust 1880–1913," *Explorations in Economic History* 52: 1–21.

Chodorow-Reich, Gabriel. 2019. "Geographic Cross-Sectional Fiscal Spending Multipliers: What Have We Learned?" *American Economic Journal: Economic Policy* 11: 1–34.

Chopra, Ajai, Kenneth Kang, Meral Karasulu, Hong Liang, Henry Ma, and Anthony Richards. 2002. "From Crisis to Recovery in Korea: Strategy, Achievements and Lessons," in David Coe and Se-Jik Kim, eds., *Korean Crisis and Recovery*. Washington, DC: IMF, pp. 13–104.

Clarke, Stephen V. O. 1967. *Central Bank Cooperation, 1923–1931*. New York: Federal Reserve Bank of New York.

Clavel, Damian. 2019. "Fraude financière, dette souveraine et impérialisme d'affaires: Une micro-histoire de l'échec de Poyais 1820–1824," unpublished Ph.D. dissertation, Geneva: Graduate Institute of International and Development Studies.

Clay, Christopher 2001. *Gold for the Sultan: Western Bankers and Ottoman Finance, 1856–1881*. New York: I. B. Tauris.

Cleveland, Harold van, and Thomas Heurtas. 1985. *Citibank, 1812–1970*. Cambridge, MA: Harvard University Press.

Cline, William. 1995. *International Debt Reexamined*. Washington, DC: Institute for International Economics.

Coffman, D'Maris. 2013a. "Credibility, Transparency, Accountability, and the Public Credit under the Long Parliament and Commonwealth, 1643–1653," in D'Maris Coffman, Adrian Leonard, and Larry Neal, eds., *Questioning Credible Commitment: Perspectives on the Rise of Financial Capitalism*. Cambridge: Cambridge University Press, pp. 76–103.

Coffman, D'Maris. 2013b. *Excise Taxation and the Origins of Public Debt*. London: Palgrave Macmillan.

Cogan, John, and John Taylor. 2011. "Where Did the Stimulus Go?" *Commentary* (January), https://www.commentarymagazine.com/articles/commentary-bk/where-did-the-stimulus-go/

Cohen, Darrel, and Glenn Follette. 2000. "The Automatic Fiscal Stabilizers: Quietly Doing Their Thing," *Federal Reserve Bank of New York Economic Policy Review* 6: 35–68.

Cohen-Cole, Ethan, Steven Durlauf, and Giacomo Rondina. 2012. "Nonlinearities in Growth: From Evidence to Policy," *Journal of Macroeconomics* 34: 42–58.

Cole, Harold, and Timothy Kehoe. 1996. "A Self-Fulfilling Model of Mexico's 1993–94 Debt Crisis," Research Department Staff Report no. 210. Minneapolis: Federal Reserve Bank of Minneapolis.

Collet, Stéphanie. 2012. "A Unified Italy? Sovereign Debt and Investor Scepticism," unpublished manuscript, Frankfurt University.

Committee for the Study of Economic and Monetary Union (Jacques Delors, chairman). 1989. *Report on Economic and Monetary Union in the European Community*. Brussels: European Community.

Committee on Banking, Finance and Urban Affairs, US Congress. 1980. *Foreign Bank Operations and Acquisitions in the United States*. Hearings before the Subcommittee on Financial Institutions Supervision, Regulation and Insurance, Part 1, Serial no. 96-77. Washington, DC: Government Printing Office.

Committee on National Debt and Taxation [Colwyn Committee]. 1927. *Report*, Cmd. 2800. London: HMSO.

Cong, William, Haoyu Gao, Jacopo Ponticelli, and Xiaoguang Yang. 2019. "Credit Allocation under Economic Stimulus: Evidence from China," *Review of Financial Studies* 32: 3241–60.

Congressional Budget Office. 2020. "CBO's Current Projections of Output, Employment and Interest Rates and a Preliminary Look at Federal Deficits for 2020 and 2021." Washington, DC: CBO (Apr. 24).

Congressional Budget Office. 2021. "The Long-Term Budget Outlook." Washington, DC: CBO (Mar. 4).

Conti, Elio. 1984. *L'imposta diretta a Firenze nel quattrocento (1427–1494)*. Rome: Nella Sede Dell'Istituto Palazzo Borromini.

Cooper, Richard, and Edwin Truman. 1971. "An Analysis of the Role of International Capital Markets in Providing Funds to Developing Countries," *Weltwirtschaftliches Archiv* 106: 153–83.

Copelovitch, Mark. 2010. *The International Monetary Fund in the Global Economy: Banks, Bonds and Bailouts*. Cambridge: Cambridge University Press.

Corporation of Foreign Bondholders. 1905. *Annual Report*. London: Corporation of Foreign Bondholders.

Cottrell, Philip. 2008. "A Survey of European Investment in Turkey, 1854–1914: Banks and the Finance of the State and Railway Construction," in Philip Cottrell, ed., *East Meets West: Banking, Commerce and Investment in the Ottoman Empire*. London: Routledge, pp. 59–96.

Council of Foreign Bondholders. 1876. *Egyptian Debt: Mission of the Right Hon. G.J. Goschen, M.P.* London: Council of Foreign Bondholders.

Cox, Gary. 2016. *Marketing Sovereign Promises: Monopoly Brokerage and the Growth of the English State*. Cambridge: Cambridge University Press.

Cox, Robert. 1993. *The Development of the Dutch Welfare State from Workers' Insurance to Universal Entitlement*. Pittsburgh: University of Pittsburgh Press.

Crafts, N. F. R. 2019. "The Sources of British Economic Growth since the Industrial Revolution: Not the Same Old Story," *Journal of Economic Surveys* 33: 1–13.

Crafts, N. F. R., and C. K. Harley. 1992. "Output Growth and the British Industrial Revolution: A Restatement of the Crafts-Harley View," *Economic History Review* 45: 703–30.

Crafts, Nicholas, and Terence Mills. 2015. "Self-Defeating Austerity? Evidence from 1930s Britain," *European Review of Economic History* 19: 109–27.

Cumby, Robert, and Richard Levich. 1987. "On the Definition and Magnitude of Recent Capital Flight," in Donald Lessard and John Williamson, eds., *Capital Flight and Third World Debt*. Washington, DC: Institute for International Economics, pp. 27–67.

Daseking, Christiana, and Robert Powell. 1999. "From Toronto Terms to the HIPC Initiative: A Brief History of Debt Relief for Low-Income Countries," IMF Working Paper no. 99/142 (October).

Dasgupta, Dipak, Dilip Ratha, Dennis Botman, and Ashish Narain. 2000. "Short-Term Debt in Financial Crises," in Charles Adams, Robert Litan, and Michael Pomerleano, eds., *Managing Financial and Corporate Distress: Lessons from Asia*. Washington, DC: Brookings Institution Press, pp. 325–60.

Daunton, Martin. 2001. *Trusting Leviathan: The Politics of Taxation in Britain, 1799–1914*. Cambridge: Cambridge University Press.

Davis, Joseph Stancliffe. 1917. *Essays in the Earlier History of American Corporations*. Cambridge, MA: Harvard University Press.

Davis, Lance, and Robert Cull. 1994. *International Capital Markets and American Economic Growth 1820–1914*. Cambridge: Cambridge University Press.

Davis, Lance, and Robert Huttenback. 1986. *Mammon and the Pursuit of Empire: The Political Economy of British Imperialism, 1860–1912*. Cambridge: Cambridge University Press.

De Luca, Giuseppe. 2008. "Government Debt and Financial Markets: Exploring Pro-Cyclical Effects in Northern Italy during the Sixteenth and the Seventeenth Centuries," in Fausto Caselli, ed., *Government Debts and Financial Markets in Europe*. London: Pickering and Chatto, pp. 45–66.

De Roover, Raymond. 1953. *L'Evolution de la Lettre de Change, XIVe–XVIIIe siècles*. Paris: Armand Colin.

De Rugy, Veronique. 2009. "Spending under President George W. Bush," Working Paper no. 09-04, Mercatus Center, George Mason University (March).

De Vries, Jan, and Ad van der Woude. 1997. *The First Modern Economy: Success, Failure, and Perseverance of the Dutch Economy, 1500–1815*. Cambridge: Cambridge University Press.

Del Punta, Ignazio. 2010. "Tuscan Merchant-Bankers and Moneyers and Their Relations with the Roman Curia in the XIIIth and early XIVth Centuries," *Rivista di storia della Chiesa in Italia* 64: 39–53.

Della Paolera, Gerardo, and Alan Taylor. 2001. *Straining at the Anchor: The Argentine Currency Board and the Search for Macroeconomic Stability, 1880–1935*. Chicago: University of Chicago Press.

Denzel, Markus. 2006. "The European Bill of Exchange," paper presented to the International Economic History Conference, Helsinki (August).

Descimon, Robert. 2006. "La venalité des offices comme dette publique sous l'Ancien Régime français. Le bien commun au pays des intérêts privés," in J. Andreau, G. Béaur, and J.-Y. Grenier, eds., *La dette publique dans l'histoire*. Paris: Institut de la gestion publique et du développement économique.

Detrixhe, John. 2020. "Investors Are Bracing for an Epidemic of Government Borrowing," *Quartz* (Mar. 18), https://qz.com/1820632/bond-yields-climb-as-governments-plan-2-8-trillion-coronavirus-stimulus/

Di Matteo, Livio. 2017. *A Federal Fiscal History: Canada, 1867–2017*. Vancouver, BC: Fraser Institute.

Dicks, M.J. 1991. "The LDC Debt Crisis," *Bank of England Quarterly Bulletin* (November): 498–507.

Dincecco, Mark. 2009. "Fiscal Centralization, Limited Government, and Public Revenues in Europe, 1650–1913," *Journal of Economic History* 69: 48–103.

Dincecco, Mark. 2011. *Political Transformations and Public Finances: Europe, 1650–1913*. New York: Cambridge University Press.

Dincecco, Mark, and Massimiliano Gaetano Onorato. 2018. *From Warfare to Wealth: The Military Origins of Urban Prosperity in Europe*. Cambridge: Cambridge University Press.

Donovan, Donal, and Antoin Murphy. 2013. *The Fall of the Celtic Tiger: Ireland and the Euro Debt Crisis*. Oxford: Oxford University Press.

Dornbusch, Rudiger, Ilan Goldfajn, and Rodrigo Valdés. 1995. "Currency Crises and Collapses," *Brookings Papers on Economic Activity* 2: 219–70.

Dornbusch, Rudiger, and Alejandro Werner. 1994. "Mexico: Stabilization, Reform and No Growth," *Brookings Papers on Economic Activity* 1: 253–315.

Doyle, William. 1984. "The Price of Offices in Pre-Revolutionary France," *Historical Journal* 27: 831–60.

Drelichman, Mauricio, and Hans-Joachim Voth. 2014. *Lending to the Borrower from Hell: Debt, Taxes, and Default in the Age of Philip II*. Princeton, NJ: Princeton University Press.

Dulles, Eleanor. 1929. *The French Franc, 1914–1928: The Facts, and Their Interpretation*. New York: Macmillan.

Dyson, Kenneth. 2014. *States, Debt and Power: "Saints" and "Sinners" in European History and Integration*. New York: Oxford University Press.

Ebbinghaus, Bernhard, and Jelle Visser. 2000. *Trade Unions in Western Europe since 1945*. London: Macmillan.

Edelstein, Michael. 1982. *Overseas Investment in the Age of High Imperialism: The United Kingdom, 1850–1914*. New York: Columbia University Press.

Edwards, Chris. 2020. "State Rainy Day Funds," Cato Institute (Apr. 13), https://www.cato.org/blog/state-rainy-day-funds

Edwards, Sebastian. 2018. *American Default: The Untold Story of FDR, the Supreme Court, and the Battle over Gold*. Princeton, NJ: Princeton University Press.

Edwards, Sebastian, and Julio Santaella. 1993. "Devaluation Controversies in Developing Countries: Lessons from the Bretton Woods Era," in Michael Bordo and Barry Eichengreen, eds., *A Retrospective on the Bretton Woods System: Lessons for International Monetary Reform*. Chicago: University of Chicago Press, pp. 405–55.

Ehrenberg, Richard. 1928. *Capital and Finance in the Age of the Renaissance: A Study of the Fuggers and Their Connections*. London: Jonathan Cape.

Eichengreen, Barry. 1989. "The U.S. Capital Market and Foreign Lending, 1929–1955," in Jeffrey Sachs, ed., *Developing Country Debt and Economic Performance*, Vol. 2. Chicago: University of Chicago Press, pp. 107–58.

Eichengreen, Barry. 1990. "The Capital Levy in Theory and Practice," in Rudiger Dornbusch and Mario Draghi, eds., *Public Debt Management: Theory and History*. Cambridge: Cambridge University Press, pp. 191–221.

Eichengreen, Barry. 1991. "Historical Research on International Lending and Debt," *Journal of Economic Perspectives* 5: 149–69.

Eichengreen, Barry. 1996. "Institutions and Economic Growth: Europe since 1945," in Nicholas Crafts and Gianni Toniolo, eds., *Economic Growth in Europe since 1945*. Cambridge: Cambridge University Press, pp. 38–72.

Eichengreen, Barry. 2018. *The Populist Temptation: Economic Grievance and Political Reaction in the Modern Era*. New York: Oxford University Press.

Eichengreen, Barry, and Michael Bordo. 2003. "Crises Now and Then: What Lessons from the Last Era of Financial Globalization?" in Paul Mizen, ed., *Monetary History, Exchange Rates and Financial Markets: Essays in Honour of Charles Goodhart*, Vol. 2. Cheltenham, UK: Edward Elgar, pp. 52–91.

Eichengreen, Barry, Asmaa El-Ganainy, Rui Esteves, and Kris James Mitchener. 2020. "Public Debt Through the Ages," in S. Ali Abbas, Alex Pienkowski, and Kenneth Rogoff, eds., *Sovereign Debt: A Guide for Economists and Practitioners*. New York: Oxford University Press, pp. 7–55.

Eichengreen, Barry, and Ricardo Hausmann. 1999. "Exchange Rates and Financial Fragility," in Federal Reserve Bank of Kansas City, ed., *New Challenges for Monetary Policy*. Kansas City, MO: Federal Reserve Bank of Kansas City, pp. 329–68.

Eichengreen, Barry, and Kris James Mitchener. 2004. "The Great Depression as a Credit Boom Gone Wrong," *Research in Economic History* 22: 183–237.

Eichengreen, Barry, and Ugo Panizza. 2016. "A Surplus of Ambition: Can Europe Rely on Large Primary Surpluses to Solve Its Debt Problem?" *Economic Policy* 31: 5–49.

Eichengreen, Barry, and Richard Portes. 1989. "Dealing with Debt: The 1930s and the 1980s," in Ishrat Husain and Ishac Diwan, eds., *Dealing with the Debt Crisis*. Washington, DC: World Bank, pp. 69–86.

Eichengreen, Barry, and Charles Wyplosz. 1998. "The Stability Pact: More than a Minor Nuisance?" *Economic Policy* 13: 66–113.

Eisenbeis, Robert, and Paul Horvitz. 1993. "The Role of Forbearance and Its Costs in Handling Troubled and Failed Depository Institutions," in George Kaufman, ed., *Reforming Financial Institutions and Markets in the United States*. Dordrecht, the Netherlands: Kluwer Academic, pp. 49–68.

Elmendorf, Douglas, Jeffrey Liebman, and David Wilcox. 2002. "Fiscal Policy and Social Security Policy during the 1990s," in Jeffrey Frankel and Peter Orszag, eds., *American Economic Policy in the 1990s*. Cambridge, MA: MIT Press, pp. 61–119.

Engle, Robert. 1982. "Autoregressive Conditional Heteroscedasticity with Estimates of the Variance of United Kingdom Inflation," *Econometrica* 50: 987–1007.

English, William. 1996. "Understanding the Costs of Sovereign Default: American State Debts in the 1840s," *American Economic Review* 86: 259–75.

Epstein, Stephan. 2000. *Freedom and Growth: The Rise of States and Markets in Europe, 1300–1750*. London: Routledge.

Esteves, Rui. 2013. "The Bondholder, the Sovereign and the Banker: Sovereign Debt and Bondholders' Protection before 1914," *European Review of Economic History* 17: 389–407.

Esteves, Rui, and Marc Flandreau. 2019. "The Value of a Quote: Stock Market Listing for Sovereign Bonds, 1872–1911," mimeo.

Esteves, Rui, and Ali Tunçer. 2016. "Feeling the Blues: Moral Hazard and Debt Dilution in Eurobonds before 1914," *Journal of International Money and Finance* 65: 46–68.

Estrin, Saul, and Peter Holmes. 1990. "Indicative Planning in Developed Economies," *Journal of Comparative Economics* 14: 531–54.

European Central Bank. 2015a. "The Fiscal Impact of Financial Sector Support during the Crisis," *Economic Bulletin* 6: 74–87.

European Central Bank. 2015b. "The State of the House Price Cycle in the Euro Area," *Economic Bulletin* 6: 9–24.

European Parliament, Committee on Economic and Monetary Affairs. 2011. "Trichet Testimony" (Oct. 4), https://www.ecb.europa.eu/press/key/date/2011/html/sp111004.en.html

Federal Deposit Insurance Corporation. 2009. "The Sand States: Anatomy of a Perfect Housing-Market Storm," *FDIC Quarterly* 3: 30–32.

Federal Reserve Bank of Cleveland. 2020. "Inflation Expectations," Cleveland: Federal Reserve Bank of Cleveland, accessed June 9, 2020, https://www.clevelandfed.org/our-research/indicators-and-data/inflation-expectations.aspx

Federal Reserve Bank of Philadelphia. 2021. "Partisan Conflict Index," Philadelphia: Federal Reserve Bank of Philadelphia, https://www.philadelphiafed.org/surveys-and-data/real-time-data-research/partisan-conflict-index

Federico, Giovanni, and Antonio Tena. 2017. "A Tale of Two Globalizations: Gains from Trade and Openness 1800–2010," *Review of World Economics (Weltwirtschaftliches Archiv)* 153: 601–26.

Feis, Herbert. 1930. *Europe, the World's Banker, 1870–1914: An Account of European Foreign Investment and the Connection of World Finance with Diplomacy before the War*. New Haven, CT: Council on Foreign Relations.

Feldman, Robert. 2003. "Japanese Realities: Challenges to Macroeconomic Theory," Center on Japanese Economy and Business, Columbia Business School, Jan. 28.

Fenochietto, Ricardo, and Carola Pessino. 2013. "Understanding Countries' Tax Effort," IMF Working Paper 13/244 (November).

Ferguson, Niall. 1999. *The Pity of War*. New York: Basic Books.

Ferguson, Niall, Andreas Schaab, and Moritz Schularick. 2014. "Central Bank Balance Sheets: Expansion and Reduction since 1900," paper for the ECB Forum on Central Banking (May 26).

Fernald, John, and Bing Wang. 2015. "The Recent Rise and Fall of Rapid Productivity Growth," *Economic Letter 2015-04*. San Francisco: Federal Reserve Bank of San Francisco (February).

Ferns, H. S. 1992. "The Baring Crisis Revisited," *Journal of Latin American Studies* 24: 241–73.

Fetter, Frank. 1947. "History of Public Debt in Latin America," *American Economic Review* 37: 142–50.

Field, Alexander. 2012. *A Great Leap Forward: 1930s Depression and U.S. Economic Growth*. New Haven, CT: Yale University Press.

Fishlow, Albert. 1985. "Lessons from the Past: Capital Markets during the 19th Century and the Interwar Period," *International Organization* 39: 38–93.

Fisk, Harvey Edward. 1922. *French Public Finance in the Great War and To-Day*. New York: Bankers Trust Publications.

Fitz-Gibbon, Bryan, and Marianne Gizycki. 2001. "A History of Last Resort Lending and Other Support for Troubled Financial Institutions in Australia," Research Discussion 2001-07. Sydney: Reserve Bank of Australia (October).

Flandreau, Marc. 2013. "Sovereign States, Bondholders Committees, and the London Stock Exchange in the Nineteenth Century (1827–68): New Facts and Old Fictions," *Oxford Review of Economic Policy* 29: 668–96.

Flandreau, Marc. 2016. *Anthropologists in the Stock Exchange: A Financial History of Victorian Science*. Chicago: University of Chicago Press.

Flandreau, Marc, and Juan Flores. 2009. "Bonds and Brands: Foundations of Sovereign Debt Markets, 1820–1830," *Journal of Economic History* 69: 646–84.

Flandreau, Marc, and Juan Flores. 2012. "Bondholders versus Bond Sellers? Investment Banks and Conditionality Lending in the London Market for Foreign Government Debt 1815–1913," *European Review of Economic History* 16: 356–83.

Flandreau, Marc, Juan Flores, Norbert Gaillard, and Sebastián Nieto-Parra. 2010. "The End of Gatekeeping: Underwriters and the Quality of Sovereign Bond Markets, 1815–2007," *NBER International Seminar on Macroeconomics* 6. Chicago: University of Chicago Press: 53–92.

Flandreau, Marc, and Nathan Sussman. 2005. "Old Sins: Exchange Clauses and European Foreign Lending in the 19th Century," in Barry Eichengreen and Ricardo Hausmann, eds., *Other People's Money: Debt Denomination and Financial Instability in Emerging Market Economies*. Chicago: University of Chicago Press, pp. 154–89.

Flandreau, Marc, and Frederic Zumer. 2004. *The Making of Global Finance, 1880–1913*. Paris: OECD.

Flora, Peter, Franz Kraus, and Winfried Pfennig. 1983. *State, Economy and Society in Western Europe, 1815–1975*. Frankfurt: Campus Verlag.

Flores, Juan. 2011. "Information Asymmetries and Conflict of Interest during the Baring Crisis, 1880–1890," *Financial History Review* 18: 191–215.

Flores, Juan. 2020. "Explaining Latin America's Persistent Defaults: An Analysis of Debtor-Creditor Relations in London, 1822–1914," *Financial History Review* 27: 319–39.

Flores, Juan, and Yann Decorzant. 2016. "Going Multilateral? Financial Markets' Access and the League of Nations Loans, 1923–8," *Economic History Review* 69: 653–78.

Folkerts-Landau, David, and Peter Garber. 1992. "The ECB: A Bank or a Monetary Policy Rule?" in Matthew Canzoneri, Vittorio Grilli, and Paul Masson, eds., *Establishing a Central Bank: Issues in Europe and Lessons from the US*. Cambridge: Cambridge University Press, pp. 86–110.

Ford, Franklin. 1953. *Robe and Sword: The Regrouping of the French Aristocracy after Louis XIV*. Cambridge, MA: Harvard University Press.

Frederiksen, Martin. 1966. "Caesar, Cicero and the Problem of Debt," *Journal of Roman Studies* 56: 128–41.

Frey, Carl Benedikt. 2019. *The Technology Trap: Capital, Labor, and Power in the Age of Automation*. Princeton, NJ: Princeton University Press.

Friedman, Irving. 1977. *The Emerging Role of Private Banks in the Developing World.* New York: Citicorp.

Friedman, Milton, and Anna Schwartz. 1963. *A Monetary History of the United States, 1867–1960.* Princeton, NJ: Princeton University Press.

Fryde, E. B., and M. M. Fryde. 1963. "Public Credit, with Special Reference to North-Western Europe," in M. M. Postan, E. E. Rich, and Edward Miller, eds., *The Cambridge Economic History of Europe, Vol. III: Economic Organization and Policies in the Middle Ages.* Cambridge: Cambridge University Press, pp. 430–543.

Fuerbringer, Jonathan. 2001. "U.S. Treasury: No Lending; With Big Budget Surpluses, Some See the End of New Bonds and Notes," *New York Times* (Apr. 6), https://www.nytimes.com/2001/04/06/business/us-treasury-no-lending-with-big-budget-surpluses-some-see-end-new-bonds-notes.html

Funke, Manuel, Moritz Schularick, and Christoph Trebesch. 2016. "Going to Extremes: Politics after Financial Crises, 1870–2014," *European Economic Review* 88: 227–60.

Galofré-Vilà, Gregori, Christopher Meissner, Martin McKee, and David Stuckler. 2019. "The Economic Consequences of the 1953 London Debt Agreement," *European Review of Economic History* 23: 1–29.

Gayer, Arthur, Walt Whitman Rostow, and Anna Schwartz. 1953. *The Growth and Fluctuation of the British Economy, 1790–1850.* Oxford: Clarendon Press.

Gelderblom, Oscar, ed. 2009. *The Political Economy of the Dutch Republic.* Farnham, UK: Ashgate.

Gelderblom, Oscar, and Joost Jonker. 2006. "Exploring the Market for Government Bonds in the Dutch Republic (1600–1800)," unpublished manuscript, Utrecht University.

Gelderblom, Oscar, and Joost Jonker. 2011. "Public Finance and Economic Growth: The Case of Holland in the Seventeenth Century," *Journal of Economic History* 71: 1–39.

Gennaioli, Nicola, Alberto Martin, and Stefano Rossi. 2018. "Banks, Government Bonds and Default: What Do the Data Say?" *Journal of Monetary Economics* 98: 98–113.

Gentry, Judith. 1970. "A Confederate Success in Europe: The Erlanger Loan," *Journal of Southern History* 36: 157–88.

Giffen, Robert. [1872] 1904. *Economic Inquiries and Studies.* London: G. Bell and Sons.

Giuliano, Paola, and Antonio Spilimbergo. 2014. "Growing Up in a Recession," *Review of Economic Studies* 81: 787–817.

Gleckman, Howard. 2019. "Can a Wealth Tax Raise the Revenue Its Sponsors Hope?" Tax Policy Center (Sep. 24), https://www.taxpolicycenter.org/taxvox/can-wealth-tax-raise-revenue-its-sponsors-hope

Goetzmann, William, and Andrey Ukhov. 2006. "British Investment Overseas 1870–1913: A Modern Portfolio Theory Approach," *Review of Finance* 10: 261–300.

Goetzmann, William, Andrey Ukhov, and Ning Zhu. 2007. "China and the World Financial Markets 1870–1939: Modern Lessons from Historical Globalization," *Economic History Review* 60: 267–312.

Goldin, Claudia, and Frank Lewis. 1975. "The Economic Cost of the American Civil War: Estimates and Implications," *Journal of Economic History* 35: 299–326.

Goldstein, Morris. 1998. *The Asian Financial Crisis: Causes, Cures and Systemic Implications.* Policy Analyses in International Economics, no. 55. Washington, DC: Institute for International Economics.

Goldthwaite, Richard. 2009. *The Economy of Renaissance Florence.* Baltimore: Johns Hopkins University Press.

Goodhart, Charles, and Manoj Pradhan. 2020. *The Great Demographic Reversal.* Zurich: Springer Nature.

Graeber, David. 2011. *Debt: The First 5,000 Years.* London: Melville House.

Grafe, Regina, and Maria Alejandra Irigoin. 2006. "The Spanish Empire and Its Legacy: Fiscal Redistribution and Political Conflict in Colonial and Post-Colonial Spanish America," *Journal of Global History* 1: 241–67.

Greenspan, Alan. 1999a. "Currency Reserves and Debt," Remarks to the World Bank Conference on Recent Trends in Reserve Management, Washington, DC (Apr. 29), https://www.federalreserve.gov/boarddocs/speeches/1999/19990429.htm

Greenspan, Alan. 1999b. "Do Efficient Financial Markets Mitigate Financial Crises?" Remarks before the 1999 Financial Markets Conference of the Federal Reserve Bank of Atlanta, Sea Island, GA (Oct. 19), https://www.federalreserve.gov/boarddocs/speeches/1999/19991019.htm

Grossman, Herschel, and Taejoon Han. 1996. "War Finance, Moral Hazard, and the Financing of the Confederacy," *Journal of Money, Credit and Banking* 28: 200–215.

Grossman, Herschel, and John van Huyck. 1988. "Sovereign Debt as a Contingent Claim: Excusable Default, Repudiation, and Reputation," *American Economic Review* 78: 1088–97.

Guajardo, Jaime, Daniel Leigh, and Andrea Pescatori. 2014. "Expansionary Austerity: New International Evidence," *Journal of the European Economic Association* 12: 949–68.

Guidotti, Pablo. 1999. "Remarks at G33 Seminar in Bonn, Germany," unpublished manuscript (Mar. 11).

Haber, Stephen. 2005. "Mexico's Experiments with Bank Privatization and Liberalization," *Journal of Banking and Finance* 29: 2325–53.

Hackett, John, and Anne-Marie Hackett. 1964. *Economic Planning in France.* Cambridge, MA: Harvard University Press.

Hagen, Sean. 2020. "Sovereign Debt Restructuring: The Centrality of the IMF's Role," Working Paper no. 20-13. Washington, DC: Peterson Institute of International Economics (July).

Haggard, Stephan. 2000. *The Political Economy of the Asian Financial Crisis.* Washington, DC: Institute for International Economics.

Hall, Nigel. 1998. "The Liverpool Cotton Market and the American Civil War," *Northern History* 34: 149–69.

Hammerman, Felix, Kiernan Leonard, Stefano Nardelli, and Julian von Landesberger. 2019. "Taking Stock of the Eurosystem's Asset Purchase Programme after the End of Net Asset Purchases," *ECB Economic Bulletin* (Mar. 18).

Hannon, Paul. 2021. "Savings to Fire up Growth—If Spent," *Wall Street Journal* (May 3), p. A2.

Hargreaves, Eric. 1967. *The National Debt.* London: Routledge.

Harley, C. Knick. 1988. "Ocean Freight Rates and Productivity, 1740–1913: The Primacy of Mechanical Invention Reaffirmed," *Journal of Economic History* 48: 851–76.

Harris, William. 2006. "A Revisionist View of Roman Money," *Journal of Roman Studies* 89: 62–75.

Heim, Carol, and Philip Mirowski. 1987. "Interest Rates and Crowding-Out during Britain's Industrial Revolution," *Journal of Economic History* 47: 117–39.

Hendriksen, Ingrid. n.d. "An Economic History of Denmark," *EH.net Encyclopedia,* https://eh.net/encyclopedia/an-economic-history-of-denmark/

Hillhouse, Albert Miller. 1936. *Municipal Bonds: A Century of Experience.* New York: Prentice-Hall.

HM Treasury. 2010. *Budget 2010.* London: HMSO.

Ho, Chun-Yo, and Dan Li. 2014. "A Mirror of History: Chinese Bond Market from 1921 to 1942," *Economic History Review* 67: 409–34.

Hoffman, Philip. 2015. *Why Did Europe Conquer the World?* Princeton, NJ: Princeton University Press.

Hoffman, Philip, Gilles Postel-Vinay, and Jean-Laurent Rosenthal. 2007. *Surviving Large Losses: Financial Crises, the Middle Class, and the Development of Capital Markets.* Cambridge, MA: Belknap Press of Harvard University Press.

Hofmann, Boris, Ilhyock Shim, and Hyun Song Shin. 2020. "Emerging Market Economy Exchange Rates and Local Currency Bond Markets Amid the Covid-19 Pandemic," *BIS Bulletin* no. 5 (Apr. 7).

Holtfrerich, Carl. 1986. *The German Inflation 1914–1923.* Berlin: De Gruyter.

Hopkin, Jonathan. 2020. *Anti-System Politics: The Crisis of Market Liberalism in Rich Democracies.* New York: Oxford University Press.

Horn, Sebastian, Carmen Reinhart, and Christoph Trebesch. 2019. "China's Overseas Lending," NBER Working Paper no. 26050 (July).

House of Commons. 1875. *Report from the Select Committee on Loans to Foreign States; with Proceedings of the Committee.* London: Ordered by the House of Commons to be printed, July 29.

Hozier, Henry Montague, ed. 1872. *The Franco-Prussian War: Its Causes, Incidents and Consequences.* London: William Mackenzie.

Huang, Tianlei, and Nicholas Lardy. 2020. "China's Fiscal Stimulus Is Good News, But Will It Be Enough?" China Economic Watch (May 26). Washington, DC: Peterson Institute for International Economics, https://www.piie.com/blogs/china-economic-watch/chinas-fiscal-stimulus-good-news-will-it-be-enough

Huang, Yi, Marco Pagano, and Ugo Panizza. 2020. "Local Crowding Out in China," *Journal of Finance* 75: 2855–98.

Hutchinson, Martin, and Kevin Dowd. 2018. "The Apotheosis of the Rentier: How Napoleonic War Finance Kick-Started the Industrial Revolution," *Cato Journal* 38: 655–78.

Hutson, Elaine. 2005. "The Early Managed Fund Industry: Investment Trusts in 19th Century Britain," *International Review of Financial Analysis* 14: 439–54.

Hyde Clarke, Henry Harcourt. "On the Debts of Sovereign and Quasi-Sovereign States, Owing by Foreign Countries," *Journal of the Statistical Society of London* 41: 299–347.

Independent Evaluation Office. 2016. "The IMF and the Crises in Greece, Ireland, and Portugal." Washington, DC: IMF.

International Monetary Fund (IMF). 2010. "Historical Public Debt Database," Washington, DC: IMF, https://data.imf.org/?sk=806ED027-520D-497F-9052-63EC199F5E63.

International Monetary Fund (IMF). 2013. "Historical Public Finance Database," Washington, DC: IMF, https://www.imf.org/external/np/fad/histdb/.

International Monetary Fund (IMF). 2018. *Fiscal Transparency Handbook.* Washington, DC: IMF.

International Monetary Fund (IMF). 2019. "A Strategy for IMF Engagement on Social Spending: Staff Report." Washington, DC: IMF (June).

International Monetary Fund (IMF). Various years. *World Economic Outlook.* Washington, D.C.: IMF.

International Monetary Fund (IMF). 2020a. *Fiscal Monitor.* Washington, DC: IMF (October).

International Monetary Fund (IMF). 2020b. "The Evolution of Public Debt Vulnerabilities in Lower Income Countries," IMF Policy Paper (February).

International Monetary Fund (IMF). 2021. "Sovereign Debt Investor Base for Emerging Markets." Washington, DC: IMF (February).

Isenmann, Eberhard. 1999. "The Holy Roman Empire in the Middle Ages," in Richard Bonney, ed., *The Rise of the Fiscal State in Europe, c. 1200–1815,* New York: Oxford University Press, pp. 243–80.

Israel, Jonathan. 1995. *The Dutch Republic: Its Rise, Greatness, and Fall, 1477–1806.* Oxford: Clarendon Press.

Ito, Hiro. 2003. "Was Japan's Real Interest Rate Really Too High during the 1990s?" unpublished manuscript, Claremont McKenna College (November).

Jacks, David, Christopher Meissner, and Denis Novy. 2011. "Trade Booms, Trade Busts and Trade Costs," *Journal of International Economics* 83: 185–201.

Jackson, R. V. 1977. *Australian Economic Development in the Nineteenth Century.* Canberra: ANU Press.

Jacobson, Margaret, Eric Leeper, and Bruce Preston. 2019. "Recovery of 1933," unpublished manuscript, Indiana University and University of Melbourne.

Jafarov, Etibar, Rodolfo Maino, and Marco Pani. 2019. "Financial Repression Is Knocking at the Door, Again," IMF Working Paper no. 19/211 (September).

Jaffee, Dwight, and Thomas Russell. 1976. "Imperfect Information, Uncertainty, and Credit Rationing," *Quarterly Journal of Economics* 90: 651–66.

James, Frank. 2011. "Speaker Boehner: National Debt Level Is Immoral," *It's All Politics: Political News from NPR* (Feb. 28), https://www.npr.org/sections/itsallpolitics/2011/02/28/134127811/speaker-boehner-national-debt-is-immoral

James, Harold. 1999. "The Reichsbank 1876–1945," in Deutsche Bundesbank, ed., *Fifty Years of the Deutsche Mark: Central Bank and the Currency in Germany since 1948*. Oxford: Oxford University Press, pp. 3–54.

Japan Securities Research Institute. 2014. *Securities Market in Japan 2014*. Tokyo: Japan Securities Research Institute.

Jeanne, Olivier, and Romain Rancière. 2006. "The Optimal Level of International Reserves for Emerging Market Countries, Formulas and Applications," IMF Working Paper no. 06/229 (October).

Jellnick, Frank. 2008. *The Paris Commune of 1871*. Hong Kong: Hesperides Press.

Jenks, Leland. 1927. *The Migration of British Capital to 1875*. New York: Knopf.

Jha, Saumitra, Kris James Mitchener, and Masanori Takashima. 2015. "Swords into Bank Shares: Finance, Conflict, and Political Reform in Meiji Japan," unpublished manuscript, Santa Clara University.

Jordà, Oscar, Moritz Schularick, Alan Taylor, and Felix Ward. 2018. "Global Financial Cycles and Risk Premiums," NBER Working Paper no. 24677 (June).

Kelly, Trish. 1998. "Ability and Willingness to Pay in the Age of Pax Britannica, 1890–1914," *Explorations in Economic History* 35: 31–38.

Kennan, John, and Robert Wilson. 1988. "Strategic Bargaining Methods and Interpretation of Strike Data," unpublished manuscript, New York University.

Kennedy, William. 1987. *Industrial Structure, Capital Markets, and the Origins of British Industrial Decline*. Cambridge: Cambridge University Press.

Kent, R. G. 1920. "The Edict of Diocletian Fixing Maximum Prices," *University of Pennsylvania Law Review* 69: 35–47.

Kessler, David, and Peter Temin. 2008. "Money and Prices in the Early Roman Empire," in W. V. Harris, ed., *The Monetary Systems of the Greeks and Romans*. New York: Oxford University Press, pp. 137–59.

Keynes, John Maynard. 1927. "The Colwyn Report on National Debt and Taxation," *Economic Journal* 37: 198–212.

Khan, Zorina. 2020. *Inventing Ideas: Patents, Prizes and the Knowledge Economy*. New York: Oxford University Press.

King, Frank. 1987. *The Hongkong Bank in Late Imperial China, 1864–1902*, Vol. 1. Cambridge: Cambridge University Press.

King, Frank. 1988. *The History of the Hongkong and Shanghai Banking Corporation*, Vol. 2. Cambridge: Cambridge University Press.

Klemm, Alexander, Shafik Hebous, Geerten Michielse, and Narine Nersesyan. 2021. "COVID-19 Recovery Contributions," Fiscal Affairs Department, Special Series on COVID-19. Washington, DC: IMF (Apr. 16).

Krishmadas, Devadas. 2013. "Sovereign Wealth Funds as Tools of National Strategy: Singapore's Approach," CIWAG Case Study 11-2013. Newport, RI: US Naval War College.

Kroszner, Randall. 1998. "Is It Better to Forgive Than to Receive? Repudiation of the Gold Index Clause in Long-Term Debt during the Great Depression," unpublished manuscript, University of Chicago.

Krueger, Anne, and Aaron Tornell. 1999. "The Role of Bank Restructuring in Recovering from Crises: Mexico 1995–98," NBER Working Paper no. 7042 (March).

Kuznets, Simon. 1966. *Modern Economic Growth*. New Haven, CT: Yale University Press.

Landais, Camille, Emmanuel Saez, and Gabriel Zucman. 2020. "A Progressive European Wealth Tax to Fund the European COVID Response," *VoxEU* (Apr. 3), https://voxeu.org/article/progressive-european-wealth-tax-fund-european-covid-response

Landes, David. 1958. *Bankers and Pashas: International Finance and Economic Imperialism in Egypt*. Cambridge, MA: Harvard University Press.

Lee, Tahirih. 1997. *Chinese Law: Social, Political, Historical and Economic Perspectives.* New York: Garland.

Lefevre Pontalis, M. Antonin. 1885. *Johan De Witt: Grand Pensionary of Holland,* S. E. and A. Stephenson, trans. Boston: Houghton, Mifflin.

Lévy-Leboyer, Maurice, and François Bourguignon. 1985. *L'économie française au XIXe siècle. Analyse macro-économique.* Paris: Economica.

Lewis, W. Arthur. 1949. *Economic Survey 1919–1939.* London: Allen & Unwin.

Liesse, André. 1909. *Evolution of Credit and Banks in France from the Founding of the Bank of France to the Present Time.* Washington, DC: Government Printing Office.

Lindbeck, Assar. 1997. "The Swedish Experiment," *Journal of Economic Literature* 35: 1273–1319.

Lindert, Peter. 1994. "The Rise of Social Spending, 1880–1930," *Explorations in Economic History* 31: 1–37.

Lindert, Peter, and Peter Morton. 1989. "How Sovereign Debt Worked," in Jeffrey Sachs, ed., *Developing Country Debt and Economic Performance,* Vol. 1. Chicago: University of Chicago Press, pp. 39–106.

Lindholm, Richard. 1947. "German Finance in World War II," *American Economic Review* 37: 121–34.

Lo Cascio, Elio. 2006. "The Finances of the Roman Empire: Budgetary Policy," in Anne Kolb, ed. *Herrschaftsstrukturen und Herrschaftspraxis. Konzepte, Prinzipien und Strategien der Administration im römischen Kaiserreich.* Berlin: Akademie Verlag, pp. 32–44.

Lopez, Jose, and Kris James Mitchener. 2021. "Uncertainty and Hyperinflation: European Inflation Dynamics after World War I," *Economic Journal* 131, pp. 450–75.

López-Córdova, J. Ernesto, and Christopher Meissner. 2003. "Exchange-Rate Regimes and International Trade: Evidence from the Classical Gold Standard Era," *American Economic Review* 93: 344–53.

Loriaux, Michael, Meredith Woo-Cumings, Kent Calder, Sylvia Maxfield, and Sofia Perez. 1997. *Capital Ungoverned: Liberalizing Finance in Interventionist States.* Ithaca, NY: Cornell University Press.

Lowenfeld, H. 1910. *All about Investment,* 2nd ed. London: Financial Review of Reviews.

Lubin, David. 2015. *Dance of the Trillions: Developing Countries and Global Finance.* Washington, DC: Brookings Institution Press.

Lustig, Nora. 1995. "The Mexican Peso Crisis: The Foreseeable and the Surprise," Brookings Discussion Papers in International Economics no. 114 (June).

Luzzatto, Gino. 1963. *Il Debito pubblico della Repubblica di Venezia: Dagli ultimi decenni del XII secolo alla fine del XV.* Milan: Istituto Editoriale Cisalpino.

Ma, Debin. 2019. "Financial Revolution in Republican China during 1900–37: A Survey and a New Interpretation," *Australian Economic History Review* 59: 242–62.

MacClintock, Samuel. 1911. "Refunding the Foreign Debt of Honduras," *Journal of Political Economy* 19: 216–28.

MacDonald, James. 2003. *A Free Nation Deep in Debt: The Financial Roots of Democracy.* New York: Farrar, Straus and Giroux.

Machlup, Fritz. 1976. "The Transfer Problem: Theme and Four Variations," in Fritz Machlup, *International Payments, Debts and Gold.* New York: New York University Press, pp. 374–95.

Maddison, Angus. 1969. *Economic Growth in Japan and the USSR.* London: Allen & Unwin.

Maddison, Angus. 2001. *The World Economy: A Millennial Perspective.* Paris: OECD.

Maier, Charles. 1975. *Recasting Bourgeois Europe: Stabilization in France, Germany and Italy in the Decade after World War I.* Princeton, NJ: Princeton University Press.

Makinen, Gail, and G. Thomas Woodward. 1989. "A Monetary Interpretation of the Poincaré Stabilization of 1926," *Southern Economic Journal* 56: 191–211.

Malmendier, Ulrike, and Stefan Nagel. 2011. "Depression Babies: Do Macroeconomic Experiences Affect Risk-Taking?" *Quarterly Journal of Economics* 126: 373–416.

Maloney, John. 1998. "Gladstone and Sound Victorian Finance," in John Maloney, ed., *Debt and Deficits: An Historical Perspective.* Cheltenham, UK: Edward Elgar, pp. 154–89.

Marichal, Carlos. 1989. *A Century of Debt Crises in Latin America: From Independence to the Great Depression, 1820–1930.* Princeton, NJ: Princeton University Press.

Marks, Louis. 1954. "La crisi finanziaria a Firenze dal 1494 al 1502." *Archivio Storico Italiano* 112: 40–72.

Mata, Eugénia. 1993. *As finanças públicas portuguesas da Regeneração à Primeira Guerra Mundial.* Lisbon: Banco de Portugal.

Maurer, Henri, and Patrick Grussenmeyer. 2015. "Financial Assistance Measures in the Euro Area from 2008 to 2013: Statistical Framework and Fiscal Impact," Statistics Paper Series no. 7. Frankfurt: European Central Bank.

Mauro, Paolo, and Yishay Yafeh. 2003. "The Corporation of Foreign Bondholders," IMF Working Paper 03/107 (May).

Mauro, Paolo, and Jing Zhou. 2020. "r-g<0: Can We Sleep More Soundly?" IMF Working Paper no. 20/52 (March).

Mauro, Paolo, and Jan Zilinsky. 2016. "Reducing Government Debt Ratios in an Era of Low Growth," Policy Brief 16-10. Washington, DC: Peterson Institute for International Economics (July).

McCallum, Bennett. 1986. "Some Issues Concerning Interest Rate Pegging, Price Level Determinacy, and the Real Bills Doctrine," *Journal of Monetary Economics* 17: 135–60.

McCarty, Nolan, Keith Poole, and Howard Rosenthal. 2016. *Polarized America: The Dance of Ideology and Unequal Riches*, 2nd ed. Cambridge, MA: MIT Press.

McCauley, Robert. 2018. "The 2008 Crisis: Transpacific or Transatlantic?" *BIS Quarterly Review* (December): 39–58.

McCulloch, John Ramsey, ed. 1888. *The Works of David Ricardo.* London: John Murray.

McGrane, Reginald. 1935. *Foreign Bondholders and American State Debt.* New York: Macmillan.

McLean, Ian. 2013. *Why Australia Prospered: The Shifting Sources of Economic Growth.* Princeton, NJ: Princeton University Press.

Mehrotra, Neil. 2017. "Debt Sustainability in a Low Interest Rate World," Hutchins Center Working Paper no. 32 (June 2).

Meltzer, Allan. 2003. *A History of the Federal Reserve*, Vol. 1: *1913–1951*. Chicago: University of Chicago Press.

Meltzer, Allan, and Scott Richard. 1981. "A Rational Theory of the Size of Government," *Journal of Political Economy* 89: 914–27.

Merriam, Ida. 1955. "Social Welfare in the United States, 1934–54," *Social Security Bulletin* 18 (October): 3–31.

Meyer, Josefin, Carmen Reinhart, and Christoph Trebesch. 2019. "Sovereign Bonds since Waterloo," NBER Working Paper no. 25543 (February).

Meyers, Roy. 1998. "Regulatory Budgeting: A Bad Idea Whose Time Has Come?" *Policy Science* 31: 371–84.

Meyland, Dominik, and Dorothea Schäfer. 2017. "Risk Weighting for Government Bonds: Challenge for Italian Banks," *DIW Economic Bulletin* 7: 283–90.

Michie, Ranald. 1999. *The London Stock Exchange: A History.* Oxford: Oxford University Press.

Miller, Grant. 2008. "Women's Suffrage, Political Responsiveness, and Child Survival in American History," *Quarterly Journal of Economics* 123: 1287–1327.

Mintz, Ilse. 1951. *Deterioration in the Quality of Foreign Bonds Issued in the United States, 1920–1930.* New York: National Bureau of Economic Research.

Miranda, José Augusto Ribas. 2017. "Small Money, Big Problems: How an Investigation on Small Latin American Republics Shaped the Financial Market for Sovereign Debt in the 19th Century," *Estudios Históricos* 30: 55–70.

Mitchell, Brian. 2003. *International Historical Statistics: 1750–2000, Europe*, 4th ed. New York and Basingstoke: Palgrave Macmillan.

Mitchener, Kris James, and Gonçalo Pina. 2020. "Pegxit Pressure: Evidence from the Classical Gold Standard," *Journal of International Money and Finance* 107: 1–14.

Mitchener, Kris James, Masato Shizume, and Marc Weidenmier. 2010. "Why Did Countries Adopt the Gold Standard? Lessons from Japan," *Journal of Economic History* 70: 27–56.

Mitchener, Kris James, and Hans-Joachim Voth. 2011. "Trading Silver for Gold: Nineteenth-Century Asian Exports and the Political Economy of Currency Unions," in Robert Barro and Jong-Wha Lee, eds., *Costs and Benefits of Economic Integration in Asia*. Oxford: Oxford University Press, pp. 126–56.

Mitchener, Kris James, and Marc Weidenmier. 2005. "Empire, Public Goods, and the Roosevelt Corollary," *Journal of Economic History* 65: 658–92.

Mitchener, Kris James, and Marc Weidenmier. 2008. "The Baring Crisis and the Great Latin American Meltdown of the 1890s," *Journal of Economic History* 68: 462–500.

Mitchener, Kris James, and Marc Weidenmier. 2010. "Supersanctions and Sovereign Debt Repayment," *Journal of International Money and Finance* 29: 19–36.

Mitchener, Kris James, and Marc Weidenmier. 2015. "Was the Classical Gold Standard Credible on the Periphery? Evidence from Currency Risk," *Journal of Economic History* 75: 479–511.

Monnet, Eric. 2018. *Controlling Credit: Central Banking and the Planned Economy in Postwar France, 1948–1973*. New York: Cambridge University Press.

Morecroft, Nigel. 2017. *The Origins of Asset Management from 1700 to 1960*. London: Palgrave Macmillan.

Mueller, Reinhold. 1997. *The Venetian Money Market: Banks, Panics, and the Public Debt, 1200–1500*. Baltimore: Johns Hopkins University Press.

Munro, John. 2013. "Rentes and the European 'Financial Revolution,'" in Gerard Caprio, ed., *Handbook of Key Global Financial Markets, Institutions, and Infrastructure*, Vol. I. Oxford: Elsevier, pp. 235–49.

Najemy, John. 2006. *A History of Florence 1200–1575*. Oxford: Blackwell.

Nash, Robert Lucas. 1874. *Fenn's Compendium of English and Foreign Funds*, 12th ed. London: Effingham Wilson.

Nash, Robert Lucas. 1883. *Fenn's Compendium of English and Foreign Funds*, 13th ed. London: Effingham Wilson.

Neal, Larry. 1990. *The Rise of Financial Capitalism: International Capital Markets in the Age of Reason*. Cambridge: Cambridge University Press.

Neal, Larry. 1998. "The Financial Crisis of 1825 and the Restructuring of the British Financial System," *Federal Reserve Bank of St. Louis Review* (May/June): 53–76.

Neal, Larry. 2015. *A Concise History of International Finance: From Babylon to Bernanke*. Cambridge: Cambridge University Press.

Neal, Larry, and Lance Davis. 2006. "The Evolution of the Structure and Performance of the London Stock Exchange in the First Global Financial Market, 1812–1914," *European Review of Economic History* 10: 279–300.

Nickel, Christiane, and Andreas Tudyka. 2013. "Fiscal Stimulus in Times of High Debt: Reconsidering Multipliers and Twin Deficits," ECB Working Paper no. 1513 (February).

North, Douglass. 1958. "Ocean Freight Rates and Economic Development 1750–1913," *Journal of Economic History* 18: 537–55.

North, Douglass, and Barry Weingast. 1989. "Constitutions and Commitment: The Evolution of Institutions Governing Public Choice in Seventeenth-Century England," *Journal of Economic History* 49: 803–32.

Oakley, Ann. 2011. *A Critical Woman: Barbara Wootton, Social Science and Public Policy in the Twentieth Century*. London: Bloomsbury Academic.

O'Brien, Patrick. 1989. "The Impact of the Revolutionary and Napoleonic Wars, 1793–1815, on the Long-Run Growth of the British Economy," *Review (Fernand Braudel Center)* 12: 335–95.

O'Brien, Patrick, and Nuno Palma. 2020. "Danger to the Old Lady of Threadneedle Street? The Bank Restriction Act and the Regime Shift to Paper Money, 1797–1821," *European Review of Economic History* 24: 390–426.

Obstfeld, Maurice, and Alan Taylor. 2004. *Global Capital Markets: Integration, Crisis, and Growth.* Cambridge: Cambridge University Press.

Office of the Historian, US Department of State. n.d. "Lend-Lease and Military Aid to the Allies in the Early Years of World War II," https://history.state.gov/milestones/1937-1945/lend-lease

Ohkawa, Kazushi, and Henry Rosovsky. 1973. *Japanese Economic Growth: Trend Acceleration in the Twentieth Century.* Stanford, CA: Stanford University Press.

Oliner, Stephen, and Daniel Sichel. 2000. "The Resurgence of Growth in the Late 1990s: Is Information Technology the Story?" *Journal of Economic Perspectives* 14: 3–22.

Oosterlinck, Kim. 2016. *Hope Springs Eternal: French Bondholders and the Repudiation of Russian Sovereign Debt.* New Haven, CT: Yale University Press.

Organisation for Economic Co-operation and Development (OECD). 1985. *Social Expenditure 1960–1990: Problems of Growth and Control.* Paris: OECD.

Organisation for Economic Co-operation and Development (OECD). 2010. *National Accounts of OECD Countries.* Paris: OECD.

Organisation for Economic Co-operation and Development (OECD). 2019. *OECD Economic Outlook* no. 106. Paris: OECD (November).

Ormrod, W. W. 1995. "The West European Monarchies in the Later Middle Ages," in Richard Bonney, ed., *Economic Systems and State Finance.* Oxford: Clarendon Press, pp. 123–60.

Padgett, John F. 2009. "The Emergence of Large, Unitary Merchant Banks in Dugento Tuscany," Working Paper no. 8, Political Networks Paper Archive, OpenSIUC.

Palma, Gabriel. 2000. "From an Export-Led to an Import-Substituting Economy: Chile 1914–1939," in Rosemary Thorp, ed., *Latin America in the 1930s: The Role of the Periphery in the World Crisis.* Oxford: Palgrave Macmillan, pp. 50–80.

Pamuk, Şevket. 2013. "Finance in the Ottoman Empire, 1453–1854," in Gerard Caprio, ed., *Handbook of Key Global Financial Markets, Institutions, and Infrastructure,* Vol. I. Oxford: Elsevier, pp. 197–206.

Pamuk, Şevket. 2018. *Uneven Centuries: Economic Development of Turkey since 1820.* Princeton, NJ: Princeton University Press.

Parent, Antoine, and Christophe Rault. 2004. "The Influences Affecting French Assets Abroad Prior to 1914," *Journal of Economic History* 64: 328–62.

Pastor, Manuel, Jr. 1989. "Latin America, the Debt Crisis, and the International Monetary Fund," *Latin American Perspectives* 16: 79–110.

Pavlović, Dušan, and Dimitrios Xefteris. 2020. "Quantifying the Common Pool Problem in Government Spending: The Role of Positional Externalities," *Constitutional Political Economy* 31: 446–457.

Persson, Torsten, Gerard Roland, and Guido Tabellini. 2007. "Electoral Rules and Government Spending in Parliamentary Democracies," *Quarterly Journal of Political Science* 2: 155–88.

Pew Research Center. 2009. "Trends in Political Values and Core Attitudes: 1987–2009." Washington, DC: Pew Research Center for the People and the Press.

Pezzolo, Luciano. 1990. *L'oro dello Stato: Società, finanze e fisco nella Repubblica Veneta del secondo 500.* Venice: Il Cardo.

Pezzolo, Luciano. 2003. "The Venetian Government Debt 1350–1650," in K. Davids, P. Janssens, and M. Boone, eds., *Urban Public Debts, Urban Governments and the Market for Annuities in Western Europe, 14th–18th Centuries.* Leuven: Brepols, pp. 61–74.

Phillipson, Nicholas. 2010. *Adam Smith: An Enlightened Life.* New Haven, CT, and London: Yale University Press.

Platt, D. C. M. 1968. *Finance, Trade and Politics: British Foreign Policy 1815–1914.* Oxford: Clarendon Press.

Platt, D. C. M. 1983. "Foreign Finance in Argentina for the First Half-Century of Independence," *Journal of Latin American Studies* 15: 23–47.

Polanyi, Karl. 1944. *The Great Transformation.* New York: Farrar & Reinhart.

Pollack, Sheldon. 2014. "The First National Income Tax, 1861–1872," *The Tax Lawyer* 67: 311–330.

Poole, Keith, and Howard Rosenthal. 2007. *Ideology and Congress*. New Brunswick, NJ: Transaction.

Poovey, Mary. 2002. "Writing about Finance in Victorian England: Disclosure and Secrecy in the Culture of Investment," *Victorian Studies* 45: 17–41.

Powell, Jerome. 2021. "Semiannual Monetary Policy Report to the Congress," before the Committee on Banking, Housing and Urban Affairs, U.S. Senate (Feb. 23), https://www.federalreserve.gov/newsevents/testimony/powell20210223a.htm

Prati, Alessandro. 1991. "Poincaré's Stabilization: Stopping a Run on Government Debt," *Journal of Monetary Economics* 27: 213–39.

Rayl, Nelson. 2020. "Cost of Austerity: Effect of Fiscal Consolidation in Europe Post 2010," unpublished manuscript, Occidental College (May), https://privpapers.ssrn.com/sol3/papers.cfm?abstract_id=3596470&dgcid=ejournal_htmlemail_european:economics:macroeconomics:monetary:economics:ejournal_abstracnk

Reinhart, Carmen, and Kenneth Rogoff. 2009. *This Time Is Different: Eight Centuries of Financial Folly*. Princeton, NJ: Princeton University Press.

Reinhart, Carmen, and Kenneth Rogoff. 2010. "Growth in a Time of Debt," *American Economic Association Papers and Proceedings* 100: 573–78.

Reinhart, Carmen, and Kenneth Rogoff. 2011. "The Forgotten History of Domestic Debt," *Economic Journal* 121: 319–50.

Reinhart, Carmen, Kenneth Rogoff, and Miguel Savastano. 2003. "Debt Intolerance," *Brookings Papers on Economic Activity* 34: 1–74.

Reinhart, Carmen, and Belen Sbrancia. 2015. "The Liquidation of Government Debt," IMF Working Paper no. 15/7 (January).

Reisen, Helmut. 1998. "Sustainable and Excessive Current Account Deficits," *Empirica* 25: 111–31.

Remes, Jaana, and Sajal Kohli. 2021. "The Varieties of Consumer Revival," Project Syndicate (May 5), https://www.project-syndicate.org/commentary/covid19-uneven-consumer-spending-recovery-by-jaana-remes-and-sajal-kohli-2021-05

Ritschl, Albrecht. 2012. "The German Transfer Problem, 1920–33: A Sovereign-Debt Perspective," *European Review of History* 19: 943–64.

Ritschl, Albrecht. 2013. "Reparations, Deficits and Debt Default: The Great Depression in Germany," in Nicholas Crafts and Peter Fearon, eds., *The Great Depression of the 1930s: Lessons for Today*. Oxford: Oxford University Press, pp. 110–39.

Ritschl, Albrecht, and Samad Sarferaz. 2014. "Currency versus Banking in the Financial Crisis of 1931," *International Economic Review* 55: 349–73.

Roberds, Will, and François Velde. 2016. "Early Public Banks II," in David Fox and Wolfgang Ernst, eds., *Money in the Western Legal Tradition: Middle Ages to Bretton Woods*. Oxford: Oxford University Press, pp. 465–86.

Roberts, Russell. 2008. "Don't Jump the Gun on Stimulus Plans," *All Things Considered* (Jan. 16), https://www.npr.org/templates/story/story.php?storyId=18159629

Rodrik, Dani. 2006. "The Social Cost of Foreign Exchange Reserves," *International Economic Journal* 20: 253–66.

Romer, Christina, and David Romer. 1989. "Does Monetary Policy Matter? A New Test in the Spirit of Friedman and Schwartz," *NBER Macroeconomics Annual* 4: 121–84.

Romer, Christina, and David Romer. 2009. "Do Tax Cuts Starve the Beast? The Effect of Tax Changes on Government Spending," *Brookings Papers on Economic Activity* (Spring): 139–214.

Romer, Christina, and David Romer. 2019. "Fiscal Space and the Aftermath of Financial Crises: How It Matters and Why," *Brookings Papers on Economic Activity* (Spring) 239–313.

Rose, Andrew. 2005. "One Reason Countries Pay Their Debts: Renegotiation and International Trade," *Journal of Development Economics* 77: 189–205.

Rose, Andrew, and Mark Spiegel. 2004. "A Gravity Model of Sovereign Lending: Trade, Default and Credit," *IMF Staff Papers* 51: 50–63.

Roubini, Nouriel, and Jeffrey Sachs. 1989. "Government Spending and Budget Deficits in the Industrial Countries," *Economic Policy* 8: 99–127.

Rouwenhorst, K. Geert. 2005. "The Origins of Mutual Funds," in William Goetzmann and K. Geert Rouwenhorst, eds., *The Origins of Value: The Financial Innovations That Created Modern Capital Markets*. Oxford: Oxford University Press, pp. 249–70.

Rowen, Herbert. 1986. *Johan De Witt: Statesman of "True Freedom."* Cambridge: Cambridge University Press.

Rubin, Robert. 2003. *In an Uncertain World: Tough Choices from Wall Street to Washington*. New York: Random House.

Sacks, David Harris. 1994. "The Paradox of Taxation: Fiscal Crises, Parliament, and Liberty in England, 1450–1640," in Philip Hoffman and Kathryn Norberg, eds., *Fiscal Crises, Liberty, and Representative Government, 1450–1789*. Stanford, CA: Stanford University Press, pp. 7–66.

Saez, Emmanuel, and Gabriel Zucman. 2019. *The Triumph of Injustice: How the Rich Dodge Taxes and How to Make Them Pay*. New York: Norton.

Santarosa, Veronica. 2015. "Financing Long-Distance Trade: The Joint Liability Rule and Bills of Exchange in Eighteenth-Century France," *Journal of Economic History* 75: 690–719.

Sapori, Armando. 1970. *The Italian Merchant in the Middle Ages*. New York: Norton.

Sargent, Thomas, and François Velde. 1995. "Macroeconomic Features of the French Revolution," *Journal of Political Economy* 103: 474–518.

Schedvin, Boris. 1970. *Australia and the Great Depression*. Sydney: Sydney University Press.

Schefferes, Steve, and Richard Roberts, eds. 2014. *The Media and Financial Crises: Comparative and Historical Perspectives*. London: Routledge.

Scheidel, Walter. 2019. *Escape from Rome: The Failure of Empire and the Road to Prosperity*. Princeton, NJ: Princeton University Press.

Schinasi, Garry, Todd Smith, and Charles Kramer. 2001. "Financial Implications of the Shrinking Supply of U.S. Treasury Securities," IMF Working Paper no. 01/61 (May).

Schmelzing, Paul. 2020. "Eight Centuries of Global Real Interest Rates, R–G, and the 'Suprasecular' Decline, 1311–2018," *Staff Working Paper no. 845*, London: Bank of England (Jan. 3).

Schularick, Moritz, and Thomas Steger. 2010. "Financial Integration, Investment and Economic Growth," *Review of Economics and Statistics* 92: 756–68.

Scratchley, Arthur. 1875. *On Average Investment Trusts*. London: Shaw and Sons.

Seidman, William. 1993. *Full Faith and Credit: The Great S&L Debacle and Other Washington Sagas*. New York: Crown Books.

Sexton, Jay. 2005. *Debtor Diplomacy: Finance and American Foreign Relations in the Civil War Era, 1837–1873*. New York: Oxford University Press.

Shackleton, Robert. 2018. "Estimating and Projecting Potential Output Using CBO's Forecasting Growth Model," Working Paper 2018-03. Washington, DC: CBO (February).

Shepherd, Henry, Jr. 1933. *Default and Adjustment of Argentine Foreign Debts, 1890–1906*. Washington, DC: US Government Printing Office.

Singh, Manmohan. 2013. "The Changing Collateral Space," IMF Working Paper no. 13/25 (January).

Slater, Martin. 2018. *The National Debt: A Short History*. Oxford: Oxford University Press.

Slivinski, Al, and Nathan Sussman. 2019. "Tax Administration and Compliance: Evidence from Medieval Paris," CEPR Discussion Paper no. 13512.

Smethurst, Richard. 2007. "American Capital and Japan's Victory in the Russo-Japanese War," in John Chapman and Inaba Chiharu, eds., *Rethinking the Russo-Japanese War, 1904–5*, Vol. 2. Folkstone, Kent: Global Oriental, pp. 61–72.

Smith, Adam. [1776] 1904. *An Inquiry into the Nature and Causes of the Wealth of Nations*. London: Methuen.

Solberg, Carl. 1987. *The Prairies and the Pampas: Agrarian Policy in Canada and Argentina 1880–1930*. Stanford, CA: Stanford University Press.

Sonenscher, Michael. 2007. *Before the Deluge: Public Debt, Inequality, and the Intellectual Origins of the French Revolution*. Princeton, NJ: Princeton University Press.

Sosin, Joshua. 2001. "Accounting and Endowments," *Tyche: Beiträge zur Alten Geschichte, Papyrologie und Epigraphik* 16: 161–75.

Spinner, Thomas, Jr. 1973. *George Joachim Goschen: The Transformation of a Victorian Liberal.* Cambridge: Cambridge University Press.

Spolaore, Enrico. 2016. "The Political Economy of European Integration," in Harald Badinger and Volker Nitsch, eds., *Routledge Handbook of the Economics of European Integration.* London: Routledge, pp. 435–48.

Sraffa, Piero. 1955. *The Works and Correspondence of David Ricardo, Vol. X, Biographic Miscellany.* Cambridge: Cambridge University Press.

Stasavage, David. 2003. *Public Debt and the Birth of the Democratic State: France and Great Britain, 1688–1789.* Cambridge: Cambridge University Press.

Stasavage, David. 2011. *States of Credit: Size, Power, and the Development of European Polities.* Princeton, NJ: Princeton University Press.

Steele, E. D. 1991. *Palmerston and Liberalism 1855–1865.* Cambridge: Cambridge University Press.

Stone, Irving. 1999. *The Global Export of British Capital: A Statistical Survey.* London: Palgrave Macmillan.

Strachan, Hew. 2004. *Financing the First World War.* New York: Oxford University Press.

Strayer, Joseph. 1970. *On the Medieval Origins of the Modern State.* Princeton, NJ: Princeton University Press.

Summers, Lawrence. 2014. "U.S. Economic Prospects: Secular Stagnation, Hysteresis, and the Zero Lower Bound," *Business Economics* 49: 65–73.

Sussman, Nathan, and Yishay Yafeh. 2000. "Institutions, Reforms, and Country Risk: Lessons from Japanese Government Debt in the Meiji Era," *Journal of Economic History* 60: 442–67.

Sutch, Richard. 2015. "Financing the Great War: A Class Tax for the Wealthy, Liberty Bonds for All," Berkeley Economic History Laboratory Working Paper WP 2015-09 (September).

Suter, Christian. 1992. *Debt Cycles in the World Economy: Foreign Loans, Financial Crises, and Debt Settlement, 1820–1990.* New York: Avalon.

Suzuki, Toshio. 1994. *Japanese Government Loan Issues on the London Capital Market 1870–1913.* London: Bloomsbury.

Swanson, Eric. 2011. "Let's Twist Again: A High-Frequency Event-Study Analysis of Operation Twist and Its Implications for QE2," *Brookings Papers on Economic Activity* (Spring): 151–88.

Sylla, Richard. 2011. "Financial Foundations: Public Credit, the National Bank, and Securities Markets," in Douglas Irwin and Richard Sylla, eds., *Founding Choices: American Economic Policy in the 1790s.* Chicago: University of Chicago Press, pp. 59–88.

Tacitus. 1931. *Histories,* Books IV–V, *Annals* Books I–III, Loeb Classical Library No. 248. Cambridge, MA: Harvard University Press.

Tang, Frank, Jun Mai, and Sarah Zheng. 2020. "China Pledges Largest-Ever Economic Rescue Package to Save Jobs and Livelihoods Amid Coronavirus," *South China Morning Post* (May 29), https://www.scmp.com/economy/china-economy/article/3086569/china-pledges-larg est-ever-economic-rescue-package-save-jobs

Temin, Peter. 2002. "The Golden Age of European Growth Reconsidered," *European Review of Economic History* 6: 3–22.

Temin, Peter. 2012. *The Roman Market Economy.* Princeton, NJ: Princeton University Press.

Temin, Peter, and Hans-Joachim Voth. 2005. "Credit Rationing and Crowding Out during the Industrial Revolution: Evidence from Hoare's Bank, 1702–1862," *Explorations in Economic History* 42: 325–48.

Thomson, David. 2019. "Financing the War," in Aaron Sheehan-Dean, ed., *The Cambridge History of the American Civil War.* Cambridge: Cambridge University Press, pp. 174–92.

Tilly, Charles. 1975. *The Formation of Nation States in Western Europe.* Princeton, NJ: Princeton University Press.

Tilly, Charles. 1992. *Coercion, Capital, and European States AD 990–1992.* New York: Wiley-Blackwell.

Todd, Richard. 1954. *Confederate Finance.* Athens: University of Georgia Press.

Tomz, Michael. 2007. *Sovereign Debt and International Cooperation*. Princeton, NJ: Princeton University Press.

Tomz, Michael, and Mark Wright. 2013. "Empirical Research on Sovereign Debt and Default." *Annual Review of Economics* 5: 247–72.

Tooze, Adam. 2015. "Applying the 'Debt Brake': The Political Construction of the German Anti-Debt Agenda," unpublished manuscript, Columbia University (June).

Tracy, James. 1985. *A Financial Revolution in the Habsburg Netherlands: "Renten" and "Renteniers" in the County of Holland, 1515–1565*. Berkeley: University of California Press.

Tracy, James. 2003. "On the Dual Origins of Long-Term Urban Debt in Medieval Europe," in M. Boone, K. Davids, and P. Jenssens, eds., *Urban Public Debts: Urban Government and the Market for Annuities in Western Europe (14th–18th Centuries)*. Turnhout, Belgium: Brepols, pp. 13–26.

Tsebelis, George. 2002. *Veto Players: How Political Institutions Work*. Princeton, NJ: Princeton University Press.

Tujula, Mika, and Guido Wolswijk. 2004. "What Determines Fiscal Balances? An Empirical Investigation in Determinants of Changes in OECD Budget Balances," ECB Working Paper no. 422 (December).

Tunçer, Ali Coşkun. 2015. *Sovereign Debt and International Financial Control: The Middle East and the Balkans, 1870–1914*. Houndmills, UK: Palgrave Macmillan.

Tunçsiper, Bedriye, and Hasan Abdioğlu. 2018. "The Ottoman Public Debt Administration (OPDA) in the Debt Process of the Ottoman Empire," unpublished manuscript, Balikesir University of Turkey.

Ugolini, Stefano. 2018. "The Historical Evolution of Central Banking," in Stefano Battilossi, Youssef Cassis, and Kazuhiko Yago, eds., *Handbook of the History of Money and Currency*. Berlin: Springer Nature, pp. 835–56.

United Nations. 1948. *Public Debt 1914–1946*. New York: United Nations.

Vam Malle Sabouret, Camille. 2008. "De la naissance de la dette publique au plafond souverain; Rôle des gouvernements régionaux dans l'évolution de la dette publique," unpublished Ph.D. dissertation, Institut d'Études Politiques de Paris.

Van de Ven, Hans. 2014. *Breaking with the Past: The Maritime Customs Service and the Global Origins of Modernity in China*. New York: Columbia University Press.

Van den Noord, Paul. 2000. "The Size and Role of Automatic Fiscal Stabilisers in the 1990s and Beyond," OECD Economics Department Working Paper no. 230 (January).

Van Zanden, Jan Luiten, Eltjo Buringh, and Maarten Bosker. 2012. "The Rise and Decline of European Parliaments, 1188–1789," *Economic History Review* 65: 835–61.

Van Zanden, Jan Luiten, and Arthur van Riel. 2004. *The Strictures of Inheritance: The Dutch Economy in the Nineteenth Century*. Princeton, NJ: Princeton University Press.

Velde, François. 2008. "French Public Finance between 1683 and 1726," in Fausto Caselli, ed., *Government Debts and Financial Markets in Europe*. London: Pickering and Chatto, pp. 135–66.

Velde, François, and David Weir. 1992. "The Financial Market and Government Debt Policy in France, 1746–1793," *Journal of Economic History* 52: 1–39.

Veloso, Fernando, André Villela, and Fabio Giambiagi. 2008. "Determinantes do 'Milagre' Econômico Brasileiro (1968–1973): Uma Análise Empírica," *Revista Brasileira de Economia* 62: 221–46.

von Glahn, Richard. 2013. "Chinese Finance, 1348–1700," in Gerard Caprio, ed., *Handbook of Key Global Financial Markets, Institutions, and Infrastructure*, Vol. I. Oxford: Elsevier, pp. 47–56.

von Reden, Sitta. 2013. "Money and Finance," in Walter Scheidel, ed., *The Cambridge Companion to the Roman Economy*. Cambridge: Cambridge University Press, pp. 266–86.

Vonyó, Tamás. 2018. *The Economic Consequences of the War: West Germany's Growth Miracle after 1945*. Cambridge: Cambridge University Press.

Waibel, Michael. 2011. *Sovereign Defaults before International Courts and Tribunals*. Cambridge: Cambridge University Press.

Wagner, Adolph. 1883. *Finanzwissenschaft.* Leipzig: C. F. Winter.

Walker, Neil. 2003. *Sovereignty in Transition.* London: Hart.

Walters, Alan. 1986. *Britain's Economic Renaissance: Margaret Thatcher's Reforms 1979–1984.* Oxford: Oxford University Press.

Walters, Alan. 1990. *Sterling in Danger.* London: Fontana.

Walters, Brian. 2008. *The Fall of Northern Rock: An Insider's Story of Britain's Biggest Banking Disaster.* London: Harriman House.

Warren, George, and Frank Pearson. *Prices.* New York: Wiley.

Weber, Anke. 2012. "Stock-Flow Adjustments and Fiscal Transparency: A Cross-Country Comparison," IMF Working Paper no. 12/49 (January).

Weir, David. 1989. "Tontines, Public Finance, and Revolution in France and England, 1688–1789," *Journal of Economic History* 49: 95–124.

White, Eugene. 2001. "France and the Failure to Modernize Macroeconomic Institutions," in Michael Bordo and Roberto Cortés Conde, eds., *Transferring Wealth and Power from the Old to the New World: Monetary and Fiscal Institutions in the 17th through the 19th Centuries.* Cambridge: Cambridge University Press, pp. 59–99.

White, Eugene. 2004. "From Privatized to Government-Administered Tax Collection: Tax Farming in Eighteenth-Century France," *Economic History Review* 57: 636–63.

White, Eugene. 2018. "Censored Success: How to Prevent a Banking Panic—the Barings Crisis of 1890 Revisited," unpublished manuscript, Rutgers University.

Wilensky, Harold. 1975. *The Welfare State and Equality: Structural and Ideological Roots of Public Expenditure.* Berkeley: University of California Press.

Williams, John. 1920. *Argentine International Trade under Inconvertible Paper Money 1880–1900.* Cambridge, MA: Harvard University Press.

Williamson, Jeffrey. 1984. "Why Was British Growth So Slow During the Industrial Revolution?" *Journal of Economic History* 44: 687–712.

Wilson, Peter. 2016. *Heart of Europe: A History of the Holy Roman Empire.* Cambridge, MA: Belknap Press of Harvard University Press.

Wilson, Peter, and Michael Schaich. 2011. "Introduction," in R. J. W. Evans, Michael Schaich, and Peter Wilson, eds., *The Holy Roman Empire 1495–1806.* London: Oxford University Press for the German Historical Institute, pp. 1–25.

Winkler, Max. 1933. *Foreign Bonds: An Autopsy.* Philadelphia: Roland Sway.

Wong, Christine. 2011. "The Fiscal Stimulus Programme and Public Governance Issues in China," *OECD Journal on Budgeting* 11: 1–21.

Woodruff, William. 1967. *Impact of Western Man: A Study of Europe's Role in the World Economy 1750–1960.* New York: Macmillan.

World Bank. 2020. "World Bank Predicts Sharpest Decline of Remittances in Recent History," press release. Washington, DC: World Bank (Apr. 22).

World Bank. 2021. "World Development Indicators," Washington, DC: World Bank, https://datatopics.worldbank.org/world-development-indicators/

Wyplosz, Charles. 2001. "Financial Restraints and Liberalization in Postwar Europe," in Gerald Caprio, Patrick Honohan, and Joseph Stiglitz, eds., *Financial Liberalization: How Far? How Fast?* Cambridge: Cambridge University Press, pp. 125–58.

Yared, Pierre. 2019. "Rising Government Debt: Causes and Solutions for a Decades-Old Trend," *Journal of Economic Perspectives* 33: 115–40.

Yousef, Tarik M. 2002. "Egypt's Growth Performance under Economic Liberalism: A Reassessment with New GDP Estimates, 1886–1945," *Review of Income and Wealth* 48: 561–79.

Zamagni, Vera. 1993. *The Economic History of Italy 1860–1990.* Oxford: Clarendon Press.

Zheng, Tongian, and Sarah Tong, eds. 2010. *China and the Global Financial Crisis.* Singapore: World Scientific.

Zysman, John. 1977. *Political Strategies for Industrial Order: State, Market and Industry in France.* Berkeley: University of California Press.

# INDEX

Abdel Nasser, Gamal, 85
  and nationalization of Suez Canal, 136
admiralties, Dutch Republic, 26, 28, 231
Africa, 54, 91, 130, 162, 252
Aglen, Francis, 72
American International Group (AIG), 183
American Recovery and Reinvestment Act
      (ARRA), 22, 186
Ancien Régime, 34–35
annuities, 19, 27, 34, 125, 230. *See also* life
      annuities
Argentina, 22, 49, 51–52, 55, 58, 77, 88–90,
      123–24, 127, 130, 144, 147, 149, 162–63,
      236, 249
  independence of, 51
  provinces, 51
  bondholder claims on, 52
  cereal production, 123
  Guaranteed Banks Law, 51
Argentina-Baring Crisis. *See* Baring Brothers
arrears, on interest and principal, 11–12, 63,
      66–67, 79, 125, 144–47, 156
Asia, 54, 91, 130, 157, 159, 160, 162, 166, 197,
      215, 237, 239, 252
  financial crisis, 157, 247, 256, 260
  financial systems, 157
Asian Bond Markets Initiative, 162
Asian Development Bank, 160
Asquith, Herbert Henry, 214
assets, 130, 132–33, 136, 185, 187, 230, 234, 251,
      255–56, 259, 262, 264
  banks' liquid, 160
  financial, 4, 104, 209
  foreign, 48, 235
  safe, 6, 87, 165, 200, 218, 259, 263–64
Australia, 49, 58, 88–89, 92, 125, 195, 200
  and Great Depression, 125–26, 249
  Baring crisis and recession, 49, 55

pre-federation borrowing, 235
  largest worldwide on per capita basis, 236
Austria, 29, 107, 113, 127, 138, 144, 178–80,
      195, 234
  fiscal consolidation starting in 2010, 190
  League of Nations loan, 121
Austrian School, 46–47
automatic fiscal stabilizers, 185, 200

Baker, James, 143
  Baker Plan, 143
balance of payments, 90, 121, 134, 137, 169,
      215, 245
balance sheets, 49, 71, 132, 142, 146–47, 160, 167,
      185, 196, 202–3, 253, 263
  central-bank, 132–133, 234
  public-sector, 251, 262
  sovereign, 157
Bangkok International Banking Facilities (BIBF),
      158, 256
bank loans, 142, 147, 167, 201, 236, 262
  converted into bonds, 147
  short-term foreign, 236
  syndicated, 59, 143, 237
bankers, 10–12, 15–17, 21–24, 31, 36, 39, 41,
      46–47, 56, 62, 64, 81, 88, 143, 167
  central, 249, 264
  foreign, 66–67, 90
  merchant, 44, 81
  private, 64
  Roman (*argentarii*), 12
  Tuscan, 14–15, 238
Banker's Magazine, 60
Bank for International Settlements, 254
*Bank für deutsche Industrieobligationen*, 184
Banking Act of 1935, United States, 251
banking system, 2, 35, 73, 75, 110, 112, 156, 162,
      166, 192

banknotes, 40. *See also* Bank of England
Bank of England, 38–41, 43, 47, 50–51, 94, 97–98,
    112, 132–33, 229, 236, 244–45, 252, 259
  and HM Treasury, 47
  banknotes, 39
  balance sheet, 245
  created as a result of William III's exhausted
    credit, 39
Bank of France, 96, 115, 252
  balance sheet falsification, 115
  increase in note issue during World War I, 112
  suspension of convertibility in 1870, 96
Bank of Japan, 74, 166–67, 217, 220, 250–51, 257
  assets of, 217
  officials of, 257
Bank of Mexico, 155
banks, 2–3, 16, 21, 38–43, 46, 49–51, 53, 59–63,
    65–66, 71, 94–96, 112, 140–43, 145–47,
    151–52, 156–63, 167, 184–85, 192–93,
    196–98, 203, 233–37, 251–52, 254–
    56, 259–61
  and diabolic loop, 110, 152–53, 259
  British, 254
  chartered, 68
  commercial, 111–12, 135, 142, 156, 209
  foreign, 65, 71, 142, 163, 240, 253, 256
  gatekeeping role in debt issuance, 71
  international, 142
  money-center, 47, 127, 142–43, 145–46, 203,
    214–15, 237
  nonmembers of Federal Reserve System, 259
  public, 169, 229
  quasi-central, 71
  recapitalization of, 156, 160, 185, 188
    costs incurred, 104, 160, 202, 256
  share prices of, 143
  state-controlled, 187
  underwriting by, 81, 122, 130, 242
  universal form, 259
Banque de Paris, 65
Banque Générale. *See* John Law
Baring Brothers, 46, 51, 62, 236, 241
Baring Crisis, 49, 61, 92, 241. *See also* Australia,
    Portugal
Bear Stearns & Co., 183
Belgium, 107, 109, 111, 113, 127, 132, 138, 141,
    144, 176, 178–80, 236
  National Finance Council, 219
  persistent primary budget surpluses after
    1995, 219
Berlin, as financial center, 52–53, 60, 66, 77, 238
  and 1873 financial crisis, 55, 66
bills. *See* Treasury bills
  bills of exchange, 15, 229, 231, 245
Bischoffsheim & Goldschmidt, 63–65, 238
Bismarck, Otto von, 108, 214
Blasebalg, Jacob, 35

blockade, naval 85–86
  of Venezuela, 86
BNP Paribas, 183–84
Bolshevik Revolution, 214
bondholder committees, 7, 20, 52, 77–78, 80–82,
    114, 146, 229, 236, 241–42, 254, 258, 262
  ad hoc, 82
  *Association Nationale de Porteurs Français de
    Valeurs Mobilières*, 82
  competing, 80
  default-specific, 242
  first Greek, 242
  German bondholder association, 242
  multiple, 82
  standing, 81, 242
bondholders, 19, 33, 51, 63, 80–82, 95, 115, 151,
    169, 196, 203, 241, 243
bond markets, 66, 73, 75, 126, 152, 187, 192, 197,
    206, 211, 215
  global, 127
  international, 82, 148–49, 162
  local, development of, 162–63
bond prices, 43, 60, 66, 134, 162, 164, 197, 216,
    223, 244–45, 250
  manipulation of, 237
  volatility of, 90
bonds, 18–19, 38–39, 46–47, 49–51, 59–64, 68–
    71, 73–74, 79–80, 89–91, 123, 125–27,
    132–34, 147, 196–97, 206–09, 217–18,
    220, 230, 235–45, 262. *See also* Treasury
  brokers engaged in trading, 81–82
  corporate, 169, 173
  czarist, 242
  defaulted, 241
  emerging-market, 262
  foreign, 7, 60, 70, 90, 130
  government, 3–4, 38–39, 42–43, 62, 71, 73, 95,
    100, 103, 117, 134, 153, 156, 163, 169,
    196–97, 234, 248, 250–51
    central, 187
    colonial, 48
    domestic, 152
    foreign, 63, 75, 88, 122, 127, 130, 244
    long-term US, 121
    Union, Civil War, 67–68
  guaranteed, 160, 235
  inflation-indexed, 264
  local-currency, 215, 256
  long-term, 218, 235
  marketing of, 132
  perpetuities as special form of, 22–23, 30,
    62, 245
  redemption of, 27, 231
  tontines as special form of, 34
borrowers, 4, 6, 22–24, 53, 73, 78–79, 81, 88, 92,
    141–42, 146–47, 185, 211, 215, 238, 243
  colonial, 48

developing-country, 215
foreign, 120
new to the market, 64, 167
private, 167
seasoned, 75
subsovereign, 50. *See also* debt
unseasoned, 46, 121
borrowing costs, 29–30, 132, 151, 162, 244
Brady, Nicholas, 147
Brady bonds, 162
Brady Plan, 147, 202, 230, 255, 262
Brazil, 55, 58, 77, 89, 90, 149, 162–63
1980s debt crisis, 144, 254
and Brady Plan, 147
and Great Depression, 124, 249
importance of coffee and rubber in 1930s, 90
larger primary budget deficits in 2020 than in Global Financial Crisis, 201
Brewer, John, 37, 233
Britain, 37, 39, 46, 52, 54, 62, 64–65, 69–70, 72, 82–84, 84–86, 93–95, 99–103, 109–14, 121, 131, 137, 234–36, 240, 243–48, 260
as market for Argentine meat and cereals, 123
banks, 253
bondholders, 82–85
colonies, 252
Conservative party, 114, 243
consols, 30, 87–90, 102, 121, 245, 247
debt-to-GDP ratio 97, 101
dominions, 91–92
Finance Act of 1923, 114
investors, 60–61, 81, 239–40
Labour party, 114
first-ever government, 114
free breakfast table, policy goal, 114
post-World War II, 139
military spending, 96
occupation of Egypt, 238
Reform Acts, 100–01
soft power, 100
British Bankers Association, 242
Broda, Christian, 189
budget, government, 1–2, 13, 26, 100, 113–16, 118, 120, 135–36, 171–72, 177–78, 218–19, 260–61
balance, 104, 128–29
deficits, 66, 115, 117, 120, 139–41, 143, 155, 167, 170, 172–73, 177, 182–83, 216, 205, 236
consolidated, 157
primary, 96–99, 100, 102–05, 112–13, 120, 127, 137–38, 143, 154, 171, 176–79, 186, 201–02, 213, 218–20, 246–50, 257, 261
surpluses, 84, 93, 96, 101, 104, 113, 119, 137, 180, 202, 219
Budget Enforcement Act of 1990, United States, 171–72, 178

Buenos Aires, 51, 236
Bush, George H. W., 171–72
Bush, George W., 174, 257

Caisse d'Escompte, 41
Canada, 49, 53, 55, 88–89, 103, 107, 109, 111, 113, 138, 244, 247, 249
railways, 52
securities, 248
Canning, George, 85
capital levy. *See* wealth taxes
Carolingian Empire, 14, 228
Ceaușescu, Nicolae, 8
central banks, 46–47, 53, 71, 111–12, 125–26, 132–35, 154–55, 158–60, 191, 197–98, 200, 206, 208–09, 218, 220–21, 260–62
autonomous, during interwar period, 122
balance sheets, 112–13, 134, 257
Chabot, Benjamin, 90, 238, 241, 244
Champagne fairs, 22, 44, 229
Charles II of England, 233
Chile, 88–90, 163, 236, 247
and Great Depression, 123–24
and copper, 90, 123
first country to borrow from World Bank, 252
China, 14, 3, 56, 58, 69–72, 125–26, 130, 162–63, 186–87, 200, 203–05, 217–18, 239–40, 242, 259–60, 263
and fiscal stimulus, 184, 188
as creditor, 205
Belt & Road Initiative, 204
bond prices, 72
Customs Service, 70–72, 208, 240
inspectors, 70, 72
debt consolidation, 125, 240
Export-Import Bank, 204
market access, 70–72, 240
and Qing loans, 71
Republican leaders, 71
Treaty of Aigun, 69
*See also* Laos, debt to China
China Development Bank, 205, 263
China Merchants Port Holdings, 204
China Southern Power Grid Co., 204
Chinese Maritime Customs Service, 70
Church, 5
Roman, 15–16, 229
French, 32–33, 232
Citicorp International Banking Ltd, 253
Citigroup, 146. *See also* National City Bank
cities as debt issuers. *See* debt, subsovereign
City of London Tavern, 80
city-states. *See* Greece, Italy
civil war, finance of, 13, 36, 53, 67, 93, 96, 99, 101, 125, 140, 219
Clay, Christopher, 66, 238–39

collateral, 4, 23–25, 38–39, 65, 68, 73, 184,
      230–31, 241–42, 251, 259
   debt securities serving as, 10, 23–24,
      38–39, 73, 96, 184, 201, 212, 230–31,
      251, 259, 262
   pledging of by sovereigns, 33, 65, 68, 241, 242
collateralized debt obligations (CDOs), 184–85
colonies, 17, 48–49, 54, 235, 252
   settler, 48
Colwyn Committee (Committee on National
      Debt and Taxation), United Kingdom,
      114, 222
Commercial Revolution, 23, 212
commissions for underwriting debt issuance, 59–
      60, 65, 68, 78, 80, 89, 237, 240, 242–43
Committee of Greek Bondholders, 80, 262. See
      also bondholder committees
commodities, primary, 90–91
   non-oil, 254
   prices of, 6, 46, 90, 123
companies, 39, 110, 176, 234
   joint-stock 15, 38, 41
   state-chartered trading, 39
Confederacy, American, 68–69, 94, 96
Congress. See representative assemblies
Congressional Budget Office (CBO), United
      States, 172–74, 217, 263
consumption, 144, 151, 189, 193–94, 203, 214–
      15, 218, 261
   taxes, 33
Corporation of Foreign Bondholders, 60, 81–82,
      84, 238, 242–44
Cottrell, Philip, 65, 238–39
Council of States, Dutch Republic, 26
councilor pensionary, Holland, 27
courts, and adjudication of debt disputes, 5–6,
      31–32, 49, 227, 232
COVID-19, 199–209, 216, 219–20, 222–23,
      244, 264.
   and fiscal measures, 217
   and K-shaped recession, 265
   crisis, 9, 181, 200–04, 217, 219–20, 258,
      263–64
   See also crises, Federal Reserve System,
      International Monetary Fund
credit, 10–12, 15–17, 23–24, 37, 39, 41, 44, 47,
      50, 66–67, 73, 75, 94, 100, 120, 135, 145,
      166, 186, 188–90, 201, 203, 231, 240,
      252–53, 254
   backward-bending supply of, 230
   boom-and-bust cycles of, 47, 110, 119–20, 184,
      192, 249
   constraints, 190
   markets, 38–39, 124, 190, 228, 250
   private, 120
   rationing of, 230
Crédit Mobilier, 65

creditors, 3–5, 8, 17–18, 20–21, 25–27, 29, 31,
      33–34, 39–40, 49–52, 78–79, 84–85, 136,
      160, 212, 242
   bilateral, 204
   coordination among, 82
   domestic, 66–67, 250
   foreign, 50, 120, 160, 227, 238
   holdout, 262
   official, 147
creditworthiness, 33, 42, 56, 100, 229, 231
   maintenance of, 102
crises, 102–03, 145–47, 152–53, 157, 159–60,
      180–84, 188, 192, 194–99, 201–02, 205,
      211, 215–20, 253–57, 259–62, 264–65
   banking, 2, 140, 240
      systemic, 9, 183, 215
   commercial, 232
   currency, 253
   emerging-market, 153
   fiscal, 216
   transatlantic in 2008-9, 184
Crusades, 17
currencies, 57–58, 90–91, 94, 125–26, 136–37,
      144–45, 156, 159–60, 163, 187, 191,
      249, 255–56
   as earlier reserve units, 264
   debasement of, 10, 13–14, 232
   depreciation of, 51, 125, 135, 143, 150, 154,
      236, 244, 248
   devaluation of, 136–37, 155, 176
   emerging-market, 149
   foreign, 6, 46, 51, 73, 91, 162, 241, 256
   local, 125, 159, 162–63
   silver-based, 71
   single European, 176–77
   uniform, United States, 43
currency risk, 90
current account, 121
   deficits, 151, 255
customs house, 86, 235
cyclically adjusted budget balance, 178
   primary, 187. See also budget balance

Davis, Jefferson, 68
Dawes Loan, 118, 121–22
de Vries, Jan, 29, 231
debt
   bilateral. See intergovernmental
   consolidation episodes, 8, 18, 21, 30, 93, 99,
      102–03, 110, 112–114, 116–20, 128, 135,
      137, 140, 178–80, 246, 261
      accounting for, 96–100, 104–05, 113, 138,
         173, 179, 247
   conversions, voluntary and involuntary, 18, 102,
      116–17, 125, 250
   corporate, 143, 159, 161, 161, 167, 169, 173,
      187, 203

socialization of, 110, 157, 166, 227, 256
government-guaranteed, 157, 160–61, 185,
   196, 235, 256, 262, 263
crises, 103
and COVID-19, 199–200
emerging-market, 143, 147, 149,
   202, 214–15
cycles, 77–78, 128, 140–44, 149–52, 157–61,
   166–70, 182–88
defaults, 3, 5, 7, 24, 47–48, 51, 77–79, 80, 82,
   85, 87–88, 90, 92, 125–26, 241, 260–61
   domestic, 125–26, 131, 235, 250
   economic costs of, 87–88, 124
   endogenous, 87–88
   excusable default, theory of, 250
   exogenous, 87
   serial, 90, 232
   trade disruptions as deterrent to, 123–24
domestic, 49, 54, 73, 74, 88, 90–92, 114, 125–
   26, 130–31, 152, 157, 160, 244, 251
emerging-market, 46–55, 69, 75, 82–86, 90–92,
   126–27, 140–48, 149–64, 201–03, 205,
   215–16, 234, 237, 244, 255, 256, 262
external. See foreign
federal, 109–10
   in the EU. See mutualization of, in Europe
   in the US, 41–43, 53, 101–02
floating, See short-term
foreign, 6, 8, 53–54, 57, 67, 69–70, 72, 88, 92,
   104, 109, 123, 129, 150–52, 157, 162, 201,
   239, 244, 250, 255
   short-term, 154, 157
gross, 104, 167–68, 217, 258. See also net
in local currency 90, 125–26, 162–64, 216, 256
intergovernmental, 135, 147, 204–05, 248
   and forgiveness of, 205
internal. See domestic
international guarantees, 65, 84
intolerance, 149, 255
long-term, 17, 27, 47, 83, 130, 152, 265
   domestic currency-denominated, 240
management of, 3, 82, 102, 125, 129, 134, 149,
   153–57, 179–80, 194
   See also debt, sustainability, fiscal dominance
markets, 3, 18–19, 22–24, 38, 42, 44, 59, 71,
   73, 90, 92, 177, 197, 211–13, 227–28,
   234, 240
   backstopping by central bank, 38–39, 41, 43,
      47, 73, 94, 126, 132–35, 177, 197–98,
      201, 206, 245, 260
   maturity, 16, 21, 74–75, 109, 117, 125, 130,
      196, 221, 260, 264
moratoria, 202, 204, 248, 253
municipal. See subsovereign
mutualization of, in Europe 190, 198, 207–08
net, 168, 217, 247, 257–58, 264. See also gross
off-budget. See corporate, government-guaranteed

overhang, 84, 202, 211
perpetual. See annuities, Britain, consols, rentes
private, See corporate
reduction. See consolidation episodes
relief and the IMF, 205, 262
renegotiation of, 22, 79–82, 88–89, 202–03, 254
   See also bondholder committees, Institute of
      International Finance, London Club,
      Paris Club
repudiation of, 82, 103, 242, 248
   in the US, 50
restructurings of, 18, 21, 24, 31, 88–89, 140,
   195–96, 202–05, 230, 262
   domestic, 125–26
   of intergovernmental debts, 204
securities. See bills, bonds, consols, rentes
service, 25, 27–28, 33–34, 55, 66–67, 84, 109,
   115–16, 129, 149–50, 263
   in foreign currency, 51, 57, 144, 150–51, 153
short-term, 33, 83, 109–11, 117, 150–52, 158,
   160, 162, 221, 231, 233, 235, 247–48
subsovereign, 50–52
   in China, 187, 203
   in the US, 50–51, 174, 189
   municipalities, 22–23, 62, 123, 228, 244
   provinces or states, 27–29, 49–52, 123,
      231, 233
sustainability, 37, 39, 55–56, 119, 182, 191,
   194–98, 218, 222–23
   in Japan, 165–68
   problems, 28, 136, 193, 199, 254, 257
debt-for-equity swaps, 39, 117, 204, 241
debt-for-national patrimony swaps, 204
Debt Service Suspension Initiative, 263
defaulted debts. See debt, default
deficit finance, 229
deficit reduction, 166, 172, 194
deficits, 52, 100, 102, 104–05, 116, 118, 126,
   166–67, 171–72, 177, 185–86, 188,
   191–94, 220, 257–58, 260–61
   balance-of-payments, 143
   current-account, 216
   federal, 172
   public-sector, 149
   reduction, 166, 172, 194
   temporary, 141
deficit spending, 140, 177, 187–88, 190, 218, 250,
   258, 265
deflation, 119, 134, 165, 217, 257
Delors Committee (Committee for the Study of
   Economic and Monetary Union), 258
Delos, island and temple, 11–12
democratization and its effects, 8, 44, 62, 106, 122
Democrats, in U.S. Congress, 171–72, 174
developing countries, 93, 136, 142, 147, 149, 152,
   204, 214, 251–53, 254–55
   See also less developed countries (LDCs)

development banks, multilateral, 254
    established by Southern US states, 52
diabolic loop. *See* banks
Dionysus of Syracuse, 10–11
disinflation, 154
Doge, 17
dollar, 43, 50, 57, 69, 89, 121, 123, 136, 142,
    144, 147, 153, 155–56, 159–60, 236,
    239, 255–56
    borrowings, 159
    currency swaps, extended by Federal Reserve to
        foreign central banks, 262
    debts, 143, 160
        short-term, 159
    deposits, 134
    funding, 156
    liquidity, 262
    of constant gold content, bonds denominated
        in, 67, 126
    receivables, 159
dowry funds, 21, 230
Draghi, Mario, 197, 206
Duer, William, 42–43, 234

Eccles, Marriner, 134
economic growth, 6–7, 53, 55, 98–99, 128, 135,
    137, 139, 171, 178, 202, 208, 222, 253,
    256, 261
    in golden age, post World War II, 120, 222, 253
    modern, 4, 6, 23, 25, 263
        following definition of Simon Kuznets,
            212–213
    slowdown post-1973, 141
Edward III of England, 14–15, 22
Egypt, 65, 73, 77, 82–86, 88–89, 92, 136–37, 163,
    236, 238–39, 241, 243
    bondholders, 243
    bonds, 89, 242
    Caisse de la Dette Publique, 84
    finances, 84, 243
    khedive, 83
    loans to, 81, 242
    taxes, 242
Eighty Years War (1568-1648), 28
elections, 2, 105, 115, 117, 155, 172
emergencies, met by using debt, 2, 9, 14, 17, 94,
    114–15, 180, 209, 220, 222
emerging market economies, 46–47, 49, 73, 75,
    149, 151, 152–153, 162–63, 165, 201–03,
    215–16, 235, 237, 253, 255–56
    *See also* debt, emerging-market and developing
        countries
enfranchisement, political. *See* representative
    assemblies
England. *See* Britain
Erlanger & Co., 68
Estates General. *See* representative assemblies

Estates of Holland. *See* representative assemblies
euro, 126, 177, 179, 182, 184–85, 192, 194, 198,
    206, 216, 258–59
    and Euro Area, 126, 153, 178, 180–82, 186–87,
        191–92, 195, 256, 259, 261
Eurodollar market, 142, 253–54
Europe, 2, 4, 6, 9, 13–14, 44, 53–55, 64, 84, 86, 91,
    110, 121, 128, 162, 166, 175–78, 180, 182,
    190–91, 193, 196–98, 206, 212, 216, 229,
    236–38, 251, 258–61
    bankers, 31
    banks, 158, 184–85
    bonds, 206, 264, 261
    geography, role in sovereign borrowing, 14, 44,
        190, 229
    integration of, 207
    investors, 7, 65, 67, 239
    manufacturing, 129
    periphery during Euro Crisis, 259
    powers, in Greece, 86
    principal financial centers, 55, 68, 77, 83
    public expenditure, 54–55
    regulators, 259
    Renaissance in, 16
    Single Market, 176, 258
    Western, 14, 46, 65, 130
European Central Bank (ECB), 135, 166, 177,
    190–92, 196–98, 200, 206–07, 220, 234,
    247, 259, 261
    Pandemic Emergency Purchase Program
        (PEPP), 206–07
    role in stabilizing bond market, 199
European Commission, 177, 192, 198, 207–08
European Parliament, 261
European Union, 177, 197–98, 207–08, 260
    Excessive Deficit Procedure, 192, 198
    prohibition of subsidies and state aids, 176
exchange rate, 6, 46, 58, 65, 104, 116, 118, 135,
    153–56, 164, 176–77, 216, 251, 255
    dynamics, 115
    fixed, 191
    prespecified in debt contract, 236
    prewar, 113
    *See also* currency risk
expansionary fiscal contraction, doctrine of, 194
exports, 51, 57–58, 90–91, 124–25, 145–46, 149–
    50, 162, 166, 243, 249, 252
    growth of, 74, 166

families, role in finance, 11, 21, 59, 62, 174, 219
Federal Reserve System, 112, 121, 132, 134, 183,
    200–1, 220–21, 235, 251, 263, 265
    Federal Open Market Investment
        Committee, 12
    Federal Reserve Bank of New York, 122
    open market operations, 251
    Operation Twist, 133–34, 235, 252

response to COVID-19, 94, 200
  *See also* currency swaps
Fenn's Compendium of English and Foreign
  Funds, 54
Fetter, Frank Albert, 46
Fetter, Frank Whitson, 46, 47, 123, 125, 234–35,
  249–50
finance companies in East Asia, 160–61
financial centers, 77, 87, 213
  global, 262
  international, 6, 52, 213
  principal European, 88
financial crises, 2, 6, 9, 66, 83, 161, 181, 184, 209,
  211, 215, 223. *See also* crises
financial development, 24, 31, 38–39, 49, 75, 184,
  212, 229, 231
financial innovation, 34, 38–39, 62, 245
financial institutions, 59, 75, 143, 156, 183–84,
  196, 236, 242
  distressed, 160
  domestic, 160
  private, 254
financial instruments, 21, 38, 44, 56
financial integration, 12
financialization, 44
financial markets, 4–6, 25, 31, 45, 56, 73, 140, 143,
  166, 183, 185
  access to, 28, 31, 40–41, 48, 64, 68, 74, 78–79,
    82–83, 87, 91, 121, 124, 145, 147, 153,
    190, 236, 240
  loss of, 31, 79
  development of, 4–6, 31
  domestic, 77
  foreign, 73
  international and global, 45, 114, 153, 201
  private, 3, 18, 38
financial press, 60
financial regulation, 127, 130, 146, 153, 167, 259.
  *See also* diabolic loop, Eurodollar market
financial repression, 100, 129, 136–37, 140, 222
  and credit regulation in Europe, 135
  and crises, 140, 197
  and deregulation, 167, 183
  and regulatory forbearance, 145–46, 167
fiscal consolidation, 167, 173, 175–77, 179,
  190–91, 220, 223, 260–61
fiscal costs, 189, 199, 220
  disguised, 157
  of bank recapitalization, 260
fiscal dominance, 134, 166, 252
fiscal policy, 3, 104, 126, 129, 153–54, 167–68,
  176, 189, 191, 199, 222, 250,
  253–54, 259
  multiplier, 189–90
  stimulus, 167, 188, 205, 222, 257, 260
Fitch Record of Government Finances, 238
Flandreau, Marc, 91, 234, 237–38, 241, 244

Florence, 15, 17, 20–21, 229, 230
  bonds, 19
  *estimo*, 20
  forced loans, 17–21, 23, 29–30, 230
  *See also* city-states, merchant banks
Foreign and Colonial Investment Trust, 61
Foreign Bondholders Protective Council, 51, **60**,
  81–82, 84, 238, 241–44
foreign direct investment, 142
foreign exchange market, 159, 166, 215
foreign financial control, 77, 84–85, 121, 239, 243
foreign governments, 7, 65, 72, 85, 90, 129,
  135, 242
  barred from borrowing in London, 131
foreign investors, 6–7, 45, 50–51, 58, 62, 67–68,
  70, 154, 158, 163, 215–16, 240–41, 244
Foreign Stock Market, London, 57, 237
France, 34, 40–41, 52, 64–65, 68–70, 81–82,
  96–99, 102–03, 109–13, 115–17, 120–21,
  137–38, 178–80, 207, 232, 234, 236–37,
  243–49, 252–53
  banks, 196
  debt, 33–34, 116, 248
    and exchange rate dynamics, 115
    reduction efforts, 97
  foreign investment, 100
  investors, 245
  kings, 33, 232
  office selling, 34, 233
  *parlements*, 31–32, 232
  *rentes sur l'Hôtel de Ville*, 33–34
  waltz of the portfolios, 115
franchise, political. *See* representative assemblies
Franks and Lombards, 2
Franco-British control, 239
Franco-Prussian War, 91, 93–94, 96, 102, 110
French and Napoleonic Wars, 93–96, 219, 234
Frühling and Goschen, 81, 83

Galata bankers. *See* Ottoman Empire
Genoa, 16–18, 229
  bankers cartel, 31, 231
  delegation of tax revenues, 22
  Procurators of San Marco, 17
  War of Chioggia (1378-81), 18
George I of England, 40, 234
Germany, 36, 52, 70–71, 82, 86, 107–13, 118,
  120–21, 129, 131–32, 138, 177–80,
  187–88, 207, 243–45, 248–52
  and hyperinflation, 118
  bonds, 121, 206–7
  capital goods production, 129
  central bank, 133, 251
  clearing debt, 251
  declares debt moratorium, 253
  economics ministry, German Reich 133
  finance ministry, 250

Germany (*cont.*)
  foreign trade, 240
  investors, 48, 82, 86, 237
  public spending of, 140
  Reich and German states, 110
    debt, 133
  Reichsbank, 133, 251
  reparations, 118–22, 247, 248
  *schwarze Null*, 13
  Sparticist Uprising, 214
  unification, 19th century, 64
Giffen, Robert, 96, 245
Global Financial Crisis, 149, 153, 179–82,
    184–88, 194–95, 201, 203, 206–07, 216,
    222, 256–57, 263
  and EU double dip recession, 192
globalization, 44–45, 47–62, 121
  financial, 120
Glorious Revolution, England, 29–30
Glyn, Mills & Co. 65
God Worshiping Society, Qing China, 69
gold, 40, 43, 58, 67–68, 70, 90, 94–95, 99, 101,
    110–13, 115, 117, 239–41
  clauses in bond contracts, 126, 236, 252
  convertibility, 58, 94–95
    restoration by France, 96
  reserves, 112, 123
gold standard, 58, 122, 134, 240
  and Bank of England, 112
  and currency risk, 58
  and domestic debt, 90
  and France, 115
  and Italy, 117
  and Meiji Japan, 74
  and Qing China, 70
  and United States, 99
    and return in 1879, 101
    Gold Standard Act of 1900, 99
  classical (pre-1914), 244
  gold-coin standard, 58
  gold-exchange standard, 58
  prewar gold parity, 94–95, 112
    in France after Franco-Prussian
        War, 94–95
    in Great Britain after World War I, 112
goldsmith-bankers, 38
Goschen, George, 81, 83, 102, 125, 242–43, 250
Government Investment Corporation,
    Singapore, 219
government, 1–2, 4–9, 38–53, 66–67, 72–77,
    79–82, 103–06, 115, 124–28, 130–31,
    140–42, 149–52, 154–57, 159–64, 180–90,
    196–200, 202–05, 207–09, 211–16, 227,
    233, 239–41, 254–56, 258–61
  colonial 48–49, 61, 75, 235
  constitutional, 75
  creditor-country, 78, 147, 192, 205, 244

  federal, 1, 41–42, 50–53, 101–02, 110, 123,
      172, 189, 207–08, 250
    assumption of state debts, 52, 236
  limited, 16–17, 21, 26, 37, 102–03
  local, 5, 186, 203, 227, 262
  multiparty coalition, 141
  minority, 248
Gramm-Rudman-Hollings Balanced Budget and
    Emergency Deficit Control Act, 171
Great Britain. *see* Britain
Great Depression, 8, 109–11, 123, 135, 169, 192,
    214, 250
  legacy of countercyclical budgets, 126
Greece, 45, 47, 113, 125–27, 138–39, 184–85, 187,
    190, 192–95, 198, 206, 209, 248–49, 261
  city-states, 10–13, 228
  debt, 169, 192–96, 198, 228, 239, 242, 252,
      261–62 193
    crises, earlier history, 262
    exposures of French and German banks
        to, 196
  islands, 11
  Karamanlis government, 192
  rescue by Troika, 192
  threat to democracy, 262
Greenspan, Alan, 151, 162, 255–56
  Greenspan-Guidotti rule, 151, 154
Guatemala, 77–78, 82, 86, 201, 249
Guidotti, Pablo, 151, 255
  Greenspan-Guidotti rule, 151, 154
gunboat diplomacy, 7, 86, 246. See also Roosevelt
    corollary and sanctions
Gutierrez, Don Carlos, 64

Hamilton, Alexander, 41–43, 51, 72, 207–08. See
    *also* lender of last resort
  Europe's Hamiltonian moment, 207
hedge funds, 183, 200, 202
  vulture funds, 18, 203
Henry IV of England, 29
Henry VIII of England, 229
holdout creditors, 80–81, 196
  disenfranchisement of, 80
Holland, 26–28, 36, 231, 233
  debt service, 28
Holy Roman Empire, 35–36
  difficulty of borrowing, 35–36
Honduras, 238, 249
  Transoceanic Ship Railway, 63–64
Hongkong and Shanghai Bank (HSBC), 70–72,
    240. See also lender of last resort
Hoover, Herbert, 120
housing, 49, 107, 140, 214, 252
  markets, 185, 259
  prices, 183, 192, 259
  shortages of after World Wars, 129, 252
Hundred Years War (1337–1453), 14

import tariffs, 26, 95, 101, 137, 176, 208, 231.
  *See also* tariff revenues
income tax, 101, 186, 219, 245–46
  administration of, 95
  first, 94, 219
  in US, 95
  rates, 174, 219
incomes policy, 153
indemnity, 69, 91
  China, after Second Opium War, 69
  France, after Franco-Prussian War, 91
India, 67, 127, 130, 144, 200–01
  importance of nonbank firms as investors in
    public debt, 163
inflation, 34, 51, 89, 99–100, 110, 115, 116–20,
    129, 131, 134, 137, 141, 160, 162, 173,
    177, 188–189, 208–10, 211, 216–17,
    220–21, 246–47, 252, 257, 265
  and price controls, 13, 132–33, 220
  as target for monetary policy, 220, 264
  as tax, 13, 206
  break-even rate, 264
  causes of, 220
  expected, 141, 231, 264
information, importance of 6, 17, 38, 46, 60, 62,
    72, 80, 159, 238
  information problems, 22, 81
infrastructure, 7
  investment in, 63
  of financial markets, 65, 73
Institute of International Finance
    (IIF), 202, 262
institutions, 24, 26, 33, 41, 56, 59, 61, 80, 100,
    105, 239
  market-supporting, 212
Insurance, 59, 61–62, 152, 169, 221
  social, 7–8, 108, 214
  state-sponsored disability, 7
interbank market, 12, 160, 162, 185, 192
Interest Equalization Tax, United States, 222
interest payments, 17, 22, 51, 56, 73, 90, 96,
    131, 137, 143, 204, 208, 236, 254–55,
    257, 261–62
  delayed, 250
  in local currency, 159
  partial, 125
  reduced, 234
interest rate, 21, 27–28, 30, 55–57, 73–75, 97–100,
    105, 112–14, 117–19, 137, 155–58, 168,
    170–73, 176, 189–91, 194–97, 201, 215–18,
    220–23, 228–30, 244–48, 258–60, 263–64
  ceilings, 12, 132, 134, 213
  differentials, 112, 128, 185, 261
  nominal, 96–97, 104, 137, 141, 158, 218, 221,
    246, 249
  premium, 46, 60, 89–90, 117–18, 222
    for default-risk, 75

real, 27, 30, 119, 138, 141, 158, 173, 217, 231,
    257, 259, 264
  negative, 137
  regulation of, 140
International Committee of Bankers on
    Mexico, 88
international finance, 53, 65, 122
  management by Federal Reserve, 123
International Monetary Fund (IMF), 60, 131,
    136–38, 144–47, 156, 160–61, 168, 171,
    173, 191, 193–96, 202, 205, 254, 261–63
  and 1956 Suez crisis, 136–37
  and 2010 Greek crisis, 192
  and bailing in the banks, 145
  and European governments, 261
  and Latin American debt crisis, 145–46
  and League of Nations precedent, 249
  and Marshall Plan, 136
  and post-World War II sovereign borrowing,
    127, 141
  and proposed COVID recovery
    contribution, 264
  Fiscal Transparency Code, 17
  lending and loans, 136–37, 254, 262
  Post-Catastrophe Debt Relief Trust, 262
  stand-by loans, 137
investment banks, 59, 63–65, 67, 75, 78, 122, 159,
    183, 213, 227, 236, 238, 249
investment funds, 61–62
investment trusts, 169
investors, 3, 5–7, 16, 23–24, 26–27, 33, 40, 43,
    46–47, 59–63, 68–70, 75–83, 85–91, 117–
    18, 121–22, 126–27, 129–30,
    133–34, 154–55, 162–63, 196–97,
    220–22, 236–40, 242–44
  domestic, 33, 68, 91, 196, 201, 243
  foreign, 163
  professional, 241
  retail, 22–23, 27, 38, 46–47, 61–62, 68, 110,
    122, 142, 241
  risk-aversion on part of, 24
Ireland, 107
  Global Financial Crisis and recession, 184–85,
    187–88, 195–96, 260
  successful debt consolidation in 1990s,
    176, 178–80
Italy, 54, 56, 107, 109–11, 113, 116–18, 138,
    176, 178–80, 185, 187–88, 190, 205–06,
    247, 249
  bankers, 3, 14, 22
  bonds, 206
  city-states, 16–18, 21–23, 245
    Levant trade of, 44
  forced debt conversion in 1925-26, 117
  Lega-5Star government, 206
  newly unified, required to pay higher interest
    rates, 238

J.P. Morgan & Co., 53, 88, 110, 122, 183, 241
Japan, 14, 9, 52–53, 70–75, 88–89, 91–92, 111,
        113, 127–28, 130, 138–39, 165–70,
        185–87, 216–18, 250–51, 257–58,
        260–61, 264
    1990s recession, 166–67
    annexation of Manchuria, 125
    banks, 160, 254, 256
    bonds, 92
        issued in London prior to 1913, 74
    customs revenues, 75
    debt-to-GDP ratio, 167
    debt managers, 165
    Economic and Social Research Institute
        (ESRI), 167
    financial development, 255
    households saving and investment behavior,
        217, 220
    Japanese government bonds (JGBs), 168–69,
        217, 251
    Meiji restoration, 73–75
    yen, 75, 166–67, 217, 256
Johnson Act, United States, 131

Keynes, John Maynard, 112, 114, 132,
        222, 248
Korean War, 134, 222
Kuhn, Loeb & Co., 53, 75, 122
Kurz, Christopher, 90, 238, 244

labor, 118, 153, 252
    productivity, 154. See also productivity
Lamont, Thomas, 122
land banks, Southern US, 50
land prices, 119, 167
Laos, 204
    and debt to China, 204
Larosière, Jacques de, 145
Latin America, 6, 40, 46–48, 54–55, 57, 65, 69,
        86, 88–89, 91–92, 123, 143–45, 162, 202,
        214–15, 235, 237, 241, 250, 254–55
    natural resources, 234
    new nations of, 47, 77
    so-called rediscovery of, 47, 53
Law, John, 39–40, 46, 232
    and Banque Générale, 39
    and Company of the Mississippi, 39–40
League of Nations, 121, 123, 131, 192, 249
    loans of, 121, 135, 249
Lefevre, Charles Joachim, 64
Lehman Brothers, 183
Lend-Lease, 131
lender of last resort, 197
    and Alexander Hamilton, 43
    and Bank of England, 41
    and HSBC, 71–72
    and Imperial Ottoman Bank, 66

and liquidity provider of last resort, 201, 206
    reluctance of ECB to act as, 197–98
lending, 3–5, 7, 11, 15–16, 21–23, 53, 59, 62, 67,
        141, 143, 215, 249
    booms, 62, 77, 140
    commercial, 122
    foreign, 65
    interbank, 151
    intergovernmental, 111, 135
    international, 11, 15, 47, 53, 90
    overseas, 7, 48
    standards for, 183
less-developed countries (LDCs), 141–43, 145
    debt crisis 143, 147
    debtors, 143, 146
    governments, 147
    loans to, 143, 146, 254
        by large British banks, 254
        by US money-center banks, 143
liabilities, financial, 53, 185, 255–56
    contingent, 162
    domestic currency-denominated, 152, 169
    foreign currency-denominated, 151
    implicit, 157, 187
    short-term foreign, 151
Liberty Bonds, 122
    and Loans, 110, 248
Liesse, André, 96, 245
life annuities, 23, 27, 35–36, 62, 231
    mass-marketed, 34
    two lives, 230
limited liability, as form of business enterprise,
        12, 228
Lindert, Peter, 79, 88, 241, 244, 246
liquidity, 39
    of financial markets and assets, 43, 60, 73, 160,
        163, 200, 211, 256, 259
    problems of, 200, 254
    of secondary market, 23, 162
litigation, as response to debt problems, 262
Liverpool, as cotton entrepot center, 69
loans, 11–15, 17–18, 20–23, 43, 46–47, 59–60, 62–65,
        67–68, 70, 72–73, 79, 84–85, 111, 121–22,
        137, 142–43, 145–47, 159–61, 193, 204–05,
        228–30, 240–44, 252, 255–56, 259, 262–63
    as personal obligation of the king, 83
    commercial, 121, 147
    contractors for, 46, 59–60, 232
    contracts governing, 2, 7, 16, 21, 23, 32–33, 44,
        59, 62, 70, 227
        payment in salt, in China, 228
    emergency, 156, 193
    for stabilization purposes, 121, 192
    foreign, 65, 73, 240
    interbank, 256
    intergovernmental, 141, 205
    international, 118

jumbo, to emerging markets, 142
long-term, 18, 65, 110, 121, 143
municipal, 52
negative-amortization mortgage, 259
nonperforming, 159–60, 196, 256
  removing from bank balance sheets, 147
short-term, 30, 36, 66, 145, 230–31
Together Loan extended by Northern Rock, 184
tribute, Turkey 241
London, 37–38, 49, 51–53, 57, 59–66, 68–69, 71–75, 80, 82–83, 90–91, 121, 123, 238, 244–45, 253
  bankers, 66
  banks, 110, 235
  capital market, 240
  City of, 46
  competition from continental financial centers, 60
London and Westminster Bank, 71
London Chamber of Commerce, 81, 242
London Club of private creditors, 146, 254
London debt accord of 1926, 248
London debt agreement of 1953, 131, 140
London Stock Exchange, 38, 46, 49, 59, 80–82, 92, 237, 242
London Tavern, 80–81
London Times, 60
Long Island meeting of central bankers, 1927, 249

Maastricht Treaty (Treaty on European Union), 177–78
  Convergence Criteria, 177
Marichal, Carlos, 47, 235, 237
Marshall Plan, 135–36, 252. See also International Monetary Fund
Massieu, José Francisco Ruiz, 155
McGregor, Gregor, 46, 63–64
Melbourne, housing boom in, 49
merchant banks, 15, 22, 44, 64–65, 81, 158
merchants, 15–18, 20, 23, 25–27, 29, 33, 43–44, 59, 68, 85, 228, 233, 240
Merkel, Angela, 207
Mexico, 88–89, 92, 124, 127, 130, 145, 147, 149, 153–57, 160, 162–63, 166, 200–01, 254
  banks, 156, 255–56
  cetes, 154–55, 255
  conversion loans, unsuccessful, 89
  debt, 154
  defaults, 19th century, 79
  Economic Solidarity Pact (Pacto), 153
  financial crisis, 153, 247
  Institutional Revolutionary Party (PRI), 155
  Second Republic, 52
  suspension of debt-service payments, 153
  tesobonos, 154–57
    related financial manipulations, 255
  Tequila crisis, 153
  Zapatista movement, 155

Mississippi, Company of the. See John Law
monetary union, 177–78, 180, 258
moneylenders, traditional, 64
money market, 23–24, 65, 184–85, 233
money supply, 112, 132, 248, 251
  in modern form, 39
Monroe Doctrine, 86
moral hazard, 205, 216, 236
Moroccan crisis of 1905, 102
mortgages, 165, 259
  mortgage-backed securities, 184
    distribution of, 185
    subprime, 183
  negative amortizing, 259
Morton, Peter, 79, 88, 241, 244
multilateral finance. See development banks, International Monetary Fund, World Bank
municipalities, 22–23, 33–34, 49–50, 51, 117, 123.
  See also debt, subsovereign
Mussolini, Benito, 117

National Bank of Commerce, 75
National Banking Act, United States, 68
  and National Banking System, 68, 73
  prohibition on foreign branching, 53
National City Bank, 75. See also Citigroup
national defense, importance of, 1, 6, 48, 54–55, 92, 160, 174, 182
  spending on, 2, 174, 180, 257–58
National Economic Council, United States, 170
Necker, Jacques, 34–35
Netherlands, 26–29, 36, 37, 52, 61, 91, 141, 185, 236, 252, 253
  Dutch East India Company, 29
New Economy, United States, 1990s, 172, 178, 180
New York, 41–42, 52–53, 74–75, 95, 120, 122, 130, 240, 249, 253–54, 259
  and financing World War I, 95
  as financial center 42, 120–21
  as venue for Japanese government flotation in 1904, 75
  correspondent banks, 111
  Mexico's attempt to borrow in the nineteenth century, 52
New York Stock Exchange, 43, 52
Norman, Montagu, 133
North American Free Trade Agreement, 155
Norway 219, 259
  persistent primary budget surpluses after 1999, 219

Office of Management and Budget, United States, 172
oil prices, 153, 254
Oliner, Stephen, 172, 257
open market operations, 235, 251. See also Federal Reserve System

opium, 69. *See also* trade
  Second Opium War (1856–60), 69
  taxes on, 70
Organisation for Economic Cooperation and
      Development (OECD), 141, 191, 247,
      253, 257–58, 261
  Creditor Reporting System, 263
Organization of Petroleum Exporting Countries
      (OPEC), 141
Ottoman Bank, 65
Ottoman Empire, 14, 65, 83–84, 239
  and Egypt, 243
  and Imperial Ottoman Bank, 65
  debt of, 238
  Galata bankers, 64, 66–67, 239
  government, 65, 238–39
  Public Debt Administration, 67, 70, 239, 240
  sultan, 64–65, 67

Palmer, Francis, 80
Palmerston, Henry John, 85, 243
pandemic, 2, 9, 199, 201–03, 205–209, 220, 223,
      225, 265
  *See also* COVID-19
papacy, 15. *See also* pope
Papandreou, George, 192
Paris, 31–34, 40, 52–53, 57, 60, 63, 65–66, 91, 96,
      238, 245
  city council, 33
  Commune, 96
  urban elite, 31
Paris Club, 147, 205, 229, 255, 263
  Toronto terms, 147–48
Parliaments. *See* representative assemblies
Paul, Rand, 1, 4
pensions, 107–08, 193, 195
  pension funds, 2–9, 152, 221
  private, 169
  state, 114
petrodollars, 141–43, 237
Petroleum Fund, Norwegian, 218
Philip II of Spain, 31, 90, 232
Pitt, William (the Younger), 94–95
  and income tax, 219, 245
  as debt manager, 95
Poincaré, Raymond, 117, 248
polarization, political, 118–19, 140, 175,
      219, 258
political parties, 79, 114–15, 117, 155, 171–72,
      174–75, 204, 230–31, 241
pope, 15–16, 229. *See also* papacy
population, 99, 152, 169–70
  aging in advanced economies, 209
Porte, Sublime, 65, 67, 83, 238–39, 241–42
Portes, Richard, 124, 250
portfolio investment, 130
Portugal, 47, 113, 236, 242

Baring crisis, default and settlement, 77–78
debt consolidation
  in interwar period, 113
  in 1990s, 179–80
  Global Financial Crisis and recession, 184–85,
      187, 190, 195
Poyais, Kingdom of, 46, 234
prices, 18–19, 21, 38–43, 64–65, 68–69, 71, 80,
      123, 125–26, 132, 134, 152–53, 155–56,
      230–31, 244–45, 254, 262
  futures, 262
  grain, 237
  housing, 192
  import, 153
productivity, 98–99, 129, 172, 180, 214. *See
      also* labor
  growth of, 128, 172–73, 250
  slowdown after 1973, 140–41
public finances, 3, 20, 25, 29, 41, 71, 95, 103,
      181–82, 196, 212
public investment, 186, 213, 258
public services, 8, 117, 199, 253
public spending, 9, 107–8, 120, 145, 180, 189,
      191–93, 216, 220, 253, 260
  additional, 8, 219
  efforts at reducing, 218
  excessive, 176

Qing China, 69–71, 237
quantitative easing. *See* debt markets,
      backstopping by central bank

railways, 7, 49–50, 57, 63–64, 74, 92, 136, 213
real estate, 102, 168, 238
  developers, 159, 167
  loans, 161
  untaxed, in Greece, 193
Reinhart, Carmen, 125–26, 137, 241, 244, 250–52,
      255, 260, 263
*rentes*, 22, 33–34, 233
reparations. *See* Franco-Prussian War, Germany,
      World War I
representative assemblies
  and credible commitment 3, 17, 20–22, 26,
      29–30, 38, 44, 100, 212, 231, 233
  and federalism 207, 208, 235, 261
  and fiscal centralization, 32, 37, 176, 231–32
  and franchise extension, 100–03, 106, 108,
      214, 247
  and partisanship, 115–16, 171–72, 174–75, 219
  in France, 31–33, 233
  in the Netherlands, 26, 231
  in the UK, 29–30, 38, 100
  in the US, 42, 171, 182, 186
  members as investors in public debt, 17, 20–21,
      38, 100
Republicans, U.S. Congress, 1, 171–72, 174, 219

repurchase (repo) market, 201, 259, 262
    short-term, 262
reputation, importance of, 28, 42, 46, 60, 152,
    200, 237
reserves, 4, 58, 68, 84, 90, 146, 154–56, 200, 219
    foreign, 151–52, 158–59, 162, 215, 252, 255
revenues, government, 1–2, 8, 17–18, 20, 26,
    32–33, 36, 38, 44, 56, 83–84, 101–02,
    170–72, 204–05, 208–09, 213–14,
    231–33, 243, 257
    capital-gains-related, 261
    customs, 70
    federal, 41, 208
    from tobacco monopoly, 83
    municipal, 228
Ricardian equivalence, 188
Ricardo, David, 80, 260
Ricardo, Jacob (Jack), 80, 242
risk. See currency risk, gold standard, interest rate
    premium
Rogoff, Kenneth, 125–26, 241, 249–50, 255,
    258, 260
Rome, Republic and Empire, 11–13
Romer, Christina, 190, 244, 258, 260
Romer, David, 190, 244, 258, 260
Roosevelt, Franklin Delano, 134
    and deficit spending, 120
    and Lend-Lease, 131
Roosevelt, Theodore, 86, 244
    Roosevelt Corollary, 86
Rothschilds, 52, 238
    London, 59
    Paris, 59
Rubinomics, 170, 173, 178
Rudman, Warren, 171
Russia, 52, 65, 69–70, 75, 88, 89, 110, 130–31,
    147, 163, 234, 236, 248
    banks, 71
    default on czarist bonds, 82
Russo-Japanese War, 74

samurai, 73, 240
sanctions, 50, 85–86. See also gunboat diplomacy,
    Roosevelt corollary
Santo Domingo, 86
savings, 4–5, 62, 68, 151, 155, 169, 174, 187, 189,
    217–18, 220
    rates, 169, 218
        of China, Germany, Saudi Arabia, and
        emerging markets, 200
Scandinavian countries, 92
    originators of welfare state, 141
Schiff, Jacob, 75
securities, 5, 7, 21–23, 27, 36, 38, 40, 42–43, 46, 48, 53,
    60–61, 67, 70–71, 92, 102, 112, 123, 133–34,
    147, 156, 212, 228–29, 235, 240, 252
    asset-backed, 165

euro-denominated, 234
excise-backed, 38
fixed-interest, 169
housing-related, 259
markets in, 59, 150
negotiable, 23, 230
pledgeability of, 38
state-contingent, 95
securitization, 230, 259
    of mortgage originations, 259
Seidman, William, 143, 254
Select Committee on Loans to Foreign States,
    Great Britain, 243
sequestration, budgetary, United States, 171
Serra Puche, Jaime, 155
Seven Years War (1756-1763), 38, 102
Shanghai, 70–71, 240
Sichel, Daniel, 172, 257
Silva Herzog, Jesús, 144–45
silver, 94, 232, 239–40
Singapore, 215
    persistent primary budget surpluses after 1990, 219
    sovereign wealth funds, 264
    technocratic government, 219
sinking fund, 42–43, 94, 114, 245
    as Italian innovation, 245
    Keynes's objections to use in 1920s, 114
    reestablished by Pitt, the Younger, 94
Sino-Japanese War, 70, 74–75
Sir John Perring, Shaw, Bardo & Co., banking
    house, 46
Six Per Cent Club, 42
Smith, Adam, 4–5, 227
Snowden, Philip, 114
social programs, 106, 109, 115, 118, 126, 129, 139,
    141, 172, 174–75, 195
social security, 55, 171, 189, 214, 257
social services, 2, 7, 106, 203, 209, 220
social spending, 101, 103, 106, 108–09, 126,
    128–29, 139–40, 171, 248, 250, 252
societates, in Ancient Rome, 11, 228
South America, 47–48, 86
    trade, 40, 234
South Korea, 144, 149, 151, 157–62, 166, 200,
    215, 247
    banks, 159
    chaebol (large conglomerates), 158
    Korea Asset Management Corporation
        (KAMCO), 160, 256
South Sea Company, 40
    shares, 41
sovereign immunity, 48–49, 80, 227, 235
sovereign wealth funds, 219
Spain, 26, 31, 45, 47, 54, 58, 125–26, , 184–85,
    196, 236
    asientos, 231–32
    colonial empire, 40, 234

Spain (*cont.*)
  *juros*, 231, 233
  Philip II's ability to borrow, 31–32, 90
Sri Lanka, Port of Hambantota, 204
Stability and Growth Pact, European Union, 177–78
state-owned enterprises (SOEs), 203–04
Statesman's Yearbook, 60
sterling, 68, 71, 112, 136, 236, 239, 252
  1956 crisis, 136–37, 253
  balances, 136–37, 252
    freezing those of Egypt, 136
  bonds denominated in, 51, 70
stimulus, fiscal, 186–87, 189–90, 203, 260
stockbrokers, role in placing debt, 59
stock-flow adjustment (SFA), 97, 102, 104, 143,
    248–49, 256–57
Suez Canal
  crisis, 137
  shares, 83
Supreme Court, United States, 42, 235
Sussman, Nathan, 91, 230, 240, 244
Sweden, 107, 109, 111, 113, 127, 132, 138, 144, 253
  increase in government spending in 1960s, 141
  use of fiscal policy in 1930s, 250
Syracuse, 10–11, 13
Syriza, 194

Takahashi, Korekiyo, 75, 250
tariff revenues, 26, 101. *See also* import tariffs
tax commission, England, 37
taxes, 2–4, 15, 17, 28–30, 32, 37, 41–42, 44, 51, 83,
    94–96, 100–01, 115–17, 120, 140, 171–73,
    174, 180, 182–83, 192–94, 208–09, 219–20,
    229–30, 232, 240, 245, 257
  estate, 174
  excise, 36–38, 42, 94–95, 233
  farming, 32–33
  in Holy Roman Empire, 35, 233
  indirect, 32, 36
  municipal, 233
  on land, 36, 233
  on silk, 66
  prospectively, of European Union, 208
  provincial, 83
  value-added (VAT), 186
  *See also* wealth, taxes
Telge & Co., 240
Temasek Holdings, Singapore, 219
temples, as religious foundations and financial
    intermediaries, 11–12, 228
Thailand, 144, 149, 157–62
  baht, 159
  Financial Institutions Development Fund
    (FIDF), 160, 256
  government, 157, 160
Thatcher government, United Kingdom, 240
Thiers government, France, 96
Thirty Years War (1618–1648), 25, 35

Tilly, Charles, 14, 229
trade, 3, 15–16, 18, 23, 25, 40, 47–48, 50, 57–58,
    101, 121, 131, 230, 233, 235, 237–39
  agreements, 58
    Cobden-Chevalier Treaty, 57
    Roca-Runciman Agreement, 123
  costs, 57–58, 237
    indices measuring, 58
  in cotton, 68
  in opium, 69
  long-distance, 3, 15, 23
  policy, 135
  use of debt in financing, 15, 50, 71
trade unions, 108
  unskilled workers, 101
transfers, fiscal 28, 42, 94, 101–03, 108, 189,
    207–08, 243, 245, 247, 252–53, 260
  federal, 189
Treasury, 42, 47, 117, 126, 134, 183, 200, 248, 251,
    262, 264
  bills, 38, 47, 94, 123, 132–34, 221, 248
  bonds, 66, 122, 126, 165, 173, 201, 222, 251,
    262–63, 265
    short-term, 83
    US
      Civil War era, 65, 83, 93, 95–97, 243
      zero-coupon, 147
  need for single European, 208
Treasury-Fed Accord, United States, 134
Trichet, Jean-Claude, 196–97, 261
Troika (composed of European Commission,
    European Central Bank, IMF) and Greece,
    192, 194, 196, 261
Turkey, 66, 86, 88–89, 92, 144, 149, 163, 200–01,
    241, 243, 247
  bonds, 241
  crises prior to 2007, 149
  importance of banks as holders of domestic
    debt, 163
  larger primary budget deficits in 2020 than in
    Global Financial Crisis, 201

unemployment, 8, 108, 120, 140, 192, 205
  insurance, 7, 108, 214
United Kingdom, 97–98, 107, 109, 111–13, 125,
    127, 131–32, 136–39, 183–87, 190, 246,
    248–50, 252, 262, 265. *See also* Britain
United Nations, 54, 255
  Conference on Trade and Development
    (UNCTAD), 255
  Relief and Rehabilitation Administration
    (UNRRA), 135
United States, 43, 50, 52–53, 86, 99, 101–03,
    109–13, 119–21, 130–39, 158, 160,
    165–67, 170–71, 175–76, 178, 183–84,
    186–87, 188, 190–92, 214, 216–20,
    235–39, 245–50, 253, 258–59
  and Canadian securities, 248

banks, 156, 158, 253–24
  expansion of activities in 1920s, 122
  and Latin American debt crisis, 143
bonds, 42–43, 53, 200, 235, 264
Customs Service, 42
deficits, 52, 182–83, 249
home prices, 259
interest rates, 122, 143
investors, 52, 236
market in government debt, 110–11,
  120–21, 248
Securities and Exchange Commission, 184
securities laws, 254
Shay's Rebellion, 234
State Department, 89
Treasury Department, 110–11, 156, 259,
  262, 264
  Exchange Stabilization Fund, 145

Van der Woude, Ad, 29, 231
Venice, 17–20, 22, 229, 230
  bonds, 19
  Grand Council, 17–18, 229
  Rialto Market, 17
Venezuela, 47, 77, 79, 86, 90, 144, 147, 249
  blockade of by Britain and Germany, 86
  debt default in 1890s, 77
  serial defaults between 1800 and 1913, 79
Vienna, and 1873 financial crisis, 55, 66
Vittorio Emanuele III of Italy, 117
Volcker, Paul, 173
  and interest-rate shock, 214–15, 254
voters, enfranchisement of. See representative
  assemblies

wages, 116, 153–54, 246
Waigel, Theo, 177
war, 14, 17–18, 28–29, 41–42, 44–45, 68–69,
  74–75, 93–95, 102–3, 135–36, 181, 197,
  211–12, 220, 229, 232–34, 245, 248, 252
  and government spending, 95–96
  and postwar debt overhang, 131

bonds, 134
debts, 248
funding of, 45, 94, 106, 110–12, 130–33
loans, 19, 75, 125
wealth, 1, 15–18, 35, 232, 265
  taxes on, 20, 115–17, 209, 220, 230
welfare spending, 7, 106–08, 126
  and women's vote, 108, 247, 253
welfare state, 7, 106, 108
  as commitment to redistribution 24, 126, 213
  as legacy of Great Depression, 126
  in Scandinavia, 141, 253
William III of England, 38. See also Bank of
  England
Witt, Johan de, 27–28
World Bank (International Bank for
  Reconstruction and Development), 127,
  131, 136, 141, 147, 160, 252, 254
World War I, 48–49, 97, 99, 102–103, 109–12,
  128, 131–32, 137, 139, 213–14, 244, 246,
  248, 250–52
  and postwar debt consolidation, 93
  and postwar reparations, 118–19, 247, 248, 249
  and Dawes plan, 121–22
  financial legacy, 110–12
  reliance on seigniorage during, 94
World War II, 8, 85, 89, 115, 127–28, 130–32,
  134–35, 137, 139, 141, 213–14, 222,
  249, 252
  ability to borrow at lower rates than during
   World War I, 115
  decline in industrial production in immediate
   postwar period, 128
  economic consequences, 130–31
  German blocked balances, 251

Xiang River, 72
Xiuquan, Hong, 69

Yangtze River 72

Zedillo, Ernesto, 155